The FEDERALIST *Papers*

The FEDERALIST *Papers*

ALEXANDER HAMILTON

JAMES MADISON

JOHN JAY

**With an introduction, table of contents,
And index of ideas**

By

CLINTON ROSSITER

GYAN

ISBN : 978-81-212-1461-2(HB)

Published, 2018

Published by

Gyan Publishing House
5, Ansari Road
Daryaganj, New Delhi-110002
Phone: 011-47034999, 9811692060
www.gyanbooks.com
E-mail: books@gyanbooks.com

Printed at: G. Print Process, Delhi.

CONTENTS

Introduction

The Federalist is the most important work in political science that has ever been written, or is likely ever to be written, in the United States. It is, indeed, the one product of the American mind that is rightly counted among the classics of political theory.

This work has always commanded widespread respect as the first and still most authoritative commentary on the Constitution of the United States. It has been searched minutely by lawyers for its analysis of the powers of Congress, quoted confidently by historians for its revelations of the hopes and fears of the framers of the Constitution, and cited magisterially by the Supreme Court for its arguments in behalf of judicial review, executive independence, and national supremacy. It would not be stretching the truth more than a few inches to say that *The Federalist* stands third only to the Declaration of Independence and the Constitution itself among all the sacred writings of American political history. It has a quality of legitimacy, of authority and authenticity, that gives it the high status of a public document, one to which, as Thomas Jefferson put it, "appeal is habitually made by all, and rarely declined or denied by any" as to the "genuine meaning" of the Constitution.

In recent years respect for *The Federalist* has blossomed into admiration. It is now valued not merely as a clever defense of a particular charter, but as an exposition of certain timeless truths about constitutional government. It has caught the fancy of political scientists throughout the world, has been translated into a dozen languages, and—surely the most convincing evidence of its lofty status—has become one of the three or four staples of the American college curriculum in political science. General Washington, who was trying merely to be friendly, wrote some prophetic words to Alexander Hamilton in the summer of 1788: "When the transient circumstances and fugitive performances which attended this crisis shall have disappeared, that work will merit the notice of posterity, because in it are candidly and ably discussed the principles of freedom and the topics of government—which will be always interesting to mankind so long as they shall be connected in civil society." The "notice of posterity" for the stern yet hopeful message of *The Federalist* has never been more attentive than in these drawn-out years of peril for constitutional democracy.

The immense prestige of this work seems especially remarkable when viewed in the light of its origins. *The Federalist* is essentially a collection of eighty-five letters to the public over the pseudonym of Publius that appeared at short intervals in the newspapers of New York City beginning on October 27, 1787. These letters were still appearing in late March, 1788, when the first thirty-six were issued in a collected edition. Continuous publication was halted with number 77 on April 4, then resumed June 14, and concluded August 16. In the meantime, a second volume containing numbers 37–85 was published May 28.

Conceived in the pressure of a great crisis in human events, written with a haste that often bordered on the frantic, printed and published as if it were the most perishable kind of daily news, *The Federalist* bore few marks of immortality at birth. It was, in fact, only one of several hundred salvos in the loud war of words that accompanied the protracted struggle over ratification of the Constitution. That new charter of government, it will be remembered, had been agreed upon and signed at Philadelphia, September 17, 1787, transmitted to the Congress then existing under the Articles of Confederation, and thereupon laid, with no great show of enthusiasm, before the people of the United States. The approval of ratifying conventions in nine of the thirteen states was to bring the Constitution into effect. Few of its authors and supporters imagined that it would be easy to win such a margin of approval in the chaotic political circumstances of the world's first experiment in popular government over an extended area; all recognized that a clear-cut vote against the Constitution in any one of four key states would be enough by itself to destroy their hopes for "a more perfect Union."

One of these states was New York, among whose claims to a vital role in the affairs of the new republic were a growing population, a lively commerce, a pivotal position on the Atlantic seaboard, and New York City, then the seat of the government of the United States. It was also the home of Governor George Clinton, a doughty politician whose principles and prejudices and skills made him the most formidable of opponents to the proposed Constitution. Plainly New York was a state that could easily be lost and yet had to be won; plainly it was a state in which arguments voiced in public debate or actions taken in the ratifying convention might influence the course of events in other states.

It was with such thoughts as these in mind that Alexander Hamilton, the recognized leader of the forces of ratification in New York, turned in the fall of 1787 to the task of winning his state to the cause of the new Constitution. The story of how Hamilton persuaded and plotted and bullied his way over the months to the narrowest of victories in the New York convention is an epic of American politics that deserves to be better known. What is important to us about this amazing effort is that Hamilton found it both practically expedient and psychologically comforting to supplement his political activities with a contribution to the literary war. Without his foresight, energy, and organizational skill there would have been no *Federalist* to stiffen the friends of the Constitution and to instruct the minds of posterity. He conceived the idea of a series of thoughtful communications that would explain and support the proposed Constitution; he scrambled for worthy contributors and finally found them in John Jay and James Madison; he wrote almost two thirds of the total of 175,000 words; he carried on the project to its scheduled end long after the other two men had been forced to leave the field. While the Publius we know and cherish today is a composite of three men, one of these men, Alexander Hamilton, must ever be regarded as the political magician who brought Publius to life.

The authors of *The Federalist* made up a first-class team of thinkers and doers. John Jay (1745–1829), the oldest and at that time most distinguished of the group, was a prosperous New York lawyer who had rendered three particularly eminent services to his state and country: authorship of the admirable New York Constitution of 1777, which was a prime source of ideas for the Convention at Philadelphia; negotiation, side-by-side with Benjamin Franklin and John Adams, of the Treaty of 1783 that gave America peace and final independence; and, as Secretary for Foreign Affairs under the Articles of Confederation, direction of the diplomatic maneuverings of the almost friendless republic. James Madison (1751–1836), although he could hardly have known it at the time, had already won lasting fame as the most useful member of the Convention of 1787. The Constitution was the joint work of a half dozen or more superior men, yet even today, in part because of the notes he kept of the proceedings of the Convention, few historians begrudge Madison the title "Father of the Constitution." Alexander Hamilton (1755–1804) was another New York lawyer who had served his state and country well, notably as a youthful comrade-in-arms of General Washington and as a prime mover of the events that led to the Convention of 1787. He, like Madison, was a delegate to Philadelphia; unlike Madison, he was irregular in attendance and unpersuasive in argument. His principal services to the new Constitution came only after the Convention had adjourned.

All three authors of *The Federalist* went on after 1788 to even more splendid careers—Jay to the Chief Justiceship and to negotiation of the famous treaty that bears his name, Madison to a distinguished eight years as the leading figure in Congress and to somewhat less distinguished eight-year tenures as both Secretary of State and President of the United States, Hamilton to service under President Washington as the most influential of all Secretaries of the Treasury. For those who care about such things—and many readers of this introduction are sure to care—it should be recorded that both Hamilton and Jay were graduates of Columbia, Madison a son of Princeton.

Throughout the long months during which *The Federalist* was running in the New York newspapers, and indeed until several years after publication of the collected essays, the identity of Publius was a well-guarded secret. This mask of anonymity, put on by the authors for sound political purposes, made it possible for Hamilton, in a note written just before his death and discovered just after, to lay claim to a full sixty-three numbers of *The Federalist*, some of which very plainly belonged to Madison. Just why this man of honor and sound memory should have engaged in this extraordinary action is impossible to explain. In any case, he touched off a tortuous dispute that went on for generations between his political heirs and those of Madison over the authorship of the various papers, especially numbers 49–58, 62 and 63. Thanks chiefly to the scholarly labors of Professor Douglass Adair, we can say with some confidence that Hamilton wrote fifty-one numbers (1, 6–9, 11–13, 15–17, 21–36, 59–61, 65–85), Madison twenty-six (10, 14, 37–58, and probably 62, 63), and Jay five (2–5, 64), while three (18–20) were the product of a joint effort by Madison and Hamilton. The skimpiness of Jay's contribution is explained by an illness that overtook him in the fall of 1787, the impressive bulk of Hamilton's by the intensity of his commitment. Madison's contribution, which is far more important for the present reputation of Publius than its modest size would indicate, was made possible in the first place only because the Virginian was in New York in the fall of 1787 as a delegate to Congress. His participation ended abruptly upon his departure for home in March, 1788.

The Federalist worked only a small influence upon the course of events during the struggle over ratification. Promises, threats, bargains, and face-to-face debates, not eloquent words in even the most widely circulated newspapers, won hard-earned victories for the Constitution in the crucial states of Massachusetts, Virginia, and New York. Publius, by his own admission, spoke to a select audience of reasonable, responsible, and established men, and most such men had already been convinced of the necessity of a change in the system of government. The chief usefulness of *The Federalist* in the events of 1788 was as a kind of debater's handbook in Virginia and New York. Copies of the collected edition were rushed to Richmond at Hamilton's direction and used gratefully by advocates of the Constitution in the climactic debate over ratification.

The fame of *The Federalist* derives, therefore, not from the events of a single decisive year, but from the whole course of American history. It is a sign, as it were, of the prodigious success of the Constitution, which, as it has endured and evolved over the generations, has called attention ever more insistently to the men who, having helped to write it, first explained it. Viewed from this perspective, which is the one we are privileged to take, *The Federalist* appears as four books in one: an explanation of the blessings of federal government; an indictment of the Articles of Confederation for their failure to provide such government, or indeed to provide much in the way of government at all; an analysis and defense of the new Constitution as an instrument of federalism and constitutionalism; and, lighting up these more practical subjects with sudden bursts of brilliance, an exposition of certain enduring truths that provide an understanding of both the dangers and the delights of free government.

As an explanation of the federal form of government *The Federalist* comes closest to being an original piece of work. Other men, to be sure—most notably Althusius and "the celebrated Montesquieu"—had discoursed intelligently on some of the problems of unity and disunity among states with close emotional and commercial ties, but it remained for Publius to make the first real stab at expounding the merits of genuine federalism, which is, after all, a full and tricky step beyond mere federation in the direction of consolidation. *The Federalist* deserves lasting credit for the clarity with which it insists that both levels of government in a federal system must exercise direct authority over individuals, that the central government must enjoy unquestioned supremacy in its assigned fields, and that federalism is to be cherished not alone for its contributions to peace within the land and security without, but for the firm foundation it provides for the enjoyment of individual freedom over a wide expanse of territory. *The Federalist,* it could be said, converted federalism from an expedient into an article of faith, from an occasional accident of history into an enduring expression of the principles of constitutionalism.

Those pages of *The Federalist* which catalogue the weaknesses of the Articles of Confederation make much the least interesting reading today. In 1787–88, however, they made very interesting reading indeed, and many friends of the new Constitution valued *The Federalist* principally for its merciless indictment of the "palpable defects of the subsisting Confederation." Since the indictment was one that had to be made with force and in detail, one cannot begrudge Publius the joys he must have experienced in beating a horse that may look dead to us but was very much alive to him. And even in the muddiest parts of the hard going from numbers 15 to 22 there are solid observations on one of the major themes of *The Federalist*: the dreadful circumstance of a weak government in a disordered society.

Up to now, at least, *The Federalist* has worked its chief influence on the course of events as a uniquely authoritative commentary on the Constitution. Today, as all through the history of American constitutional development, a particular interpretation of some clause in that document can be given a special flavor of authenticity by a quotation from Publius. If he was understandably wrong in his interpretation of some details in the Constitution—for example, in assigning the Senate a share in the power of removal and in giving a purely military cast to the President's authority as commander-in-chief—he was remarkably right about many more. Publius the constitutional lawyer, in the bold person of Hamilton, reached the peak of intellectual power and of historical influence in the breathtaking assertion of judicial review in number 78.

Publius the political theorist, in the perceptive persons of both Hamilton and Madison, is the man who has brought fame and influence to *The Federalist* in recent years—this despite the fact that all the more or less speculative musings of *The Federalist* make up at best a fragment on government. What Hamilton and Madison were capable of producing as political theorists in the closet of leisurely detachment and what they managed to produce as political strategists in the arena of zestful engagement were, alas, two quite different matters. *The Federalist* is a contribution to political theory only by accident—by the happy accident, one might say, that neither of its chief authors could ever make a point in the most earth-bound debate without pausing, if only for a moment, to put the point in a larger and more abstract perspective. Yet this, after all, is the familiar way in which some of the greatest contributions to political theory were brought into being, and one should not spend too much time regretting the startling omissions and uneven quality of *The Federalist*, lest he be slow to pay the homage of painstaking study to such notable contributions as Madison's reflections on the plural society in numbers 10 and 51 and Hamilton's appraisal of executive power as an agency of free government in number 70.

If he does pay such homage, and if he also keeps an earnest eye out for the nuggets of speculation strewn all through these pages, the student of *The Federalist* will in time amass a respectable treasure of political wisdom about the problems and possibilities of freedom. While *The Federalist* has important things to say about all governments in general, it is popular government—in those days called "republican" government—with which Publius is principally concerned. His dislike of instability and downright fear of anarchy are writ large and often in these essays, but he offers us other and better ways than that recommended by Thomas Hobbes to bring peace and security to the community. To find "republican remedies" for the "diseases most incident to republican government" is the constant purpose of the authors of *The Federalist*.

In the course of their long search for these remedies, the chief of which turn out to be federalism, social pluralism, and constitutionalism (that is, divided, balanced, and limited government), Hamilton and Madison give their own answers to some of the oldest questions of political theory; and it is safe to say that no more eloquent, tough-minded, and instructive answers have ever been given by an American pen. Whether discoursing on the universal urge of mankind toward weakness and wickedness, demonstrating the existence of the saving graces of human reason and decency, accounting for the diverse interests that arise in a progressive society, finding a formula for liberty in the very fact of these clashing interests, setting both static and dynamic limits to the rule of the majority, or working out the balance of forces within a complex structure of government, *The Federalist* sends out messages of universal validity to all students of political man, and especially to those who wish him well. It is, in particular, the cold-eyed yet ultimately hopeful view of mankind that lifts *The Federalist* into the circle of classics in political theory. No one can read these pages without being reminded powerfully of both the light and dark sides of human nature—of man's capacity for reason and justice that makes free government possible, of his capacity for passion and injustice that makes it necessary.

It is, to be sure, a great pity that the authors of *The Federalist* had neither time nor inclination to sort out and restate in orderly, comprehensive fashion their many brilliant observations about the nature of political man, or indeed about liberty or society or the purposes and forms of government. It is a greater pity, a source of especially keen distress to students of political theory, that they apparently found it unnecessary to make more than a handful of explicit observations on private property as a right of man, a pillar of ordered society, and a force in politics. Nor is the occasional character of *The Federalist* as a tract in political theory its only fault. As a piece of very special pleading—some have called it a lawyer's brief—it says the same thing over and over in a half dozen ways, tiptoes delicately around many of the hard criticisms directed against the Constitution and slogs ponderously through some of the silliest, and makes at least a few arguments and appeals which its authors must have had trouble justifying to their own consciences. Hamilton, in particular, was hardly the enthusiast for the Constitution that he appears to be in these pages.

In recent years a good deal has been made of the fact that Publius was a "split personality," speaking through Madison as a federalist and an exponent of limited government, through Hamilton as a nationalist and an admirer of energetic government. Yet Publius was, on any large view, at least as whole a personality as any reasonable man can be when he has to deal with the everlasting tensions of free government. His own tensions, it might be argued, are only an honest reflection of those built into the Constitution. *The Federalist,* like the Constitution it expounds and the polity it celebrates, is a "bundle of compromises." The wonder must always be, not that Publius spoke some of the great truths of politics in an offhand manner and with a hoarse voice, but that, in the circumstances of the case, he spoke as pointedly and coherently as he did. He managed to do this principally because the thoughts of his creators, while hastily written down, had not been lightly conceived. They were, indeed, the product of years of learned study and hard experience.

Not every great political theorist has cared much for free and popular government. Of those who have cared, not every one has been candid enough to expose its diseases, or hopeful enough to counsel a broad scheme of prevention. *The Federalist* is a famous work in political science because it does just that, because it mixes candor and hope, realism and idealism, in a message to all friends of liberty wherever they ply their honorable trade. And the message of *The Federalist* reads: no happiness without liberty, no liberty without self-government, no self-government without constitutionalism, no constitutionalism without morality—and none of these great goods without stability and order.

—Clinton Rossiter

February 15, 1961

Note on Text

THE text of this edition of *The Federalist* is taken directly from the first, so-called "McLean edition" of 1788. Spelling and punctuation have been modernized, and a few glaring mistakes—solecisms, Homeric nods, and printer's lapses—have been corrected. The main heads in the table of contents are also taken from the first edition, while the subheads are my own work. So, too, is the index (including the indexed Constitution), which was conceived and compiled with particular attention to the interests of students of political theory and constitutional law. All footnotes to the text are the work of the authors of *The Federalist.*

Those readers who do not have the energy and fixed purpose to make their way through the whole of *The Federalist* may wish to know that, by common consent of learned opinion, the following numbers are the cream of the eighty-five papers: 1, 2, 6, 9, 10, 14, 15, 16, 23, 37, 39, 47, 48, 49, 51, 62, 63, 70, 78, 84, 85 (ten by Hamilton, ten by Madison, one by Jay).

C.R.

Contents of the Federalist

No. 1: Hamilton

AFTER an unequivocal experience of the inefficacy of the subsisting federal government, you are called upon to deliberate on a new Constitution for the United States of America. The subject speaks its own importance; comprehending in its consequences nothing less than the existence of the UNION, the safety and welfare of the parts of which it is composed, the fate of an empire in many respects the most interesting in the world. It has been frequently remarked that it seems to have been reserved to the people of this country, by their conduct and example, to decide the important question, whether societies of men are really capable or not of establishing good government from reflection and choice, or whether they are forever destined to depend for their political constitutions on accident and force. If there be any truth in the remark, the crisis at which we are arrived may with propriety be regarded as the era in which that decision is to be made; and a wrong election of the part we shall act may, in this view, deserve to be considered as the general misfortune of mankind.

This idea will add the inducements of philanthropy to those of patriotism, to heighten the solicitude which all considerate and good men must feel for the event. Happy will it be if our choice should be directed by a judicious estimate of our true interests, unperplexed and unbiased by considerations not connected with the public good. But this is a thing more ardently to be wished than seriously to be expected. The plan offered to our deliberations affects too many particular interests, innovates upon too many local institutions, not to involve in its discussion a variety of objects foreign to its merits, and of views, passions, and prejudices little favorable to the discovery of truth.

Among the most formidable of the obstacles which the new Constitution will have to encounter may readily be distinguished the obvious interest of a certain class of men in every State to resist all changes which may hazard a diminution of the power, emolument, and consequence of the offices they hold under the State establishments; and the perverted ambition of another class of men, who will either hope to aggrandize themselves by the confusions of their country, or will flatter themselves with fairer prospects of elevation from the subdivision of the empire into several partial confederacies than from its union under one government.

It is not, however, my design to dwell upon observations of this nature. I am well aware that it would be disingenuous to resolve indiscriminately the opposition of any set of men (merely because their situations might subject them to suspicion) into interested or ambitious views. Candor will oblige us to admit that even such men may be actuated by upright intentions; and it cannot be doubted that much of the opposition which has made its appearance, or may hereafter make its appearance, will spring from sources, blameless at least if not respectable—the honest errors of minds led astray by preconceived jealousies and fears. So numerous indeed and so powerful are the causes which serve to give a false bias to the judgment, that we, upon many occasions, see wise and good men on the wrong as well as on the right side of questions of the first magnitude to society. This circumstance, if duly attended to, would furnish a lesson of moderation to those who are ever so thoroughly persuaded of their being in the right in any controversy. And a further reason for caution, in this respect, might be drawn from the reflection that we are not always sure that those who advocate the truth are influenced by purer principles than their antagonists. Ambition, avarice, personal animosity, party opposition, and many other motives not more laudable than these, are apt to operate as well upon those who support as those who oppose the right side of a question. Were there not even these inducements to moderation, nothing could be more ill-judged than that intolerant spirit which has at all times characterized political parties. For in politics, as in religion, it is equally absurd to aim at making proselytes by fire and sword. Heresies in either can rarely be cured by persecution.

And yet, however just these sentiments will be allowed to be, we have already sufficient indications that it will happen in this as in all former cases of great national discussion. A torrent of angry and malignant passions will be let loose. To judge from the conduct of the opposite parties, we shall be led to conclude that they will mutually hope to evince the justness of their opinions, and to increase the number of their converts by the loudness of their declamations and by the bitterness of their invectives. An enlightened zeal for the energy and efficiency of government will be stigmatized as the offspring of a temper fond of despotic power and hostile to the principles of liberty. An over-scrupulous jealousy of danger to the rights of the people, which is more commonly the fault of the head than of the heart, will be represented as mere pretense and artifice, the stale bait for popularity at the expense of public good. It will be forgotten, on the one hand, that jealousy is the usual concomitant of violent love, and that the noble enthusiasm of liberty is too apt to be infected with a spirit of narrow and illiberal distrust. On the other hand, it will be equally forgotten that the vigor of government is essential to the security of liberty; that, in the contemplation of a sound and well-informed judgment, their interests can never be separated; and that a dangerous ambition more often lurks behind the specious mask of zeal for the rights of the people than under the forbidding appearance of zeal for the firmness and efficiency of government. History will teach us that the former has been found a much more certain road to the introduction of despotism than the latter, and that of those men who have overturned the liberties of republics, the greatest number have begun their career by paying an obsequious court to the people, commencing demagogues and ending tyrants.

In the course of the preceding observations, I have had an eye, my fellow-citizens, to putting you upon your guard against all attempts, from whatever quarter, to influence your decision in a matter of the utmost moment to your welfare by any impressions other than those which may result from the evidence of truth. You will, no doubt, at the same time have collected from the general scope of them that they proceed from a source not unfriendly to the new Constitution. Yes, my countrymen, I own to you that after having given it an attentive consideration, I am clearly of opinion it is your interest to adopt it. I am convinced that this is the safest course for your liberty, your dignity, and your happiness. I affect not reserves which I do not feel. I will not amuse you with an appearance of deliberation when I have decided. I frankly acknowledge to you my convictions, and I will freely lay before you the reasons on which they are founded. The consciousness of good intentions disdains ambiguity. I shall not, however, multiply professions on this head. My motives must remain in the depository of my own breast. My arguments will be open to all and may be judged of by all. They shall at least be offered in a spirit which will not disgrace the cause of truth.

I propose, in a series of papers, to discuss the following interesting particulars:—*The utility of the UNION to your political prosperity—The insufficiency of the present Confederation to preserve that Union—The necessity of a government at least equally energetic with the one proposed, to the attainment of this object—The conformity of the proposed Constitution to the true principles of republican government—Its analogy to your own State constitution*—and lastly, *The additional security which its adoption will afford to the preservation of that species of government, to liberty, and to property.*

In the progress of this discussion I shall endeavor to give a satisfactory answer to all the objections which shall have made their appearance, that may seem to have any claim to your attention.

It may perhaps be thought superfluous to offer arguments to prove the utility of the UNION, a point, no doubt, deeply engraved on the hearts of the great body of the people in every State, and one which, it may be imagined, has no adversaries. But the fact is that we already hear it whispered in the private circles of those who oppose the new Constitution, that the thirteen States are of too great extent for any general system, and that we must of necessity resort to separate confederacies of distinct portions of the whole.* This doctrine will, in all

* The same idea, tracing the arguments to their consequences, is held out in several of the late publications against the new Constitution.

probability, be gradually propagated, till it has votaries enough to countenance an open avowal of it. For nothing can be more evident to those who are able to take an enlarged view of the subject than the alternative of an adoption of the new Constitution or a dismemberment of the Union. It will therefore be of use to begin by examining the advantages of that Union, the certain evils, and the probable dangers, to which every State will be exposed from its dissolution. This shall accordingly constitute the subject of my next address.

PUBLIUS

No. 2: Jay

WHEN the people of America reflect that they are now called upon to decide a question, which in its consequences must prove one of the most important that ever engaged their attention, the propriety of their taking a very comprehensive, as well as a very serious, view of it will be evident.

Nothing is more certain than the indispensable necessity of government; and it is equally undeniable that whenever and however it is instituted, the people must cede to it some of their natural rights, in order to vest it with requisite powers. It is well worthy of consideration, therefore, whether it would conduce more to the interest of the people of America that they should, to all general purposes, be one nation, under one federal government, than that they should divide themselves into separate confederacies and give to the head of each the same kind of powers which they are advised to place in one national government.

It has until lately been a received and uncontradicted opinion that the prosperity of the people of America depended on their continuing firmly united, and the wishes, prayers, and efforts of our best and wisest citizens have been constantly directed to that object. But politicians now appear who insist that this opinion is erroneous, and that instead of looking for safety and happiness in union, we ought to seek it in a division of the States into distinct confederacies or sovereignties. However extraordinary this new doctrine may appear, it nevertheless has its advocates; and certain characters who were much opposed to it formerly are at present of the number. Whatever may be the arguments or inducements which have wrought this change in the sentiments and declarations of these gentlemen, it certainly would not be wise in the people at large to adopt these new political tenets without being fully convinced that they are founded in truth and sound policy.

It has often given me pleasure to observe that independent America was not composed of detached and distant territories, but that one connected, fertile, widespreading country was the portion of our western sons of liberty. Providence has in a particular manner blessed it with a variety of soils and productions and watered it with innumerable streams for the delight and accommodation of its inhabitants. A succession of navigable waters forms a kind of chain round its borders, as if to bind it together; while the most noble rivers in the world, running at convenient distances, present them with highways for the easy communication of friendly aids and the mutual transportation and exchange of their various commodities.

With equal pleasure I have as often taken notice that Providence has been pleased to give this one connected country to one united people—a people descended from the same ancestors, speaking the same language, professing the same religion, attached to the same principles of government, very similar in their manners and customs, and who, by their joint counsels, arms, and efforts, fighting side by side throughout a long and bloody war, have nobly established their general liberty and independence.

This country and this people seem to have been made for each other, and it appears as if it was the design of Providence that an inheritance so proper and convenient for a band of brethren, united to each other by the strongest ties, should never be split into a number of unsocial, jealous, and alien sovereignties.

Similar sentiments have hitherto prevailed among all orders and denominations of men among us. To all general purposes we have uniformly been one people; each individual citizen everywhere enjoying the same national rights, privileges, and protection. As a nation we have made peace and war; as a nation we have vanquished our common enemies; as a nation we have formed alliances, and made treaties, and entered into various compacts and conventions with foreign states.

A strong sense of the value and blessings of union induced the people, at a very early period, to institute a federal government to preserve and perpetuate it. They formed it almost as soon as they had a political existence; nay, at a time when their habitations were in flames, when many of their citizens were bleeding, and when the progress of hostility and desolation left little room for those calm and mature inquiries and reflections which must ever precede the formation of a wise and well-balanced government for a free people. It is not to be wondered at that a government instituted in times so inauspicious should on experiment be found greatly deficient and inadequate to the purpose it was intended to answer.

This intelligent people perceived and regretted these defects. Still continuing no less attached to union than enamored of liberty, they observed the danger which immediately threatened the former and more remotely the latter; and being persuaded that ample security for both could only be found in a national government more wisely framed, they, as with one voice, convened the late convention at Philadelphia to take that important subject under consideration.

This convention, composed of men who possessed the confidence of the people, and many of whom had become highly distinguished by their patriotism, virtue, and wisdom, in times which tried the minds and hearts of men, undertook the arduous task. In the mild season of peace, with minds unoccupied by other subjects, they passed many months in cool, uninterrupted, and daily consultation; and finally, without having been awed by power, or influenced by any passions except love for their country, they presented and recommended to the people the plan produced by their joint and very unanimous councils.

Admit, for so is the fact, that this plan is only *recommended,* not imposed, yet let it be remembered that it is neither recommended to *blind* approbation, nor to *blind* reprobation; but to that sedate and candid consideration which the magnitude and importance of the subject demand, and which it certainly ought to receive. But, as has been already remarked, it is more to be wished than expected that it may be so considered and examined. Experience on a former occasion teaches us not to be too sanguine in such hopes. It is not yet forgotten that well-grounded apprehensions of imminent danger induced the people of America to form the memorable Congress of 1774. That body recommended certain measures to their constituents, and the event proved their wisdom; yet it is fresh in our memories how soon the press began to teem with pamphlets and weekly papers against those very measures. Not only many of the officers of government, who obeyed the dictates of personal interest, but others, from a mistaken estimate of consequences, from the undue influence of ancient attachments or whose ambition aimed at objects which did not correspond with the public good, were indefatigable in their endeavors to persuade the people to reject the advice of that patriotic Congress. Many, indeed, were deceived and deluded, but the great majority of the people reasoned and decided judiciously; and happy they are in reflecting that they did so.

They considered that the Congress was composed of many wise and experienced men. That, being convened from different parts of the country, they brought with them and communicated to each other a variety of useful information. That, in the course of the time they passed together in inquiring into and discussing the true interests of their country, they must have acquired very accurate knowledge on that head. That they were individually interested in the public liberty and prosperity, and therefore that it was not less their inclination than their duty to recommend only such measures as, after the most mature deliberation, they really thought prudent and advisable.

These and similar considerations then induced the people to rely greatly on the judgment and integrity of the Congress; and they took their advice, notwithstanding the various arts and endeavors used to deter and dissuade them from it. But if the people at large had reason to confide in the men of that Congress, few of whom had been fully tried or generally known, still greater reason have they now to respect the judgment and advice of the convention, for it is well known that some of the most distinguished members of that Congress, who have been since tried and justly approved for patriotism and abilities, and who have grown old in acquiring political information, were also members of this convention, and carried into it their accumulated knowledge and experience.

It is worthy of remark that not only the first, but every succeeding Congress, as well as the late convention, have invariably joined with the people in thinking that the prosperity of America depended on its Union. To preserve and perpetuate it was the great object of the people in forming that convention, and it is also the great object of the plan which the convention has advised them to adopt. With what propriety, therefore, or for what good purposes, are attempts at this particular period made by some men to depreciate the importance of the Union? Or why is it suggested that three or four confederacies would be better than one? I am persuaded in my own mind that the people have always thought right on this subject, and that their universal and uniform attachment to the cause of the Union rests on great and weighty reasons, which I shall endeavor to develop and explain in some ensuing papers. They who promote the idea of substituting a number of distinct confederacies in the room of the plan of the convention seem clearly to foresee that the rejection of it would put the continuance of the Union in the utmost jeopardy. That certainly would be the case, and I sincerely wish that it may be as clearly foreseen by every good citizen that whenever the dissolution of the Union arrives, America will have reason to exclaim, in the words of the poet: "FAREWELL! A LONG FAREWELL TO ALL MY GREATNESS."

PUBLIUS

No. 3: Jay

IT IS not a new observation that the people of any country (if, like the Americans, intelligent and well-informed) seldom adopt and steadily persevere for many years in an erroneous opinion respecting their interests. That consideration naturally tends to create great respect for the high opinion which the people of America have so long and uniformly entertained of the importance of their continuing firmly united under one federal government, vested with sufficient powers for all general and national purposes.

The more attentively I consider and investigate the reasons which appear to have given birth to this opinion, the more I become convinced that they are cogent and conclusive.

Among the many objects to which a wise and free people find it necessary to direct their attention, that of providing for their *safety* seems to be the first. The *safety* of the people doubtless has relation to a great variety of circumstances and considerations, and consequently affords great latitude to those who wish to define it precisely and comprehensively.

At present I mean only to consider it as it respects security for the preservation of peace and tranquillity, as well as against dangers from *foreign arms and influence,* as from dangers of the *like kind* arising from domestic causes. As the former of these comes first in order, it is proper it should be the first discussed. Let us therefore proceed to examine whether the people are not right in their opinion that a cordial Union, under an efficient national government, affords them the best security that can be devised against *hostilities* from abroad.

The number of wars which have happened or will happen in the world will always be found to be in proportion to the number and weight of the causes, whether *real* or *pretended,* which *provoke* or *invite* them. If this remark be just, it becomes useful to inquire whether so many *just* causes of war are likely to be given by *united America* as by *disunited* America; for if it should turn out that united America will probably give the fewest, then it will follow that in this respect the Union tends most to preserve the people in a state of peace with other nations.

The *just* causes of war, for the most part, arise either from violations of treaties or from direct violence. America has already formed treaties with no less than six foreign nations, and all of them, except Prussia, are maritime, and therefore able to annoy and injure us. She has also extensive commerce with Portugal, Spain, and Britain, and, with respect to the two latter, has, in addition, the circumstance of neighborhood to attend to.

It is of high importance to the peace of America that she observe the laws of nations towards all these powers, and to me it appears evident that this will be more perfectly and punctually done by one national government than it could be either by thirteen separate States or by three or four distinct confederacies. For this opinion various reasons may be assigned.

When once an efficient national government is established, the best men in the country will not only consent to serve, but also will generally be appointed to manage it; for, although town or country, or other contracted influence, may place men in State assemblies, or senates, or courts of justice, or executive departments, yet more general and extensive reputation for talents and other qualifications will be necessary to recommend men to offices under the national government—especially as it will have the widest field for choice, and never experience that want of proper persons which is not uncommon in some of the States. Hence, it will result that the administration, the political counsels, and the judicial decisions of the national government will be more wise, systematical, and judicious than those of individual States, and consequently more satisfactory with respect to other nations, as well as more *safe* with respect to us.

Under the national government, treaties and articles of treaties, as well as the laws of nations, will always be expounded in one sense and executed in the same manner—whereas adjudications on the same points and questions in thirteen States, or in three or four confederacies, will not always accord or be consistent; and that, as well from the variety of independent courts and judges appointed by different and independent governments as from the different local laws and interests which may affect and influence them. The wisdom of the convention in committing such questions to the jurisdiction and judgment of courts appointed by and responsible only to one national government cannot be too much commended.

The prospect of present loss or advantage may often tempt the governing party in one or two States to swerve from good faith and justice; but those temptations, not reaching the other States, and consequently having little or no influence on the national government, the temptation will be fruitless, and good faith and justice be preserved. The case of the treaty of peace with Britain adds great weight to this reasoning.

If even the governing party in a State should be disposed to resist such temptations, yet, as such temptations may, and commonly do, result from circumstances peculiar to the State, and may affect a great number of the inhabitants, the governing party may not always be able, if willing, to prevent the injustice meditated, or to punish the aggressors. But the national government, not being affected by those local circumstances, will neither be induced to commit the wrong themselves, nor want power or inclination to prevent or punish its commission by others.

So far, therefore, as either designed or accidental violations of treaties and of the laws of nations afford *just* causes of war, they are less to be apprehended under one general government than under several lesser ones, and in that respect the former most favors the *safety* of the people.

As to those just causes of war which proceed from direct and unlawful violence, it appears equally clear to me that one good national government affords vastly more security against dangers of that sort than can be derived from any other quarter.

Such violences are more frequently occasioned by the passions and interests of a part than of the whole, of one or two States than of the Union. Not a single Indian war has yet been produced by aggressions of the present federal government, feeble as it is; but there are several instances of Indian hostilities having been provoked by the improper conduct of individual States, who, either unable or unwilling to restrain or punish offenses, have given occasion to the slaughter of many innocent inhabitants.

The neighborhood of Spanish and British territories, bordering on some States and not on others, naturally confines the causes of quarrel more immediately to the borderers. The bordering States, if any, will be those who, under the impulse of sudden irritation, and a quick sense of apparent interest or injury, will be most likely, by direct violence, to excite war with those nations; and nothing can so effectually obviate that danger as a national government, whose wisdom and prudence will not be diminished by the passions which actuate the parties immediately interested.

But not only fewer just causes of war will be given by the national government, but it will also be more in their power to accommodate and settle them amicably. They will be more temperate and cool, and in that respect, as well as in others, will be more in capacity to act with circumspection than the offending State. The pride of states, as well as of men, naturally disposes them to justify all their actions, and opposes their acknowledging, correcting, or repairing their errors and offenses. The national government, in such cases, will not be affected by this pride, but will proceed with moderation and candor to consider and decide on the means most proper to extricate them from the difficulties which threaten them.

Besides, it is well known that acknowledgments, explanations, and compensations are often accepted as satisfactory from a strong united nation, which would be rejected as unsatisfactory if offered by a State or confederacy of little consideration or power.

In the year 1685, the state of Genoa having offended Louis XIV, endeavored to appease him. He demanded that they should send their *Doge*, or chief magistrate, accompanied by four of their senators, to *France*, to ask his pardon and receive his terms. They were obliged to submit to it for the sake of peace. Would he on any occasion either have demanded or have received the like humiliation from Spain, or Britain, or any other *powerful* nation?

PUBLIUS

No. 4: Jay

MY LAST paper assigned several reasons why the safety of the people would be best secured by union against the danger it may be exposed to by *just* causes of war given to other nations; and those reasons show that such causes would not only be more rarely given, but would also be more easily accommodated by a national government than either by the State governments or the proposed little confederacies.

But the safety of the people of America against dangers from *foreign* force depends not only on their forbearing to give *just* causes of war to other nations, but also on their placing and continuing themselves in such a situation as not to *invite* hostility or insult; for it need not be observed that there are *pretended* as well as just causes of war.

It is too true, however disgraceful it may be to human nature, that nations in general will make war whenever they have a prospect of getting anything by it; nay, that absolute monarchs will often make war when their nations are to get nothing by it, but for purposes and objects merely personal, such as a thirst for military glory, revenge for personal affronts, ambition, or private compacts to aggrandize or support their particular families or partisans. These and a variety of other motives, which affect only the mind of the sovereign, often lead him to engage in wars not sanctified by justice or the voice and interests of his people. But, independent of these inducements to war, which are most prevalent in absolute monarchies, but which well deserve our attention, there are others which affect nations as often as kings; and some of them will on examination be found to grow out of our relative situation and circumstances.

With France and with Britain we are rivals in the fisheries, and can supply their markets cheaper than they can themselves, notwithstanding any efforts to prevent it by bounties on their own or duties on foreign fish.

With them and with most other European nations we are rivals in navigation and the carrying trade; and we shall deceive ourselves if we suppose that any of them will rejoice to see it flourish; for, as our carrying trade cannot increase without in some degree diminishing theirs, it is more their interest, and will be more their policy, to restrain than to promote it.

In the trade to China and India, we interfere with more than one nation, inasmuch as it enables us to partake in advantages which they had in a manner monopolized, and as we thereby supply ourselves with commodities which we used to purchase from them.

The extension of our own commerce in our own vessels cannot give pleasure to any nations who possess territories on or near this continent, because the cheapness and excellence of our productions, added to the circumstance of vicinity, and the enterprise and address of our merchants and navigators, will give us a greater share in the advantages which those territories afford than consists with the wishes or policy of their respective sovereigns.

Spain thinks it convenient to shut the Mississippi against us on the one side, and Britain excludes us from the Saint Lawrence on the other; nor will either of them permit the other waters which are between them and us to become the means of mutual intercourse and traffic.

From these and such like considerations, which might, if consistent with prudence, be more amplified and detailed, it is easy to see that jealousies and uneasiness may gradually slide into the minds and cabinets of other nations, and that we are not to expect that they should regard our advancement in union, in power and consequence by land and by sea, with an eye of indifference and composure.

The people of America are aware that inducements to war may arise out of these circumstances, as well as from others not so obvious at present, and that whenever such inducements may find fit time and opportunity for operation, pretenses to color and justify them will not be wanting. Wisely, therefore, do they consider union and a good national government as necessary to put and keep them in *such a situation* as, instead of *inviting* war, will tend to repress and discourage it. That situation consists in the best possible state of defense, and necessarily depends on the government, the arms, and the resources of the country.

As the safety of the whole is the interest of the whole, and cannot be provided for without government, either one or more or many, let us inquire whether one good government is not, relative to the object in question, more competent than any other given number whatever.

One government can collect and avail itself of the talents and experience of the ablest men, in whatever part of the Union they may be found. It can move on uniform principles of policy. It can harmonize, assimilate, and protect the several parts and members, and extend the benefit of its foresight and precautions to each. In the formation of treaties, it will regard the interest of the whole, and the particular interests of the parts as connected with that of the whole. It can apply the resources and power of the whole to the defense of any particular part, and that more easily and expeditiously than State governments or separate confederacies can possibly do, for want of concert and unity of system. It can place the militia under one plan of discipline, and, by putting their officers in a proper line of subordination to the Chief Magistrate, will, in a manner, consolidate them into one corps, and thereby render them more efficient than if divided into thirteen or into three or four distinct independent bodies.

What would the militia of Britain be if the English militia obeyed the government of England, if the Scotch militia obeyed the government of Scotland, and if the Welsh militia obeyed the government of Wales! Suppose an invasion; would those three governments (if they agreed at all) be able, with all their respective forces, to operate against the enemy so effectually as the single government of Great Britain would?

We have heard much of the fleets of Britain, and the time may come, if we are wise, when the fleets of America may engage attention. But if one national government had not so regulated the navigation of Britain as to make it a nursery for seamen—if one national government had not called forth all the national means and materials for forming fleets, their prowess and their thunder would never have been celebrated. Let England have its navigation and fleet—let Scotland have its navigation and fleet—let Wales have its navigation and fleet—let Ireland have its navigation and fleet—let those four of the constituent parts of the British Empire be under four independent governments, and it is easy to perceive how soon they would each dwindle into comparative insignificance.

Apply these facts to our own case. Leave America divided into thirteen or, if you please, into three or four independent governments—what armies could they raise and pay—what fleets could they ever hope to have? If one was attacked, would the others fly to its succor and spend their blood and money in its defense? Would there be no danger of their being flattered into neutrality by specious promises, or seduced by a too great fondness for peace to decline hazarding their tranquillity and present safety for the sake of neighbors, of whom perhaps they have been jealous, and whose importance they are content to see diminished. Although such conduct would not be wise, it would, nevertheless, be natural. The history of the states of Greece, and of other countries, abounds with such instances, and it is not improbable that what has so often happened would, under similar circumstances, happen again.

But admit that they might be willing to help the invaded State or confederacy. How, and when, and in what proportion shall aids of men and money be afforded? Who shall command the allied armies, and from which of them shall he receive his orders? Who shall settle the terms of peace, and in case of disputes what umpire shall decide between them and compel acquiescence? Various difficulties and inconveniences would be inseparable from such a situation; whereas one government, watching over the general and common interests and combining and directing the powers and resources of the whole, would be free from all these embarrassments and conduce far more to the safety of the people.

But whatever may be our situation, whether firmly united under one national government, or split into a number of confederacies, certain it is that foreign nations will know and view it exactly as it is; and they will act towards us accordingly. If they see that our national government is efficient and well administered, our trade prudently regulated, our militia properly organized and disciplined, our resources and finances discreetly managed, our credit re-established, our people free, contented, and united, they will be much more disposed to cultivate our friendship than provoke our resentment. If, on the other hand, they find us either destitute of an effectual government (each State doing right or wrong, as to its rulers may seem convenient), or split into three or four independent and probably discordant republics or confederacies, one inclining to Britain, another to France, and a third to Spain, and perhaps played off against each other by the three, what a poor, pitiful figure will America make in their eyes! How liable would she become not only to their contempt, but to their outrage; and how soon would dear-bought experience proclaim that when a people or family so divide, it never fails to be against themselves. PUBLIUS

No. 5: Jay

QUEEN Anne, in her letter of the 1st July, 1706, to the Scotch Parliament, makes some observations on the importance of the *Union* then forming between England and Scotland, which merit our attention. I shall present the public with one or two extracts from it: "An entire and perfect union will be the solid foundation of lasting peace: It will secure your religion, liberty, and property; remove the animosities amongst yourselves, and the jealousies and differences betwixt our two kingdoms. It must increase your strength, riches, and trade; and by this union the whole island, being joined in affection and free from all apprehensions of different interests, will be *enabled to resist all its enemies.*" "We most earnestly recommend to you calmness and unanimity in this great and weighty affair, that the union may be brought to a happy conclusion, being the only *effectual* way to secure our present and future happiness, and disappoint the designs of our and your enemies, who will doubtless, on this occasion, *use their utmost endeavors to prevent or delay this union.*"

It was remarked in the preceding paper that weakness and divisions at home would invite dangers from abroad; and that nothing would tend more to secure us from them than union, strength, and good government within ourselves. This subject is copious and cannot easily be exhausted.

The history of Great Britain is the one with which we are in general the best acquainted, and it gives us many useful lessons. We may profit by their experience without paying the price which it cost them. Although it seems obvious to common sense that the people of such an island should be but one nation, yet we find that they were for ages divided into three, and that those three were almost constantly embroiled in quarrels and wars with one another. Notwithstanding their true interest with respect to the continental nations was really the same, yet by the arts and policy and practices of those nations, their mutual jealousies were perpetually kept inflamed, and for a long series of years they were far more inconvenient and troublesome than they were useful and assisting to each other.

Should the people of America divide themselves into three or four nations, would not the same thing happen? Would not similar jealousies arise, and be in like manner cherished? Instead of their being "joined in affection and free from all apprehension of different interests," envy and jealousy would soon extinguish confidence and affection, and the partial interests of each confederacy, instead of the general interests of all America, would be the only objects of their policy and pursuits. Hence, like most other *bordering* nations, they would always be either involved in disputes and war, or live in the constant apprehension of them.

The most sanguine advocates for three or four confederacies cannot reasonably suppose that they would long remain exactly on an equal footing in point of strength, even if it was possible to form them so at first; but, admitting that to be practicable, yet what human contrivance can secure the continuance of such equality? Independent of those local circumstances which tend to beget and increase power in one part and to impede its progress in another, we must advert to the effects of that superior policy and good management which would probably distinguish the government of one above the rest, and by which their relative equality in strength and consideration would be destroyed. For it cannot be presumed that the same degree of sound policy, prudence, and foresight would uniformly be observed by each of these confederacies for a long succession of years.

Whenever, and from whatever causes, it might happen, and happen it would, that any one of these nations or confederacies should rise on the scale of political importance much above the degree of her neighbors, that moment would those neighbors behold her with envy and with fear. Both those passions would lead them to countenance, if not to promote, whatever might promise to diminish her importance; and would also restrain them from measures calculated to advance or even to secure her prosperity. Much time would not be necessary to enable her to discern these unfriendly dispositions. She would soon begin, not only to lose confidence in her neighbors, but also to feel a disposition equally unfavorable to them. Distrust naturally creates distrust, and by nothing is good will and kind conduct more speedily changed than by invidious jealousies and uncandid imputations, whether expressed or implied.

The North is generally the region of strength, and many local circumstances render it probable that the most Northern of the proposed confederacies would, at a period not very distant, be unquestionably more formidable than any of the others. No sooner would this become evident than the *Northern Hive* would excite the same ideas and sensations in the more southern parts of America which it formerly did in the southern parts of Europe. Nor does it appear to be a rash conjecture that its young swarms might often be tempted to gather honey in the more blooming fields and milder air of their luxurious and more delicate neighbors.

They who well consider the history of similar divisions and confederacies will find abundant reason to apprehend that those in contemplation would in no other sense be neighbors than as they would be borderers; that they would neither love nor trust one another, but on the contrary would be a prey to discord, jealousy, and mutual injuries; in short, that they would place us exactly in the situations in which some nations doubtless wish to see us, viz., *formidable only to each other*.

From these considerations it appears that those persons are greatly mistaken who suppose that alliances offensive and defensive might be formed between these confederacies, and would produce that combination and union of wills, of arms, and of resources, which would be necessary to put and keep them in a formidable state of defense against foreign enemies.

When did the independent states into which Britain and Spain were formerly divided combine in such alliance, or unite their forces against a foreign enemy? The proposed confederacies will be *distinct nations*. Each of them would have its commerce with foreigners to regulate by distinct treaties; and as their productions and commodities are different and proper for different markets, so would those treaties be essentially different. Different commercial concerns must create different interests, and of course different degrees of political attachment to and connection with different foreign nations. Hence it might and probably would happen that the foreign nation with whom the *Southern* confederacy might be at war would be the one with whom the *Northern* confederacy would be the most desirous of preserving peace and friendship. An alliance so contrary to their immediate interest would not therefore be easy to form, nor, if formed, would it be observed and fulfilled with perfect good faith.

Nay, it is far more probable that in America, as in Europe, neighboring nations, acting under the impulse of opposite interests and unfriendly passions, would frequently be found taking different sides. Considering our distance from Europe, it would be more natural for these confederacies to apprehend danger from one another than from distant nations, and therefore that each of them should be more desirous to guard against the others by the aid of foreign alliances, than to guard against foreign dangers by alliances between themselves. And here let us not forget how much more easy it is to receive foreign fleets into our ports, and foreign armies into our country, than it is to persuade or compel them to depart. How many conquests did the Romans and others make in the characters of allies, and what innovations did they under the same character introduce into the governments of those whom they pretended to protect.

Let candid men judge, then, whether the division of America into any given number of independent sovereignties would tend to secure us against the hostilities and improper interference of foreign nations. PUBLIUS

No. 6: Hamilton

THE three last numbers of this paper have been dedicated to an enumeration of the dangers to which we should be exposed, in a state of disunion, from the arms and arts of foreign nations. I shall now proceed to delineate dangers of a different and, perhaps, still more alarming kind—those which will in all probability flow from dissensions between the States themselves and from domestic factions and convulsions. These have been already in some instances slightly anticipated; but they deserve a more particular and more full investigation.

A man must be far gone in Utopian speculations who can seriously doubt that if these States should either be wholly disunited, or only united in partial confederacies, the subdivisions into which they might be thrown would have frequent and violent contests with each other. To presume a want of motives for such contests as an argument against their existence would be to forget that men are ambitious, vindictive, and rapacious. To look for a continuation of harmony between a number of independent, unconnected sovereignties situated in the same neighborhood would be to disregard the uniform course of human events, and to set at defiance the accumulated experience of ages.

The causes of hostility among nations are innumerable. There are some which have a general and almost constant operation upon the collective bodies of society. Of this description are the love of power or the desire of pre-eminence and dominion—the jealousy of power, or the desire of equality and safety. There are others which have a more circumscribed though an equally operative influence within their spheres. Such are the rivalships and competitions of commerce between commercial nations. And there are others, not less numerous than either of the former, which take their origin entirely in private passions; in the attachments, enmities, interests, hopes, and fears of leading individuals in the communities of which they are members. Men of this class, whether the favorites of a king or of a people, have in too many instances abused the confidence they possessed; and assuming the pretext of some public motive, have not scrupled to sacrifice the national tranquillity to personal advantage or personal gratification.

The celebrated Pericles, in compliance with the resentment of a prostitute,* at the expense of much of the

* Aspasia, *vide* Plutarch's *Life of Pericles.*

blood and treasure of his countrymen, attacked, vanquished, and destroyed the city of the *Samnians*. The same man, stimulated by private pique against the *Megarensians,** another nation of Greece, or to avoid a prosecution with which he was threatened as an accomplice in a supposed theft of the statuary of Phidias,† or to get rid of the accusations prepared to be brought against him for dissipating the funds of the state in the purchase of popularity,‡ of from a combination of all these causes, was the primitive author of that famous and fatal war, distinguished in the Grecian annals by the name of the *Peloponnesian* war; which, after various vicissitudes, intermissions, and renewals, terminated in the ruin of the Athenian commonwealth.

The ambitious cardinal, who was prime minister to Henry VIII, permitting his vanity to aspire to the triple crown,§ entertained hopes of succeeding in the acquisition of that splendid prize by the influence of the Emperor Charles V. To secure the favor and interest of this enterprising and powerful monarch, he precipitated England into a war with France, contrary to the plainest dictates of policy, and at the hazard of the safety and independence, as well of the kingdom over which he presided by his counsels as of Europe in general. For if there ever was a sovereign who bid fair to realize the project of universal monarchy, it was the Emperor Charles V, of whose intrigues Wolsey was at once the instrument and the dupe.

The influence which the bigotry of one female,|| the petulancies of another,# and the cabals of a third,** had in the contemporary policy, ferments, and pacifications of a considerable part of Europe, are topics that have been too often descanted upon not to be generally known.

To multiply examples of the agency of personal considerations in the production of great national events,

* *Ibid.*

† *Ibid.* Phidias was supposed to have stolen some public gold, with the connivance of Pericles, for the embellishment of the statue of Minerva.

‡ *Ibid.*

§ Worn by the popes.

|| Madame de Maintenon.

\# Duchess of Marlborough.

** Madame de Pompadour.

either foreign or domestic, according to their direction, would be an unnecessary waste of time. Those who have but a superficial acquaintance with the sources from which they are to be drawn will themselves recollect a variety of instances; and those who have a tolerable knowledge of human nature will not stand in need of such lights to form their opinion either of the reality or extent of that agency. Perhaps, however, a reference, tending to illustrate the general principle, may with propriety be made to a case which has lately happened among ourselves. If Shays had not been a *desperate debtor,* it is much to be doubted whether Massachusetts would have been plunged into a civil war.

But notwithstanding the concurring testimony of experience, in this particular, there are still to be found visionary or designing men, who stand ready to advocate the paradox of perpetual peace between the States, though dismembered and alienated from each other. The genius of republics (say they) is pacific; the spirit of commerce has a tendency to soften the manners of men, and to extinguish those inflammable humors which have so often kindled into wars. Commercial republics, like ours, will never be disposed to waste themselves in ruinous contentions with each other. They will be governed by mutual interest, and will cultivate a spirit of mutual amity and concord.

Is it not (we may ask these projectors in politics) the true interest of all nations to cultivate the same benevolent and philosophic spirit? If this be their true interest, have they in fact pursued it? Has it not, on the contrary, invariably been found that momentary passions, and immediate interests, have a more active and imperious control over human conduct than general or remote considerations of policy, utility, or justice? Have republics in practice been less addicted to war than monarchies? Are not the former administered by *men* as well as the latter? Are there not aversions, predilections, rivalships, and desires of unjust acquisitions that affect nations as well as kings? Are not popular assemblies frequently subject to the impulses of rage, resentment, jealousy, avarice, and of other irregular and violent propensities? Is it not well known that their determinations are often governed by a few individuals in whom they place confidence, and are, of course, liable to be tinctured by the passions and views of those individuals? Has commerce hitherto done any thing more than change the objects of war? Is not the love of wealth as domineering and enterprising a passion as that of power or glory? Have there not been as many wars founded upon commercial motives since that has become the prevailing system of nations, as were before occasioned by the cupidity of territory or dominion? Has not the spirit of commerce, in many instances, administered new incentives to the appetite, both for the one and for the other? Let experience, the least fallible guide of human opinions, be appealed to for an answer to these inquiries.

Sparta, Athens, Rome, and Carthage were all republics; two of them, Athens and Carthage, of the commercial kind. Yet were they as often engaged in wars, offensive and defensive, as the neighboring monarchies of the same times. Sparta was little better than a well-regulated camp; and Rome was never sated of carnage and conquest.

Carthage, though a commercial republic, was the aggressor in the very war that ended in her destruction. Hannibal had carried her arms into the heart of Italy and to the gates of Rome, before Scipio, in turn, gave him an overthrow in the territories of Carthage and made a conquest of the commonwealth.

Venice, in later times, figured more than once in wars of ambition, till, becoming an object to the other Italian states, Pope Julius the Second found means to accomplish that formidable league,* which gave a deadly blow to the power and pride of this haughty republic.

The provinces of Holland, till they were overwhelmed in debts and taxes, took a leading and conspicuous part in the wars of Europe. They had furious contests with England for the dominion of the sea, and were among the most persevering and most implacable of the opponents of Louis XIV.

In the government of Britain the representatives of

* The League of Cambray, comprehending the Emperor, the King of France, the King of Aragon, and most of the Italian princes and states.

the people compose one branch of the national legislature. Commerce has been for ages the predominant pursuit of that country. Few nations, nevertheless, have been more frequently engaged in war; and the wars in which that kingdom has been engaged have, in numerous instances, proceeded from the people.

There have been, if I may so express it, almost as many popular as royal wars. The cries of the nation and the importunities of their representatives have, upon various occasions, dragged their monarchs into war, or continued them in it, contrary to their inclinations, and sometimes contrary to the real interests of the state. In that memorable struggle for superiority between the rival houses of *Austria* and *Bourbon,* which so long kept Europe in a flame, it is well known that the antipathies of the English against the French, seconding the ambition, or rather the avarice, of a favorite leader,* protracted the war beyond the limits marked out by sound policy, and for a considerable time in opposition to the views of the court.

The wars of these two last-mentioned nations have in a great measure grown out of commercial considerations—the desire of supplanting and the fear of being supplanted, either in particular branches of traffic or in the general advantages of trade and navigation, and sometimes even the more culpable desire of sharing in the commerce of other nations without their consent.

The last war but two between Britain and Spain sprang from the attempts of the English merchants to prosecute an illicit trade with the Spanish main. These unjustifiable practices on their part produced severity on the part of the Spaniards towards the subjects of Great Britain which were not more justifiable, because they exceeded the bounds of a just retaliation and were chargeable with inhumanity and cruelty. Many of the English who were taken on the Spanish coast were sent to dig in the mines of Potosi; and by the usual progress of a spirit of resentment, the innocent were, after a while, confounded with the guilty in indiscriminate punishment. The complaints of the merchants kindled a violent flame

* The Duke of Marlborough.

throughout the nation, which soon after broke out in the House of Commons, and was communicated from that body to the ministry. Letters of reprisal were granted, and a war ensued, which in its consequences overthrew all the alliances that but twenty years before had been formed with sanguine expectations of the most beneficial fruits.

From this summary of what has taken place in other countries, whose situations have borne the nearest resemblance to our own, what reason can we have to confide in those reveries which would seduce us into an expectation of peace and cordiality between the members of the present confederacy, in a state of separation? Have we not already seen enough of the fallacy and extravagance of those idle theories which have amused us with promises of an exemption from the imperfections, the weaknesses, and the evils incident to society in every shape? Is it not time to awake from the deceitful dream of a golden age and to adopt as a practical maxim for the direction of our political conduct that we, as well as the other inhabitants of the globe, are yet remote from the happy empire of perfect wisdom and perfect virtue?

Let the point of extreme depression to which our national dignity and credit have sunk, let the inconveniences felt everywhere from a lax and ill administration of government, let the revolt of a part of the State of North Carolina, the late menacing disturbances in Pennsylvania, and the actual insurrections and rebellions in Massachusetts, declare——!

So far is the general sense of mankind from corresponding with the tenets of those who endeavor to lull asleep our apprehensions of discord and hostility between the States, in the event of disunion, that it has from long observation of the progress of society become a sort of axiom in politics that vicinity, or nearness of situation, constitutes nations natural enemies. An intelligent writer expresses himself on this subject to this effect: "NEIGHBORING NATIONS [says he] are naturally ENEMIES of each other, unless their common weakness forces them to league in a CONFEDERATE REPUBLIC, and their constitution prevents the differences that neighborhood occasions, extinguishing that secret jealousy which disposes all states to aggrandize themselves at the expense of their neighbors."* This passage, at the same time, points out the EVIL and suggests the REMEDY. PUBLIUS

No. 7: Hamilton

IT IS sometimes asked, with an air of seeming triumph, what inducements could the States have, if disunited, to make war upon each other? It would be a full answer to this question to say—precisely the same inducements which have, at different times, deluged in blood all the nations in the world. But, unfortunately for us, the question admits of a more particular answer. There are causes of differences within our immediate contemplation, of the tendency of which, even under the restraints of a federal constitution, we have had sufficient experience to enable us to form a judgment of what might be expected if those restraints were removed.

Territorial disputes have at all times been found one of the most fertile sources of hostility among nations. Perhaps the greatest proportion of wars that have desolated the earth have sprung from this origin. This cause would exist among us in full force. We have a vast tract of unsettled territory within the boundaries of the United States. There still are discordant and undecided claims between several of them, and the dissolution of the Union would lay a foundation for similar claims between them all. It is well known that they have heretofore had serious and animated discussions concerning the right to the lands which were ungranted at the time of the Revolution, and which usually went under the name of crown lands. The States within the limits of whose colonial governments they were comprised have claimed them as their property, the others have contended that the rights of the crown in this article devolved upon the Union; especially as to all that part of the Western territory which, either by actual possession, or through the submission of the Indian proprietors, was subjected to the jurisdiction of the king of

* *Vide Principes des Négociations* par l'Abbé de Mably.

Great Britain, till it was relinquished in the treaty of peace. This, it has been said, was at all events an acquisition to the Confederacy by compact with a foreign power. It has been the prudent policy of Congress to appease this controversy, by prevailing upon the States to make cessions to the United States for the benefit of the whole. This has been so far accomplished as, under a continuation of the Union, to afford a decided prospect of an amicable termination of the dispute. A dismemberment of the Confederacy, however, would revive this dispute, and would create others on the same subject. At present a large part of the vacant Western territory is, by cession at least, if not by any anterior right, the common property of the Union. If that were at an end, the States which have made cessions on a principle of federal compromise, would be apt, when the motive of the grant had ceased, to reclaim the lands as a reversion. The other States would no doubt insist on a proportion by right of representation. Their argument would be that a grant once made could not be revoked; and that the justice of their participating in territory acquired or secured by the joint efforts of the Confederacy remained undiminished. If, contrary to probability, it should be admitted by all the States that each had a right to a share of this common stock, there would still be a difficulty to be surmounted as to a proper rule of apportionment. Different principles would be set up by different States for this purpose; and as they would affect the opposite interests of the parties, they might not easily be susceptible of a pacific adjustment.

In the wide field of Western territory, therefore, we perceive an ample theater for hostile pretensions, without any umpire or common judge to interpose between the contending parties. To reason from the past to the future, we shall have good ground to apprehend that the sword would sometimes be appealed to as the arbiter of their differences. The circumstances of the dispute between Connecticut and Pennsylvania, respecting the lands at Wyoming, admonish us not to be sanguine in expecting an easy accommodation of such differences. The Articles of Confederation obliged the parties to submit the matter to the decision of a federal court. The submission was made, and the court decided in favor of Pennsylvania.

But Connecticut gave strong indications of dissatisfaction with that determination; nor did she appear to be entirely resigned to it, till, by negotiation and management, something like an equivalent was found for the loss she supposed herself to have sustained. Nothing here said is intended to convey the slightest censure on the conduct of that State. She no doubt sincerely believed herself to have been injured by the decision; and States, like individuals, acquiesce with great reluctance in determinations to their disadvantage.

Those who had an opportunity of seeing the inside of the transactions which attended the progress of the controversy between this State and the district of Vermont can vouch the opposition we experienced, as well from States not interested as from those which were interested in the claim, and can attest the danger to which the peace of the Confederacy might have been exposed, had this State attempted to assert its rights by force. Two motives preponderated in that opposition: one, a jealousy entertained of our future power; and the other, the interest of certain individuals of influence in the neighboring States, who had obtained grants of land under the actual government of that district. Even the States which brought forward claims in contradiction to ours seemed more solicitous to dismember this State, than to establish their own pretensions. These were New Hampshire, Massachusetts, and Connecticut. New Jersey and Rhode Island upon all occasions discovered a warm zeal for the independence of Vermont; and Maryland, until alarmed by the appearance of a connection between Canada and that place, entered deeply into the same views. These being small States, saw with an unfriendly eye the perspective of our growing greatness. In a review of these transactions we may trace some of the causes which would be likely to embroil the States with each other, if it should be their unpropitious destiny to become disunited.

Competitions of commerce would be another fruitful source of contention. The States less favorably circumstanced would be desirous of escaping from the disadvantages of local situation, and of sharing in the advantages of their more fortunate neighbors. Each State, or separate confederacy, would pursue a system of commercial policy peculiar to itself. This would occasion distinctions, preferences, and exclusions, which would beget discontent. The habits of intercourse, on the basis of equal privileges, to which we have been accustomed since the earliest settlement of the country would give a keener edge to those causes of discontent than they would naturally have independent of this circumstance. *We should be ready to denominate injuries those things which were in reality the justifiable acts of independent sovereignties consulting a distinct interest.* The spirit of enterprise, which characterizes the commercial part of America, has left no occasion of displaying itself unimproved. It is not at all probable that this unbridled spirit would pay much respect to those regulations of trade by which particular States might endeavor to secure exclusive benefits to their own citizens. The infractions of these regulations, on one side, the efforts to prevent and repel them, on the other, would naturally lead to outrages, and these to reprisals and wars.

The opportunities which some States would have of rendering others tributary to them by commercial regulations would be impatiently submitted to by the tributary States. The relative situation of New York, Connecticut, and New Jersey would afford an example of this kind. New York, from the necessities of revenue, must lay duties on her importations. A great part of these duties must be paid by the inhabitants of the two other States in the capacity of consumers of what we import. New York would neither be willing nor able to forego this advantage. Her citizens would not consent that a duty paid by them should be remitted in favor of the citizens of her neighbors; nor would it be practicable, if there were not this impediment in the way, to distinguish the customers in our own markets. Would Connecticut and New Jersey long submit to be taxed by New York for her exclusive benefit? Should we be long permitted to remain in the quiet and undisturbed enjoyment of a metropolis, from the possession of which we derived an advantage so odious to our neighbors, and, in their opinion, so oppressive? Should we be able to preserve it against the incumbent weight of Connecticut on the one side, and the co-operating pressure of New Jersey on the other? These are questions that temerity alone will answer in the affirmative.

The public debt of the Union would be a further cause of collision between the separate States or confederacies. The apportionment, in the first instance, and the progressive extinguishment afterwards, would be alike productive of ill humor and animosity. How would it be possible to agree upon a rule of apportionment satisfactory to all? There is scarcely any that can be proposed which is entirely free from real objections. These, as usual, would be exaggerated by the adverse interests of the parties. There are even dissimilar views among the States as to the general principle of discharging the public debt. Some of them, either less impressed with the importance of national credit, or because their citizens have little, if any, immediate interest in the question, feel an indifference, if not a repugnance, to the payment of the domestic debt at any rate. These would be inclined to magnify the difficulties of a distribution. Others of them, a numerous body of whose citizens are creditors to the public beyond the proportion of the State in the total amount of the national debt, would be strenuous for some equitable and effective provision. The procrastinations of the former would excite the resentments of the latter. The settlement of a rule would, in the meantime, be postponed by real differences of opinion and affected delays. The citizens of the States interested would clamor; foreign powers would urge for the satisfaction of their just demands, and the peace of the States would be hazarded to the double contingency of external invasion in internal contention.

Suppose the difficulties of agreeing upon a rule surmounted and the apportionment made. Still there is great room to suppose that the rule agreed upon would, upon experiment, be found to bear harder upon some States than upon others. Those which were sufferers by it would naturally seek for a mitigation of the burden. The others would as naturally be disinclined to a revision, which was likely to end in an increase of their own incumbrances. Their refusal would be too plausible a pretext to the complaining States to withhold their contributions, not to be embraced with avidity; and the noncompliance of these States with their engagements would be a ground of bitter dissension and altercation. If even the rule adopted should in practice justify the equality of its principle, still delinquencies in payment on the part of some of the States would result from a diversity of other causes—the real deficiency of resources; the mismanagement of their finances; accidental disorders in the administration of the government; and, in addition to the rest, the reluctance with which men commonly part with money for purposes that have outlived the exigencies which produced them and interfere with the supply of immediate wants. Delinquencies, from whatever causes, would be productive of complaints, recriminations, and quarrels. There is, perhaps, nothing more likely to disturb the tranquillity of nations than their being bound to mutual contributions for any common object that does not yield an equal and coincident benefit. For it is an observation, as true as it is trite, that there is nothing men differ so readily about as the payment of money.

Laws in violation of private contracts, as they amount to aggressions on the rights of those States whose citizens are injured by them, may be considered as another probable source of hostility. We are not authorized to expect that a more liberal or more equitable spirit would preside over the legislations of the individual States hereafter, if unrestrained by any additional checks, than we have heretofore seen in too many instances disgracing their several codes. We have observed the disposition to retaliation excited in Connecticut, in consequence of the enormities perpetrated by the legislature of Rhode Island; and we reasonably infer that, in similar cases under other circumstances, a war, not of *parchment*, but of the sword, would chastise such atrocious breaches of moral obligation and social justice.

The probability of incompatible alliances between the different States, or confederacies, and different foreign nations, and the effects of this situation upon the peace of the whole, have been sufficiently unfolded in some preceding papers. From the view they have exhibited of this part of the subject, this conclusion is to be drawn, that America, if not connected at all, or only by the feeble tie of a simple league, offensive and defensive, would, by the operation of such jarring alliances, be gradually entangled in all the pernicious labyrinths of European politics and wars; and by the destructive contentions of the parts into which she was divided, would be likely to become a prey to the artifices and machinations of powers equally the enemies of them all. *Divide et impera* * must be the motto of every nation that either hates or fears us.

PUBLIUS

No. 8: Hamilton

ASSUMING it therefore as an established truth that the several States, in case of disunion, or such combinations of them as might happen to be formed out of the wreck of the general Confederacy, would be subject to those vicissitudes of peace and war, of friendship and enmity with each other, which have fallen to the lot of all neighboring nations not united under one government, let us enter into a concise detail of some of the consequences that would attend such a situation.

War between the States, in the first period of their separate existence, would be accompanied with much greater distresses than it commonly is in those countries where regular military establishments have long obtained. The disciplined armies always kept on foot on the continent of Europe, though they bear a malignant aspect to liberty and economy, have, notwithstanding, been productive of the signal advantage of rendering sudden conquests impracticable, and of preventing that rapid desolation which used to mark the progress of war prior to their introduction. The art of fortification has contributed to the same ends. The nations of Europe are encircled with chains of fortified places, which mutually obstruct invasion. Campaigns are wasted in reducing two or three frontier garrisons to gain admittance into an enemy's country. Similar impediments occur at every step to exhaust the strength and delay the progress of an invader. Formerly an invading army would penetrate into the heart of a neighboring country almost as soon as intelligence of its approach could be received; but now a comparatively small force of disciplined troops, acting on the defensive, with the aid of posts, is able to impede, and finally to frustrate, the enterprises of one much more

* Divide and command.

considerable. The history of war in that quarter of the globe is no longer a history of nations subdued and empires overturned, but of towns taken and retaken, of battles that decide nothing, of retreats more beneficial than victories, of much effort and little acquisition.

In this country the scene would be altogether reversed. The jealousy of military establishments would postpone them as long as possible. The want of fortifications, leaving the frontiers of one State open to another, would facilitate inroads. The populous States would, with little difficulty, overrun their less populous neighbors. Conquests would be as easy to be made as difficult to be retained. War, therefore, would be desultory and predatory. PLUNDER and devastation ever march in the train of irregulars. The calamities of individuals would make the principal figure in the events which would characterize our military exploits.

This picture is not too highly wrought; though, I confess, it would not long remain a just one. Safety from external danger is the most powerful director of national conduct. Even the ardent love of liberty will, after a time, give way to its dictates. The violent destruction of life and property incident to war, the continual effort and alarm attendant on a state of continual danger, will compel nations the most attached to liberty to resort for repose and security to institutions which have a tendency to destroy their civil and political rights. To be more safe, they at length become willing to run the risk of being less free.

The institutions chiefly alluded to are STANDING ARMIES and the correspondent appendages of military establishments. Standing armies, it is said, are not provided against in the new Constitution; and it is thence inferred that they may exist under it. This inference, from the very form of the proposition, is, at best, problematical and uncertain.* But standing armies, it may be replied, must inevitably result from a dissolution of the

* This objection will be fully examined in its proper place, and it will be shown that the only rational precaution which could have been taken on this subject has been taken; and a much better one than is to be found in any constitution that has been heretofore framed in America, most of which contain no guard at all on this subject.

Confederacy. Frequent war and constant apprehension, which require a state of as constant preparation, will infallibly produce them. The weaker States, or confederacies, would first have recourse to them to put themselves upon an equality with their more potent neighbors. They would endeavor to supply the inferiority of population and resources by a more regular and effective system of defense, by disciplined troops, and by fortifications. They would, at the same time, be necessitated to strengthen the executive arm of government, in doing which their constitutions would acquire a progressive direction towards monarchy. It is of the nature of war to increase the executive at the expense of the legislative authority.

The expedients which have been mentioned would soon give the States, or confederacies, that made use of them a superiority over their neighbors. Small states, or states of less natural strength, under vigorous governments, and with the assistance of disciplined armies, have often triumphed over large states, or states of greater natural strength, which have been destitute of these advantages. Neither the pride nor the safety of the more important States, or confederacies, would permit them long to submit to this mortifying and adventitious superiority. They would quickly resort to means similar to those by which it had been effected, to reinstate themselves in their lost pre-eminence. Thus we should, in a little time, see established in every part of this country the same engines of despotism which have been the scourge of the old world. This, at least, would be the natural course of things; and our reasonings will be the more likely to be just in proportion as they are accommodated to this standard.

These are not vague inferences drawn from supposed or speculative defects in a Constitution, the whole power of which is lodged in the hands of a people, or their representatives and delegates, but they are solid conclusions, drawn from the natural and necessary progress of human affairs.

It may, perhaps, be asked, by way of objection to this, why did not standing armies spring up out of the contentions which so often distracted the ancient republics of Greece? Different answers, equally satisfactory, may be given to this question. The industrious habits of the people of the present day, absorbed in the pursuits of gain and devoted to the improvements of agriculture and commerce, are incompatible with the condition of a nation of soldiers, which was the true condition of the people of those republics. The means of revenue, which have been so greatly multiplied by the increase of gold and silver and of the arts of industry, and the science of finance, which is the offspring of modern times, concurring with the habits of nations, have produced an entire revolution in the system of war, and have rendered disciplined armies, distinct from the body of the citizens, the inseparable companion of frequent hostility.

There is a wide difference, also, between military establishments in a country seldom exposed by its situation to internal invasions, and in one which is often subject to them and always apprehensive of them. The rulers of the former can have no good pretext, if they are even so inclined, to keep on foot armies so numerous as must of necessity be maintained in the latter. These armies being, in the first case, rarely if at all called into activity for interior defense, the people are in no danger of being broken to military subordination. The laws are not accustomed to relaxation in favor of military exigencies; the civil state remains in full vigor, neither corrupted, nor confounded with the principles or propensities of the other state. The smallness of the army renders the natural strength of the community an overmatch for it; and the citizens, not habituated to look up to the military power for protection, or to submit to its oppressions, neither love nor fear the soldiery; they view them with a spirit of jealous acquiescence in a necessary evil and stand ready to resist a power which they suppose may be exerted to the prejudice of their rights.

The army under such circumstances may usefully aid the magistrate to suppress a small faction, or an occasional mob, or insurrection; but it will be unable to enforce encroachments against the united efforts of the great body of the people.

In a country in the predicament last described, the contrary of all this happens. The perpetual menacings of danger oblige the government to be always prepared to repel it; its armies must be numerous enough for instant defense. The continual necessity for their services enhances the importance of the soldier, and proportionably degrades the condition of the citizen. The military state becomes elevated above the civil. The inhabitants of territories, often the theater of war, are unavoidably subjected to frequent infringements on their rights, which serve to weaken their sense of those rights; and by degrees the people are brought to consider the soldiery not only as their protectors but as their superiors. The transition from this disposition to that of considering them masters is neither remote nor difficult; but it is very difficult to prevail upon a people under such impressions to make a bold or effectual resistance to usurpations supported by the military power.

The kingdom of Great Britain falls within the first description. An insular situation, and a powerful marine, guarding it in a great measure against the possibility of foreign invasion, supersede the necessity of a numerous army within the kingdom. A sufficient force to make head against a sudden descent, till the militia could have time to rally and embody, is all that has been deemed requisite. No motive of national policy has demanded, nor would public opinion have tolerated, a larger number of troops upon its domestic establishment. There has been, for a long time past, little room for the operation of the other causes, which have been enumerated as the consequences of internal war. This peculiar felicity of situation has, in a great degree, contributed to preserve the liberty which that country to this day enjoys, in spite of the prevalent venality and corruption. If, on the contrary, Britain had been situated on the continent, and had been compelled, as she would have been, by that situation, to make her military establishments at home coextensive with those of the other great powers of Europe, she, like them, would in all probability be, at this day, a victim to the absolute power of a single man. 'Tis possible, though not easy, that the people of that island may be enslaved from other causes; but it cannot be by the prowess of an army so inconsiderable as that which has been usually kept up within the kingdom.

If we are wise enough to preserve the Union we may for ages enjoy an advantage similar to that of an insulated situation. Europe is at a great distance from us. Her colonies in our vicinity will be likely to continue too much disproportioned in strength to be able to give us any dangerous annoyance. Extensive military establishments cannot, in this position, be necessary to our security. But if we should be disunited, and the integral parts should either remain separated, or, which is most probable, should be thrown together into two or three confederacies, we should be, in a short course of time, in the predicament of the continental powers of Europe —our liberties would be a prey to the means of defending ourselves against the ambition and jealousy of each other.

This is an idea not superficial nor futile, but solid and weighty. It deserves the most serious and mature consideration of every prudent and honest man of whatever party. If such men will make a firm and solemn pause, and meditate dispassionately on the importance of this interesting idea; if they will contemplate it in all its attitudes, and trace it to all its consequences, they will not hesitate to part with trivial objections to a Constitution, the rejection of which would in all probability put a final period to the Union. The airy phantoms that flit before the distempered imaginations of some of its adversaries would quickly give place to the more substantial prospects of dangers, real, certain, and formidable.

PUBLIUS

No. 9: Hamilton

A FIRM Union will be of the utmost moment to the peace and liberty of the States as a barrier against domestic faction and insurrection. It is impossible to read the history of the petty republics of Greece and Italy without feeling sensations of horror and disgust at the distractions with which they were continually agitated, and at the rapid succession of revolutions by which they were kept in a state of perpetual vibration between the extremes of tyranny and anarchy. If they exhibit occasional calms, these only serve as short-lived contrasts to the furious storms that are to succeed. If now and then intervals of felicity open themselves to view, we behold them with a mixture of regret, arising from the reflection that the pleasing scenes before us are soon to be overwhelmed by the tempestuous waves of sedition and party rage. If momentary rays of glory break forth from the gloom, while they dazzle us with a transient and fleeting brilliancy, they at the same time admonish us to lament that the vices of government should pervert the direction and tarnish the luster of those bright talents and exalted endowments for which the favored soils that produced them have been so justly celebrated.

From the disorders that disfigure the annals of those republics the advocates of despotism have drawn arguments, not only against the forms of republican government, but against the very principles of civil liberty. They have decried all free government as inconsistent with the order of society, and have indulged themselves in malicious exultation over its friends and partisans. Happily for mankind, stupendous fabrics reared on the basis of liberty, which have flourished for ages, have, in a few glorious instances, refuted their gloomy sophisms. And, I trust, America will be the broad and solid foundation of other edifices, not less magnificent, which will be equally permanent monuments of their errors.

But it is not to be denied that the portraits they have sketched of republican government were too just copies of the originals from which they were taken. If it had been found impracticable to have devised models of a more perfect structure, the enlightened friends to liberty would have been obliged to abandon the cause of that species of government as indefensible. The science of politics, however, like most other sciences, has received great improvement. The efficacy of various principles is now well understood, which were either not known at all, or imperfectly known to the ancients. The regular distribution of power into distinct departments; the introduction of legislative balances and checks; the institution of courts composed of judges holding their offices during good behavior; the representation of the people in the legislature by deputies of their own election: these are wholly new discoveries, or have made their principal progress towards perfection in modern times. They are means, and powerful means, by which the excellencies of republican government may be retained and its imperfections lessened or avoided. To this catalogue of circumstances that tend to the amelioration of popular systems of civil government, I shall venture, however novel it may appear to some, to add one more, on a principle which has been made the foundation of an objection to the new Constitution; I mean the ENLARGEMENT of the ORBIT within which such systems are to revolve, either in respect to the dimensions of a single State, or to the consolidation of several smaller States into one great Confederacy. The latter is that which immediately concerns the object under consideration. It will, however, be of use to examine the principle in its application to a single State, which shall be attended to in another place.

The utility of a Confederacy, as well to suppress faction and to guard the internal tranquillity of States as to increase their external force and security, is in reality not a new idea. It has been practised upon in different countries and ages, and has received the sanction of the most applauded writers on the subjects of politics. The opponents of the PLAN proposed have, with great assiduity, cited and circulated the observations of Montesquieu on the necessity of a contracted territory for a republican government. But they seem not to have been apprised of the sentiments of that great man expressed in another part of his work, nor to have adverted to the consequences of the principle to which they subscribe with such ready acquiescence.

When Montesquieu recommends a small extent for republics, the standards he had in view were of dimensions far short of the limits of almost every one of these States. Neither Virginia, Massachusetts, Pennsylvania, New York, North Carolina, nor Georgia can by any means be compared with the models from which he reasoned and to which the terms of his description apply. If we therefore take his ideas on this point as the criterion of truth, we shall be driven to the alternative either of taking refuge at once in the arms of monarchy, or of splitting ourselves into an infinity of little, jealous, clashing, tumultuous commonwealths, the wretched nurseries of unceasing discord and the miserable objects of universal pity or contempt. Some of the writers who have come forward on the other side of the question seem to have been aware of the dilemma; and have even been bold enough to hint at the division of the larger States as a desirable thing. Such an infatuated policy, such a desperate expedient, might, by the multiplication of petty offices, answer the views of men who possess not qualifications to extend their influence beyond the narrow circles of personal intrigue, but it could never promote the greatness or happiness of the people of America.

Referring the examination of the principle itself to another place, as has been already mentioned, it will be sufficient to remark here that, in the sense of the author who has been most emphatically quoted upon the occasion, it would only dictate a reduction of the SIZE of the more considerable MEMBERS of the Union, but would not militate against their being all comprehended in one confederate government. And this is the true question, in the discussion of which we are at present interested.

So far are the suggestions of Montesquieu from standing in opposition to a general Union of the States that he explicitly treats of a CONFEDERATE REPUBLIC as the expedient for extending the sphere of popular government and reconciling the advantages of monarchy with those of republicanism.

"It is very probable" (says he*) "that mankind would have been obliged at length to live constantly under the government of a SINGLE PERSON, had they not contrived a kind of constitution that has all the internal advantages of a republican, together with the external force of a monarchical, government. I mean a CONFEDERATE REPUBLIC.

"This form of government is a convention by which several smaller *states* agree to become members of a larger *one,* which they intend to form. It is a kind of assemblage of societies that constitute a new one, capable of increasing, by means of new associations, till they arrive to such a degree of power as to be able to provide for the security of the united body.

"A republic of this kind, able to withstand an external force, may support itself without any internal corrup-

* *Spirit of Laws,* Vol. I., Book IX., Chap. I.

tions. The form of this society prevents all manner of inconveniences.

"If a single member should attempt to usurp the supreme authority, he could not be supposed to have an equal authority and credit in all the confederate states. Were he to have too great influence over one, this would alarm the rest. Were he to subdue a part, that which would still remain free might oppose him with forces independent of those which he had usurped, and overpower him before he could be settled in his usurpation.

"Should a popular insurrection happen in one of the confederate states, the others are able to quell it. Should abuses creep into one part, they are reformed by those that remain sound. The state may be destroyed on one side, and not on the other; the confederacy may be dissolved, and the confederates preserve their sovereignty.

"As this government is composed of small republics, it enjoys the internal happiness of each; and with respect to its external situation, it is possessed, by means of the association, of all the advantages of large monarchies."

I have thought it proper to quote at length these interesting passages, because they contain a luminous abridgment of the principal arguments in favor of the Union, and must effectually remove the false impressions which a misapplication of other parts of the world was calculated to produce. They have, at the same time, an intimate connection with the more immediate design of this paper, which is to illustrate the tendency of the Union to repress domestic faction and insurrection.

A distinction, more subtle than accurate, has been raised between a *confederacy* and a *consolidation* of the States. The essential characteristic of the first is said to be the restriction of its authority to the members in their collective capacities, without reaching to the individuals of whom they are composed. It is contended that the national council ought to have no concern with any object of internal administration. An exact equality of suffrage between the members has also been insisted upon as a leading feature of a confederate government. These positions are, in the main, arbitrary; they are supported neither by principle nor precedent. It has indeed happened that governments of this kind have generally operated in the manner which the distinction, taken notice of, supposes to be inherent in their nature; but there have been in most of them extensive exceptions to the practice, which serve to prove, as far as example will go, that there is no absolute rule on the subject. And it will be clearly shown, in the course of this investigation, that as far as the principle contended for has prevailed, it has been the cause of incurable disorder and imbecility in the government.

The definition of a *confederate republic* seems simply to be "an assemblage of societies," or an association of two or more states into one state. The extent, modifications, and objects of the federal authority are mere matters of discretion. So long as the separate organization of the members be not abolished; so long as it exists, by a constitutional necessity, for local purposes; though it should be in perfect subordination to the general authority of the union, it would still be, in fact and in theory, an association of states, or a confederacy. The proposed Constitution, so far from implying an abolition of the State governments, makes them constituent parts of the national sovereignty, by allowing them a direct representation in the Senate, and leaves in their possession certain exclusive and very important portions of sovereign power. This fully corresponds, in every rational import of the terms, with the idea of a federal government.

In the Lycian confederacy, which consisted of twenty-three CITIES, or republics, the largest were entitled to *three* votes in the COMMON COUNCIL, those of the middle class to *two,* and the smallest to *one*. The COMMON COUNCIL had the appointment of all the judges and magistrates of the respective CITIES. This was certainly the most delicate species of interference in their internal administration; for if there be any thing that seems exclusively appropriated to the local jurisdictions, it is the appointment of their own officers. Yet Montesquieu, speaking of this association, says: "Were I to give a model of an excellent Confederate Republic, it would be that of Lycia." Thus we perceive that the distinctions insisted upon were not within the contemplation of this enlightened civilian; and we shall be led to conclude that they are the novel refinements of an erroneous theory.

PUBLIUS

No. 10: Madison

AMONG the numerous advantages promised by a well-constructed Union, none deserves to be more accurately developed than its tendency to break and control the violence of faction. The friend of popular governments never finds himself so much alarmed for their character and fate as when he contemplates their propensity to this dangerous vice. He will not fail, therefore, to set a due value on any plan which, without violating the principles to which he is attached, provides a proper cure for it. The instability, injustice, and confusion introduced into the public councils have, in truth, been the mortal diseases under which popular governments have everywhere perished, as they continue to be the favorite and fruitful topics from which the adversaries to liberty derive their most specious declamations. The valuable improvements made by the American constitutions on the popular models, both ancient and modern, cannot certainly be too much admired; but it would be an unwarrantable partiality to contend that they have as effectually obviated the danger on this side, as was wished and expected. Complaints are everywhere heard from our most considerate and virtuous citizens, equally the friends of public and private faith and of public and personal liberty, that our governments are too unstable, that the public good is disregarded in the conflicts of rival parties, and that measures are too often decided, not according to the rules of justice and the rights of the minor party, but by the superior force of an interested and overbearing majority. However anxiously we may wish that these complaints had no foundation, the evidence of known facts will not permit us to deny that they are in some degree true. It will be found, indeed, on a candid review of our situation, that some of the distresses under which we labor have been erroneously charged on the operation of our governments; but it will be found, at the same time, that other causes will not alone account for many of our heaviest misfortunes; and, particularly, for that prevailing and increasing distrust of public engagements and alarm for private rights which are echoed from one end of the continent to the other. These must be chiefly, if not wholly, effects of the unsteadiness and injustice with which a factious spirit has tainted our public administration.

By a faction I understand a number of citizens, whether amounting to a majority or minority of the whole, who are united and actuated by some common impulse of passion, or of interest, adverse to the rights of other citizens, or to the permanent and aggregate interests of the community.

There are two methods of curing the mischiefs of faction: the one, by removing its causes; the other, by controlling its effects.

There are again two methods of removing the causes of faction: the one, by destroying the liberty which is essential to its existence; the other, by giving to every citizen the same opinions, the same passions, and the same interests.

It could never be more truly said than of the first remedy that it was worse than the disease. Liberty is to faction what air is to fire, an aliment without which it instantly expires. But it could not be a less folly to abolish liberty, which is essential to political life, because it nourishes faction than it would be to wish the annihilation of air, which is essential to animal life, because it imparts to fire its destructive agency.

The second expedient is as impracticable as the first would be unwise. As long as the reason of man continues fallible, and he is at liberty to exercise it, different opinions will be formed. As long as the connection subsists between his reason and his self-love, his opinions and his passions will have a reciprocal influence on each other; and the former will be objects to which the latter will attach themselves. The diversity in the faculties of men, from which the rights of property originate, is not less an insuperable obstacle to a uniformity of interests. The protection of these faculties is the first object of government. From the protection of different and unequal faculties of acquiring property, the possession of different degrees and kinds of property immediately results; and from the influence of these on the sentiments and views of the respective proprietors ensues a division of the society into different interests and parties.

The latent causes of faction are thus sown in the nature of man; and we see them everywhere brought into different degrees of activity, according to the different circumstances of civil society. A zeal for different opinions concerning religion, concerning government, and many other points, as well of speculation as of practice; an attachment to different leaders ambitiously contending for pre-eminence and power; or to persons of other descriptions whose fortunes have been interesting to the human passions, have, in turn, divided mankind into parties, inflamed them with mutual animosity, and rendered them much more disposed to vex and oppress each other than to co-operate for their common good. So strong is this propensity of mankind to fall into mutual animosities that where no substantial occasion presents itself the most frivolous and fanciful distinctions have been sufficient to kindle their unfriendly passions and excite their most violent conflicts. But the most common and durable source of factions has been the verious and unequal distribution of property. Those who hold and those who are without property have ever formed distinct interests in society. Those who are creditors, and those who are debtors, fall under a like discrimination. A landed interest, a manufacturing interest, a mercantile interest, a moneyed interest, with many lesser interests, grow up of necessity in civilized nations, and divide them into different classes, actuated by different sentiments and views. The regulation of these various and interfering interests forms the principal task of modern legislation and involves the spirit of party and faction in the necessary and ordinary operations of government.

No man is allowed to be a judge in his own cause, because his interest would certainly bias his judgment, and, not improbably, corrupt his integrity. With equal, nay with greater reason, a body of men are unfit to be both judges and parties at the same time; yet what are many of the most important acts of legislation but so many judicial determinations, not indeed concerning the rights of single persons, but concerning the rights of large bodies of citizens? And what are the different classes of legislators but advocates and parties to the causes which they determine? Is a law proposed concerning private debts? It is a question to which the creditors are parties on one side and the debtors on the other. Justice ought to hold the balance between them. Yet the parties are, and must be, themselves the judges; and the most numerous party, or in other words, the most powerful faction must be expected to prevail. Shall domestic manufacturers be encouraged, and in what degree, by restrictions on foreign manufacturers? are questions which would be differently decided by the landed and the manufacturing classes, and probably by neither with a sole regard to justice and the public good. The apportionment of taxes on the various descriptions of property is an act which seems to require the most exact impartiality; yet there is, perhaps, no legislative act in which greater opportunity and temptation are given to a predominant party to trample on the rules of justice. Every shilling with which they overburden the inferior number is a shilling saved to their own pockets.

It is in vain to say that enlightened statesmen will be able to adjust these clashing interests and render them all subservient to the public good. Enlightened statesmen will not always be at the helm. Nor, in many cases, can such an adjustment be made at all without taking into view indirect and remote considerations, which will rarely prevail over the immediate interest which one party may find in disregarding the rights of another or the good of the whole.

The inference to which we are brought is that the *causes* of faction cannot be removed and that relief is only to be sought in the means of controlling its *effects*.

If a faction consists of less than a majority, relief is supplied by the republican principle, which enables the majority to defeat its sinister views by regular vote. It may clog the administration, it may convulse the society; but it will be unable to execute and mask its violence under the forms of the Constitution. When a majority is included in a faction, the form of popular government, on the other hand, enables it to sacrifice to its ruling passion or interest both the public good and the rights of other citizens. To secure the public good and private rights against the danger of such a faction, and at the same time to preserve the spirit and the form of popular government, is then the great object to which our inquiries are directed. Let me add that it is the great desideratum by which alone this form of government can be rescued from the opprobrium under which it has so long labored and be recommended to the esteem and adoption of mankind.

By what means is this object attainable? Evidently by one of two only. Either the existence of the same passion or interest in a majority at the same time must be prevented, or the majority, having such coexistent passion or interest, must be rendered, by their number and local situation, unable to concert and carry into effect schemes of oppression. If the impulse and the opportunity be suffered to coincide, we well know that neither moral nor religious motives can be relied on as an adequate control. They are not found to be such on the injustice and violence of individuals, and lose their efficacy in proportion to the number combined together, that is, in proportion as their efficacy becomes needful.

From this view of the subject it may be concluded that a pure democracy, by which I mean a society consisting of a small number of citizens, who assemble and administer the government in person, can admit of no cure for the mischiefs of faction. A common passion or interest will, in almost every case, be felt by a majority of the whole; a communication and concert results from the form of government itself; and there is nothing to check the inducements to sacrifice the weaker party or an obnoxious individual. Hence it is that such democracies have ever been spectacles of turbulence and contention; have ever been found incompatible with personal security or the rights of property; and have in general been as short in their lives as they have been violent in their deaths. Theoretic politicians, who have patronized this species of government, have erroneously supposed that by reducing mankind to a perfect equality in their political rights, they would at the same time be perfectly equalized and assimilated in their possessions, their opinions, and their passions.

A republic, by which I mean a government in which the scheme of representation takes place, opens a different prospect and promises the cure for which we are seeking. Let us examine the points in which it varies from pure democracy, and we shall comprehend both the nature of the cure and the efficacy which it must derive from the Union.

The two great points of difference between a democracy and a republic are: first, the delegation of the government, in the latter, to a small number of citizens elected by the rest; secondly, the greater number of citizens and greater sphere of country over which the latter may be extended.

The effect of the first difference is, on the one hand, to refine and enlarge the public views by passing them through the medium of a chosen body of citizens, whose wisdom may best discern the true interest of their country and whose patriotism and love of justice will be least likely to sacrifice it to temporary or partial considerations. Under such a regulation it may well happen that the public voice, pronounced by the representatives of the people, will be more consonant to the public good than if pronounced by the people themselves, convened for the purpose. On the other hand, the effect may be inverted. Men of factious tempers, of local prejudices, or of sinister designs, may, by intrigue, by corruption, or by other means, first obtain the suffrages, and then betray the interests of the people. The question resulting is, whether small or extensive republics are most favorable to the election of proper guardians of the public weal; and it is clearly decided in favor of the latter by two obvious considerations.

In the first place it is to be remarked that however small the republic may be the representatives must be raised to a certain number in order to guard against the cabals of a few; and that however large it may be they must be limited to a certain number in order to guard against the confusion of a multitude. Hence, the number of representatives in the two cases not being in proportion to that of the constituents, and being proportionally greatest in the small republic, it follows that if the proportion of fit characters be not less in the large than in the small republic, the former will present a greater option, and consequently a greater probability of a fit choice.

In the next place, as each representative will be chosen by a greater number of citizens in the large than in the small republic, it will be more difficult for unworthy candidates to practise with success the vicious arts by which elections are too often carried; and the suffrages of the people being more free, will be more likely to center on men who possess the most attractive merit and the most diffusive and established characters.

It must be confessed that in this, as in most other cases, there is a mean, on both sides of which inconveniencies will be found to lie. By enlarging too much the number of electors, you render the representative too little acquainted with all their local circumstances and lesser interests; as by reducing it too much, you render him unduly attached to these, and too little fit to comprehend and pursue great and national objects. The federal Constitution forms a happy combination in this respect; the great and aggregate interests being referred to the national, the local and particular to the State legislatures.

The other point of difference is the greater number of citizens and extent of territory which may be brought within the compass of republican than of democratic government; and it is this circumstance principally which renders factious combinations less to be dreaded in the former than in the latter. The smaller the society, the fewer probably will be the distinct parties and interests composing it; the fewer the distinct parties and interests, the more frequently will a majority be found of the same party; and the smaller the number of individuals composing a majority, and the smaller the compass within which they are placed, the more easily will they concert and execute their plans of oppression. Extend the sphere and you take in a greater variety of parties and interests; you make it less probable that a majority of the whole will have a common motive to invade the rights of other citizens; or if such a common motive exists, it will be more difficult for all who feel it to discover their own strength and to act in unison with each other. Besides other impediments, it may be remarked that, where there is a consciousness of unjust or dishonorable purposes, communication is always checked by distrust in proportion to the number whose concurrence is necessary.

Hence, it clearly appears that the same advantage which a republic has over a democracy in controlling the effects of faction is enjoyed by a large over a small republic—is enjoyed by the Union over the States composing it. Does this advantage consist in the substitution of representatives whose enlightened views and virtuous sentiments render them superior to local prejudices and to schemes of injustice? It will not be denied that the representation of the Union will be most likely to possess these requisite endowments. Does it consist in the greater security afforded by a greater variety of parties, against the event of any one party being able to outnumber and oppress the rest? In an equal degree does the increased variety of parties comprised within the Union increase this security. Does it, in fine, consist in the greater obstacles opposed to the concert and accomplishment of the secret wishes of an unjust and interested majority? Here again the extent of the Union gives it the most palpable advantage.

The influence of factious leaders may kindle a flame within their particular States but will be unable to spread a general conflagration through the other States. A religious sect may degenerate into a political faction in a part of the Confederacy; but the variety of sects dispersed over the entire face of it must secure the national councils against any danger from that source. A rage for paper money, for an abolition of debts, for an equal division of property, or for any other improper or wicked project, will be less apt to pervade the whole body of the Union than a particular member of it, in the same proportion as such a malady is more likely to taint a particular county or district than an entire State.

In the extent and proper structure of the Union, therefore, we behold a republican remedy for the diseases most incident to republican government. And according to the degree of pleasure and pride we feel in being republicans ought to be our zeal in cherishing the spirit and supporting the character of federalists. PUBLIUS

No. 11: Hamilton

THE importance of the Union, in a commercial light, is one of those points about which there is least room to entertain a difference of opinion, and which has, in fact, commanded the most general assent of men who have any acquaintance with the subject. This applies as well to our intercourse with foreign countries as with each other.

There are appearances to authorize a supposition that the adventurous spirit, which distinguishes the commercial character of America, has already excited uneasy sensations in several of the maritime powers of Europe. They seem to be apprehensive of our too great interference in that carrying trade, which is the support of their navigation and the foundation of their naval strength. Those of them which have colonies in America look forward to what this country is capable of becoming with painful solicitude. They foresee the dangers that may threaten their American dominions from the neighborhood of States, which have all the dispositions and would possess all the means requisite to the creation of a powerful marine. Impressions of this kind will naturally indicate the policy of fostering divisions among us and of depriving us, as far as possible, of an ACTIVE COMMERCE in our own bottoms. This would answer the threefold purpose of preventing our interference in their navigation, of monopolizing the profits of our trade, and of clipping the wings by which we might soar to a dangerous greatness. Did not prudence forbid the detail, it would not be difficult to trace, by facts, the workings of this policy to the cabinets of ministers.

If we continue united, we may counteract a policy so unfriendly to our prosperity in a variety of ways. By prohibitory regulations, extending at the same time throughout the States, we may oblige foreign countries to bid against each other for the privileges of our markets. This assertion will not appear chimerical to those who are able to appreciate the importance to any manufacturing nation of the markets of three millions of people—increasing in rapid progression, for the most part exclusively addicted to agriculture, and likely from local circumstances to remain in this disposition; and the immense difference there would be to the trade and navigation of such a nation, between a direct communication in its own ships and an indirect conveyance of its products and returns, to and from America, in the ships of another country. Suppose, for instance, we had a government in America capable of excluding Great Britain (with whom we have at present no treaty of commerce) from all our ports; what would be the probable operation of this step upon her politics? Would it not enable us to negotiate, with the fairest prospect of success, for commercial privileges of the most valuable and extensive kind in the dominions of that kingdom? When these questions have been asked upon other occasions, they have received a plausible, but not a solid or satisfactory answer. It has been said that prohibitions on our part would produce no change in the system of Britain, because she could prosecute her trade with us through the medium of the Dutch, who would be her immediate customers and paymasters for those articles which were wanted for the supply of our markets. But would not her navigation be materially injured by the loss of the important advantage of being her own carrier in that trade? Would not the principal part of its profits be intercepted by the Dutch as a compensation for their agency and risk? Would not the mere circumstance of freight occasion a considerable deduction? Would not so circuitous an intercourse facilitate the competitions of other nations, by enhancing the price of British commodities in our markets and by transferring to other hands the management of this interesting branch of the British commerce?

A mature consideration of the objects suggested by these questions will justify a belief that the real disadvantages to Great Britain from such a state of things, conspiring with the prepossessions of a great part of the nation in favor of the American trade and with the importunities of the West India islands, would produce a relaxation in her present system and would let us into the enjoyment of privileges in the markets of those islands and elsewhere, from which our trade would derive the most substantial benefits. Such a point gained from the British government, and which could not be expected without an equivalent in exemptions and immunities in our markets, would be likely to have a correspondent effect on the conduct of other nations, who would not be inclined to see themselves altogether supplanted in our trade.

A further resource for influencing the conduct of European nations towards us, in this respect, would arise from the establishment of a federal navy. There can be no doubt that the continuance of the Union under an efficient government would put it in our power, at a period not very distant, to create a navy which, if it could not vie with those of the great maritime powers, would at least be of respectable weight if thrown into the scale of either of two contending parties. This would be more particularly the case in relation to operations in the West Indies. A few ships of the line, sent opportunely to the reinforcement of either side, would often be sufficient to decide the fate of a campaign on the event of which interests of the greatest magnitude were suspended. Our position is in this respect a very commanding one. And if to this consideration we add that of the usefulness of supplies from this country, in the prosecution of military operations in the West Indies, it will readily be perceived that a situation so favorable would enable us to bargain with great advantage for commercial privileges. A price would be set not only upon our friendship, but upon our neutrality. By a steady adherence to the Union, we may hope, erelong, to become the arbiter of Europe in America, and to be able to incline the balance of European competitions in this part of the world as our interest may dictate.

But in the reverse of this eligible situation, we shall discover that the rivalships of the parts would make them checks upon each other and would frustrate all the tempting advantages which nature has kindly placed within our reach. In a state so insignificant our commerce would be a prey to the wanton intermeddlings of all nations at war with each other, who, having nothing to fear from us, would with little scruple or remorse supply their wants by depredations on our property as often as it fell in their way. The rights of neutrality will only be respected when they are defended by an adequate power. A nation, despicable by its weakness, forfeits even the privilege of being neutral.

Under a vigorous national government, the natural strength and resources of the country, directed to a common interest, would baffle all the combinations of European jealousy to restrain our growth. This situation would even take away the motive to such combinations by inducing an impracticability of success. An active commerce, an extensive navigation, a flourishing marine would then be the inevitable offspring of moral and physical necessity. We might defy the little arts of little politicians to control or vary the irresistible and unchangeable course of nature.

But in a state of disunion, these combinations might exist and might operate with success. It would be in the power of the maritime nations, availing themselves of our universal impotence, to prescribe the conditions of our political existence; and as they have a common interest in being our carriers, and still more in preventing our being theirs, they would in all probability combine to embarrass our navigation in such a manner as would in effect destroy it and confine us to a PASSIVE COMMERCE. We should thus be compelled to content ourselves with the first price of our commodities and to see the profits of our trade snatched from us to enrich our enemies and persecutors. That unequaled spirit of enterprise, which signalizes the genius of the American merchants and navigators and which is in itself an inexhaustible mine of national wealth, would be stifled and lost, and poverty and disgrace would overspread a country which with wisdom might make herself the admiration and envy of the world.

There are rights of great moment to the trade of America which are rights of the Union—I allude to the fisheries, to the navigation of the lakes, and to that of the Mississippi. The dissolution of the Confederacy would give room for delicate questions concerning the future existence of these rights, which the interest of more powerful partners would hardly fail to solve to our disadvantage. The disposition of Spain with regard to the Mississippi needs no comment. France and Britain are concerned with us in the fisheries, and view them as of the utmost moment to their navigation. They, of course, would hardly remain long indifferent to that decided mastery of which experience has shown us to be possessed in this valuable branch of traffic and by which we are able to undersell those nations in their own markets. What more natural than that they should be disposed to exclude from the lists such dangerous competitors?

This branch of trade ought not to be considered as a partial benefit. All the navigating States may, in different degrees, advantageously participate in it, and under circumstances of a greater extension of mercantile capital would not be unlikely to do it. As a nursery of seamen, it now is, or, when time shall have more nearly assimilated the principles of navigation in the several States, will become a universal resource. To the establishment of a navy it must be indispensable.

To this great national object, a NAVY, union will contribute in various ways. Every institution will grow and flourish in proportion to the quantity and extent of the means concentered towards its formation and support. A navy of the United States, as it would embrace the resources of all, is an object far less remote than a navy of any single State or partial confederacy, which would only embrace the resources of a part. It happens, indeed, that different portions of confederated America possess each some peculiar advantage for this essential establishment. The more southern States furnish in greater abundance certain kinds of naval stores—tar, pitch, and turpentine. Their wood for the construction of ships is also of a more solid and lasting texture. The difference in the duration of the ships of which the navy might be composed, if chiefly constructed of Southern wood, would be of signal importance, either in the view of naval strength or of national economy. Some of the Southern and of the Middle States yield a greater plenty of iron, and of better quality. Seamen must chiefly be drawn from the Northern hive. The necessity of naval protection to external or maritime commerce, and the conduciveness of that species of commerce to the prosperity of a navy, are points too manifest to require a particular elucidation. They, by a kind of reaction, mutually beneficial, promote each other.

An unrestrained intercourse between the States themselves will advance the trade of each by an interchange of their respective productions, not only for the supply of reciprocal wants at home, but for exportation to foreign markets. The veins of commerce in every part will be replenished and will acquire additional motion and vigor from a free circulation of the commodities of every part. Commercial enterprise will have much greater scope from the diversity in the productions of different States. When the staple of one fails from a bad harvest or unproductive crop, it can call to its aid the staple of another. The variety, not less than the value, of products for exportation contributes to the activity of foreign commerce. It can be conducted upon much better terms with a large number of materials of a given value than with a small number of materials of the same value, arising from the competitions of trade and from the fluctuations of markets. Particular articles may be in great demand at certain periods and unsalable at others; but if there be a variety of articles, it can scarcely happen that they should all be at one time in the latter predicament, and on this account the operations of the merchant would be less liable to any considerable obstruction or stagnation. The speculative trader will at once perceive the force of these observations, and will acknowledge that the aggregate balance of the commerce of the United States would bid fair to be much more favorable than that of the thirteen States without union or with partial unions.

It may perhaps be replied to this that whether the States are united or disunited there would still be an intimate intercourse between them which would answer the same ends; but this intercourse would be fettered, interrupted, and narrowed by a multiplicity of causes, which in the course of these papers have been amply detailed. A unity of commercial, as well as political, interests can only result from a unity of government.

There are other points of view in which this subject might be placed, of a striking and animating kind. But they would lead us too far into the regions of futurity, and would involve topics not proper for a newspaper discussion. I shall briefly observe that our situation invites and our interests prompt us to aim at an ascendant in the system of American affairs. The world may politically, as well as geographically, be divided into four parts, each having a distinct set of interests. Unhappily for the other three, Europe, by her arms and by her negotiations, by force and by fraud, has in different degrees extended her dominion over them all. Africa, Asia, and America have successively felt her domination. The superiority she has long maintained has tempted her to plume herself as the mistress of the world, and to consider the rest of mankind as created for her benefit. Men admired as profound philosophers have in direct terms attributed to her inhabitants a physical superiority and have gravely asserted that all animals, and with them the human species, degenerate in America—that even dogs cease to bark after having breathed awhile in our atmosphere.* Facts have too long supported these arrogant pretensions of the European. It belongs to us to vindicate the honor of the human race, and to teach that assuming brother moderation. Union will enable us to do it. Disunion will add another victim to his triumphs. Let Americans disdain to be the instruments of European greatness! Let the thirteen States, bound together in a strict and indissoluble Union, concur in erecting one great American system superior to the control of all transatlantic force or influence and able to dictate the terms of the connection between the old and the new world!

PUBLIUS

No. 12: Hamilton

THE effects of Union upon the commercial prosperity of the States have been sufficiently delineated. Its tendency to promote the interests of revenue will be the subject of our present inquiry.

The prosperity of commerce is now perceived and acknowledged by all enlightened statesmen to be the most useful as well as the most productive source of national wealth, and has accordingly become a primary object of their political cares. By multiplying the means of gratification, by promoting the introduction and circulation of the precious metals, those darling objects of human avarice and enterprise, it serves to vivify and invigorate all the channels of industry and to make them flow with greater activity and copiousness. The assiduous merchant, the laborious husbandman, the active mechanic, and the industrious manufacturer—all orders of men look forward with eager expectation and growing alacrity to this pleasing reward of their toils. The often-agitated question between agriculture and commerce has from indubitable experience received a decision which has silenced the rivalship that once subsisted between them, and has proved, to the entire satisfaction of their friends, that their interests are intimately blended and inter-

* "Recherches philosophiques sur les Américains."

woven. It has been found in various countries that in proportion as commerce has flourished land has risen in value. And how could it have happened otherwise? Could that which procures a freer vent for the products of the earth, which furnishes new incitements to the cultivators of land, which is the most powerful instrument in increasing the quantity of money in a state—could that, in fine, which is the faithful handmaid of labor and industry in every shape fail to augment the value of that article, which is the prolific parent of far the greatest part of the objects upon which they are exerted? It is astonishing that so simple a truth should ever have had an adversary; and it is one among a multitude of proofs how apt a spirit of ill-informed jealousy, or of too great abstraction and refinement, is to lead men astray from the plainest paths of reason and conviction.

The ability of a country to pay taxes must always be proportioned in a great degree to the quantity of money in circulation and to the celerity with which it circulates. Commerce, contributing to both these objects, must of necessity render the payment of taxes easier and facilitate the requisite supplies to the treasury. The hereditary dominions of the Emperor of Germany contain a great extent of fertile, cultivated, and populous territory, a large proportion of which is situated in mild and luxuriant climates. In some parts of this territory are to be found the best gold and silver mines in Europe. And yet from the want of the fostering influence of commerce that monarch can boast but slender revenues. He has several times been compelled to owe obligations to the pecuniary succors of other nations for the preservation of his essential interests, and is unable, upon the strength of his own resources, to sustain a long or continued war.

But it is not in this aspect of the subject alone that Union will be seen to conduce to the purposes of revenue. There are other points of view in which its influence will appear more immediate and decisive. It is evident from the state of the country, from the habits of the people, from the experience we have had on the point itself that it is impracticable to raise any very considerable sums by direct taxation. Tax laws have in vain been multiplied; new methods to enforce the collection have in vain been tried; the public expectation has been uniformly disappointed, and the treasuries of the States have remained empty. The popular system of administration inherent in the nature of popular government, coinciding with the real scarcity of money incident to a languid and mutilated state of trade, has hitherto defeated every experiment for extensive collections, and has at length taught the different legislatures the folly of attempting them.

No person acquainted with what happens in other countries will be surprised at this circumstance. In so opulent a nation as that of Britain, where direct taxes from superior wealth must be much more tolerable, and from the vigor of the government, much more practicable than in America, far the greatest part of the national revenue is derived from taxes of the indirect kind, from imposts and from excises. Duties on imported articles form a large branch of this latter description.

In America it is evident that we must a long time depend for the means of revenue chiefly on such duties. In most parts of it excises must be confined within a narrow compass. The genius of the people will ill brook the inquisitive and peremptory spirit of excise laws. The pockets of the farmers, on the other hand, will reluctantly yield but scanty supplies in the unwelcome shape of impositions on their houses and lands; and personal property is too precarious and invisible a fund to be laid hold of in any other way than by the imperceptible agency of taxes on consumption.

If these remarks have any foundation, that state of things which will best enable us to improve and extend so valuable a resource must be the best adapted to our political welfare. And it cannot admit of a serious doubt that this state of things must rest on the basis of a general Union. As far as this would be conducive to the interests of commerce, so far it must tend to the extension of the revenue to be drawn from that source. As far as it would contribute to rendering regulations for the collection of the duties more simple and efficacious, so far it must serve to answer the purposes of making the same rate of duties more productive and of putting it into the power of the government to increase the rate without prejudice to trade.

The relative situation of these States; the number of

rivers with which they are intersected and of bays that wash their shores; the facility of communication in every direction; the affinity of language and manners; the familiar habits of intercourse—all these are circumstances that would conspire to render an illicit trade between them a matter of little difficulty and would insure frequent evasions of the commercial regulations of each other. The separate States, or confederacies, would be necessitated by mutual jealousy to avoid the temptations to that kind of trade by the lowness of their duties. The temper of our governments for a long time to come would not permit those rigorous precautions by which the European nations guard the avenues into their respective countries, as well by land as by water; and which, even there, are found insufficient obstacles to the adventurous stratagems of avarice.

In France there is an army of patrols (as they are called) constantly employed to secure her fiscal regulations against the inroads of the dealers in contraband. Mr. Neckar computes the number of these patrols at upwards of twenty thousand. This proves the immense difficulty in preventing that species of traffic where there is an inland communication and shows in a strong light the disadvantages with which the collection of duties in this country would be encumbered, if by disunion the States should be placed in a situation with respect to each other resembling that of France with respect to her neighbors. The arbitrary and vexatious powers with which the patrols are necessarily armed would be intolerable in a free country.

If, on the contrary, there be but one government pervading all the States, there will be, as to the principal part of our commerce, but ONE SIDE to guard—the ATLANTIC COAST. Vessels arriving directly from foreign countries, laden with valuable cargoes, would rarely choose to hazard themselves to the complicated and critical perils which would attend attempts to unlade prior to their coming into port. They would have to dread both the dangers of the coast and of detection, as well after as before their arrival at the places of their final destination. An ordinary degree of vigilance would be competent to the prevention of any material infractions upon the rights of the revenue. A few armed vessels, judiciously stationed at the entrances of our ports, might at small expense be made useful sentinels of the laws. And the government having the same interests to provide against violations everywhere, the co-operation of its measures in each State would have a powerful tendency to render them effectual. Here also we should preserve, by Union, an advantage which nature holds out to us and which would be relinquished by separation. The United States lie at a great distance from Europe and at a considerable distance from all other places with which they would have extensive connections of foreign trade. The passage from them to us, in a few hours or in a single night, as between the coasts of France and Britain, and of other neighboring nations, would be impracticable. This is a prodigious security against a direct contraband with foreign countries; but a circuitous contraband to one State through the medium of another would be both easy and safe. The difference between a direct importation from abroad, and an indirect importation through the channel of a neighboring State, in small parcels according to time and oportunity, with the additional facilities of inland communication, must be palpable to every man of discernment.

It is therefore evident that one national government would be able at much less expense to extend the duties on imports beyond comparison, further than would be practicable to the States separately, or to any partial confederacies. Hitherto, I believe, it may safely be asserted that these duties have not upon an average exceeded in any State three percent. In France they are estimated at about fifteen percent, and in Britain the proportion is still greater. There seems to be nothing to hinder their being increased in this country to at least treble their present amount. The single article of ardent spirits under federal regulation might be made to furnish a considerable revenue. Upon a ratio to the importation into this State, the whole quantity imported into the United States may at a low computation be estimated at four millions of gallons, which, at a shilling per gallon, would produce two hundred thousand pounds. That article would well bear this rate of duty; and if it should tend to diminish the consumption of it, such an effect would be equally favorable to the agriculture, to the economy, to the morals, and to the health of the society. There is, perhaps, nothing so much a subject of national extravagance as this very article.

What will be the consequence if we are not able to avail ourselves of the resource in question in its full extent? A nation cannot long exist without revenue. Destitute of this essential support, it must resign its independence and sink into the degraded condition of a province. This is an extremity to which no government will of choice accede. Revenue, therefore, must be had at all events. In this country if the principal part be not drawn from commerce, it must fall with oppressive weight upon land. It has been already intimated that excises in their true signification are too little in unison with the feelings of the people to admit of great use being made of that mode of taxation; nor, indeed, in the States where almost the sole employment is agriculture are the objects proper for excise sufficiently numerous to permit very ample collections in that way. Personal estate (as has been before remarked), from the difficulty of tracing it, cannot be subjected to large contributions by any other means than by taxes on consumption. In populous cities it may be enough the subject of conjecture to occasion the oppression of individuals, without much aggregate benefit to the State; but beyond these circles it must, in a great measure, escape the eye and the hand of the tax-gatherer. As the necessities of the State, nevertheless, must be satisfied in some mode or other, the defect of other resources must throw the principal weight of the public burdens on the possessors of land. And as on the other hand the wants of the government can never obtain an adequate supply, unless all the sources of revenue are open to its demands, the finances of the community, under such embarrassments, cannot be put into a situation consistent with its respectability or its security. Thus we shall not even have the consolations of a full treasury to atone for the oppression of that valuable class of the citizens who are employed in the cultivation of the soil. But public and private distress will keep pace with each other in gloomy concert and unite in deploring the infatuation of those counsels which led to disunion.

PUBLIUS

No. 13: Hamilton

As CONNECTED with the subject of revenue, we may with propriety consider that of economy. The money saved from one object may be usefully applied to another, and there will be so much the less to be drawn from the pockets of the people. If the States are united under one government, there will be but one national civil list to support; if they are divided into several confederacies, there will be as many different national civil lists to be provided for—and each of them, as to the principal departments, coextensive with that which would be necessary for a government of the whole. The entire separation of the States into thirteen unconnected sovereignties is a project too extravagant and too replete with danger to have many advocates. The ideas of men who speculate upon the dismemberment of the empire seem generally turned towards three confederacies—one consisting of the four Northern, another of the four Middle, and a third of the five Southern States. There is little probability that there would be a greater number. According to this distribution each confederacy would comprise an extent of territory larger than that of the kingdom of Great Britain. No well-informed man will suppose that the affairs of such a confederacy can be properly regulated by a government less comprehensive in its origins or institutions than that which has been proposed by the convention. When the dimensions of a State attain to a certain magnitude, it requires the same energy of government and the same forms of administration which are requisite in one of much greater extent. This idea admits not of precise demonstration, because there is no rule by which we can measure the momentum of civil power necessary to the government of any given number of individuals; but when we consider that the island of Britain, nearly commensurate with each of the supposed confederacies, contains about eight millions of people, and when we reflect upon the degree of authority required to direct the passions of so large a society to the public good, we shall see no reason to doubt that the like portion of power would be sufficient to perform the same task in a society far more numerous. Civil power, properly organized and exerted, is capable of diffusing its force to a very great extent, and can in a manner reproduce itself in every part of a great empire by a judicious arrangement of subordinate institutions.

The supposition that each confederacy into which the States would be likely to be divided would require a government not less comprehensive than the one proposed will be strengthened by another supposition, more probable than that which presents us with three confederacies as the alternative to a general Union. If we attend carefully to geographical and commercial considerations, in conjunction with the habits and prejudices of the different States, we shall be led to conclude that in case of disunion they will most naturally league themselves under two governments. The four Eastern States, from all the causes that form the links of national sympathy and connection, may with certainty be expected to unite. New York, situated as she is, would never be unwise enough to oppose a feeble and unsupported flank to the weight of that confederacy. There are other obvious reasons that would facilitate her accession to it. New Jersey is too small a State to think of being a frontier in opposition to this still more powerful combination; nor do there appear to be any obstacles to her admission into it. Even Pennsylvania would have strong inducements to join the Northern league. An active foreign commerce, on the basis of her own navigation, is her true policy, and coincides with the opinions and dispositions of her citizens. The more Southern States, from various circumstances, may not think themselves much interested in the encouragement of navigation. They may prefer a system which would give unlimited scope to all nations to be the carriers as well as the purchasers of their commodities. Pennsylvania may not choose to confound her interests in a connection so adverse to her policy. As she must at all events be a frontier, she may deem it most consistent with her safety to have her exposed side turned towards the weaker power of the Southern, rather than towards the stronger power of the Northern, Confederacy. This would give her the fairest chance to avoid being the Flanders of

America. Whatever may be the determination of Pennsylvania, if the Northern Confederacy includes New Jersey, there is no likelihood of more than one confederacy to the south of that State.

Nothing can be more evident than that the thirteen States will be able to support a national government better than one half, or one third, or any number less than the whole. This reflection must have great weight in obviating that objection to the proposed plan, which is founded on the principle of expense; an objection, however, which, when we come to take a nearer view of it, will appear in every light to stand on mistaken ground.

If, in addition to the consideration of a plurality of civil lists, we take into view the number of persons who must necessarily be employed to guard the inland communication between the different confederacies against illicit trade, and who in time will infallibly spring up out of the necessities of revenue; and if we also take into view the military establishments which it has been shown would unavoidably result from the jealousies and conflicts of the several nations into which the States would be divided, we shall clearly discover that a separation would be not less injurious to the economy than to the tranquillity, commerce, revenue, and liberty of every part.

PUBLIUS

No. 14: Madison

WE HAVE seen the necessity of the Union as our bulwark against foreign danger, as the conservator of peace among ourselves, as the guardian of our commerce and other common interests, as the only substitute for those military establishments which have subverted the liberties of the old world, and as the proper antidote for the diseases of faction, which have proved fatal to other popular governments, and of which alarming symptoms have been betrayed by our own. All that remains within this branch of our inquiries is to take notice of an objection that may be drawn from the great extent of country which the Union embraces. A few observations on this subject will be the more proper as it is perceived that the adversaries of the new Constitution are availing themselves of a prevailing prejudice with regard to the practicable sphere of republican administration, in order to supply by imaginary difficulties the want of those solid objections which they endeavor in vain to find.

The error which limits republican government to a narrow district has been unfolded and refuted in preceding papers. I remark here only that it seems to owe its rise and prevalence chiefly to the confounding of a republic with a democracy, and applying to the former reasonings drawn from the nature of the latter. The true distinction between these forms was also adverted to on a former occasion. It is that in a democracy the people meet and exercise the government in person; in a republic they assemble and administer it by their representatives and agents. A democracy, consequently, must be confined to a small spot. A republic may be extended over a large region.

To this accidental source of the error may be added the artifice of some celebrated authors, whose writings have had a great share in forming the modern standard of political opinions. Being subjects either of an absolute or limited monarchy, they have endeavored to heighten the advantages, or palliate the evils of those forms, by placing in comparison with them the vices and defects of the republican and by citing as specimens of the latter the turbulent democracies of ancient Greece and modern Italy. Under the confusion of names, it has been an easy task to transfer to a republic observations applicable to a democracy only; and among others, the observation that it can never be established but among a small number of people, living within a small compass of territory.

Such a fallacy may have been the less perceived, as most of the popular governments of antiquity were of the democratic species; and even in modern Europe, to which we owe the great principle of representation, no example is seen of a government wholly popular and founded, at the same time, wholly on that principle. If Europe has the merit of discovering this great mechanical power in government, by the simple agency of which the will of the largest political body may be concentered and its force directed to any object which the public good requires, America can claim the merit of making the discovery the basis of unmixed and extensive republics. It is only to be lamented that any of her citizens should wish to deprive her of the additional merit of displaying its full efficacy in the establishment of the comprehensive system now under her consideration.

As the natural limit of a democracy is that distance from the central point which will just permit the most remote citizens to assemble as often as their public functions demand, and will include no greater number than can join in those functions, so the natural limit of a republic is that distance from the center which will barely allow the representatives of the people to meet as often as may be necessary for the administration of public affairs. Can it be said that the limits of the United States exceed this distance? It will not be said by those who recollect that the Atlantic coast is the longest side of the Union, that during the term of thirteen years the representatives of the States have been almost continually assembled, and that the members from the most distant States are not chargeable with greater intermissions of attendance than those from the States in the neighborhood of Congress.

That we may form a juster estimate with regard to this interesting subject, let us resort to the actual dimensions of the Union. The limits, as fixed by the treaty of peace, are: on the east the Atlantic, on the south the latitude of thirty-one degrees, on the west the Mississippi, and on the north an irregular line running in some instances beyond the forty-fifth degree, in others falling as low as the forty-second. The southern shore of Lake Erie lies below that latitude. Computing the distance between the thirty-first and forty-fifth degrees, it amounts to nine hundred and seventy-three common miles; computing it from thirty-one to forty-two degrees, to seven hundred, sixty-four miles and a half. Taking the mean for the distance, the amount will be eight hundred, sixty-eight miles and three fourths. The mean distance from the Atlantic to the Mississippi does not probably exceed seven hundred and fifty miles. On a comparison of this extent with that of several countries in Europe, the practicability of rendering our system commensurate to it appears to be demonstrable. It is not a great deal larger than Germany, where a diet representing the whole empire is continually assembled; or than Poland before the late dismemberment, where another national diet was the depositary of the supreme power. Passing by France and Spain, we find that in Great Britain, inferior as it may be in size, the representatives of the northern extremity of the island have as far to travel to the national council as will be required of those of the most remote parts of the Union.

Favorable as this view of the subject may be, some observations remain which will place it in a light still more satisfactory.

In the first place it is to be remembered that the general government is not to be charged with the whole power of making and administering laws. Its jurisdiction is limited to certain enumerated objects, which concern all the members of the republic, but which are not to be attained by the separate provisions of any. The subordinate governments, which can extend their care to all those other objects which can be separately provided for, will retain their due authority and activity. Were it proposed by the plan of the convention to abolish the governments of the particular States, its adversaries would have some ground for their objection; though it would not be difficult to show that if they were abolished the general government would be compelled by the principle of self-preservation to reinstate them in their proper jurisdiction.

A second observation to be made is that the immediate object of the federal Constitution is to secure the union of the thirteen primitive States, which we know to be practicable; and to add to them such other States as may arise in their own bosoms, or in their neighborhoods, which we cannot doubt to be equally practicable. The arrangements that may be necessary for those angles and fractions of our territory which lie on our northwestern frontier must be left to those whom further discoveries and experience will render more equal to the task.

Let it be remarked, in the third place, that the intercourse throughout the Union will be facilitated by new improvements. Roads will everywhere be shortened and kept in better order; accommodations for travelers will be multiplied and meliorated; an interior navigation on our eastern side will be opened throughout, or nearly throughout, the whole extent of the thirteen States. The communication between the Western and Atlantic districts, and between different parts of each, will be rendered more and more easy by those numerous canals with which the beneficence of nature has intersected our country, and which art finds it so little difficult to connect and complete.

A fourth and still more important consideration is that as almost every State will on one side or other be a frontier, and will thus find, in a regard to its safety, an inducement to make some sacrifices for the sake of the general protection; so the States which lie at the greatest distance from the heart of the Union, and which, of course, may partake least of the ordinary circulation of its benefits, will be at the same time immediately contiguous to foreign nations, and will consequently stand, on particular occasions, in greatest need of its strength and resources. It may be inconvenient for Georgia, or the States forming our western or northeastern borders, to send their representatives to the seat of government; but they would find it more so to struggle alone against an invading enemy, or even to support alone the whole expense of those precautions which may be dictated by the neighborhood of continual danger. If they should derive less benefit, therefore, from the Union in some respects than the less distant States, they will derive greater benefit from it in other respects, and thus the proper equilibrium will be maintained throughout.

I submit to you, my fellow-citizens, these considerations, in full confidence that the good sense which has so often marked your decisions will allow them their due weight and effect; and that you will never suffer difficulties, however formidable in appearance or however fashionable the error on which they may be founded, to drive you into the gloomy and perilous scene into which the advocates for disunion would conduct you. Hearken not to the unnatural voice which tells you that the people of America, knit together as they are by so many cords of affection, can no longer live together as members of the same family; can no longer continue the mutual guardians of their mutual happiness; can no longer be fellow-citizens of one great, respectable, and flourishing empire. Hearken not to the voice which petulantly tells you that the form of government recommended for your adoption is a novelty in the political world; that it has never yet had a place in the theories of the wildest projectors; that it rashly attempts what it is impossible to accomplish. No, my countrymen, shut your ears against this unhallowed language. Shut your hearts against the poison which it conveys; the kindred blood which flows in the veins of American citizens, the mingled blood which they have shed in defense of their sacred rights, consecrate their Union and excite horror at the idea of their becoming aliens, rivals, enemies. And if novelties are to be shunned, believe me, the most alarming of all novelties, the most wild of all projects, the most rash of all attempts, is that of rending us in pieces in order to preserve our liberties and promote our happiness. But why is the experiment of an extended republic to be rejected merely because it may comprise what is new? Is it not the glory of the people of America that, whilst they have paid a decent regard to the opinions of former times and other nations, they have not suffered a blind veneration for antiquity, for custom, or for names, to overrule the suggestions of their own good sense, the knowledge of their own situation, and the lessons of their own experience? To this manly spirit posterity will be indebted for the possession, and the world for the example, of the numerous innovations displayed on the American theater in favor of private rights and public happiness. Had no important step been taken by the leaders of the Revolution for which a precedent could not be discovered, no government established of which an exact model did not present itself, the people of the United States might at this moment have been numbered among the melancholy victims of misguided councils, must at best have been laboring under the weight of some of those forms which have crushed the liberties of the rest of mankind. Happily for America, happily we trust for the whole human race, they pursued a new and more noble course. They accomplished a revolution which has no parallel in the annals of human society. They reared the fabrics of governments which have no model on the face of the globe. They formed the design of a great Confederacy, which it is incumbent on their successors to improve and perpetuate. If their works betray imperfections, we wonder at the fewness of them. If they erred most in the structure of the Union, this was the work most difficult to be executed; this is the work which has been new modeled by the act of your convention, and it is that act on which you are now to deliberate and to decide. PUBLIUS

No. 15: Hamilton

IN THE course of the preceding papers I have endeavored, my fellow-citizens, to place before you in a clear and convincing light the importance of Union to your political safety and happiness. I have unfolded to you a complication of dangers to which you would be exposed, should you permit that sacred knot which binds the people of America together to be severed or dissolved by ambition or by avarice, by jealousy or by misrepresentation. In the sequel of the inquiry through which I propose to accompany you, the truths intended to be inculcated will receive further confirmation from facts and arguments hitherto unnoticed. If the road over which you will still have to pass should in some places appear to you tedious or irksome, you will recollect that you are in quest of information on a subject the most momentous which can engage the attention of a free people, that the field through which you have to travel is in itself spacious, and that the difficulties of the journey have been unnecessarily increased by the mazes with which sophistry has beset the way. It will be my aim to remove the obstacles to your progress in as compendious a manner as it can be done, without sacrificing utility to dispatch.

In pursuance of the plan which I have laid down for the discussion of the subject, the point next in order to be examined is the "insufficiency of the present Confederation to the preservation of the Union." It may perhaps be asked what need there is of reasoning or proof to illustrate a position which is not either controverted or doubted, to which the understandings and feelings of all classes of men assent, and which in substance is admitted by the opponents as well as by the friends of the new Constitution. It must in truth be acknowledged that, however these may differ in other respects, they in general appear to harmonize in this sentiment at least: that there are material imperfections in our national system and that something is necessary to be done to rescue us from impending anarchy. The facts that support this opinion are no longer objects of speculation. They have forced themselves upon the sensibility of the people at large, and have at length extorted from those, whose mistaken policy has had the principal share in precipitating the extremity at which we are arrived, a reluctant confession of the reality of those defects in the scheme of our federal government which have been long pointed out and regretted by the intelligent friends of the Union.

We may indeed with propriety be said to have reached almost the last stage of national humiliation. There is scarcely anything that can wound the pride or degrade the character of an independent nation which we do not experience. Are there engagements to the performance of which we are held by every tie respectable among men? These are the subjects of constant and unblushing violation. Do we owe debts to foreigners and to our own citizens contracted in a time of imminent peril for the preservation of our political existence? These remain without any proper or satisfactory provision for their discharge. Have we valuable territories and important posts in the possession of a foreign power which, by express stipulations, ought long since to have been surrendered? These are still retained to the prejudice of our interests, not less than of our rights. Are we in a condition to resent or to repel the aggression? We have neither troops, nor treasury, nor government.* Are we even in a condition to remonstrate with dignity? The just imputations on our own faith in respect to the same treaty ought first to be removed. Are we entitled by nature and compact to a free participation in the navigation of the Mississippi? Spain excludes us from it. Is public credit an indispensable resource in time of public danger? We seem to have abandoned its cause as desperate and irretrievable. Is commerce of importance to national wealth? Ours

* "I mean for the Union."

is at the lowest point of declension. Is respectability in the eyes of foreign powers a safeguard against foreign encroachments? The imbecility of our government even forbids them to treat with us. Our ambassadors abroad are the mere pageants of mimic sovereignty. Is a violent and unnatural decrease in the value of land a symptom of national distress? The price of improved land in most parts of the country is much lower than can be accounted for by the quantity of waste land at market, and can only be fully explained by that want of private and public confidence, which are so alarmingly prevalent among all ranks and which have a direct tendency to depreciate property of every kind. Is private credit the friend and patron of industry? That most useful kind which relates to borrowing and lending is reduced within the narrowest limits, and this still more from an opinion of insecurity than from a scarcity of money. To shorten an enumeration of particulars which can afford neither pleasure nor instruction, it may in general be demanded, what indication is there of national disorder, poverty, and insignificance that could befall a community so peculiarly blessed with natural advantages as we are, which does not form a part of the dark catalogue of our public misfortunes?

This is the melancholy situation to which we have been brought by those very maxims and counsels which would now deter us from adopting the proposed Constitution; and which, not content with having conducted us to the brink of a precipice, seem resolved to plunge us into the abyss that awaits us below. Here, my countrymen, impelled by every motive that ought to influence an enlightened people, let us make a firm stand for our safety, our tranquillity, our dignity, our reputation. Let us at last break the fatal charm which has too long seduced us from the paths of felicity and prosperity.

It is true, as has been before observed, that facts too stubborn to be resisted have produced a species of general assent to the abstract proposition that there exist material defects in our national system; but the usefulness of the concession on the part of the old adversaries of federal measures is destroyed by a strenuous opposition to a remedy upon the only principles that can give it a chance of success. While they admit that the government of the

United States is destitute of energy, they contend against conferring upon it those powers which are requisite to supply that energy. They seem still to aim at things repugnant and irreconcilable; at an augmentation of federal authority without a diminution of State authority; at sovereignty in the Union and complete independence in the members. They still, in fine, seem to cherish with blind devotion the political monster of an *imperium in imperio*. This renders a full display of the principal defects of the Confederation necessary in order to show that the evils we experience do not proceed from minute or partial imperfections, but from fundamental errors in the structure of the building, which cannot be amended otherwise than by an alteration in the first principles and main pillars of the fabric.

The great and radical vice in the construction of the existing Confederation is in the principle of LEGISLATION for STATES or GOVERNMENTS, in their CORPORATE or COLLECTIVE CAPACITIES, and as contradistinguished from the INDIVIDUALS of whom they consist. Though this principle does not run through all the powers delegated to the Union, yet it pervades and governs those on which the efficacy of the rest depends. Except as to the rule of apportionment, the United States have an indefinite discretion to make requisitions for men and money; but they have no authority to raise either by regulations extending to the individual citizens of America. The consequence of this is that though in theory their resolutions concerning those objects are laws constitutionally binding on the members of the Union, yet in practice they are mere recommendations which the States observe or disregard at their option.

It is a singular instance of the capriciousness of the human mind that after all the admonitions we have had from experience on this head, there should still be found men who object to the new Constitution for deviating from a principle which has been found the bane of the old and which is in itself evidently incompatible with the idea of GOVERNMENT; a principle, in short, which, if it is to be executed at all, must substitute the violent and sanguinary agency of the sword to the mild influence of the magistracy.

There is nothing absurd or impracticable in the idea of a league or alliance between independent nations for certain defined purposes precisely stated in a treaty regulating all the details of time, place, circumstance, and quantity, leaving nothing to future discretion, and depending for its execution on the good faith of the parties. Compacts of this kind exist among all civilized nations, subject to the usual vicissitudes of peace and war, of observance and nonobservance, as the interests or passions of the contracting powers dictate. In the early part of the present century there was an epidemical rage in Europe for this species of compacts, from which the politicians of the times fondly hoped for benefits which were never realized. With a view to establishing the equilibrium of power and the peace of that part of the world, all the resources of negotiations were exhausted, and triple and quadruple alliances were formed; but they were scarcely formed before they were broken, giving an instructive but afflicting lesson to mankind how little dependence is to be placed on treaties which have no other sanction than the obligations of good faith, and which oppose general considerations of peace and justice to the impulse of any immediate interest or passion.

If the particular States in this country are disposed to stand in a similar relation to each other, and to drop the project of a general DISCRETIONARY SUPERINTENDENCE, the scheme would indeed be pernicious and would entail upon us all the mischiefs which have been enumerated under the first head; but it would have the merit of being, at least, consistent and practicable. Abandoning all views towards a confederate government, this would bring us to a simple alliance offensive and defensive; and would place us in a situation to be alternate friends and enemies of each other, as our mutual jealousies and rivalships, nourished by the intrigues of foreign nations, should prescribe to us.

But if we are unwilling to be placed in this perilous situation; if we still will adhere to the design of a national government, or, which is the same thing, of a superintending power under the direction of a common council, we must resolve to incorporate into our plan those ingredients which may be considered as forming the characteristic difference between a league and a government; we must extend the authority of the Union to the persons of the citizens—the only proper objects of government.

Government implies the power of making laws. It is essential to the idea of a law that it be attended with a sanction; or, in other words, a penalty or punishment for disobedience. If there be no penalty annexed to disobedience, the resolutions or commands which pretend to be laws will, in fact, amount to nothing more than advice or recommendation. This penalty, whatever it may be, can only be inflicted in two ways: by the agency of the courts and ministers of justice, or by military force; by the COERCION of the magistracy, or by the COERCION of arms. The first kind can evidently apply only to men; the last kind must of necessity be employed against bodies politic, or communities, or States. It is evident that there is no process of a court by which the observance of the laws can in the last resort be enforced. Sentences may be denounced against them for violations of their duty; but these sentences can only be carried into execution by the sword. In an association where the general authority is confined to the collective bodies of the communities that compose it, every breach of the laws must involve a state of war; and military execution must become the only instrument of civil obedience. Such a state of things can certainly not deserve the name of government, nor would any prudent man choose to commit his happiness to it.

There was a time when we were told that breaches by the States of the regulations of the federal authority were not to be expected; that a sense of common interest would preside over the conduct of the respective members, and would beget a full compliance with all the constitutional requisitions of the Union. This language, at the present day, would appear as wild as a great part of what we now hear from the same quarter will be thought, when we shall have received further lessons from that best oracle of wisdom, experience. It at all times betrayed an ignorance of the true springs by which human conduct is actuated, and belied the original inducements to the establishment of civil power. Why has government been instituted at all? Because the passions of men will not conform to the dictates of reason and justice without constraint. Has it been found that bodies of men act with more rectitude or greater disinterestedness than individuals? The contrary of this has been inferred by all accurate observers of the conduct of mankind; and the inference is founded upon obvious reasons. Regard to reputation has a less active influence when the infamy of a bad action is to be divided among a number than when it is to fall singly upon one. A spirit of faction, which is apt to mingle its poison in the deliberations of all bodies of men, will often hurry the persons of whom they are composed into improprieties and excesses for which they would blush in a private capacity.

In addition to all this, there is in the nature of sovereign power an impatience of control that disposes those who are invested with the exercise of it to look with an evil eye upon all external attempts to restrain or direct its operations. From this spirit it happens that in every political association which is formed upon the principle of uniting in a common interest a number of lesser sovereignties, there will be found a kind of eccentric tendency in the subordinate or inferior orbs by the operation of which there will be a perpetual effort in each to fly off from the common center. This tendency is not difficult to be accounted for. It has its origin in the love of power. Power controlled or abridged is almost always the rival and enemy of that power by which it is controlled or abridged. This simple proposition will teach us how little reason there is to expect that the persons intrusted with the administration of the affairs of the particular members of a confederacy will at all times be ready with perfect good humor and an unbiased regard to the public weal to execute the resolutions or decrees of the general authority. The reverse of this results from the constitution of man.

If, therefore, the measures of the Confederacy cannot be executed without the intervention of the particular administrations, there will be little prospect of their being executed at all. The rulers of the respective members, whether they have a constitutional right to do it or not, will undertake to judge of the propriety of the measures themselves. They will consider the conformity of the thing proposed or required to their immediate interests or aims; the momentary conveniences or inconveniences that would attend its adoption. All this will be done; and in a spirit of interested and suspicious scrutiny, without that knowledge of national circumstances and reasons of state, which is essential to a right judgment, and with that strong predilection in favor of local objects, which can hardly fail to mislead the decision. The same process must be repeated in every member of which the body is constituted; and the execution of the plans, framed by the councils of the whole, will always fluctuate on the discretion of the ill-informed and prejudiced opinion of every part. Those who have been conversant in the proceedings of popular assemblies; who have seen how difficult it often is, when there is no exterior pressure of circumstances, to bring them to harmonious resolutions on important points, will readily conceive how impossible it must be to induce a number of such assemblies, deliberating at a distance from each other, at different times and under different impressions, long to co-operate in the same views and pursuits.

In our case the concurrence of thirteen distinct sovereign wills is requisite under the Confederation to the complete execution of every important measure that proceeds from the Union. It has happened as was to have been foreseen. The measures of the Union have not been executed; and the delinquencies of the States have step by step matured themselves to an extreme, which has, at length, arrested all the wheels of the national government and brought them to an awful stand. Congress at this time scarcely possess the means of keeping up the forms of administration, till the States can have time to agree upon a more substantial substitute for the present shadow of a federal government. Things did not come to this desperate extremity at once. The causes which have been specified produced at first only unequal and disproportionate degrees of compliance with the requisitions of the Union. The greater deficiencies of some States furnished the pretext of example and the temptation of interest to the complying, or to the least delinquent States. Why should we do more in proportion than those who are embarked with us in the same political voyage? Why should we consent to bear more than our proper share of the common burden? There were suggestions which human selfishness could not withstand, and which even speculative men, who looked forward to remote consequences, could not without hesitation combat. Each State yielding to the persuasive voice of immediate interest or convenience has successively withdrawn its support, till the frail and tottering edifice seems ready to fall upon our heads and to crush us beneath its ruins.

PUBLIUS

No. 16: Hamilton

THE tendency of the principle of legislation for States, or communities, in their political capacities, as it has been exemplified by the experiment we have made of it, is equally attested by the events which have befallen all other governments of the confederate kind of which we have any account in exact proportion to its prevalence in those systems. The confirmations of this fact will be worthy of a distinct and particular examination. I shall content myself with barely observing here that of all the confederacies of antiquity which history has handed down to us, the Lycian and Achæan leagues, as far as there remain vestiges of them, appear to have been most free from the fetters of that mistaken principle, and were accordingly those which have best deserved and have most liberally received the applauding suffrages of political writers.

This exceptionable principle may as truly as emphatically be styled the parent of anarchy: It has been seen that delinquencies in the members of the Union are its natural and necessary offspring; and that whenever they happen, the only constitutional remedy is force, and the immediate effect of the use of it, civil war.

It remains to inquire how far so odious an engine of government in its application to us would even be capable of answering its end. If there should not be a large army constantly at the disposal of the national government it would either not be able to employ force at all, or, when this could be done, it would amount to a war between different parts of the Confederacy concerning the infractions of a league in which the strongest combination would be most likely to prevail, whether it consisted of those who supported or of those who resisted the general authority. It would rarely happen that the delinquency to be redressed would be confined to a single member, and if there were more than one who had neglected their duty, similarity of situation would induce them to unite for common defense. Independent of this motive of sympathy, if a large and influential State should happen to be the aggressing member, it would commonly have weight enough with its neighbors to win over some of them as associates to its cause. Specious arguments of danger to the general liberty could easily be contrived; plausible excuses for the deficiencies of the party could without difficulty be invented to alarm the apprehensions, inflame the passions, and conciliate the good will even of those States which were not chargeable with any violation or omission of duty. This would be the more likely to take place, as the delinquencies of the larger members might be expected sometimes to proceed from an ambitious premeditation in their rulers, with a view to getting rid of all external control upon their designs of personal aggrandizement; the better to effect which it is presumable they would tamper beforehand with leading individuals in the adjacent States. If associates could not be found at home, recourse would be had to the aid of foreign powers, who would seldom be disinclined to encouraging the dissensions of a Confederacy from the firm union of which they had so much to fear. When the sword is once drawn, the passions of men observe no bounds of moderation. The suggestions of wounded pride, the instigations of irritated resentment, would be apt to carry the States against which the arms of the Union were exerted to any extremes necessary to avenge the affront or to avoid the disgrace of submission. The first war of this kind would probably terminate in a dissolution of the Union.

This may be considered as the violent death of the Confederacy. Its more natural death is what we now seem to be on the point of experiencing, if the federal system be not speedily renovated in a more substantial form. It is not probable, considering the genius of this country, that the complying States would often be inclined to support the authority of the Union by engaging in a war against the noncomplying States. They would always be more ready to pursue the milder course of putting themselves upon an equal footing with the delinquent members by an imitation of their example. And the guilt of all would thus become the security of all. Our past experience has exhibited the operation of this spirit in its full light. There would, in fact, be an insuperable difficulty in ascertaining when force could with propriety by employed. In the article of pecuniary contribution, which would be the most usual source of delinquency, it would often be impossible to decide whether it had proceeded from disinclination or inability. The pretense of the latter would always be at hand. And the case must be very flagrant in which its fallacy could be detected with sufficient certainty to justify the harsh expedient of compulsion. It is easy to see that this problem alone, as often as it should occur, would open a wide field to the majority that happened to prevail in the national council for the exercise of factious views, of partiality, and of oppression.

It seems to require no pains to prove that the States ought not to prefer a national Constitution which could only be kept in motion by the instrumentality of a large army continually on foot to execute the ordinary requisitions or decrees of the government. And yet this is the plain alternative involved by those who wish to deny it the power of extending its operations to individuals. Such a scheme, if practicable at all, would instantly degenerate into a military despotism; but it will be found in every light impracticable. The resources of the Union would not be equal to the maintenance of an army considerable enough to confine the larger States within the limits of their duty; nor would the means ever be furnished of forming such an army in the first instance. Whoever considers the populousness and strength of several of these States singly at the present juncture, and looks forward to what they will become even at the distance of half a century, will at once dismiss as idle and visionary any scheme which aims at regulating their movements by laws to operate upon them in their collective capacities and to be executed by a coercion applicable to them in the same capacities. A project of this kind is little less romantic than the monster-taming spirit, attributed to the fabulous heroes and demigods of antiquity.

Even in those confederacies which have been composed of members smaller than many of our counties, the principle of legislation for sovereign States supported by military coercion has never been found effectual. It has rarely been attempted to be employed, but against the weaker members; and in most instances attempts to coerce the refractory and disobedient have been the signals of bloody wars in which one half of the Confederacy has displayed its banners against the other half.

The result of these observations to an intelligent mind must be clearly this, that if it be possible at any rate to construct a federal government capable of regulating the common concerns and preserving the general tranquillity, it must be founded, as to the objects committed to its care, upon the reverse of the principle contended for by the opponents of the proposed Constitution. It must carry its agency to the persons of the citizens. It must stand in need of no intermediate legislations, but must itself be empowered to employ the arm of the ordinary magistrate to execute its own resolutions. The majesty of the national authority must be manifested through the medium of the courts of justice. The government of the Union, like that of each State, must be able to address itself immediately to the hopes and fears of individuals; and to attract to its support those passions which have the strongest influence upon the human heart. It must, in short, possess all the means, and have a right to resort to all the methods, of executing the powers with which it is intrusted, that are possessed and exercised by the governments of the particular States.

To this reasoning it may perhaps be objected that if any State should be disaffected to the authority of the Union it could at any time obstruct the execution of its laws, and bring the matter to the same issue of force, with the necessity of which the opposite scheme is reproached.

The plausibility of this objection will vanish the moment we advert to the essential difference between a mere NONCOMPLIANCE and a DIRECT and ACTIVE RESISTANCE. If the interposition of the State lelgislatures be necessary to give effect to a measure of the Union, they have only NOT TO ACT, or TO ACT EVASIVELY, and the measure is defeated. This neglect of duty may be disguised under affected but unsubstantial provisions so as not to appear, and of course not to excite any alarm in the people for the safety of the Constitution. The State leaders may even make a merit of their surreptitious invasions of it on the ground of some temporary convenience, exemption, or advantage.

But if the execution of the laws of the national government should not require the intervention of the State legislatures, if they were to pass into immediate operation upon the citizens themselves, the particular governments could not interrupt their progress without an open and violent exertion of an unconstitutional power. No omissions nor evasions would answer the end. They would be obliged to act, and in such a manner as would leave no doubt that they had encroached on the national rights. An experiment of this nature would always be hazardous in the face of a constitution in any degree competent to its own defense, and of a people enlightened enough to distinguish between a legal exercise and an illegal usurpation of authority. The success of it would require not merely a factious majority in the legislature, but the concurrence of the courts of justice and of the body of the people. If the judges were not embarked in a conspiracy with the legislature, they would pronounce the resolutions of such a majority to be contrary to the supreme law of the land, unconstitutional, and void. If the people were not tainted with the spirit of their State representatives, they, as the natural guardians of the Constitution, would throw their weight into the national scale and give it a decided preponderancy in the contest. Attempts of this kind would not often be made with levity or rashness, because they could seldom be made without danger to the authors, unless in cases of a tyrannical exercise of the federal authority.

If opposition to the national government should arise from the disorderly conduct of refractory or seditious individuals, it could be overcome by the same means which are daily employed against the same evil under the State governments. The magistracy, being equally the ministers of the law of the land from whatever source it might emanate, would doubtless be as ready to guard the national as the local regulations from the inroads of private licentiousness. As to those partial commotions and insurrections which sometimes disquiet society from the intrigues of an inconsiderable faction, or from sudden or occasional ill humors that do not infect the great body of the community, the general government could command more extensive resources for the suppression of disturbances of that kind than would be in the power of any single member. And as to those mortal feuds which in certain conjunctures spread a conflagration through a whole nation, or through a very large proportion of it, proceeding either from weighty causes of discontent given by the government or from the contagion of some violent popular paroxysm, they do not fall within any ordinary rules of calculation. When they happen, they commonly amount to revolutions and dismemberments of empire. No form of government can always either avoid or control them. It is in vain to hope to guard against events too mighty for human foresight or precaution, and it would be idle to object to a government because it could not perform impossibilities. PUBLIUS

No. 17: Hamilton

AN OBJECTION of a nature different from that which has been stated and answered in my last address may perhaps be likewise urged against the principle of legislation for the individual citizens of America. It may be said that it would tend to render the government of the Union too powerful, and to enable it to absorb those residuary authorities, which it might be judged proper to leave with the States for local purposes. Allowing the utmost latitude to the love of power which any reasonable man can require, I confess I am at a loss to discover what temptation the persons intrusted with the administration of the general government could ever feel to divest the States of the authorities of that description. The regulation of the mere domestic police of a State appears to me to hold out slender allurements to ambition. Commerce, finance, negotiation, and war seem to comprehend all the objects which have charms for minds governed by that passion; and all the powers necessary to those objects ought in the first instance to be lodged in the national depository. The administration of private justice between the citizens of the same State, the supervision of agriculture and of other concerns of a similar nature, all those things, in short, which are proper to be provided for by local legislation, can never be desirable cares of a general jurisdiction. It is therefore improbable that there should exist a disposition in the federal councils to usurp the powers with which they are connected; because the attempt to exercise those powers would be as troublesome as it would be nugatory; and the possession of them, for that reason, would contribute nothing to the dignity, to the importance, or to the splendor of the national government.

But let it be admitted, for argument's sake, that mere wantonness and lust of domination would be sufficient to beget that disposition; still it may be safely affirmed that the sense of the constituent body of the national representatives, or, in other words, the people of the several States, would control the indulgence of so extravagant an appetite. It will always be far more easy for the State governments to encroach upon the national authorities than for the national government to encroach upon the State authorities. The proof of this proposition turns upon the greater degree of influence which the State governments, if they administer their affairs with uprightness and prudence, will generally possess over the people; a circumstance which at the same time teaches us that there is an inherent and intrinsic weakness in all federal constitutions; and that too much pains cannot be taken in their organization to give them all the force which is compatible with the principles of liberty.

The superiority of influence in favor of the particular governments would result partly from the diffusive construction of the national government, but chiefly from the nature of the objects to which the attention of the State administrations would be directed.

It is a known fact in human nature that its affections are commonly weak in proportion to the distance or diffusiveness of the object. Upon the same principle that a man is more attached to his family than to his neighborhood, to his neighborhood than to the community at large, the people of each State would be apt to feel a stronger bias towards their local governments than towards the government of the Union; unless the force of that principle should be destroyed by a much better administration of the latter.

This strong propensity of the human heart would find powerful auxiliaries in the objects of State regulation.

The variety of more minute interests, which will necessarily fall under the superintendence of the local administrations and which will form so many rivulets of influence, running through every part of the society, cannot be particularized without involving a detail too tedious and uninteresting to compensate for the instruction it might afford.

There is one transcendent advantage belonging to the province of the State governments, which alone suffices to place the matter in a clear and satisfactory light—I mean the ordinary administration of criminal and civil justice. This, of all others, is the most powerful, most universal, and most attractive source of popular obedience and attachment. It is this which, being the immediate and visible guardian of life and property, having its benefits and its terrors in constant activity before the public eye, regulating all those personal interests and familiar concerns to which the sensibility of individuals is more immediately awake, contributes more than any other circumstance to impressing upon the minds of the people affection, esteem, and reverence towards the government. This great cement of society, which will diffuse itself almost wholly through the channels of the particular governments, independent of all other causes of influence, would insure them so decided an empire over their respective citizens as to render them at all times a complete counterpoise, and, not unfrequently, dangerous rivals to the power of the Union.

The operations of the national government, on the other hand, falling less immediately under the observation of the mass of the citizens, the benefits derived from it will chiefly be perceived and attended to by speculative men. Relating to more general interests, they will be less apt to come home to the feelings of the people; and, in proportion, less likely to inspire an habitual sense of obligation and an active sentiment of attachment.

The reasoning on this head has been abundantly exemplified by the experience of all federal constitutions with which we are acquainted, and of all others which have borne the least analogy to them.

Though the ancient feudal systems were not, strictly speaking, confederacies, yet they partook of the nature of that species of association. There was a common head, chieftain, or sovereign, whose authority extended over the whole nation; and a number of subordinate vassals, or feudatories, who had large portions of land allotted to them, and numerous trains of *inferior* vassals or retainers, who occupied and cultivated that land upon the tenure of fealtv or obedience to the persons of whom they held it. Each principal vassal was a kind of sovereign within his particular demesnes. The consequences of this situation were a continual opposition to the authority of the sovereign and frequent wars between the great barons or chief feudatories themselves. The power of the head of the nation was commonly too weak either to preserve the public peace or to protect the people against the oppressions of their immediate lords. This period of European affairs is emphatically styled by historians the times of feudal anarchy.

When the sovereign happened to be a man of vigorous and warlike temper and of superior abilities, he would acquire a personal weight and influence, which answered for the time the purposes of a more regular authority. But in general the power of the barons triumphed over that of the prince; and in many instances his dominion was entirely thrown off, and the great fiefs were erected into independent principalities or states. In those instances in which the monarch finally prevailed over his vassals, his success was chiefly owing to the tyranny of those vassals over their dependents. The barons, or nobles, equally the enemies of the sovereign and the oppressors of the common people, were dreaded and detested by both; till mutual danger and mutual interest effected a union between them fatal to the power of the aristocracy. Had the nobles, by a conduct of clemency and justice, preserved the fidelity and devotion of their retainers and followers, the contests between them and the prince must almost always have ended in their favor and in the abridgment or subversion of the royal authority.

This is not an assertion founded merely in speculation or conjecture. Among other illustrations of its truth which might be cited, Scotland will furnish a cogent example. The spirit of clanship which was at an early day introduced into that kingdom, uniting the nobles and their dependents by ties equivalent to those of kindred, rendered the aristocracy a constant overmatch for the power of the monarch, till the incorporation with

England subdued its fierce and ungovernable spirit and reduced it within those rules of subordination which a more rational and more energetic system of civil polity had previously established in the latter kingdom.

The separate governments in a confederacy may aptly be compared with the feudal baronies; with this advantage in their favor: that from the reasons already explained they will generally possess the confidence and good will of the people, and with so important a support will be able effectually to oppose all encroachments of the national government. It will be well if they are not able to counteract its legitimate and necessary authority. The points of similitude consist in the rivalship of power applicable to both; and in the CONCENTRATION of large portions of the strength of the community into particular DEPOSITORIES, in one case at the disposal of individuals, in the other case at the disposal of political bodies.

A concise review of the events that have attended confederate governments will further illustrate this important doctrine; an inattention to which has been the great source of our political mistakes and has given our jealousy a direction to the wrong side. This review shall form the subject of some ensuing papers. PUBLIUS

No. 18: Madison (with Hamilton)

AMONG the confederacies of antiquity the most considerable was that of the Grecian republics, associated under the Amphictyonic council. From the best accounts transmitted of this celebrated institution it bore a very instructive analogy to the present Confederation of the American States.

The members retained the character of independent and sovereign states and had equal votes in the federal council. This council had a general authority to propose and resolve whatever it judged necessary for the common welfare of Greece; to declare and carry on war; to decide in the last resort all controversies between the members; to fine the aggressing party; to employ the whole force of the Confederacy against the disobedient; to admit new members. The Amphictyons were the guardians of religion and of the immense riches belonging to the temple of Delphos, where they had the right of jurisdiction in controversies between the inhabitants and those who came to consult the oracle. As a further provision for the efficacy of the federal powers, they took an oath mutually to defend and protect the united cities, to punish the violators of this oath, and to inflict vengeance on sacrilegious despoilers of the temple.

In theory and upon paper, this apparatus of powers seems amply sufficient for all general purposes. In several material instances they exceed the powers enumerated in the Articles of Confederation. The Amphictyons had in their hands the superstition of the times, one of the principal engines by which government was then maintained; they had a declared authority to use coercion against refractory cities, and were bound by oath to exert this authority on the necessary occasions.

Very different, nevertheless, was the experiment from the theory. The powers, like those of the present Congress, were administered by deputies appointed wholly by the cities in their political capacities; and exercised over them in the same capacities. Hence the weakness, the disorders, and finally the destruction of the confederacy. The more powerful members, instead of being kept in awe and subordination, tyrannized successively over all the rest. Athens, as we learn from Demosthenes, was the arbiter of Greece seventy-three years. The Lacedæmonians next governed it twenty-nine years; at a subsequent period, after the battle of Leuctra, the Thebans had their turn of domination.

It happened but too often, according to Plutarch, that the deputies of the strongest cities awed and corrupted those of the weaker; and that judgment went in favor of the most powerful party.

Even in the midst of defensive and dangerous wars with Persia and Macedon, the members never acted in concert, and were, more or fewer of them, eternally the dupes or the hirelings of the common enemy. The intervals of foreign war were filled up by domestic vicissitudes, convulsions, and carnage.

After the conclusion of the war with Xerxes, it appears that the Lacedæmonians required that a number of the cities should be turned out of the confederacy for the unfaithful part they had acted. The Athenians, finding that the Lacedæmonians would lose fewer partisans by such a measure than themselves and would become masters of the public deliberations, vigorously opposed and defeated the attempt. This piece of history proves at once the inefficiency of the union, the ambition and jealousy of its most powerful members, and the dependent and degraded condition of the rest. The smaller members, though entitled by the theory of their system to revolve in equal pride and majesty around the common center, had become, in fact, satellites of the orbs of primary magnitude.

Had the Greeks, says the Abbé Milot, been as wise as they were courageous, they would have been admonished by experience of the necessity of closer union, and would have availed themselves of the peace which followed their success against the Persian arms to establish such a reformation. Instead of this obvious policy, Athens and Sparta, inflated with the victories and the glory they had acquired, became first rivals and then enemies; and did each other infinitely more mischief than they had suffered from Xerxes. Their mutual jealousies, fears, hatreds, and injuries ended in the celebrated Peloponnesian war, which itself ended in the ruin and slavery of the Athenians who had begun it.

As a weak government when not at war is ever agitated by internal dissensions, so these never fail to bring on fresh calamities from abroad. The Phocians having plowed up some consecrated ground belonging to the temple of Apollo, the Amphictyonic council, according to the superstition of the age, imposed a fine on the sacrilegious offenders. The Phocians, being abetted by Athens and Sparta, refused to submit to the decree. The Thebans, with others of the cities, undertook to maintain the authority of the Amphictyons and to avenge the violated god. The latter, being the weaker party, invited the assistance of Philip of Macedon, who had secretly fostered the contest. Philip gladly seized the opportunity of executing the designs he had long planned against the liberties of Greece. By his intrigues and bribes he won over to his interests the popular leaders of several cities; by their influence and votes, gained admission into the

Amphictyonic council; and by his arts and his arms, made himself master of the confederacy.

Such were the consequences of the fallacious principle on which this interesting establishment was founded. Had Greece, says a judicious observer on her fate, been united by a stricter confederation and persevered in her union she would never have worn the chains of Macedon; and might have proved a barrier to the vast projects of Rome.

The Achæan league, as it is called, was another society of Grecian republics which supplies us with valuable instruction.

The Union here was far more intimate, and its organization much wiser than in the preceding instance. It will accordingly appear that though not exempt from a similar catastrophe, it by no means equally deserved it.

The cities composing this league retained their municipal jurisdiction, appointed their own officers, and enjoyed a perfect equality. The senate, in which they were represented, had the sole and exclusive right of peace and war; of sending and receiving ambassadors; of entering into treaties and alliances; of appointing a chief magistrate or prætor, as he was called, who commanded their armies and who, with the advice and consent of ten of the senators, not only administered the government in the recess of the senate, but had a great share in its deliberations, when assembled. According to the primitive constitution, there were two prætors associated in the administration; but on trial a single one was preferred.

It appears that the cities had all the same laws and customs, the same weights and measures, and the same money. But how far this effect proceeded from the authority of the federal council is left in uncertainty. It is said only that the cities were in a manner compelled to receive the same laws and usages. When Lacedæmon was brought into the league by Philopœmen, it was attended with an abolition of the institutions and laws of Lycurgus, and an adoption of those of the Achæans. The Amphictyonic confederacies, of which she had been a member, left her in the full exercise of her government and her legislation. This circumstance alone proves a very material difference in the genius of the two systems.

It is much to be regretted that such imperfect monuments remain of this curious political fabric. Could its interior structure and regular operation be ascertained, it is probable that more light would be thrown by it on the science of federal government than by any of the like experiments with which we are acquainted.

One important fact seems to be witnessed by all the historians who take notice of Achæan affairs. It is that as well after the renovation of the league by Aratus as before its dissolution by the arts of Macedon, there was infinitely more of moderation and justice in the administration of its government, and less of violence and sedition in the people, than were to be found in any of the cities exercising *singly* all the prerogatives of sovereignty. The Abbé Mably, in his observations on Greece, says that the popular government, which was so tempestuous elsewhere, caused no disorders in the members of the Achæan republic, *because it was there tempered by the general authority and laws of the confederacy.*

We are not to conclude too hastily, however, that faction did not, in a certain degree, agitate the particular cities; much less than a due subordination and harmony reigned in the general system. The contrary is sufficiently displayed in the vicissitudes and fate of the republic.

Whilst the Amphictyonic confederacy remained, that of the Achæans, which comprehended the less important cities only, made little figure on the theater of Greece. When the former became a victim to Macedon, the latter was spared by the policy of Philip and Alexander. Under the successors of these princes, however, a different policy prevailed. The arts of division were practiced among the Achæans; each city was seduced into a separate interest; the union was dissolved. Some of the cities fell under the tyranny of Macedonian garrisons, others under that of usurpers springing out of their own confusions. Shame and oppression erelong awakened their love of liberty. A few cities reunited. Their example was followed by others as opportunities were found of cutting off their tyrants. The league soon embraced almost the whole Peloponnesus. Macedon saw its progress, but was hindered by internal dissensions from stopping it. All Greece caught the enthusiasm and seemed ready to unite in one confederacy, when the jealousy and envy in Sparta and

Athens of the rising glory of the Achæans threw a fatal damp on the enterprise. The dread of the Macedonian power induced the league to court the alliance of the kings of Egypt and Syria, who, as successors of Alexander, were rivals of the king of Macedon. This policy was defeated by Cleomenes, King of Sparta, who was led by his ambition to make an unprovoked attack on his neighbors, the Achæans, and who, as an enemy to Macedon, had interest enough with the Egyptian and Syrian princes to effect a breach of their engagements with the league. The Achæans were now reduced to the dilemma of submitting to Cleomenes, or of supplicating the aid of Macedon, its former oppressor. The latter expedient was adopted. The contests of the Greeks always afforded a pleasing opportunity to that powerful neighbor of intermeddling in their affairs. A Macedonian army quickly appeared. Cleomenes was vanquished. The Achæans soon experienced, as often happens, that a victorious and powerful ally is but another name for a master. All that their most abject compliances could obtain from him was a toleration of the exercise of their laws. Philip, who was now on the throne of Macedon, soon provoked by his tyrannies fresh combinations among the Greeks. The Achæans, though weakened by internal dissensions and by the revolt of Messene, one of its members, being joined by the Ætolians and Athenians, erected the standard of opposition. Finding themselves, though thus supported, unequal to the undertaking, they once more had recourse to the dangerous expedient of introducing the succor of foreign arms. The Romans, to whom the invitation was made, eagerly embraced it. Philip was conquered; Macedon subdued. A new crisis ensued to the league. Dissensions broke out among its members. These the Romans fostered. Callicrates and other popular leaders became mercenary instruments for inveigling their countrymen. The more effectually to nourish discord and disorder the Romans had, to the astonishment of those who confided in their sincerity, already proclaimed universal liberty* throughout Greece. With the same insidious views, they now seduced the members from the league by representing to

* This was but another name more specious for the independence of the members on the federal head.

their pride the violation it committed on their sovereignty. By these arts this union, the last hope of Greece, the last hope of ancient liberty, was torn into pieces; and such imbecility and distraction introduced, that the arms of Rome found little difficulty in completing the ruin which their arts had commenced. The Achæans were cut to pieces, and Achaia loaded with chains, under which it is groaning at this hour.

I have thought it not superfluous to give the outlines of this important portion of history, both because it teaches more than one lesson and because, as a supplement to the outlines of the Achæan constitution, it emphatically illustrates the tendency of federal bodies rather to anarchy among the members than to tyranny in the head.

PUBLIUS

No. 19: Madison (with Hamilton)

THE examples of ancient confederacies cited in my last paper have not exhausted the source of experimental instruction on this subject. There are existing institutions founded on a similar principle which merit particular consideration. The first which presents itself is the Germanic body.

In the early ages of Christianity, Germany was occupied by seven distinct nations, who had no common chief. The Franks, one of the number, having conquered the Gauls, established the kingdom which has taken its name from them. In the ninth century Charlemagne, its warlike monarch, carried his victorious arms in every direction; and Germany became a part of his vast dominions. On the dismemberment which took place under his sons this part was erected into a separate and independent empire. Charlemagne and his immediate descendants possessed the reality, as well as the ensigns and dignity of imperial power. But the principal vassals, whose fiefs had become hereditary, and who composed the national diets which Charlemagne had not abolished, gradually threw off the yoke and advanced to sovereign jurisdiction and independence. The force of imperial sovereignty was insufficient to restrain such powerful dependents, or to preserve the unity and tranquillity of the empire. The most furious private wars, accompanied with every species of calamity, were carried on between the different princes and states. The imperial authority, unable to maintain the public order, declined by degrees till it was almost extinct in the anarchy, which agitated the long interval between the death of the last emperor of the Suabian and the accession of the first emperor of the Austrian lines. In the eleventh century the emperors enjoyed full sovereignty; in the fifteenth they had little more than the symbols and decorations of power.

Out of this feudal system, which has itself many of the important features of a confederacy, has grown the federal system which constitutes the Germanic empire. Its powers are vested in a diet representing the component members of the confederacy; in the emperor, who is the executive magistrate, with a negative on the decrees of the diet; and in the imperial chamber and the aulic council, two judiciary tribunals having supreme jurisdiction in controversies which concern the empire, or which happen among its members.

The diet possesses the general power of legislating for the empire; of making war and peace; contracting alliances; assessing quotas of troops and money; constructing fortresses; regulating coin; admitting new members; and subjecting disobedient members to the ban of the empire, by which the party is degraded from his sovereign rights and his possessions forfeited. The members of the confederacy are expressly restricted from entering into compacts prejudicial to the empire; from imposing tolls and duties on their mutual intercourse, without the consent of the emperor and diet; from altering the value of money; from doing injustice to one another; or from affording assistance or retreat to disturbers of the public peace. And the ban is denounced against such as shall violate any of these restrictions. The members of the diet, as such, are subject in all cases to be judged by the emperor and diet, and in their private capacities by the aulic council and imperial chamber.

The prerogatives of the emperor are numerous. The most important of them are: his exclusive right to make propositions to the diet; to negative its resolutions; to name ambassadors; to confer dignities and titles; to fill vacant electorates; to found universities; to grant privileges not injurious to the states of the empire; to receive and apply the public revenues; and generally to watch over the public safety. In certain cases the electors form a council to him. In quality of emperor, he possesses no territory within the empire, nor receives any revenue for his support. But his revenue and dominions, in other qualities, constitute him one of the most powerful princes in Europe.

From such a parade of constitutional powers in the representatives and head of this Confederacy, the natural supposition would be that it must form an exception to the general character which belongs to its kindred systems. Nothing would be farther from the reality. The fundamental principle on which it rests, that the empire is a community of sovereigns, that the diet is a representation of sovereigns, and that the laws are addressed to sovereigns, renders the empire a nerveless body, incapable of regulating its own members, insecure against external dangers, and agitated with unceasing fermentations in its own bowels.

The history of Germany is a history of wars between the emperor and the princes and states; of wars among the princes and states themselves; of the licentiousness of the strong and the oppression of the weak; of foreign intrusions and foreign intrigues; of requisitions of men and money disregarded, or partially complied with; of attempts to enforce them, altogether abortive, or attended with slaughter and desolation, involving the innocent with the guilty; of general imbecility, confusion, and misery.

In the sixteenth century, the emperor, with one part of the empire on his side, was seen engaged against the other princes and states. In one of the conflicts, the emperor himself was put to flight, and very near being made prisoner by the elector of Saxony. The late king of Prussia was more than once pitted against his imperial sovereign, and commonly proved an overmatch for him. Controversies and wars among the members themselves have been so common that the German annals are crowded with the bloody pages which describe them. Previous to the peace of Westphalia, Germany was desolated by a war of thirty years, in which the emperor, with one half of the empire, was on one side, and Sweden, with the other half, on the opposite side. Peace was at length negotiated and dictated by foreign powers; and the articles of it, to which foreign powers are parties, made a fundamental part of the Germanic constitution.

If the nation happens, on any emergency, to be more united by the necessity of self-defense, its situation is still deplorable. Military preparations must be preceded by so many tedious discussions, arising from the jealousies, pride, separate views, and clashing pretensions of sovereign bodies, that before the diet can settle the arrangements, the enemy are in the field; and before the federal troops are ready to take it, are retiring into winter quarters.

The small body of national troops, which has been judged necessary in time of peace, is defectively kept up, badly paid, infected with local prejudices, and supported by irregular and disproportionate contributions to the treasury.

The impossibility of maintaining order and dispensing justice among these sovereign subjects produced the experiment of dividing the empire into nine or ten circles or districts; of giving them an interior organization; and of charging them with the military execution of the laws against delinquent and contumacious members. This experiment has only served to demonstrate more fully the radical vice of the constitution. Each circle is the miniature picture of the deformities of this political monster. They either fail to execute their commissions, or they do it with all the devastation and carnage of civil war. Sometimes whole circles are defaulters; and then they increase the mischief which they were instituted to remedy.

We may form some judgment of this scheme of military coercion from a sample given by Thuanus. In Donawerth, a free and imperial city of the circle of Suabia, the Abbé de St. Croix enjoyed certain immunities which had been reserved to him. In the exercise of these, on some public occasion, outrages were committed on him by the people of the city. The consequence was that the city was put under the ban of the empire, and the Duke of Bavaria, though director of another circle, obtained an appointment to enforce it. He soon appeared before the city with a corps of ten thousand troops, and finding it a fit occasion, as he had secretly intended from the beginning, to revive an antiquated claim on the pretext that his ancestors had suffered the place to be dismembered from his territory,* he took possession of it in his own name, disarmed and punished the inhabitants, and reannexed the city to his domains.

It may be asked, perhaps, what has so long kept this disjointed machine from falling entirely to pieces? The answer is obvious: The weakness of most of the members, who are unwilling to expose themselves to the mercy of foreign powers; the weakness of most of the principal members, compared with the formidable powers all around them; the vast weight and influence which the emperor derives from his separate and hereditary dominions; and the interest he feels in preserving a system with which his family pride is connected, and which constitutes him the first prince in Europe. These causes support a feeble and precarious Union, whilst the repellent quality incident to the nature of sovereignty, and which time continually strengthens, prevents any reform whatever founded on a proper consolidation. Nor is it to be imagined, if this obstacle could be surmounted, that the neighboring powers would suffer a revolution to take place, which would give to the empire the force and pre-eminence to which it is entitled. Foreign nations have long considered themselves as interested in the changes made by events in this constitution, and have on various occasions betrayed their policy of perpetuating its anarchy and weakness.

If more direct examples were wanting, Poland, as a government over local sovereigns, might not improperly be taken notice of. Nor could any proof more striking be given of the calamities flowing from such institutions. Equally unfit for self-government and self-defense, it has long been at the mercy of its powerful neighbors, who have lately had the mercy to disburden it of one third of its people and territories.

The connection among the Swiss cantons scarcely

* Pfeffel, "Nouvel Abrég. Chronol. de l'Hist., etc., d'Allemagne," says the pretext was to indemnify himself for the expense of the expedition.

amounts to a confederacy, though it is sometimes cited as an instance of the stability of such institutions.

They have no common treasury; no common troops even in war; no common coin; no common judicatory; nor any other common mark of sovereignty.

They are kept together by the peculiarity of their topographical position; by their individual weakness and insignificancy; by the fear of powerful neighbors, to one of which they were formerly subject; by the few sources of contention among a people of such simple and homogeneous manners; by their joint interest in their dependent possessions; by the mutual aid they stand in need of for suppressing insurrections and rebellions, an aid expressly stipulated and often required and afforded; and by the necessity of some regular and permanent provision for accommodating disputes among the cantons. The provision is that the parties at variance shall each choose four judges out of the neutral cantons, who, in case of disagreement, choose an umpire. This tribunal, under an oath of impartiality, pronounces definitive sentence, which all the cantons are bound to enforce. The competency of this regulation may be estimated by a clause in their treaty of 1683 with Victor Amadeus of Savoy, in which he obliges himself to interpose as mediator in disputes between the cantons, and to employ force, if necessary, against the contumacious party.

So far as the pecularity of their case will admit of comparison with that of the United States, it serves to confirm the principle intended to be established. Whatever efficacy the union may have had in ordinary cases, it appears that the moment a cause of difference sprang up capable of trying its strength it failed. The controversies on the subject of religion, which in three instances have kindled violent and bloody contests, may be said, in fact, to have severed the league. The Protestant and Catholic cantons have since had their separate diets, where all the most important concerns are adjusted, and which have left the general diet little other business than to take care of the common bailages.

That separation had another consequence which merits attention. It produced opposite alliances with foreign powers: of Berne, as the head of the Protestant association, with the United Provinces; and of Luzerne, as the head of the Catholic association, with France.

PUBLIUS

No. 20: Madison (with Hamilton)

THE United Netherlands are a confederacy of republics, or rather of aristocracies of a very remarkable texture, yet confirming all the lessons derived from those which we have already reviewed.

The union is composed of seven coequal and sovereign states, and each state or province is a composition of equal and independent cities. In all important cases, not only the provinces but the cities must be unanimous.

The sovereignty of the union is represented by the States-General, consisting usually of about fifty deputies appointed by the provinces. They hold their seats, some for life, some for six, three, and one years; from two provinces they continue in appointment during pleasure.

The States-General have authority to enter into treaties and alliances; to make war and peace; to raise armies and equip fleets; to ascertain quotas and demand contributions. In all these cases, however, unanimity and the sanction of their constituents are requisite. They have authority to appoint and receive ambassadors; to execute treaties and alliances already formed; to provide for the collection of duties on imports and exports; to regulate the mint with a saving to the provincial rights; to govern as sovereigns the dependent territories. The provinces are restrained, unless with the general consent, from entering into foreign treaties; from establishing imposts injurious to others, or charging their neighbors with higher duties than their own subjects. A council of state, a chamber of accounts, with five colleges of admiralty, aid and fortify the federal administration.

The executive magistrate of the Union is the stadtholder, who is now an hereditary prince. His principal weight and influence in the republic are derived from his independent title; from his great patrimonial estates; from his family connections with some of the chief potentates of Europe; and, more than all, perhaps, from his being stadtholder in the several provinces, as well as for the Union; in which provincial quality he has the appointment of town magistrates under certain regulations, executes provincial decrees, presides when he pleases in the provincial tribunals, and has throughout the power of pardon.

As stadtholder of the Union, he has, however, considerable prerogatives.

In his political capacity he has authority to settle disputes between the provinces, when other methods fail; to assist at the deliberations of the States-General and at their particular conferences; to give audiences to foreign ambassadors and to keep agents for his particular affairs at foreign courts.

In his military capacity he commands the federal troops, provides for garrisons, and in general regulates military affairs; disposes of all appointments, from colonels to ensigns, and of the governments and posts of fortified towns.

In his marine capacity he is admiral-general and superintends and directs every thing relative to naval forces and other naval affairs; presides in the admiralties in person or by proxy; appoints lieutenant-admirals and other officers; and establishes councils of war, whose sentences are not executed till he approves them.

His revenue, exclusive of his private income, amounts to 300,000 florins. The standing army which he commands consists of about 40,000 men.

Such is the nature of the celebrated Belgic confederacy, as delineated on parchment. What are the characters which practice has stamped upon it? Imbecility in the government; discord among the provinces; foreign influence and indignities; a precarious existence in peace, and peculiar calamities from war.

It was long ago remarked by Grotius that nothing but the hatred of his countrymen to the house of Austria kept them from being ruined by the vices of their constitution.

The Union of Utrecht, says another respectable writer, reposes an authority in the States-General seemingly sufficient to secure harmony, but the jealousy in each province renders the practice very different from the theory.

The same instrument, says another, obliges each province to levy certain contributions; but this article never could, and probably never will, be executed; because the inland provinces, who have little commerce, cannot pay an equal quota.

In matters of contribution it is the practice to waive the articles of the constitution. The danger of delay obliges the consenting provinces to furnish their quotas, without waiting for the others; and then to obtain reimbursement from the others by deputations, which are frequent, or otherwise, as they can. The great wealth and influence of the province of Holland enable her to effect both these purposes.

It has more than once happened that the deficiencies have been ultimately to be collected at the point of the bayonet, a thing practicable, though dreadful, in a confederacy where one of the members exceeds in force all the rest, and where several of them are too small to meditate resistance; but utterly impracticable in one composed of members, several of which are equal to each other in strength and resources and equal singly to a vigorous and persevering defense.

Foreign ministers, says Sir William Temple, who was himself a foreign minister, elude matters taken *ad referendum* by tampering with the provinces and cities. In 1726 the treaty of Hanover was delayed by these means a whole year. Instances of a like nature are numerous and notorious.

In critical emergencies the States-General are often compelled to overleap their constitutional bounds. In 1688 they concluded a treaty of themselves at the risk of their heads. The treaty of Westphalia in 1648, by which their independence was formally and finally recognized, was concluded without the consent of Zealand. Even as recently as the last treaty of peace with Great Britain, the constitutional principle of unanimity was departed from. A weak constitution must necessarily terminate in dissolution for want of proper powers, or the usurpation of powers requisite for the public safety. Whether the usurpation, when once begun, will stop at the salutary point, or go forward to the dangerous extreme, must depend on the contingencies of the moment. Tyranny has perhaps oftener grown out of the assumptions of power called for, on pressing exigencies, by a defective constitution, than out of the full exercise of the largest constitutional authorities.

Notwithstanding the calamities produced by the stadtholdership, it has been supposed that without his influence in the individual provinces, the causes of anarchy manifest in the confederacy would long ago have dissolved it. "Under such a government," says the Abbé Mably, "the Union could never have subsisted, if the provinces had not a spring within themselves capable of quickening their tardiness, and compelling them to the same way of thinking. This spring is the stadtholder." It is remarked by Sir William Temple "that in the intermissions of the stadtholdership, Holland, by her riches and her authority, which drew the others into a sort of dependence, supplied the place."

These are not the only circumstances which have controlled the tendency to anarchy and dissolution. The surrounding powers impose an absolute necessity of union to a certain degree, at the same time that they nourish by their intrigues the constitutional vices which keep the republic in some degree always at their mercy.

The true patriots have long bewailed the fatal tendency of these vices, and have made no less than four regular experiments by *extraordinary assemblies,* convened for the special purpose to apply a remedy. As many times has their laudable zeal found it impossible to *unite the public councils* in reforming the known, the acknowledged, the fatal evils of the existing constitution. Let us pause, my fellow-citizens, for one moment over this melancholy and monitory lesson of history; and with the tear that drops for the calamities brought on mankind by their adverse opinions and selfish passions, let our gratitude mingle an ejaculation to Heaven for the propitious concord which has distinguished the consultations for our political happiness.

The design was also conceived of establishing a general tax to be administered by the federal authority. This also had its adversaries and failed.

This unhappy people seem to be now suffering from popular convulsions, from dissensions among the states, and from the actual invasion of foreign arms, the crisis of their destiny. All nations have their eyes fixed on the awful spectacle. The first wish prompted by humanity is that this severe trial may issue in such a revolution of their government as will establish their union and render it the parent of tranquillity, freedom, and happiness. The next, that the asylum under which, we trust, the enjoyment of these blessings will speedily be secured in this country may receive and console them for the catastrophe of their own.

I make no apology for having dwelt so long on the contemplation of these federal precedents. Experience is the oracle of truth; and where its responses are unequivocal, they ought to be conclusive and sacred. The important truth, which it unequivocally pronounces in the present case, is that a sovereignty over sovereigns, a government over governments, a legislation for communities, as contradistinguished from individuals, as it is a solecism in theory, so in practice it is subversive of the order and ends of civil polity, by substituting *violence* in place of the mild and salutary *coercion* of the *magistracy*.

PUBLIUS

No. 21: Hamilton

HAVING in the three last numbers taken a summary review of the principal circumstances and events which depict the genius and fate of other confederate governments, I shall now proceed in the enumeration of the most important of those defects which have hitherto disappointed our hopes from the system established among ourselves. To form a safe and satisfactory judgment of the proper remedy, it is absolutely necessary that we should be well acquainted with the extent and malignity of the disease.

The next most palpable defect of the existing Confederation is the total want of a SANCTION to its laws. The United States as now composed have no power to exact obedience, or punish disobedience to their resolutions, either by pecuniary mulcts, by a suspension or divestiture of privileges, or by any other constitutional means. There is no express delegation of authority to them to use force against delinquent members; and if such a right should be ascribed to the federal head, as resulting from the nature of the social compact between the States, it must be by inference and construction in the face of that part of the second article by which it is declared "that each State shall retain every power, jurisdiction, and right, not *expressly* delegated to the United States in Congress assembled." The want of such a right involves, no doubt, a striking absurdity; but we are reduced to the dilemma either of supposing that deficiency, preposterous as it may seem, or of contravening or explaining away a provision, which has been of late a repeated theme of the eulogies of those who oppose the new Constitution; and the omission of which in that plan has been the subject of much plausible animadversion and severe criticism. If we are unwilling to impair the force of this applauded provision, we shall be obliged to conclude that the United States afford the extraordinary spectacle of a government destitute even of the shadow of constitutional power to enforce the execution of its own laws. It will appear from the specimens which have been cited that the American Confederacy, in this particular, stands discriminated from every other institution of a similar kind, and exhibits a new and unexampled phenomenon in the political world.

The want of a mutual guaranty of the State governments is another capital imperfection in the federal plan. There is nothing of this kind declared in the articles that compose it; and to imply a tacit guaranty from considerations of utility would be a still more flagrant departure from the clause which has been mentioned, than to imply a tacit power of coercion from the like considerations. The want of a guaranty, though it might in its consequences endanger the Union, does not so immediately attack its existence as the want of a constitutional sanction to its laws.

Without a guaranty the assistance to be derived from the Union in repelling those domestic dangers which may sometimes threaten the existence of the State constitutions must be renounced. Usurpation may rear its crest in each State and trample upon the liberties of the people, while the national government could legally do nothing more than behold its encroachments with indignation and regret. A successful faction may erect a tyranny on the ruins of order and law, while no succor could constitutionally be afforded by the Union to the friends and supporters of the government. The tempestuous situation from which Massachusetts has scarcely emerged evinces that dangers of this kind are not merely speculative. Who can determine what might have been the issue of her late convulsions if the malcontents had been headed by a Cæsar or by a Cromwell? Who can predict what effect a despotism established in Massachusetts would have upon the liberties of New Hampshire or Rhode Island, of Connecticut or New York?

The inordinate pride of State importance has suggested to some minds an objection to the principle of a guaranty in the federal government, as involving an officious interference in the domestic concerns of the members. A scruple of this kind would deprive us of one of the principal advantages to be expected from union, and can only flow from a misapprehension of the nature of the provision itself. It could be no impediment to reforms of the State constitutions by a majority of the people in a legal and peaceable mode. This right would remain undiminished. The guaranty could only operate against changes to be effected by violence. Towards the preventions of calamities of this kind, too many checks cannot be provided. The peace of society and the stability of government depend absolutely on the efficacy of the precautions adopted on this head. Where the whole power of the government is in the hands of the people, there is the less pretense for the use of violent remedies in partial or occasional distempers of the State. The natural cure for an ill administration in a popular or representative constitution is a change of men. A guaranty by the national authority would be as much leveled against the usurpations of rulers as against the ferments and outrages of faction and sedition in the community.

The principle of regulating the contributions of the States to the common treasury by QUOTAS is another fundamental error in the Confederation. Its repugnancy to an adequate supply of the national exigencies has been already pointed out, and has sufficiently appeared from the trial which has been made of it. I speak of it now solely with a view to equality among the States. Those who have been accustomed to contemplate the circumstances which produce and constitute national wealth must be satisfied that there is no common standard or barometer by which the degrees of it can be ascertained. Neither the value of lands, nor the numbers of the people, which have been successively proposed as the rule of State contributions, has any pretension to being a just representative. If we compare the wealth of the United Netherlands with that of Russia or Germany, or even of France, and if we at the same time compare the total value of the lands and the aggregate population of the contracted territory of that republic with the total value of the lands and the aggregate population of the immense regions of either of those kingdoms, we shall at once discover that there is no comparison between the proportion of either of these two objects and that of the relative wealth of those nations. If the like parallel were to be run between several of the American States, it would furnish a like result. Let Virginia be contrasted with North Carolina, Pennsylvania with Connecticut, or Maryland with New Jersey, and we shall be convinced that the respective abilities of those States in relation to revenue bear little or no analogy to their comparative stock in lands or to their comparative population. The position may be equally illustrated by a similar process between the counties of the same State. No man acquainted with the State of New York will doubt that the active wealth of Kings County bears a much greater proportion to that of Montgomery than it would appear to do if we should take either the total value of the lands or the total number of the people as a criterion!

The wealth of nations depends upon an infinite variety of causes. Situation, soil, climate, the nature of the productions, the nature of the government, the genius of the citizens, the degree of information they possess, the state of commerce, of arts, of industry—these circumstances and many more, too complex, minute, or adventitious to admit of a particular specification, occasion differences hardly conceivable in the relative opulence and riches of different countries. The consequence clearly is that there can be no common measure of national wealth, and, of course, no general or stationary rule by which the ability of a state to pay taxes can be determined. The attempt, therefore, to regulate the contributions of the members of a confederacy by any such rule cannot fail to be productive of glaring inequality and extreme oppression.

This inequality would of itself be sufficient in America to work the eventual destruction of the Union, if any mode of enforcing a compliance with its requisitions could be devised. The suffering States would not long consent to remain associated upon a principle which distributed the public burdens with so unequal a hand, and which was calculated to impoverish and oppress the citizens of some States, while those of others would scarcely be conscious of the small proportion of the weight they were required to sustain. This, however, is an evil inseparable from the principle of quotas and requisitions.

There is no method of steering clear of this inconvenience, but by authorizing the national government to raise its own revenues in its own way. Imposts, excises, and, in general, all duties upon articles of consumption, may be compared to a fluid, which will in time find its level with the means of paying them. The amount to be contributed by each citizen will in a degree be at his own option, and can be regulated by an attention to his resources. The rich may be extravagant, the poor can be frugal; and private oppression may always be avoided by a judicious selection of objects proper for such impositions. If inequalities should arise in some States from duties on particular objects, these will in all probability be counterbalanced by proportional inequalities in other States, from the duties on other objects. In the course of time and things, an equilibrium, as far as it is attainable in so complicated a subject, will be established everywhere. Or, if inequalities should still exist, they would neither be so great in their degree, so uniform in their operation, nor so odious in their appearance, as those which would necessarily spring from quotas upon any scale that can possibly be devised.

It is a signal advantage of taxes on articles of consumption that they contain in their own nature a security against excess. They prescribe their own limit, which cannot be exceeded without defeating the end proposed—that is, an extension of the revenue. When applied to this object, the saying is as just as it is witty that, "in political arithmetic, two and two do not always make four." If duties are too high, they lessen the consumption; the collection is eluded; and the product to the treasury is not so great as when they are confined within proper and moderate bounds. This forms a complete barrier against any material oppression of the citizens by taxes of this class, and is itself a natural limitation of the power of imposing them.

Impositions of this kind usually fall under the denomination of indirect taxes, and must for a long time constitute the chief part of the revenue raised in this country. Those of the direct kind, which principally relate to land and buildings, may admit of a rule of apportionment. Either the value of land, or the number of the people, may serve as a standard. The state of agriculture and the populousness of a country are considered as having a near relation with each other. And, as a rule, for the purpose intended, numbers, in the view of simplicity and certainty, are entitled to a preference. In every country it is an herculean task to obtain a valuation of the land; in a country imperfectly settled and progressive in improvement, the difficulties are increased almost to impracticability. The expense of an accurate valuation is, in all situations, a formidable objection. In a branch of taxation where no limits to the discretion of the government are to be found in the nature of the thing, the establishment of a fixed rule, not incompatible with the end, may be attended with fewer inconveniences than to leave that discretion altogether at large. PUBLIUS

No. 22: Hamilton

IN ADDITION to the defects already enumerated in the existing federal system, there are others of not less importance which concur in rendering it altogether unfit for the administration of the affairs of the Union.

The want of a power to regulate commerce is by all parties allowed to be of the number. The utility of such a power has been anticipated under the first head of our inquiries; and for this reason, as well as from the universal conviction entertained upon the subject, little need be added in this place. It is indeed evident, on the most superficial view, that there is no object, either as it respects the interest of trade or finance, that more strongly demands a federal superintendence. The want of it has already operated as a bar to the formation of beneficial treaties with foreign powers, and has given occasions of dissatisfaction between the States. No nation acquainted with the nature of our political association would be unwise enough to enter into stipulations with the United States, conceding on their part privileges of importance, while they were apprised that the engagements on the part of the Union might at any moment be violated by its members, and while they found from experience that they might enjoy every advantage they desired in our markets without granting us any return but such as their momentary convenience might suggest. It is not, therefore, to be wondered at that Mr. Jenkinson in ushering into the House of Commons a bill for regulating the temporary intercourse between the two countries should preface its introduction by a declaration that similar provisions in former bills had been found to answer every purpose to the commerce of Great Britain, and that it would be prudent to persist in the plan until it should appear whether the American government was likely or not to acquire greater consistency.*

Several States have endeavored by separate prohibitions, restrictions, and exclusions to influence the conduct of that kingdom in this particular, but the want of concert, arising from the want of a general authority and from clashing and dissimilar views in the States, has hitherto frustrated every experiment of the kind, and will continue to do so as long as the same obstacles to a uniformity of measures continue to exist.

The interfering and unneighborly regulations of some States, contrary to the true spirit of the Union, have, in different instances, given just cause of umbrage and complaint to others, and it is to be feared that examples of this nature, if not restrained by a national control, would be multiplied and extended till they became not less serious sources of animosity and discord than injurious impediments to the intercourse between the different parts

* This, as nearly as I can recollect, was the sense of his speech in introducing the last bill.

of the Confederacy. "The commerce of the German empire * is in continual trammels from the multiplicity of the duties which the several princes and states exact upon the merchandises passing through their territories, by means of which the fine streams and navigable rivers with which Germany is so happily watered are rendered almost useless." Though the genius of the people of this country might never permit this description to be strictly applicable to us, yet we may reasonably expect from the gradual conflicts of State regulations that the citizens of each would at length come to be considered and treated by the others in no better light than that of foreigners and aliens.

The power of raising armies by the most obvious construction of the articles of the Confederation is merely a power of making requisitions upon the States for quotas of men. This practice in the course of the late war was found replete with obstructions to a vigorous and to an economical system of defense. It gave birth to a competition between the States which created a kind of auction for men. In order to furnish the quotas required of them, they outbid each other till bounties grew to an enormous and insupportable size. The hope of a still further increase afforded an inducement to those who were disposed to serve to procrastinate their enlistment, and disinclined them from engaging for any considerable periods. Hence, slow and scanty levies of men, in the most critical emergencies of our affairs; short enlistments at an unparalleled expense; continual fluctuations in the troops, ruinous to their discipline and subjecting the public safety frequently to the perilous crisis of a disbanded army. Hence, also, those oppressive expedients for raising men which were upon several occasions practiced, and which nothing but the enthusiasm of liberty would have induced the people to endure.

This method of raising troops is not more unfriendly to economy and vigor than it is to an equal distribution of the burden. The States near the seat of war, influenced by motives of self-preservation, made efforts to furnish their quotas, which even exceeded their abilities; while those at a distance from danger were for the most part

* Encyclopedia, article "Empire."

as remiss as the others were diligent in their exertions. The immediate pressure of this inequality was not in this case, as in that of the contributions of money, alleviated by the hope of a final liquidation. The States which did not pay their proportions of money might at least be charged with their deficiencies; but no account could be formed of the deficiences in the supplies of men. We shall not, however, see much reason to regret the want of this hope, when we consider how little prospect there is, that the most delinquent States will ever be able to make compensation for their pecuniary failures. The system of quotas and requisitions, whether it be applied to men or money, is in every view a system of imbecility in the Union, and of inequality and injustice among the members.

The right of equal suffrage among the States is another exceptionable part of the Confederation. Every idea of proportion and every rule of fair representation conspire to condemn a principle, which gives to Rhode Island an equal weight in the scale of power with Massachusetts, or Connecticut, or New York; and to Delaware an equal voice in the national deliberations with Pennsylvania, or Virginia, or North Carolina. Its operation contradicts that fundamental maxim of republican government, which requires that the sense of the majority should prevail. Sophistry may reply that sovereigns are equal, and that a majority of the votes of the States will be a majority of confederated America. But this kind of logical legerdemain will never counteract the plain suggestions of justice and common sense. It may happen that this majority of States is a small minority of the people of America;* and two thirds of the people of America could not long be persuaded upon the credit of artificial distinctions and syllogistic subtleties to submit their interests to the management and disposal of one third. The larger States would after a while revolt from the idea of receiving the law from the smaller. To acquiesce in such a privation of their due importance in the political scale would be not merely to be insensible to the love of power, but even to sacrifice the desire of equality. It is neither rational to

* New Hampshire, Rhode Island, New Jersey, Delaware, Georgia, South Carolina, and Maryland are a majority of the whole number of the States, but they do not contain one third of the people.

expect the first, nor just to require the last. The smaller States, considering how peculiarly their safety and welfare depend on union, ought readily to renounce a pretension which, if not relinquished, would prove fatal to its duration.

It may be objected to this that not seven but nine States, or two thirds of the whole number, must consent to the most important resolutions; and it may be thence inferred that nine States would always comprehend a majority of the Union. But this does not obviate the impropriety of an equal vote between States of the most unequal dimensions and populousness; nor is the inference accurate in point of fact; for we can enumerate nine States which contain less than a majority of the people;* and it is constitutionally possible that these nine may give the vote. Besides, there are matters of considerable moment determinable by a bare majority; and there are others, concerning which doubts have been entertained, which, if interpreted in favor of the sufficiency of a vote of seven States, would extend its operation to interests of the first magnitude. In addition to this it is to be observed that there is a probability of an increase in the number of States, and no provision for a proportional augmentation of the ratio of votes.

But this is not all: what at first sight may seem a remedy, is in reality a poison. To give a minority a negative upon the majority (which is always the case where more than a majority is requisite to a decision) is, in its tendency, to subject the sense of the greater number to that of the lesser number. Congress, from the non-attendance of a few States, have been frequently in the situation of a Polish diet, where a single veto has been sufficient to put a stop to all their movements. A sixtieth part of the Union, which is about the proportion of Delaware and Rhode Island, has several times been able to oppose an entire bar to its operations. This is one of those refinements which, in practice, has an effect the reverse of what is expected from it in theory. The necessity of unanimity in public bodies, or of something approaching towards it, has been founded upon a supposition that it

* Add New York and Connecticut to the foregoing seven, and they will be less than a majority.

would contribute to security. But its real operation is to embarrass the administration, to destroy the energy of the government, and to substitute the pleasure, caprice, or artifices of an insignificant, turbulent, or corrupt junto to the regular deliberations and decisions of a respectable majority. In those emergencies of a nation in which the goodness or badness, the weakness or strength, of its government is of the greatest importance, there is commonly a necessity for action. The public business must in some way or other go forward. If a pertinacious minority can control the opinion of a majority, respecting the best mode of conducting it, the majority in order that something may be done must conform to the views of the minority; and thus the sense of the smaller number will overrule that of the greater and give a tone to the national proceedings. Hence, tedious delays; continual negotiation and intrigue; contemptible compromises of the public good. And yet, in such a system it is even happy when such compromises can take place: for upon some occasions things will not admit of accommodation; and then the measures of government must be injuriously suspended, or fatally defeated. It is often by the impracticability of obtaining the concurrence of the necessary number of votes kept in a state of inaction. Its situation must always savor of weakness, sometimes border upon anarchy.

It is not difficult to discover that a principle of this kind gives greater scope to foreign corruption, as well as to domestic faction, than that which permits the sense of the majority to decide; though the contrary of this has been presumed. The mistake has proceeded from not attending with due care to the mischiefs that may be occasioned by obstructing the progress of government at certain critical seasons. When the concurrence of a large number is required by the Constitution to the doing of any national act, we are apt to rest satisfied that all is safe, because nothing improper will be likely *to be done;* but we forget how much good may be prevented, and how much ill may be produced, by the power of hindering that which is necessary from being done, and of keeping affairs in the same unfavorable posture in which they may happen to stand at particular periods.

Suppose, for instance, we were engaged in a war in

conjunction with one foreign nation against another. Suppose the necessity of our situation demanded peace, and the interest or ambition of our ally led him to seek the prosecution of the war, with views that might justify us in making separate terms. In such a state of things, this ally of ours would evidently find it much easier by his bribes and intrigues to tie up the hands of government from making peace, where two thirds of all the votes were requisite to that object, than where a simple majority would suffice. In the first case, he would have to corrupt a smaller number; in the last, a greater number. Upon the same principle, it would be much easier for a foreign power with which we were at war to perplex our councils and embarrass our exertions. And, in a commercial view, we may be subjected to similar inconveniences. A nation, with which we might have a treaty of commerce, could with much greater facility prevent our forming a connection with her competitor in trade, though such a connection should be ever so beneficial to ourselves.

Evils of this description ought not to be regarded as imaginary. One of the weak sides of republics, among their numerous advantages, is that they afford too easy an inlet to foreign corruption. An hereditary monarch, though often disposed to sacrifice his subjects to his ambition, has so great a personal interest in the government and in the external glory of the nation, that it is not easy for a foreign power to give him an equivalent for what he would sacrifice by treachery to the state. The world has accordingly been witness to few examples of this species of royal prostitution, though there have been abundant specimens of every other kind.

In republics, persons elevated from the mass of the community by the suffrages of their fellow-citizens to stations of great pre-eminence and power may find compensations for betraying their trust, which, to any but minds actuated by superior virtue may appear to exceed the proportion of interest they have in the common stock, and to overbalance the obligations of duty. Hence it is that history furnishes us with so many mortifying examples of the prevalency of foreign corruption in republican governments. How much this contributed to the ruin of the ancient commonwealths has been already disclosed. It is well known that the deputies of the United Provinces have, in various instances, been purchased by the emissaries of the neighboring kingdoms. The Earl of Chesterfield (if my memory serves me right), in a letter to his court, intimates that his success in an important negotiation must depend on his obtaining a major's commission for one of those deputies. And in Sweden the parties were alternately bought by France and England in so barefaced and notorious a manner that it excited universal disgust in the nation, and was a principal cause that the most limited monarch in Europe, in a single day, without tumult, violence, or opposition, became one of the most absolute and uncontrolled.

A circumstance which crowns the defects of the Confederation remains yet to be mentioned—the want of a judiciary power. Laws are a dead letter without courts to expound and define their true meaning and operation. The treaties of the United States, to have any force at all, must be considered as part of the law of the land. Their true import, as far as respects individuals, must, like all other laws, be ascertained by judicial determinations. To produce uniformity in these determinations, they ought to be submitted, in the last resort, to one SUPREME TRIBUNAL. And this tribunal ought to be instituted under the same authority which forms the treaties themselves. These ingredients are both indispensable. If there is in each State a court of final jurisdiction, there may be as many different final determinations on the same point as there are courts. There are endless diversities in the opinions of men. We often see not only different courts but the judges of the same court differing from each other. To avoid the confusion which would unavoidably result from the contradictory decisions of a number of independent judicatories, all nations have found it necessary to establish one court paramount to the rest, possessing a general superintendence and authorized to settle and declare in the last resort a uniform rule of civil justice.

This is the more necessary where the frame of the government is so compounded that the laws of the whole are in danger of being contravened by the laws of the parts. In this case, if the particular tribunals are invested with a right of ultimate jurisdiction, besides the contradictions to be expected from difference of opinion there will be much to fear from the bias of local views and prejudices and from the interference of local regulations. As often as such an interference was to happen, there would be reason to apprehend that the provisions of the particular laws might be preferred to those of the general laws; from the deference with which men in office naturally look up to that authority to which they owe their official existence.

The treaties of the United States under the present Constitution are liable to the infractions of thirteen different legislatures, and as many different courts of final jurisdiction, acting under the authority of those legislatures. The faith, the reputation, the peace of the whole Union are thus continually at the mercy of the prejudices, the passions, and the interests of every member of which it is composed. Is it possible that foreign nations can either respect or confide in such a government? Is it possible that the people of America will longer consent to trust their honor, their happiness, their safety, on so precarious a foundation?

In this review of the Confederation, I have confined myself to the exhibition of its most material defects; passing over those imperfections in its details by which even a considerable part of the power intended to be conferred upon it has been in a great measure rendered abortive. It must be by this time evident to all men of reflection, who are either free from erroneous prepossessions, or can divest themselves of them, that it is a system so radically vicious and unsound as to admit not of amendment but by an entire change in its leading features and characters.

The organization of Congress is itself utterly improper for the exercise of those powers which are necessary to be deposited in the Union. A single assembly may be a proper receptacle of those slender, or rather fettered, authorities, which have been heretofore delegated to the federal head; but it would be inconsistent with all the principles of good government to intrust it with those additional powers which even the moderate and more rational adversaries of the proposed Constitution admit ought to reside in the United States. If that plan should not be adopted, and if the necessity of Union should be able to withstand the ambitious aims of those men who may indulge magnificent schemes of personal aggrandizement from its dissolution, the probability would be that we should run into the project of conferring supplementary powers upon Congress as they are now constituted. And either the machine, from the intrinsic feebleness of its structure, will moulder into pieces, in spite of our ill-judged efforts to prop it; or, by successive augmentations of its force and energy, as necessity might prompt, we shall finally accumulate in a single body all the most important prerogatives of sovereignty, and thus entail upon our posterity one of the most execrable forms of government that human infatuation ever contrived. Thus we should create in reality that very tyranny which the adversaries of the new Constitution either are, or affect to be, solicitous to avert.

It has not a little contributed to the infirmities of the existing federal system that it never had a ratification by the PEOPLE. Resting on no better foundation than the consent of the several legislatures, it has been exposed to frequent and intricate questions concerning the validity of its powers, and has in some instances given birth to the enormous doctrine of a right of legislative repeal. Owing its ratification to the law of a State, it has been contended that the same authority might repeal the law by which it was ratified. However gross a heresy it may be to maintain that a *party* to a *compact* has a right to revoke that *compact*, the doctrine itself has had respectable advocates. The possibility of a question of this nature proves the necessity of laying the foundations of our national government deeper than in the mere sanction of delegated authority. The fabric of American empire ought to rest on the solid basis of THE CONSENT OF THE PEOPLE. The streams of national power ought to flow immediately from that pure, original fountain of all legitimate authority.

PUBLIUS

No. 23: Hamilton

THE necessity of a Constitution, at least equally energetic with the one proposed, to the preservation of the Union is the point at the examination of which we are now arrived.

This inquiry will naturally divide itself into three branches—the objects to be provided for by a federal government, the quantity of power necessary to the accomplishment of those objects, the persons upon whom that power ought to operate. Its distribution and organization will more properly claim our attention under the succeeding head.

The principal purposes to be answered by union are these—the common defense of the members; the preservation of the public peace, as well against internal convulsions as external attacks; the regulation of commerce with other nations and between the States; the superintendence of our intercourse, political and commercial, with foreign countries.

The authorities essential to the common defense are these: to raise armies; to build and equip fleets; to prescribe rules for the government of both; to direct their operations; to provide for their support. These powers ought to exist without limitation, *because it is impossible to foresee or to define the extent and variety of national exigencies, and the correspondent extent and variety of the means which may be necessary to satisfy them.* The circumstances that endanger the safety of nations are infinite, and for this reason no constitutional shackles can wisely be imposed on the power to which the care of it is committed. This power ought to be coextensive with all the possible combinations of such circumstances; and ought to be under the direction of the same councils which are appointed to preside over the common defense.

This is one of those truths which to a correct and unprejudiced mind carries its own evidence along with it, and may be obscured, but cannot be made plainer by argument or reasoning. It rests upon axioms as simple as they are universal; the *means* ought to be proportioned to the *end;* the persons from whose agency the attainment of any *end* is expected ought to possess the *means* by which it is to be attained.

Whether there ought to be a federal government intrusted with the care of the common defense is a question in the first instance open to discussion; but the moment it is decided in the affirmative, it will follow that that government ought to be clothed with all the powers requisite to complete execution of its trust. And unless it can be shown that the circumstances which may affect the public safety are reducible within certain determinate limits; unless the contrary of this position can be fairly and rationally disputed, it must be admitted as a necessary consequence that there can be no limitation of that authority which is to provide for the defense and protection of the community in any matter essential to its efficacy—that is, in any matter essential to the *formation, direction,* or *support* of the NATIONAL FORCES.

Defective as the present Confederation has been proved to be, this principle appears to have been fully recognized by the framers of it; though they have not made proper or adequate provision for its exercise. Congress have an unlimited discretion to make requisitions of men and money; to govern the army and navy; to direct their operations. As their requisitions are made constitutionally binding upon the States, who are in fact under the most solemn obligations to furnish the supplies required of them, the intention evidently was that the United States should command whatever resources were by them judged requisite to the "common defense and general welfare." It was presumed that a sense of their true interests, and a regard to the dictates of good faith, would be found sufficient pledges for the punctual performance of the duty of the members to the federal head.

The experiment has, however, demonstrated that this expectation was ill-founded and illusory; and the observations made under the last head will, I imagine, have sufficed to convince the impartial and discerning that there is an absolute necessity for an entire change in the first principles of the system; that if we are in earnest about giving the Union energy and duration we must abandon the vain project of legislating upon the States in their collective capacities; we must extend the laws of the federal government to the individual citizens of America; we must discard the fallacious scheme of quotas and requisitions as equally impracticable and unjust. The result from all this is that the Union ought to be invested with full power to levy troops; to build and equip fleets; and to raise the revenues which will be required for the formation and support of an army and navy in the customary and ordinary modes practiced in other governments.

If the circumstances of our country are such as to demand a compound instead of a simple, a confederate instead of a sole, government, the essential point which will remain to be adjusted will be to discriminate the OBJECTS, as far as it can be done, which shall appertain to the different provinces or departments of power; allowing to each the most ample authority for fulfilling the objects committed to its charge. Shall the Union be constituted the guardian of the common safety? Are fleets and armies and revenues necessary to this purpose? The government of the Union must be empowered to pass all laws, and to make all regulations which have relation to them. The same must be the case in respect to commerce, and to every other matter to which its jurisdiction is permitted to extend. Is the administration of justice between the citizens of the same State the proper department of the local governments? These must possess all the authorities which are connected with this object, and with every other that may be allotted to their particular cognizance and direction. Not to confer in each case a degree of power commensurate to the end would be to violate the most obvious rules of prudence and propriety, and improvidently to trust the great interests of the nation to hands which are disabled from managing them with vigor and success.

Who so likely to make suitable provisions for the public defense as that body to which the guardianship of the public safety is confided; which, as the center of information, will best understand the extent and urgency of the dangers that threaten; as the representative of the WHOLE, will feel itself most deeply interested in the preservation of every part; which, from the responsibility implied in the duty assigned to it, will be most sensibly impressed with the necessity of proper exertions; and which, by the extension of its authority throughout the States, can alone establish uniformity and concert in the plans and measures by which the common safety is to be secured? Is there not a manifest inconsistency in devolving upon the federal government the care of the general defense and leaving in the State governments the *effective* powers by which it is to be provided for? Is not a want of co-operation the infallible consequence of such a system? And will not weakness, disorder, an undue distribution of the burdens and calamities of war, an unnecessary and intolerable increase of expense, be its natural and inevitable concomitants? Have we not had unequivocal experience of its effects in the course of the revolution which we have just achieved?

Every view we may take of the subject, as candid inquirers after truth, will serve to convince us that it is both unwise and dangerous to deny the federal government an unconfined authority in respect to all those objects which are intrusted to its management. It will indeed deserve the most vigilant and careful attention of the people to see that it be modeled in such a manner as to admit of its being safely vested with the requisite powers. If any plan which has been, or may be, offered to our consideration should not, upon a dispassionate inspection, be found to answer this description, it ought to be rejected. A government, the constitution of which renders it unfit to be trusted with all the powers which a free people *ought to delegate to any government*, would be an unsafe and improper depositary of the NATIONAL INTERESTS. Wherever THESE can with propriety be confided, the co-incident powers may safely accompany them. This is the true result of all just reasoning upon the subject. And the adversaries of the plan promulgated by the convention would have given a better impression of their candor if they had confined themselves to showing that the internal structure of the proposed government was such as to render it unworthy of the confidence of the people. They ought not to have wandered into inflammatory declamations and unmeaning cavils about the extent of the powers. The POWERS are not too extensive for the OBJECTS of federal administration, or, in other words, for the management of our NATIONAL INTERESTS; nor can any satisfactory argument be framed to show that they are chargeable with such an excess. If it be true, as has been insinuated by some of the writers on the other side, that the difficulty arises from the nature of the thing, and that the extent of the country will not permit us to form a government in which such ample powers can safely be reposed, it would prove that we ought to contract our views, and resort to the expedient of separate confederacies, which will move within more practicable spheres. For the absurdity must continually stare us in the face of confiding to a government the direction of the most essential national interests, without daring to trust it to the authorities which are indispensable to their proper and efficient management. Let us not attempt to reconcile contradictions, but firmly embrace a rational alternative.

I trust, however, that the impracticability of one general system cannot be shown. I am greatly mistaken if anything of weight has yet been advanced of this tendency; and I flatter myself that the observations which have been made in the course of these papers have served to place the reverse of that position in as clear a light as any matter still in the womb of time and experience is susceptible of. This, at all events, must be evident, that the very difficulty itself, drawn from the extent of the country, is the strongest argument in favor of an energetic government; for any other can certainly never preserve the Union of so large an empire. If we embrace the tenets of those who oppose the adoption of the proposed Constitution as the standard of our political creed we cannot fail to verify the gloomy doctrines which predict the impracticability of a national system pervading the entire limits of the present Confederacy.

PUBLIUS

No. 24: Hamilton

TO THE powers proposed to be conferred upon the federal government, in respect to the creation and direction of the national forces, I have met with but one specific objection, which, if I understand it rightly, is this—that proper provision has not been made against the existence of standing armies in time of peace; an objection which I shall now endeavor to show rests on weak and unsubstantial foundations.

It has indeed been brought forward in the most vague and general form, supported only by bold assertions without the appearance of argument; without even the sanction of theoretical opinions; in contradiction to the practice of other free nations, and to the general sense of America, as expressed in most of the existing constitutions. The propriety of this remark will appear the moment it is recollected that the objection under consideration turns upon a supposed necessity of restraining the LEGISLATIVE authority of the nation in the article of military establishments; a principle unheard of, except in one or two of our State constitutions, and rejected in all the rest.

A stranger to our politics, who was to read our newspapers at the present juncture without having previously inspected the plan reported by the convention, would be naturally led to one of two conclusions: either that it contained a positive injunction and standing armies should be kept up in time of peace; or that it vested in the EXECUTIVE the whole power of levying troops without subjecting his discretion, in any shape, to the control of the legislature.

If he came afterwards to peruse the plan itself, he would be surprised to discover that neither the one nor the other was the case; that the whole power of raising armies was lodged in the *legislature,* not in the *executive;* that this legislature was to be a popular body, consisting of the representatives of the people periodically elected; and that instead of the provision he had supposed in favor of standing armies, there was to be found in respect to this object an important qualification even of the legislative discretion in that clause which forbids the appropriation of money for the support of an army for any longer period than two years—a precaution which upon a nearer view of it will appear to be a great and real security against military establishments without evident necessity.

Disappointed in his first surmise, the person I have supposed would be apt to pursue his conjectures a little further. He would naturally say to himself, it is impossible that all this vehement and pathetic declamation can be without some colorable pretext. It must needs be that this people, so jealous of their liberties, have, in all the preceding models of the constitutions which they have established, inserted the most precise and rigid precautions on this point, the omission of which in the new plan has given birth to all this apprehension and clamor.

If under this impression he proceeded to pass in review the several State constitutions, how great would be his disappointment to find that *two* only of them* contained an interdiction of standing armies in time of peace; that the other eleven had either observed a profound silence on the subject, or had in express terms admitted the right of the legislature to authorize their existence.

Still, however, he would be persuaded that there must be some plausible foundation for the cry raised on this head. He would never be able to imagine, while any source of information remained unexplored, that it was nothing more than an experiment upon the public credulity, dictated either by a deliberate intention to deceive, or by the overflowings of a zeal too intemperate to be ingenuous. It would probably occur to him that he would be likely to find the precautions he was in search of in the primitive compact between the States. Here, at length, he would expect to meet with a solution of the enigma. No doubt he would observe to himself the existing Confederation must contain the most explicit provisions against military establishments in time of peace; and a departure from this model in a favorite point has occasioned the discontent which appears to influence these political champions.

If he should now apply himself to a careful and critical survey of the articles of Confederation, his astonishment

* This statement of the matter is taken from the printed collections of State constitutions. Pennsylvania and North Carolina are the two which contain the interdiction in these words: "As standing armies in time of peace are dangerous to liberty, THEY OUGHT NOT to be kept up." This is, in truth, rather a CAUTION than a PROHIBITION. New Hampshire, Massachusetts, Delaware, and Maryland have, in each of their bills of rights, a clause to this effect: "Standing armies are dangerous to liberty, and ought not to be raised or kept up WITHOUT THE CONSENT OF THE LEGISLATURE"; which is a formal admission of authority of the legislature. New York has no bill of her rights, and her constitution says not a word about the matter. No bills of rights appear annexed to the constitutions of the other States, except the foregoing, and their constitutions are equally silent. I am told, however, that one or two States have bills of rights which do not appear in this collection; but that those also recognize the right of the legislative authority in this respect.

would not only be increased, but would acquire a mixture of indignation at the unexpected discovery that these articles, instead of containing the prohibition he looked for, and though they had with a jealous circumspection restricted the authority of the State legislatures in this particular, had not imposed a single restraint on that of the United States. If he happened to be a man of quick sensibility, or ardent temper, he could now no longer refrain from pronouncing these clamors to be the dishonest artifices of a sinister and unprincipled opposition to a plan which ought at least to receive a fair and candid examination from all sincere lovers of their country! How else, he would say, could the authors of them have been tempted to vent such loud censures upon that plan about a point in which it seems to have conformed itself to the general sense of America as declared in its different forms of government, and in which it has even superadded a new and powerful guard unknown to any of them? If, on the contrary, he happened to be a man of calm and dispassionate feelings, he would indulge a sigh for the frailty of human nature, and would lament that in a matter so interesting to the happiness of millions the true merits of the question should be perplexed and obscured by expedients so unfriendly to an impartial and right determination. Even such a man could hardly forbear remarking that a conduct of this kind has too much the appearance of an intention to mislead the people by alarming their passions, rather than to convince them by arguments addressed to their understandings.

But however little this objection may be countenanced, even by precedents among ourselves, it may be satisfactory to take a nearer view of its intrinsic merits. From a close examination it will appear that restraints upon the discretion of the legislature in respect to military establishments would be improper to be imposed, and if imposed, from the necessities of society, would be unlikely to be observed.

Though a wide ocean separates the United States from Europe, yet there are various considerations that warn us against an excess of confidence or security. On one side of us, and stretching far into our rear, are growing settlements subject to the dominion of Britain. On the other side, and extending to meet the British settlements, are colonies and establishments subject to the dominion of Spain. This situation and the vicinity of the West India Islands, belonging to these two powers, create between them, in respect to their American possessions and in relation to us, a common interest. The savage tribes on our Western frontier ought to be regarded as our natural enemies, their natural allies, because they have most to fear from us, and most to hope from them. The improvements in the art of navigation have, as to the facility of communication, rendered distant nations, in a great measure, neighbors. Britain and Spain are among the principal maritime powers of Europe. A future concert of views between these nations ought not to be regarded as improbable. The increasing remoteness of consanguinity is every day diminishing the force of the family compact between France and Spain. And politicians have ever with great reason considered the ties of blood as feeble and precarious links of political connection. These circumstances combined admonish us not to be too sanguine in considering ourselves as entirely out of the reach of danger.

Previous to the Revolution, and ever since the peace, there has been a constant necessity for keeping small garrisons on our Western frontier. No person can doubt that these will continue to be indispensable, if it should only be against the ravages and depredations of the Indians. These garrisons must either be furnished by occasional detachments from the militia, or by permanent corps in the pay of the government. The first is impracticable; and if practicable, would be pernicious. The militia would not long, if at all, submit to be dragged from their occupations and families to perform that most disagreeable duty in times of profound peace. And if they could be prevailed upon or compelled to do it, the increased expense of a frequent rotation of service, and the loss of labor and disconcertion of the industrious pursuits of individuals, would form conclusive objections to the scheme. It would be as burdensome and injurious to the public as ruinous to private citizens. The latter resource of permanent corps in the pay of the government amounts to a standing army in time of peace; a small one, indeed, but not the less real for being small.

Here is a simple view of the subject that shows us at once the impropriety of a constitutional interdiction of such establishments, and the necessity of leaving the matter to the discretion and prudence of the legislature.

In proportion to our increase in strength, it is probable, nay, it may be said certain, that Britain and Spain would augment their military establishments in our neighborhood. If we should not be willing to be exposed in a naked and defenseless condition to their insults and encroachments, we should find it expedient to increase our frontier garrisons in some ratio to the force by which our Western settlements might be annoyed. There are, and will be, particular posts, the possession of which will include the command of large districts of territory, and facilitate future invasions of the remainder. It may be added that some of those posts will be keys to the trade with the Indian nations. Can any man think it would be wise to leave such posts in a situation to be at any instant seized by one or the other of two neighboring and formidable powers? To act this part would be to desert all the usual maxims of prudence and policy.

If we mean to be a commercial people, or even to be secure on our Atlantic side, we must endeavor, as soon as possible, to have a navy. To this purpose there must be dockyards and arsenals; and for the defense of these, fortifications, and probably garrisons. When a nation has become so powerful by sea that it can protect its dockyards by its fleets, this supersedes the necessity of garrisons for that purpose; but where naval establishments are in their infancy, moderate garrisons will, in all likelihood, be found an indispensable security against descents for the destruction of the arsenals and dockyards, and sometimes of the fleet itself.

PUBLIUS

No. 25: Hamilton

IT MAY perhaps be urged that the objects enumerated in the preceding number ought to be provided for by the State governments, under the direction of the Union. But this would be in reality an inversion of the primary principle of our political association, as it would in practice transfer the care of the common defense from the federal head to the individual members: a project oppressive to some States, dangerous to all, and baneful to the Confederacy.

The territories of Britain, Spain, and of the Indian nations in our neighborhood do not border on particular States, but encircle the Union from Maine to Georgia. The danger, though in different degrees, is therefore common. And the means of guarding against it ought in like manner to be the objects of common councils, and of a common treasury. It happens that some States, from local situation, are more directly exposed. New York is of this class. Upon the plan of separate provisions, New York would have to sustain the whole weight of the establishments requisite to her immediate safety, and to the mediate or ultimate protection of her neighbors. This would neither be equitable as it respected New York, nor safe as it respected the other States. Various inconveniences would attend such a system. The States, to whose lot it might fall to support the necessary establishments, would be as little able as willing for a considerable time to come to bear the burden of competent provisions. The security of all would thus be subjected to the parsimony, improvidence, or inability of a part. If the resources of such part becoming more abundant and extensive, its provisions should be proportionally enlarged, the other States would quickly take the alarm at seeing the whole military force of the Union in the hands of two or three of its members, and those probably amongst the most powerful. They would each choose to have some counterpoise, and pretenses could easily be contrived. In this situation, military establishments, nourished by mutual jealousy, would be apt to swell beyond their natural or proper size; and being at the separate disposal of the members, they would be engines for the abridgment or demolition of the national authority.

Reasons have been already given to induce a supposition that the State governments will too naturally be prone to a rivalship with that of the Union, the foundation of which will be the love of power; and that in any contest between the federal head and one of its members, the people will be most apt to unite with their local government. If, in addition to this immense advantage, the ambition of the members should be stimulated by the separate and independent possession of military forces, it would afford too strong a temptation and too great facility to them to make enterprises upon, and finally to subvert, the constitutional authority of the Union. On the other hand, the liberty of the people would be less safe in this state of things than in that which left the national forces in the hands of the national government. As far as an army may be considered as a dangerous weapon of power, it had better be in those hands of which the people are most likely to be jealous than in those of which they are least likely to be jealous. For it is a truth, which the experience of all ages has attested, that the people are commonly most in danger when the means of injuring their rights are in the possession of those of whom they entertain the least suspicion.

The framers of the existing Confederation, fully aware of the dangers to the Union from the separate possession of military forces by the States, have in express terms prohibited them from having either ships or troops, unless with the consent of Congress. The truth is, that the existence of a federal government and military establishments under State authority are not less at variance with each other than a due supply of the federal treasury and the system of quotas and requisitions.

There are other lights besides those already presented in which the impropriety of restraints on the discretion of the national legislature will be equally manifest. The design of the objection which has been mentioned is to preclude standing armies in time of peace, though we have never been informed how far it is desired the prohibition should extend: whether to raising armies as well as to *keeping them up* in a season of tranquillity or not. If it be confined to the latter it will have no precise signification, and it will be ineffectual for the purpose intended. When armies are once raised what shall be denominated "keeping them up," contrary to the sense of the Constitution? What time shall be requisite to ascertain the violation? Shall it be a week, a month, or a year? Or shall we say they may be continued as long as the danger which occasioned their being raised continues? This would be to admit that they might be kept up *in time of peace*, against threatening or impending danger, which would be at once to deviate from the literal meaning of the prohibition and to introduce an extensive latitude of construction. Who shall judge of the continuance of the danger? This must undoubtedly be submitted to the national government, and the matter would then be brought to this issue, that the national government to provide against apprehended danger might in the first instance raise troops, and might afterwards keep them on foot as long as they supposed the peace or safety of the community was in any degree of jeopardy. It is easy to perceive that a discretion so latitudinary as this would afford ample room for eluding the force of the provision.

The supposed utility of a provision of this kind must be founded upon a supposed probability, or at least possibility, of a combination between the executive and legislative in some scheme of usurpation. Should this at any time happen, how easy would it be to fabricate pretenses of approaching danger? Indian hostilities, instigated by Spain or Britain, would always be at hand. Provocations to produce the desired appearances might even be given to some foreign power, and appeased again by timely concessions. If we can reasonably presume such a combination to have been formed, and that the enterprise is warranted by a sufficient prospect of success, the army, when once raised from whatever cause, or on whatever pretext, may be applied to the execution of the project.

If, to obviate this consequence, it should be resolved to extend the prohibition to the *raising* of armies in time of peace, the United States would then exhibit the most extraordinary spectacle which the world has yet seen—that of a nation incapacitated by its Constitution to prepare for defense before it was actually invaded. As the ceremony of a formal denunciation of war has of late fallen into disuse, the presence of an enemy within our territories must be waited for as the legal warrant to the government to begin its levies of men for the protection of the State. We must receive the blow before we could even prepare to return it. All that kind of policy by which nations anticipate distant danger and meet the gathering storm must be abstained from, as contrary to the genuine maxims of a free government. We must expose our property and liberty to the mercy of foreign invaders and invite them by our weakness to seize the naked and defenseless prey, because we are afraid that rulers, created by our choice, dependent on our will, might endanger that liberty by an abuse of the means necessary to its preservation.

Here I expect we shall be told that the militia of the country is its natural bulwark, and would be at all times equal to the national defense. This doctrine, in substance, had like to have lost us our independence. It cost millions to the United States that might have been saved. The facts which from our own experience forbid a reliance of this kind are too recent to permit us to be the dupes of such a suggestion. The steady operations of war against a regular and disciplined army can only be successfully conducted by a force of the same kind. Considerations of economy, not less than of stability and vigor, confirm this position. The American militia, in the course of the late war, have, by their valor on numerous occasions, erected eternal monuments to their fame; but the bravest of them feel and know that the liberty of their country could not have been established by their efforts alone, however great and valuable they were. War, like most other things, is a science to be acquired and perfected by diligence, by perseverance, by time, and by practice.

All violent policy, contrary to the natural and experienced course of human affairs, defeats itself. Pennsylvania at this instant affords an example of the truth of this remark. The Bill of Rights of that State declares that standing armies are dangerous to liberty, and ought not to be kept up in time of peace. Pennsylvania, nevertheless, in a time of profound peace from the existence of partial disorders in one or two of her counties, has resolved to raise a body of troops; and in all probability will keep them up as long as there is any appearance of danger to the public peace. The conduct of Massachusetts affords a lesson on the same subject, though on different ground. That State (without waiting for the sanction of Congress, as the articles of the Confederation require) was compelled to raise troops to quell a domestic insurrection, and still keeps a corps in pay to prevent a revival of the spirit of revolt. The particular constitution of Massachusetts opposed no obstacle to the measure; but the instance is still of use to instruct us that cases are likely to occur under our government, as well as under those of other nations, which will sometimes render a military force in time of peace essential to the security of the society, and that it is therefore improper in this respect to control the legislative discretion. It also teaches us, in its application to the United States, how little the rights of a feeble government are likely to be respected, even by its own constituents. And it teaches us, in addition to the rest, how unequal parchment provisions are to a struggle with public necessity.

It was a fundamental maxim of the Lacedæmonian commonwealth that the post of admiral should not be conferred twice on the same person. The Peloponnesian confederates, having suffered a severe defeat at sea from the Athenians, demanded Lysander, who had before served with success in that capacity, to command the combined fleets. The Lacedæmonians, to gratify their allies and yet preserve the semblance of an adherence to their ancient institutions, had recourse to the flimsy subterfuge of investing Lysander with the real power of admiral under the nominal title of vice-admiral. This instance is selected from among a multitude that might be cited to confirm the truth already advanced and illustrated by domestic examples; which is, that nations pay little regard to rules and maxims calculated in their very nature to run counter to the necessities of society. Wise politicians will be cautious about fettering the government with restrictions that cannot be observed, because they know that every breach of the fundamental laws, though dictated by necessity, impairs that sacred reverence which ought to be maintained in the breast of rulers towards the constitution of a country, and forms a precedent for other breaches where the same plea of necessity does not exist at all, or is less urgent and palpable. PUBLIUS

No. 26: Hamilton

IT WAS a thing hardly to be expected that in a popular revolution the minds of men should stop at that happy mean which marks the salutary boundary between POWER and PRIVILEGE, and combines the energy of government with the security of private rights. A failure in this delicate and important point is the great source of the inconveniences we experience, and if we are not cautious to avoid a repetition of the error in our future attempts to rectify and ameliorate our system we may travel from one chimerical project to another; we may try change after change; but we shall never be likely to make any material change for the better.

The idea of restraining the legislative authority in the means of providing for the national defense is one of those refinements which owe their origin to a zeal for liberty more ardent than enlightened. We have seen, however, that it has not had thus far an extensive prevalency; that even in this country, where it made its first appearance, Pennsylvania and North Carolina are the only two States by which it has been in any degree patronized; and that all the others have refused to give it the least countenance; wisely judging that confidence must be placed somewhere; that the necessity of doing it is implied in the very act of delegating power; and that it is better to hazard the abuse of that confidence than to embarrass the government and endanger the public safety by impolitic restrictions on the legislative authority. The opponents of the proposed Constitution combat, in this respect, the general decision of America; and instead of being taught by experience the propriety of correcting any extremes into which we may have heretofore run, they appear disposed to conduct us into others still more dangerous and more extravagant. As if the tone of government had been found too high, or too rigid, the doctrines they teach are calculated to induce us to depress or to relax it by expedients which, upon other occasions, have been condemned or forborne. It may be affirmed without the imputation of invective that if the principles they inculcate on various points could so far obtain as to become the popular creed, they would utterly unfit the people of this country for any species of government whatever. But a danger of this kind is not to be apprehended. The citizens of America have too much discernment to be argued into anarchy. And I am much mistaken if experience has not wrought a deep and solemn conviction in the public mind that greater energy of government is essential to the welfare and prosperity of the community.

It may not be amiss in this place concisely to remark the origin and progress of the idea, which aims at the exclusion of military establishments in time of peace. Though in speculative minds it may arise from a contemplation of the nature and tendency of such institutions, fortified by the events that have happened in other ages and countries, yet as a national sentiment it must be traced to those habits of thinking which we derive from the nation from whom the inhabitants of these States have in general sprung.

In England, for a long time after the Norman Conquest, the authority of the monarch was almost unlimited. Inroads were gradually made upon the prerogative in favor of liberty, first by the barons and afterwards by the people, till the greatest part of its most formidable pretensions became extinct. But it was not till the revolution in 1688, which elevated the Prince of Orange to the throne of Great Britain, that English liberty was completely triumphant. As incident to the undefined power of making war an acknowledged prerogative of the crown, Charles II had, by his own authority, kept on foot in time of peace a body of 5,000 regular troops. And this number James II increased to 30,000, which were paid out of his civil list. At the revolution, to abolish the exercise of so dangerous an authority, it became an article of the Bill of Rights then framed that "the raising or keeping a standing army within the kingdom in time of peace, *unless with the consent of Parliament*, was against law."

In that kingdom, when the pulse of liberty was at its highest pitch, no security against the danger of standing armies was thought requisite, beyond a prohibition of their being raised or kept up by the mere authority of the executive magistrate. The patriots who effected that memorable revolution were too temperate, too well-informed, to think of any restraint on the legislative discretion. They were aware that a certain number of troops for guards and garrisons were indispensable; that no precise bounds could be set to the national exigencies; that a power equal to every possible contingency must exist somewhere in the government: and that when they referred the exercise of that power to the judgment of the legislature, they had arrived at the ultimate point of precaution which was reconcilable with the safety of the community.

From the same source, the people of America may be said to have derived an hereditary impression of danger to liberty from standing armies in time of peace. The circumstances of a revolution quickened the public sensibility on every point connected with the security of popular rights, and in some instances raised the warmth of our zeal beyond the degree which consisted with the due temperature of the body politic. The attempts of two of the States to restrict the authority of the legislature in the article of military establishments are of the number of these instances. The principles which had taught us to be jealous of the power of an hereditary monarch were by an injudicious excess extended to the representatives of the people in their popular assemblies. Even in some of the States, where this error was not adopted, we find unnecessary declarations that standing armies ought not to be kept up in time of peace WITHOUT THE CONSENT OF THE LEGISLATURE. I call them unnecessary, because the reason which had introduced a similar provision into the English Bill of Rights is not applicable to any of the State constitutions. The power of raising armies at all under those constitutions can by no construction be deemed to reside anywhere else than in the legislatures themselves; and it was superfluous, if not absurd, to declare that a matter should not be done without the consent of a body, which alone had the power of doing it. Accordingly, in some of those constitutions, and among others, in that of the State of New York, which has been justly celebrated both in Europe and America as one of the best of the forms of government established in this country, there is a total silence upon the subject.

It is remarkable that even in the two States which seem to have meditated an interdiction of military establishments in time of peace, the mode of expression made use of is rather monitory than prohibitory. It is not said that standing armies *shall not be* kept up, but that they *ought not* to be kept up, in time of peace. This ambiguity of terms appears to have been the result of a conflict between jealousy and conviction; between the desire of excluding such establishments at all events and the persuasion that an absolute exclusion would be unwise and unsafe.

Can it be doubted that such a provision, whenever the situation of public affairs was understood to require a departure from it, would be interpreted by the legislature into a mere admonition, and would be made to yield to the necessities or supposed necessities of the State? Let the fact already mentioned with respect to Pennsylvania decide. What then (it may be asked) is the use of such a provision, if it cease to operate the moment there is an inclination to disregard it?

Let us examine whether there be any comparison in point of efficacy between the provision alluded to and that which is contained in the new Constitution for restraining the appropriations of money for military purposes to the period of two years. The former, by aiming at too much, is calculated to effect nothing; the latter, by steering clear of an imprudent extreme, and by being perfectly compatible with a proper provision for the exigencies of the nation, will have a salutary and powerful operation.

The legislature of the United States will be *obliged* by this provision, once at least in every two years, to deliberate upon the propriety of keeping a military force on foot; to come to a new resolution on the point; and to declare their sense of the matter by a formal vote in the face of their constituents. They are not *at liberty* to vest in the executive department permanent funds for the support of an army, if they were even incautious enough to be willing to repose in it so improper a confidence. As the spirit of party in different degrees must be expected to infect all political bodies, there will be, no doubt, persons in the national legislature willing enough to arraign the measures and criminate the views of the majority. The provision for the support of a military force will always be a favorable topic for declamation. As often as the question comes forward, the public attention will be roused and attracted to the subject by the party in opposition; and if the majority should be really disposed to exceed the proper limits, the community will be warned of the danger, and will have an opportunity of taking measures to guard against it. Independent of parties in the national legislature itself, as often as the period of discussion arrived, the State legislatures, who will always be not only vigilant but suspicious and jealous guardians of the rights of the citizens against encroachments from the federal government, will constantly have their attention awake to the conduct of the national rulers, and will be ready enough, if anything improper appears, to sound the alarm to the people, and not only to be the VOICE, but, if necessary, the ARM of their discontent.

Schemes to subvert the liberties of a great community *require time* to mature them for execution. An army, so large as seriously to menace those liberties, could only be formed by progressive augmentations; which would suppose not merely a temporary combination between the legislature and executive, but a continued conspiracy for a series of time. Is it probable that such a combination would exist at all? Is it probable that it would be persevered in, and transmitted along through all the successive variations in a representative body, which biennial elections would naturally produce in both houses? Is it presumable that every man the instant he took his seat in the national Senate or House of Representatives would commence a traitor to his constituents and to his country? Can it be supposed that there would not be found one man discerning enough to detect so atrocious a conspiracy, or bold or honest enough to apprise his constituents of their danger? If such presumptions can fairly be made, there ought to be at once an end of all delegated authority. The people should resolve to recall all the powers they have heretofore parted with out of their own hands, and to divide themselves into as many States as there are counties in order that they may be able to manage their own concerns in person.

If such suppositions could even be reasonably made,

still the concealment of the design for any duration would be impracticable. It would be announced by the very circumstance of augmenting the army to so great an extent in time of profound peace. What colorable reason could be assigned in a country so situated for such vast augmentations of the military force? It is impossible that the people could be long deceived; and the destruction of the project and of the projectors would quickly follow the discovery.

It has been said that the provision which limits the appropriation of money for the support of an army to the period of two years would be unavailing, because the executive, when once possessed of a force large enough to awe the people into submission, would find resources in that very force sufficient to enable him to dispense with supplies from the acts of the legislature. But the question again recurs, upon what pretense could he be put in possession of a force of that magnitude in time of peace? If we suppose it to have been created in consequence of some domestic insurrection or foreign war, then it becomes a case not within the principle of the objection; for this is leveled against the power of keeping up troops in time of peace. Few persons will be so visionary as seriously to contend that military forces ought not to be raised to quell a rebellion or resist an invasion; and if the defense of the community under such circumstances should make it necessary to have an army so numerous as to hazard its liberty, this is one of those calamities for which there is neither preventative nor cure. It cannot be provided against by any possible form of government; it might even result from a simple league offensive and defensive, if it should ever be necessary for the confederates or allies to form an army for common defense.

But it is an evil infinitely less likely to attend us in a united than in a disunited state; nay, it may be safely asserted that it is an evil altogether unlikely to attend us in the former situation. It is not easy to conceive a possibility that dangers so formidable can assail the whole Union as to demand a force considerable enough to place our liberties in the least jeopardy, especially if we take into our view the aid to be derived from the militia, which ought always to be counted upon as a valuable and powerful auxiliary. But in a state of disunion (as has been fully shown in another place), the contrary of this supposition would become not only probable, but almost unavoidable.

PUBLIUS

No. 27: Hamilton

IT HAS been urged in different shapes that a Constitution of the kind proposed by the convention cannot operate without the aid of a military force to execute its laws. This, however, like most other things that have been alleged on that side, rests on mere general assertion, unsupported by any precise or intelligible designation of the reasons upon which it is founded. As far as I have been able to divine the latent meaning of the objectors, it seems to originate in a presupposition that the people will be disinclined to the exercise of federal authority in any matter of an internal nature. Waiving any exception that might be taken to the inaccuracy of inexplicitness of the distinction between internal and external, let us inquire what ground there is to presuppose that disinclination in the people. Unless we presume at the same time that the powers of the general government will be worse administered than those of the State governments, there seems to be no room for the presumption of ill will, disaffection, or opposition in the people. I believe it may be laid down as a general rule that their confidence in and obedience to a government will commonly be proportioned to the goodness or badness of its administration. It must be admitted that there are exceptions to this rule; but these exceptions depend so entirely on accidental causes that they cannot be considered as having any relation to the intrinsic merits or demerits of a constitution. These can only be judged of by general principles and maxims.

Various reasons have been suggested in the course of these papers to induce a probability that the general government will be better administered than the particular governments: the principal of which are that the extension of the spheres of election will present a greater option, or latitude of choice, to the people; that through the medium of the State legislatures—who are select bodies of men and who are to appoint the members of the national Senate—there is reason to expect that this branch will generally be composed with peculiar care and judgment; that these circumstances promise greater knowledge and more comprehensive information in the national councils. And that on account of the extent of the country from which those, to whose direction they will be committed, will be drawn, they will be less apt to be tainted by the spirit of faction, and more out of the reach of those occasional ill humors, or temporary prejudices and propensities, which in smaller societies frequently contaminate the public deliberations, beget injustice and oppression of a part of the community, and engender schemes which, though they gratify a momentary inclination or desire, terminate in general distress, dissatisfaction, and disgust. Several additional reasons of considerable force to fortify that probability will occur when we come to survey with a more critical eye the interior structure of the edifice which we are invited to erect. It will be sufficient here to remark that until satisfactory reasons can be assigned to justify an opinion that the federal government is likely to be administered in such a manner as to render it odious or contemptible to the people, there can be no reasonable foundation for the supposition that the laws of the Union will meet with any greater obstruction from them, or will stand in need of any other methods to enforce their execution, than the laws of the particular members.

The hope of impunity is a strong incitement to sedition; the dread of punishment, a proportionately strong discouragement to it. Will not the government of the Union, which, if possessed of a due degree of power, can call to its aid the collective resources of the whole Confederacy, be more likely to repress the *former* sentiment and to inspire the *latter,* than that of a single State, which can only command the resources within itself? A turbulent faction in a State may easily suppose itself able to contend with the friends to the government in that State; but it can hardly be so infatuated as to imagine itself a match for the combined efforts of the Union. If this reflection be just, there is less danger of resistance from irregular combinations of individuals to the authority of the Confederacy than to that of a single member.

I will, in this place, hazard an observation which will not be the less just because to some it may appear new; which is, that the more the operations of the national authority are intermingled in the ordinary exercise of government, the more the citizens are accustomed to meet with it in the common occurrences of their political life, the more it is familiarized to their sight and to their feelings, the further it enters into those objects which touch the most sensible chords and put in motion the most active springs of the human heart, the greater will be the probability that it will conciliate the respect and attachment of the community. Man is very much a creature of habit. A thing that rarely strikes his senses will generally have but a transient influence upon his mind. A government continually at a distance and out of sight can hardly be expected to interest the sensations of the people. The inference is that the authority of the Union and the affections of the citizens towards it will be strengthened, rather than weakened, by its extension to what are called matters of internal concern; and that it will have less occasion to recur to force, in proportion to the familiarity and comprehensiveness of its agency. The more it circulates through those channels and currents in which the passions of mankind naturally flow, the less will it require the aid of the violent and perilous expedients of compulsion.

One thing at all events must be evident, that a government like that proposed would bid much fairer to avoid the necessity of using force than the species of league contended for by most of its opponents; the authority of which should only operate upon the States in their political or collective capacities. It has been shown that in such a Confederacy there can be no sanction for the laws but force; that frequent delinquencies in the members are the natural offspring of the very frame of the government; and that as often as these happen, they can only be redressed, if at all, by war and violence.

The plan reported by the convention, by extending the authority of the federal head to the individual citizens of the several States, will enable the government to employ the ordinary magistracy of each in the execution of its laws. It is easy to perceive that this will tend to destroy, in the common apprehension, all distinction between the sources from which they might proceed; and will give the federal government the same advantage for securing a due obedience to its authority which is enjoyed by the government of each State, in addition to the influence on public opinion which will result from the important consideration of its having power to call to its assistance and support the resources of the whole Union. It merits particular attention in this place, that the laws of the Confederacy as to the *enumerated* and *legitimate* objects of its jurisdiction will become the SUPREME LAW of the land; to the observance of which all officers, legislative, executive, and judicial in each State will be bound by the sanctity of an oath. Thus the legislatures, courts, and magistrates, of the respective members will be incorporated into the operations of the national government *as far as its just and constitutional authority extends;* and will be rendered auxiliary to the enforcement of its laws.* Any man who will pursue by his own reflections the consequences of this situation will perceive that there is good ground to calculate upon a regular and peaceable execution of the laws of the Union, if its powers are administered with a common share of prudence. If we will arbitrarily suppose the contrary, we may deduce any inferences we please from the supposition; for it is certainly possible, by an injudicious exercise of the authorities of the best government that ever was, or ever can be instituted, to provoke and precipitate the people into the wildest excesses. But though the adversaries of the proposed Constitution should presume that the national rulers would be insensible to the motives of public good, or to the obligations of duty, I would still ask them how the interests of ambition, or the views of encroachment, can be promoted by such a conduct?

PUBLIUS

* The sophistry which has been employed to show that this will tend to the destruction of the State governments will, in its proper place, be fully detected.

No. 28: Hamilton

THAT there may happen cases in which the national government may be necessitated to resort to force cannot be denied. Our own experience has corroborated the lessons taught by the examples of other nations; that emergencies of this sort will sometimes exist in all societies, however constituted; that seditions and insurrections are, unhappily, maladies as inseparable from the body politic as tumors and eruptions from the natural body; that the idea of governing at all times by the simple force of law (which we have been told is the only admissible principle of republican government) has no place but in the reveries of those political doctors whose sagacity disdains the admonitions of experimental instruction.

Should such emergenices at any time happen under the national government, there could be no remedy but force. The means to be employed must be proportioned to the extent of the mischief. If it should be a slight commotion in a small part of a State, the militia of the residue would be adequate to its suppression; and the natural presumption is that they would be ready to do their duty. An insurrection, whatever may be its immediate cause, eventually endangers all government. Regard to the public peace, if not to the rights of the Union, would engage the citizens to whom the contagion had not communicated itself to oppose the insurgents; and if the general government should be found in practice conducive to the prosperity and felicity of the people, it were irrational to believe that they would be disinclined to its support.

If, on the contrary, the insurrection should pervade a whole State, or a principal part of it, the employment of a different kind of force might become unavoidable. It appears that Massachusetts found it necessary to raise troops for suppressing the disorders within that State; that Pennsylvania, from the mere apprehension of commotions among a part of her citizens, has thought proper to have recourse to the same measure. Suppose the State of New York had been inclined to re-establish her lost jurisdiction over the inhabitants of Vermont, could she have hoped for success in such an enterprise from the efforts of the militia alone? Would she not have been compelled to raise and to maintain a more regular force for the execution of her design? If it must then be admitted that the necessity of recurring to a force different from the militia, in cases of this extraordinary nature, is applicable to the State governments themselves, why should the possibility that the national government might be under a like necessity, in similar extremities, be made an objection to its existence? Is it not surprising that men who declare an attachment to the Union in the abstract should urge as an objection to the proposed Constitution what applies with tenfold weight to the plan for which they contend; and what, as far as it has any foundation in truth, is an inevitable consequence of civil society upon an enlarged scale? Who would not prefer that possibility to the unceasing agitations and frequent revolutions which are the continual scourges of petty republics?

Let us pursue this examination in another light. Suppose, in lieu of one general system, two, or three, or even four Confederacies were to be formed, would not the same difficulty oppose itself to the operations of either of these Confederacies? Would not each of them be exposed to the same casualties; and when these happened, be obliged to have recourse to the same expedients for upholding its authority which are objected to in a government for all the States? Would the militia in this supposition be more ready or more able to support the federal authority than in the case of a general union? All candid and intelligent men must, upon due consideration, acknowledge that the principle of the objection is equally applicable to either of the two cases; and that whether we have one government for all the States, or different governments for different parcels of them, or as many unconnected governments as there are States, there might sometimes be a necessity to make use of a force constituted differently from the militia to preserve the peace of the community and to maintain the just authority of the laws against those violent invasions of them which amount to insurrections and rebellions.

Independent of all other reasonings upon the subject,

it is a full answer to those who require a more peremptory provision against military establishments in time of peace to say that the whole power of the proposed government is to be in the hands of the representatives of the people. This is the essential, and, after all, the only efficacious security for the rights and privileges of the people which is attainable in civil society.*

If the representatives of the people betray their constituents, there is then no resource left but in the exertion of that original right of self-defense which is paramount to all positive forms of government, and which against the usurpations of the national rulers may be exerted with infinitely better prospect of success than against those of the rulers of an individual State. In a single State, if the persons intrusted with supreme power become usurpers, the different parcels, subdivisions, or districts of which it consists, having no distinct government in each, can take no regular measures for defense. The citizens must rush tumultuously to arms, without concert, without system, without resource; except in their courage and despair. The usurpers, clothed with the forms of legal authority, can too often crush the opposition in embryo. The smaller the extent of the territory, the more difficult will it be for the people to form a regular or systematic plan of opposition, and the more easy will it be to defeat their early efforts. Intelligence can be more speedily obtained of their preparations and movements, and the military force in the possession of the usurpers can be more rapidly directed against the part where the opposition has begun. In this situation there must be a peculiar coincidence of circumstances to insure success to the popular resistance.

The obstacles to usurpation and the facilities of resistance increase with the increased extent of the state, provided the citizens understand their rights and are disposed to defend them. The natural strength of the people in a large community, in proportion to the artificial strength of the government, is greater than in a small, and of course more competent to a struggle with the attempts of the government to establish a tyranny. But in a confederacy the people, without exaggeration, may be

* Its full efficacy will be examined hereafter.

said to be entirely the masters of their own fate. Power being almost always the rival of power, the general government will at all times stand ready to check the usurpations of the state governments, and these will have the same disposition towards the general government. The people, by throwing themselves into either scale, will infallibly make it preponderate. If their rights are invaded by either, they can make use of the other as the instrument of redress. How wise will it be in them by cherishing the union to preserve to themselves an advantage which can never be too highly prized!

It may safely be received as an axiom in our political system that the State governments will, in all possible contingencies, afford complete security against invasions of the public liberty by the national authority. Projects of usurpation cannot be masked under pretenses so likely to escape the penetration of select bodies of men, as of the people at large. The legislatures will have better means of information. They can discover the danger at a distance; and possessing all the organs of civil power and the confidence of the people, they can at once adopt a regular plan of opposition, in which they can combine all the resources of the community. They can readily communicate with each other in the different States, and unite their common forces for the protection of their common liberty.

The great extent of the country is a further security. We have already experienced its utility against the attacks of a foreign power. And it would have precisely the same effect against the enterprises of ambitious rulers in the national councils. If the federal army should be able to quell the resistance of one State, the distant States would be able to make head with fresh forces. The advantages obtained in one place must be abandoned to subdue the opposition in others; and the moment the part which had been reduced to submission was left to itself, its efforts would be renewed, and its resistance revive.

We should recollect that the extent of the military force must, at all events, be regulated by the resources of the country. For a long time to come it will not be possible to maintain a large army; and as the means of doing this increase, the population and natural strength of the community will proportionably increase. When will the time arrive that the federal government can raise and maintain an army capable of erecting a despotism over the great body of the people of an immense empire, who are in a situation, through the medium of their State governments, to take measures for their own defense, with all the celerity, regularity, and system of independent nations? The apprehension may be considered as a disease, for which there can be found no cure in the resources of argument and reasoning. PUBLIUS

No. 29: Hamilton

THE power of regulating the militia and of commanding its services in times of insurrection and invasion are natural incidents to the duties of superintending the common defense, and of watching over the internal peace of the Confederacy.

It requires no skill in the science of war to discern that uniformity in the organization and discipline of the militia would be attended with the most beneficial effects, whenever they were called into service for the public defense. It would enable them to discharge the duties of the camp and of the field with mutual intelligence and concert—an advantage of peculiar moment in the operations of an army; and it would fit them much sooner to acquire the degree of proficiency in military functions which would be essential to their usefulness. This desirable uniformity can only be accomplished by confiding the regulation of the militia to the direction of the national authority. It is, therefore, with the most evident propriety that the plan of the convention proposes to empower the Union "to provide for organizing, arming, and disciplining the militia, and for governing such part of them as may be employed in the service of the United States, *reserving to the States respectively the appointment of the officers, and the authority of training the militia according to the discipline prescribed by Congress.*"

Of the different grounds which have been taken in opposition to this plan there is none that was so little to have been expected, or is so untenable in itself, as the one from which this particular provision has been attacked. If a well-regulated militia be the most natural defense of a free country, it ought certainly to be under the regulation and at the disposal of that body which is constituted the guardian of the national security. If standing armies are dangerous to liberty, an efficacious power over the militia in the same body ought, as far as possible, to take away the inducement and the pretext to such unfriendly institutions. If the federal government can command the aid of the militia in those emergencies which call for the military arm in support of the civil magistrate, it can the better dispense with the employment of a different kind of force. If it cannot avail itself of the former, it will be obliged to recur to the latter. To render an army unnecessary will be a more certain method of preventing its existence than a thousand prohibitions upon paper.

In order to cast an odium upon the power of calling forth the militia to execute the laws of the Union, it has been remarked that there is nowhere any provision in the proposed Constitution for requiring the aid of the POSSE COMITATUS to assist the magistrate in the execution of his duty; whence it has been inferred that military force was intended to be his only auxiliary. There is a striking incoherence in the objections which have appeared, and sometimes even from the same quarter, not much calculated to inspire a very favorable opinion of the sincerity or fair dealing of their authors. The same persons who tell us in one breath that the powers of the federal government will be despotic and unlimited inform us in the next that it has not authority sufficient even to call out the POSSE COMITATUS. The latter, fortunately, is as much short of the truth as the former exceeds it. It would be absurd to doubt that a right to pass all laws *necessary* and *proper* to execute its declared powers would include that of requiring the assistance of the citizens to the officers who may be intrusted with the execution of those laws as it would be to believe that a right to enact laws necessary and proper for the imposition and collection of taxes would involve that of varying the rules of descent and of the alienation of landed property, or of abolishing the trial by jury in cases relating to it. It being therefore evident that the supposition of a want of power to require the aid of the POSSE COMITATUS is entirely destitute of color, it will follow that the conclusion which has been drawn from it, in its application to the authority of the federal government over the militia, is as uncandid as it is illogical. What reason could there be to infer that force was intended to be the sole instrument of authority, merely because there is a power to make use of it when necessary? What shall we think of the motives which could induce men of sense to reason in this extraordinary manner? How shall we prevent a conflict between charity and conviction?

By a curious refinement upon the spirit of republican jealousy, we are even taught to apprehend danger from the militia itself in the hands of the federal government. It is observed that select corps may be formed, composed of the young and the ardent, who may be rendered subservient to the views of arbitrary power. What plan for the regulation of the militia may be pursued by the national government is impossible to be foreseen. But so far from viewing the matter in the same light with those who object to select corps as dangerous, were the Constitution ratified and were I to deliver my sentiments to a member of the federal legislature on the subject of a militia establishment, I should hold to him, in the substance, the following discourse:

"The project of disciplining all the militia of the United States is as futile as it would be injurious if it were capable of being carried into execution. A tolerable expertness in military movements is a business that requires time and practice. It is not a day, nor a week nor even a month, that will suffice for the attainment of it. To oblige the great body of the yeomanry and of the other classes of the citizens to be under arms for the purpose of going through military exercises and evolutions, as often as might be necessary to acquire the degree of perfection which would entitle them to the character of a well-regulated militia, would be a real grievance to the people and a serious public inconvenience and loss. It would form an annual deduction from the productive labor of the country to an amount which, calculating upon the present numbers of the people, would not fall far short of a million pounds. To attempt a thing which would abridge the mass of labor and industry to so considerable an extent would be unwise: and the experiment, if made, could not succeed, because it would not long be endured. Little more can reasonably be aimed at with respect to the people at large than to have them properly armed and equipped; and in order to see that this be not neglected, it will be necessary to assemble them once or twice in the course of a year.

"But though the scheme of disciplining the whole nation must be abandoned as mischievous or impracticable; yet it is a matter of the utmost importance that a well-digested plan should, as soon as possible, be adopted for the proper establishment of the militia. The attention of the government ought particularly to be directed to the formation of a select corps of moderate size, upon such principles as will really fit it for service in case of need. By thus circumscribing the plan, it will be possible to have an excellent body of well-trained militia ready to take the field whenever the defense of the State shall require it. This will not only lessen the call for military establishments, but if circumstances should at any time oblige the government to form an army of any magnitude that army can never be formidable to the liberties of the people while there is a large body of citizens, little if at all inferior to them in discipline and the use of arms, who stand ready to defend their own rights and those of their fellow-citizens. This appears to me the only substitute that can be devised for a standing army, and the best possible security against it, if it should exist."

Thus differently from the adversaries of the proposed Constitution should I reason on the same subject, deducing arguments of safety from the very sources which they represent as fraught with danger and perdition. But how the national legislature may reason on the point is a thing which neither they nor I can foresee.

There is something so far-fetched and so extravagant in the idea of danger to liberty from the militia that one is at a loss whether to treat it with gravity or with raillery; whether to consider it as a mere trial of skill, like the paradoxes of rhetoricians; as a disingenuous artifice to instil prejudices at any price; or as the serious offspring of political fanaticism. Where in the name of common sense are our fears to end if we may not trust our sons, our brothers, our neighbors, our fellow-citizens? What shadow of danger can there be from men who are daily mingling with the rest of their countrymen and who participate with them in the same feelings, sentiments, habits, and interests? What reasonable cause of apprehension can be inferred from a power in the Union to prescribe regulations for the militia and to command its services when necessary, while the particular States are to have the *sole and exclusive appointment of the officers?* If it were possible seriously to indulge a jealousy of the militia upon any conceivable establishment under the federal government, the circumstance of the officers being in the appointment of the States ought at once to extinguish it. There can be no doubt that this circumstance will always secure to them a preponderating influence over the militia.

In reading many of the publications against the Constitution, a man is apt to imagine that he is perusing some ill-written tale or romance, which, instead of natural and agreeable images, exhibits to the mind nothing but frightful and distorted shapes—

"Gorgons, Hydras, and Chimeras dire;"

discoloring and disfiguring whatever it represents, and transforming everything it touches into a monster.

A sample of this is to be observed in the exaggerated and improbable suggestions which have taken place respecting the power of calling for the services of the militia. That of New Hampshire is to be marched to Georgia, of Georgia to New Hampshire, of New York to Kentucky, and of Kentucky to Lake Champlain. Nay, the debts due to the French and Dutch are to be paid in militiamen instead of Louis d'ors and ducats. At one moment there is to be a large army to lay prostrate the liberties of the people; at another moment the militia of Virginia are to be dragged from their homes five or six hundred miles to tame the republican contumacy of Massachusetts; and that of Massachusetts is to be transported an equal distance to subdue the refractory haughtiness of the aristocratic Virginians. Do the persons who rave at this rate imagine that their art or their eloquence can impose any conceits or absurdities upon the people of America for infallible truths?

If there should be an army to be made use of as the engine of despotism, what need of the militia? If there should be no army, whither would the militia, irritated at being required to undertake a distant and distressing expedition for the purpose of riveting the chains of slavery upon a part of their countrymen, direct their course, but to the seat of the tyrants, who had meditated so foolish as well as so wicked a project to crush them in their imagined intrenchments of power, and to make them an example of the just vengeance of an abused and incensed people? Is this the way in which usurpers stride to dominion over a numerous and enlightened nation? Do they begin by exciting the detestation of the very instruments of their intended usurpations? Do they usually commence their career by wanton and disgustful acts of power, calculated to answer no end, but to draw upon themselves universal hatred and execration? Are suppositions of this sort the sober admonitions of discerning patriots to a discerning people? Or are they the inflammatory ravings of chagrined incendiaries or distempered enthusiasts? If we were even to suppose the national rulers actuated by the most ungovernable ambition, it is impossible to believe that they would employ such preposterous means to accomplish their designs.

In times of insurrection, or invasion, it would be natural and proper that the militia of a neighboring State should be marched into another, to resist a common enemy, or to guard the republic against the violence of faction or sedition. This was frequently the case in respect to the first object in the course of the late war; and this mutual succor is, indeed, a principal end of our political association. If the power of affording it be placed under the direction of the Union, there will be no danger of a supine and listless inattention to the dangers of a neighbor till its near approach had superadded the incitements of self-preservation to the too feeble impulses of duty and sympathy.

PUBLIUS

No. 30: Hamilton

IT HAS been already observed that the federal government ought to possess the power of providing for the support of the national forces; in which proposition was intended to be included the expense of raising troops, of building and equipping fleets, and all other expenses in any wise connected with military arrangements and operations. But these are not the only objects to which the jurisdiction of the Union in respect to revenue must necessarily be empowered to extend. It must embrace a provision for the support of the national civil list; for the payment of the national debts contracted, or that may be contracted; and, in general, for all those matters which will call for disbursements out of the national treasury. The conclusion is that there must be interwoven in the frame of the government a general power of taxation, in one shape or another.

Money is, with propriety, considered as the vital principle of the body politic; as that which sustains its life and motion and enables it to perform its most essential functions. A complete power, therefore, to procure a regular and adequate supply of revenue, as far as the resources of the community will permit, may be regarded as an indispensable ingredient in every constitution. From a deficiency in this particular, one of two evils must ensue: either the people must be subjected to continual plunder, as a substitute for a more eligible mode of supplying the public wants, or the government must sink into a fatal atrophy, and, in a short course of time, perish.

In the Ottoman or Turkish empire the sovereign, though in other respects absolute master of the lives and fortunes of his subjects, has no right to impose a new tax. The consequence is that he permits the bashaws or governors of provinces to pillage the people at discretion, and, in turn, squeezes out of them the sums of which he stands in need to satisfy his own exigencies and those of the state. In America, from a like cause, the government of the Union has gradually dwindled into a state of decay, approaching nearly to annihilation. Who can doubt that the happiness of the people in both countries would be promoted by competent authorities in the proper hands to provide the revenues which the necessities of the public might require?

The present Confederation, feeble as it is, intended to repose in the United States an unlimited power of providing for the pecuniary wants of the Union. But proceeding upon an erroneous principle, it has been done in such a manner as entirely to have frustrated the intention. Congress, by the articles which compose that compact (as has already been stated), are authorized to ascertain and call for any sums of money necessary in their judgment to the service of the United States; and their requisitions, if conformable to the rule of apportionment, are in every constitutional sense obligatory upon the States. These have no right to question the propriety of the demand; no discretion beyond that of devising the ways and means of furnishing the sums demanded. But though this be strictly and truly the case; though the assumption of such a right would be an infringement of the articles of Union; though it may seldom or never have been avowedly claimed, yet in practice it has been constantly exercised and would continue to be so, as long as the revenues of the Confederacy should remain dependent on the intermediate agency of its members. What the consequences of this system have been is within the knowledge of every man the least conversant in our public affairs, and has been abundantly unfolded in different parts of these inquiries. It is this which affords ample cause of mortification to ourselves, and of triumph to our enemies.

What remedy can there be for this situation, but in a change of the system which has produced it—in a change of the fallacious and delusive system of quotas and requisitions? What substitute can there be imagined for this *ignis fatuus* in finance, but that of permitting the national government to raise its own revenues by the ordinary methods of taxation authorized in every well-ordered constitution of civil government? Ingenious men may declaim with plausibility on any subject; but no human ingenuity can point out any other expedient to rescue us from the inconveniences and embarrassments naturally resulting from defective supplies of the public treasury.

The more intelligent adversaries of the new Constitution admit the force of this reasoning; but they qualify their admission by a distinction between what they call *internal* and *external* taxation. The former they would reserve to the State governments; the latter, which they explain into commercial imposts, or rather duties on imported articles, they declare themselves willing to concede to the federal head. This distinction, however, would violate that fundamental maxim of good sense and sound policy, which dictates that every POWER ought to be proportionate to its OBJECT; and would still leave the general government in a kind of tutelage to the State governments, inconsistent with every idea of vigor or efficiency. Who can pretend that commercial imposts are, or would be, alone equal to the present and future exigencies of the Union? Taking into the account the existing debt, foreign and domestic, upon any plan of extinguishment which a man moderately impressed with the importance of public justice and public credit could approve, in addition to the establishments which all parties will acknowledge to be necessary, we could not reasonably flatter ourselves that this resource alone, upon the most improved scale, would even suffice for its present necessities. Its future necessities admit not of calcuation or limitation; and upon the principle more than once adverted to the power of making provision for them as they arise ought to be equally unconfined. I believe it may be regarded as a position warranted by the history of mankind that, *in the usual progress of things, the necessities of a nation, in every stage of its existence, will be found at least equal to its resources.*

To say that deficiencies may be provided for by requisitions upon the States is on the one hand to acknowledge that this system cannot be depended upon, and on the other hand to depend upon it for every thing beyond a certain limit. Those who have carefully attended to its vices and deformities as they have been exhibited by experience or delineated in the course of these papers must feel an invincible repugnancy to trusting the national interests in any degree to its operation. Its inevitable tendency, whenever it is brought into activity, must be to enfeeble the Union, and sow the seeds of discord and contention between the federal head and its members, and between the members themselves. Can it be expected that the deficiencies would be better supplied in this mode than the total wants of the Union have heretofore been supplied in the same mode? It ought to be recollected that if less will be required from the States, they will have proportionably less means to answer the demand. If the opinions of those who contend for the distinction which has been mentioned were to be received as evidence of truth, one would be led to conclude that there was some known point in the economy of national affairs at which it would be safe to stop and to say: Thus far the ends of public happiness will be promoted by supplying the wants of government, and all beyond this is unworthy of our care or anxiety. How is it possible that a government half supplied and always necessitous can fulfil the purposes of its institution, can provide for the security, advance the prosperity, or support the reputation of the commonwealth? How can it ever possess either energy or stability, dignity or credit, confidence at home or respectability abroad? How can its administration be anything else than a succession of expedients temporizing, impotent, disgraceful? How will it be able to avoid a frequent sacrifice of its engagements to immediate necessity? How can it undertake or execute any liberal or enlarged plans of public good?

Let us attend to what would be the effects of this situation in the very first war in which we should happen to be engaged. We will presume, for argument's sake, that the revenue arising from the impost duties answers the purposes of a provision for the public debt and of a peace establishment for the Union. Thus circumstanced, a war breaks out. What would be the probable conduct of the government in such an emergency? Taught by experience that proper dependence could not be placed on the success of requisitions, unable by its own authority to lay hold of fresh resources, and urged by considerations of national danger, would it not be driven to the expedient of diverting the funds already appropriated from their proper objects to the defense of the State? It is not easy to see how a step of this kind could be avoided; and if it should be taken, it is evident that it would prove the destruction of public credit at the very moment that it was becoming essential to the public safety. To imagine that at such a crisis credit might be dispensed with would be the extreme of infatuation. In the modern system of war, nations the most wealthy are obliged to have recourse to large loans. A country so little opulent as ours must feel this necessity in a much stronger degree. But who would lend to a government that prefaced its overtures for borrowing by an act which demonstrated that no reliance could be placed on the steadiness of its measures for paying? The loans it might be able to procure would be as limited in their extent as burdensome in their conditions. They would be made upon the same principles that usurers commonly lend to bankrupt and fraudulent debtors—with a sparing hand and at enormous premiums.

It may perhaps be imagined that from the scantiness of the resources of the country the necessity of diverting the established funds in the case supposed would exist, though the national government should possess an unrestrained power of taxation. But two considerations will serve to quiet all apprehension on this head: one is that we are sure the resources of the community, in their full extent, will be brought into activity for the benefit of the Union; the other is that whatever deficiencies there may be can without difficulty be supplied by loans.

The power of creating new funds upon new objects of taxation by its own authority would enable the national government to borrow as far as its necessities might require. Foreigners, as well as the citizens of America, could then reasonably repose confidence in its engagements; but to depend upon a government that must itself depend upon thirteen other governments for the means of fulfilling its contracts, when once its situation is clearly understood, would require a degree of credulity not often to be met with in the pecuniary transactions of mankind, and little reconcilable with the usual sharp-sightedness of avarice.

Reflections of this kind may have trifling weight with men who hope to see realized in America the halcyon scenes of the poetic or fabulous age; but to those who believe we are likely to experience a common portion of the vicissitudes and calamities which have fallen to the lot of other nations, they must appear entitled to serious attention. Such men must behold the actual situation of their country with painful solicitude, and deprecate the evils which ambition or revenge might, with too much facility, inflict upon it.

PUBLIUS

No. 31: Hamilton

IN DISQUISITIONS of every kind there are certain primary truths, or first principles, upon which all subsequent reasonings must depend. These contain an internal evidence which, antecedent to all reflection or combination, commands the assent of the mind. Where it produces not this effect, it must proceed either from some disorder in the organs of perception, or from the influence of some strong interest, or passion, or prejudice. Of this nature are the maxims in geometry that the whole is greater than its parts; that things equal to the same are equal to one another; that two straight lines cannot enclose a space; and that all right angles are equal to each other. Of the same nature are these other maxims in ethics and politics, that there cannot be an effect without a cause; that the means ought to be proportioned to the end; that every power ought to be commensurate with its object; that there ought to be no limitation of a power destined to effect a purpose which is itself incapable of limitation. And there are other truths in the two latter sciences which, if they cannot pretend to rank in the class of axioms, are yet such direct inferences from them, and so obvious in themselves, and so agreeable to the natural and unsophisticated dictates of common sense that they challenge the assent of a sound and unbiased mind with a degree of force and conviction almost equally irresistible.

The objects of geometrical inquiry are so entirely abstracted from those pursuits which stir up and put in motion the unruly passions of the human heart that mankind, without difficulty, adopt not only the more simple theorems of the science, but even those abstruse paradoxes which, however they may appear susceptible of demonstration, are at variance with the natural conceptions which the mind, without the aid of philosophy, would be led to entertain upon the subject. The INFINITE DIVISIBILITY of matter, or, in other words, the INFINITE divisibility of a FINITE thing, extending even to the minutest atom, is a point agreed among geometricians, though not less incomprehensible to common sense than any of those mysteries in religion against which the batteries of infidelity have been so industriously leveled.

But in the sciences of morals and politics, men are found far less tractable. To a certain degree it is right and useful that this should be the case. Caution and investigation are a necessary armor against error and imposition. But this untractableness may be carried too far, and may degenerate into obstinacy, perverseness, or disingenuity. Though it cannot be pretended that the principles of moral and political knowledge have, in general, the same degree of certainty with those of the mathematics, yet they have much better claims in this respect than to judge from the conduct of men in particular situations we should be disposed to allow them. The obscurity is much oftener in the passions and prejudices of the reasoner than in the subject. Men, upon too many occasions, do not give their own understandings fair play; but, yielding to some untoward bias, they entangle themselves in words and confound themselves in subtleties.

How else could it happen (if we admit the objectors to be sincere in their opposition) that positions so clear as those which manifest the necessity of a general power of taxation in the government of the Union should have to encounter any adversaries among men of discernment? Though these positions have been elsewhere fully stated, they will perhaps not be improperly recapitulated in this place as introductory to an examination of what may have been offered by way of objection to them. They are in substance as follows:

A government ought to contain in itself every power requisite to the full accomplishment of the objects committed to its care, and to the complete execution of the trusts for which it is responsible, free from every other control but a regard to the public good and to the sense of the people.

As the duties of superintending the national defense and of securing the public peace against foreign or domestic violence involve a provision for casualties and dangers to which no possible limits can be assigned, the power of making that provision ought to know no other bounds than the exigencies of the nation and the resources of the community.

As revenue is the essential engine by which the means of answering the national exigencies must be procured, the power of procuring that article in its full extent must necessarily be comprehended in that of providing for those exigencies.

As theory and practice conspire to prove that the power of procuring revenue is unavailing when exercised over the States in their collective capacities, the federal government must of necessity be invested with an unqualified power of taxation in the ordinary modes.

Did not experience evince the contrary, it would be natural to conclude that the propriety of a general power of taxation in the national government might safely be permitted to rest on the evidence of these propositions, unassisted by any additional arguments or illustrations. But we find, in fact, that the antagonists of the proposed Constitution, so far from acquiescing in their justness or truth, seem to make their principal and most zealous effort against this part of the plan. It may therefore be satisfactory to analyze the arguments with which they combat it.

Those of them which have been most labored with that view seem in substance to amount to this: "It is not true, because the exigencies of the Union may not be susceptible of limitation, that its power of laying taxes ought to be unconfined. Revenue is as requisite to the purposes of the local administrations as to those of the Union; and the former are at least of equal importance with the latter to the happiness of the people. It is, therefore, as necessary that the State governments should be able to command the means of supplying their wants, as that the national government should possess the like faculty in respect to the wants of the Union. But an indefinite power of taxation in the *latter* might, and probably would in time, deprive the *former* of the means of providing for their own necessities; and would subject them entirely to the mercy of the national legislature. As the laws of the Union are to become the supreme law of the land, as it is to have power to pass all laws that may be NECESSARY for carrying into execution the authorities with which it is proposed to vest it, the national government might at any time abolish the taxes imposed for State objects upon the pretense of an interference with its own. It might allege a necessity of doing this in order to give efficacy to the national revenues. And thus all the resources of taxation might by degrees become the subjects of federal monopoly to the entire exclusion and destruction of the State governments."

This mode of reasoning appears sometimes to turn upon the supposition of usurpation in the national government; at other times it seems to be designed only as a deduction from the constitutional operation of its intended powers. It is only in the latter light that it can be admitted to have any pretensions to fairness. The moment we launch into conjectures about the usurpations of the federal government, we get into an unfathomable abyss and fairly put ourselves out of the reach of all reasoning. Imagination may range at pleasure till it gets bewildered amidst the labyrinths of an enchanted castle, and knows not on which side to turn to escape from the apparitions which itself has raised. Whatever may be the limits or modifications of the powers of the Union, it is easy to imagine an endless train of possible dangers; and by indulging an excess of jealousy and timidity, we may bring ourselves to a state of absolute skepticism and irresolution. I repeat here what I have observed in substance in another place, that all observations founded upon the danger of usurpation ought to be referred to the composition and structure of the government, not to the nature or extent of its powers. The State governments by their original constitutions are invested with complete sovereignty. In what does our security consist against usurpations from that quarter? Doubtless in the manner of their formation, and in a due dependence of those who are to administer them upon the people. If the proposed construction of the federal government be found, upon an impartial examination of it, to be such as to afford to a proper extent the same species of security, all apprehensions on the score of usurpation ought to be discarded.

It should not be forgotten that a disposition in the

State governments to encroach upon the rights of the Union is quite as probable as a disposition in the Union to encroach upon the rights of the State governments. What side would be likely to prevail in such a conflict must depend on the means which the contending parties could employ towards insuring success. As in republics strength is always on the side of the people, and as there are weighty reasons to induce a belief that the State governments will commonly possess most influence over them, the natural conclusion is that such contests will be most apt to end to the disadvantage of the Union; and that there is greater probability of encroachments by the members upon the federal head than by the federal head upon the members. But it is evident that all conjectures of this kind must be extremely vague and fallible: and that it is by far the safest course to lay them altogether aside and to confine our attention wholly to the nature and extent of the powers as they are delineated in the Constitution. Everything beyond this must be left to the prudence and firmness of the people; who, as they will hold the scales in their own hands, it is to be hoped will always take care to preserve the constitutional equilibrium between the general and the State governments. Upon this ground, which is evidently the true one, it will not be difficult to obviate the objections which have been made to an indefinite power of taxation in the United States.

PUBLIUS

No. 32: Hamilton

ALTHOUGH I am of opinion that there would be no real danger of the consequences which seem to be apprehended to the State governments from a power in the Union to control them in the levies of money, because I am persuaded that the sense of the people, the extreme hazard of provoking the resentments of the State governments, and a conviction of the utility and necessity of local administrations for local purposes, would be a complete barrier against the oppressive use of such a power; yet I am willing here to allow, in its full extent, the justness of the reasoning which requires that the individual

States should possess an independent and uncontrollable authority to raise their own revenues for the supply of their own wants. And making this concession, I affirm that (with the sole exception of duties on imports and exports) they would, under the plan of the convention, retain that authority in the most absolute and unqualified sense; and that an attempt on the part of the national government to abridge them in the exercise of it would be a violent assumption of power, unwarranted by any article or clause of its Constitution.

An entire consolidation of the States into one complete national sovereignty would imply an entire subordination of the parts; and whatever powers might remain in them would be altogether dependent on the general will. But as the plan of the convention aims only at a partial union or consolidation, the State governments would clearly retain all the rights of sovereignty which they before had, and which were not, by that act, *exclusively* delegated to the United States. This exclusive delegation, or rather this alienation, of State sovereignty would only exist in three cases: where the Constitution in express terms granted an exclusive authority to the Union; where it granted in one instance an authority to the Union, and in another prohibited the States from exercising the like authority; and where it granted an authority to the Union to which a similar authority in the States would be absolutely and totally *contradictory* and *repugnant*. I use these terms to distinguish this last case from another which might appear to resemble it, but which would, in fact, be essentially different; I mean where the exercise of a concurrent jurisdiction might be productive of occasional interferences in the *policy* of any branch of administration, but would not imply any direct contradiction or repugnancy in point of constitutional authority. These three cases of exclusive jurisdiction in the federal government may be exemplified by the following instances: The last clause but one in the eighth section of the first article provides expressly that Congress shall exercise *"exclusive legislation"* over the district to be appropriated as the seat of government. This answers to the first case. The first clause of the same section empowers Congress *"to lay and collect taxes, duties, imposts, and excises"*; and the second clause of the tenth section of the same article declares that "*no State shall* without the consent of Congress *lay any imposts or duties on imports or exports,* except for the purpose of executing its inspection laws." Hence would result an exclusive power in the Union to lay duties on imports and exports, with the particular exception mentioned; but this power is abridged by another clause, which declares that no tax or duty shall be laid on articles exported from any State; in consequence of which qualification it now only extends to the *duties on imports.* This answers to the second case. The third will be found in that clause which declares that Congress shall have power "to establish an UNIFORM RULE of naturalization throughout the United States." This must necessarily be exclusive; because if each State had power to prescribe a DISTINCT RULE, there could not be a UNIFORM RULE.

A case which may perhaps be thought to resemble the latter, but which is in fact widely different, affects the question immediately under consideration. I mean the power of imposing taxes on all articles other than exports and imports. This, I contend, is manifestly a concurrent and coequal authority in the United States and in the individual States. There is plainly no expression in the granting clause which makes that power *exclusive* in the Union. There is no independent clause or sentence which prohibits the States from exercising it. So far is this from being the case that a plain and conclusive argument to the contrary is to be deducible from the restraint laid upon the States in relation to duties on imports and exports. This restriction implies an admission that if it were not inserted the States would possess the power it excludes; and it implies a further admission that as to all other taxes, the authority of the States remains undiminished. In any other view it would be both unnecessary and dangerous; it would be unnecessary, because if the grant to the Union of the power of laying such duties implied the exclusion of the States, or even their subordination in this particular there could be no need of such a restriction; it would be dangerous, because the introduction of it leads directly to the conclusion which has been mentioned, and which, if the reasoning of the objectors be just, could not have been intended; I mean that the States, in all cases to which the restriction did not apply, would have a concurrent power of taxation with the Union. The restriction in question amounts to what lawyers call a NEGATIVE PREGNANT—that is, a *negation* of one thing, and an *affirmance* of another; a negation of the authority of the States to impose taxes on imports and exports, and an affirmance of their authority to impose them on all other articles. It would be mere sophistry to argue that it was meant to exclude them *absolutely* from the imposition of taxes of the former kind, and to leave them at liberty to lay others *subject to the control* of the national legislature. The restraining or prohibitory clause only says, that they shall not, *without the consent of Congress,* lay such duties; and if we are to understand this in the sense last mentioned, the Constitution would then be made to introduce a formal provision for the sake of a very absurd conclusion; which is, that the States, *with the consent* of the national legislature, might tax imports and exports; and that they might tax every other article, *unless controlled* by the same body. If this was the intention, why was it not left in the first instance, to what is alleged to be the natural operation of the original clause, conferring a general power of taxation upon the Union? It is evident that this could not have been the intention, and that it will not bear a construction of the kind.

As to a supposition of repugnancy between the power of taxation in the States and in the Union, it cannot be supported in that sense which would be requisite to work an exclusion of the States. It is, indeed, possible that a tax might be laid on a particular article by a State which might render it *inexpedient* that a further tax should be laid on the same article by the Union; but it would not imply a constitutional inability to impose a further tax. The quantity of the imposition, the expediency or inexpediency of an increase on either side, would be mutually questions of prudence; but there would be involved no direct contradiction of power. The particular policy of the national and of the State systems of finance might now and then not exactly coincide, and might require reciprocal forbearances. It is not, however, a mere possibility of inconvenience in the exercise of powers, but an immediate constitutional repugnancy that can by implication alienate and extinguish a pre-existing right of sovereignty.

The necessity of a concurrent jurisdiction in certain cases results from the division of the sovereign power; and the rule that all authorities, of which the States are not explicitly divested in favor of the Union, remain with them in full vigor is not only a theoretical consequence of that division, but is clearly admitted by the whole tenor of the instrument which contains the articles of the proposed Constitution. We there find that, notwithstanding the affirmative grants of general authorities, there has been the most pointed care in those cases where it was deemed improper that the like authorities should reside in the States to insert negative clauses prohibiting the exercise of them by the States. The tenth section of the first article consists altogether of such provisions. This circumstance is a clear indication of the sense of the convention, and furnishes a rule of interpretation out of the body of the act, which justifies the position I have advanced and refutes every hypothesis to the contrary.

PUBLIUS

No. 33: Hamilton

THE residue of the argument against the provisions of the Constitution in respect to taxation is ingrafted upon the following clauses. The last clause of the eighth section of the first article authorizes the national legislature "to make all laws which shall be *necessary* and *proper* for carrying into execution *the powers* by that Constitution vested in the government of the United States, or in any department or officer thereof"; and the second clause of the sixth article declares that "the Constitution and the laws of the United States made *in pursuance thereof* and the treaties made by their authority shall be the *supreme law* of the land, anything in the constitution or laws of any State to the contrary notwithstanding."

These two clauses have been the source of much virulent invective and petulant declamation against the proposed Constitution. They have been held up to the people in all the exaggerated colors of misrepresentation as the pernicious engines by which their local governments were to be destroyed and their liberties exterminated; as the hideous monster whose devouring jaws would spare neither sex nor age, nor high nor low, nor sacred nor profane; and yet, strange as it may appear, after all this clamor, to those who may not have happened to contemplate them in the same light, it may be affirmed with perfect confidence that the constitutional operation of the intended government would be precisely the same if these clauses were entirely obliterated as if they were repeated in every article. They are only declaratory of a truth which would have resulted by necessary and unavoidable implication from the very act of constituting a federal government and vesting it with certain specified powers. This is so clear a proposition that moderation itself can scarcely listen to the railings which have been so copiously vented against this part of the plan without emotions that disturb its equanimity.

What is a power but the ability or faculty of doing a thing? What is the ability to do a thing but the power of employing the *means* necessary to its execution? What is a LEGISLATIVE power but a power of making LAWS? What are the *means* to execute a LEGISLATIVE power but LAWS? What is the power of laying and collecting taxes but a *legislative power,* or a power of *making laws* to lay and collect taxes? What are the proper means of executing such a power but *necessary* and *proper* laws?

This simple train of inquiry furnishes us at once with a test of the true nature of the clause complained of. It conducts us to this palpable truth that a power to lay and collect taxes must be a power to pass all laws *necessary* and *proper* for the execution of that power; and what does the unfortunate and calumniated provision in question do more than declare the same truth, to wit, that the national legislature to whom the power of laying and collecting taxes had been previously given might, in the execution of that power, pass all laws *necessary* and *proper* to carry it into effect? I have applied these observations thus particularly to the power of taxation, because it is the immediate subject under consideration and because it is the most important of the authorities proposed to be conferred upon the Union. But the same process will lead to the same result in relation to all other powers declared in the Constitution. And it is *expressly* to execute these powers that the sweeping clause, as it has been affectedly called, authorizes the national legislature to pass all *necessary* and *proper* laws. If there be anything exceptionable, it must be sought for in the specific powers upon which this general declaration is predicated. The declaration itself, though it may be chargeable with tautology or redundancy, is at least perfectly harmless.

But SUSPICION may ask, Why then was it introduced? The answer is that it could only have been done for greater caution, and to guard against all cavilling refinements in those who might hereafter feel a disposition to curtail and evade the legitimate authorities of the Union. The Convention probably foresaw what it has been a principal aim of these papers to inculcate, that the danger which most threatens our political welfare is that the State governments will finally sap the foundations of the Union; and might therefore think it necessary, in so cardinal a point, to leave nothing to construction. Whatever may have been the inducement to it, the wisdom of the precaution is evident from the cry which has been raised against it; as that very cry betrays a disposition to question the great and essential truth which it is manifestly the object of that provision to declare.

But it may be again asked, Who is to judge of the *necessity* and *propriety* of the laws to be passed for executing the powers of the Union? I answer first that this question arises as well and as fully upon the simple grant of those powers as upon the declaratory clause; and I answer in the second place that the national government, like every other, must judge, in the first instance, of the proper exercise of its powers, and its constituents in the last. If the federal government should overpass the just bounds of its authority and make a tyrannical use of its powers, the people, whose creature it is, must appeal to the standard they have formed, and take such measures to redress the injury done to the Constitution as the exigency may suggest and prudence justify. The propriety of a law, in a constitutional light, must always be determined by the nature of the powers upon which it is founded. Suppose, by some forced constructions of its authority (which, indeed, cannot easily be imagined), the federal legislature should attempt to vary the law of descent in any State, would it not be evident that in making such an attempt it had exceeded its jurisdiction and infringed upon that of the State? Suppose, again, that upon the pretense of an interference with its revenues, it should undertake to abrogate a land tax imposed by the authority of a State; would it not be equally evident that this was an invasion of that concurrent jurisdiction in respect to this species of tax, which its Constitution plainly supposes to exist in the State governments? If there ever should be a doubt on this head, the credit of it will be entirely due to those reasoners who, in the imprudent zeal of their animosity to the plan of the convention, have labored to envelop it in a cloud calculated to obscure the plainest and simplest truths.

But it is said that the laws of the Union are to be the *supreme law* of the land. What inference can be drawn from this, or what would they amount to, if they were not to be supreme? It is evident they would amount to nothing. A LAW, by the very meaning of the term, includes supremacy. It is a rule which those to whom it is prescribed are bound to observe. This results from every political association. If individuals enter into a state of society, the laws of that society must be the supreme regulator of their conduct. If a number of political societies enter into a larger political society, the laws which the latter may enact, pursuant to the powers intrusted to it by its constitution, must necessarily be supreme over those societies and the individuals of whom they are composed. It would otherwise be a mere treaty, dependent on the good faith of the parties, and not a government, which is only another word for POLITICAL POWER AND SUPREMACY. But it will not follow from this doctrine that acts of the larger society which are *not pursuant* to its constitutional powers, but which are invasions of the residuary authorities of the smaller societies, will become the supreme law of the land. These will be merely acts of usurpation, and will deserve to be treated as such. Hence we perceive that the clause which declares the supremacy of the laws of the Union, like the one we have just before considered, only declares a truth which flows immediately and necessarily from the institution of a federal government. It will not, I presume, have escaped observation that it *expressly* confines this supremacy to laws made *pursuant to the Constitution;* which I mention merely as an instance of caution in the convention; since that limitation would have been to be understood, though it had not been expressed.

Though a law, therefore, for laying a tax for the use of the United States would be supreme in its nature and could not legally be opposed or controlled, yet a law for abrogating or preventing the collection of a tax laid by the authority of a State (unless upon imports and exports) would not be the supreme law of the land, but a usurpation of power not granted by the Constitution. As far as an improper accumulation of taxes on the same object might tend to render the collection difficult or precarious, this would be a mutual inconvenience, not arising from a superiority or defect of power on either side, but from an injudicious exercise of power by one or the other in a manner equally disadvantageous to both. It is to be hoped and presumed, however, that mutual interest would dictate a concert in this respect which would avoid any material inconvenience. The inference from the whole is that the individual States would, under the proposed Constitution, retain an independent and uncontrollable authority to raise revenue to any extent of which they may stand in need, by every kind of taxation, except duties on imports and exports. It will be shown in the next paper that this *concurrent jurisdiction* in the article of taxation was the only admissible substitute for an entire subordination, in respect to this branch of power, of the State authority to that of the Union.

PUBLIUS

No. 34: Hamilton

I FLATTER myself it has been clearly shown in my last number that the particular States, under the proposed Constitution, would have COEQUAL authority with the

Union in the article of revenue, except as to duties on imports. As this leaves open to the States far the greatest part of the resources of the community, there can be no color for the assertion that they would not possess means as abundant as could be desired for the supply of their own wants, independent of all external control. That the field is sufficiently wide will more fully appear when we come to develop the inconsiderable share of the public expenses for which it will fall to the lot of the State governments to provide.

To argue upon abstract principles that this co-ordinate authority cannot exist would be to set up theory and supposition against fact and reality. However proper such reasonings might be to show that a thing *ought not to exist,* they are wholly to be rejected when they are made use of to prove that it does not exist contrary to the evidence of the fact itself. It is well known that in the Roman republic the legislative authority in the last resort resided for ages in two different political bodies—not as branches of the same legislature, but as distinct and independent legislatures, in each of which an opposite interest prevailed: in one, the patrician; in the other, the plebeian. Many arguments might have been adduced to prove the unfitness of two such seemingly contradictory authorities, each having power to *annul* or *repeal* the acts of the other. But a man would have been regarded as frantic who should have attempted at Rome to disprove their existence. It will readily be understood that I allude to the COMITIA CENTURIATA and COMITIA TRIBUTA. The former, in which the people voted by centuries, was so arranged as to give a superiority to the patrician interest; in the latter, in which numbers prevailed, the plebeian interest had an entire predominancy. And yet these two legislatures coexisted for ages, and the Roman republic attained to the pinnacle of human greatness.

In the case particularly under consideration, there is no such contradiction as appears in the example cited; there is no power on either side to annul the acts of the other. And in practice there is little reason to apprehend any inconvenience; because in a short course of time the wants of the States will naturally reduce themselves within *a very narrow compass;* and in the interim, the

United States will in all probability find it convenient to abstain wholly from those objects to which the particular States would be inclined to resort.

To form a more precise judgment of the true merits of this question it will be well to advert to the proportion between the objects that will require a federal provision in respect to revenue, and those which will require a State provision. We shall discover that the former are altogether unlimited and that the latter are circumscribed within very moderate bounds. In pursuing this inquiry, we must bear in mind that we are not to confine our view to the present period, but to look forward to remote futurity. Constitutions of civil government are not to be framed upon a calculation of existing exigencies, but upon a combination of these with the probable exigencies of ages, according to the natural and tried course of human affairs. Nothing, therefore, can be more fallacious than to infer the extent of any power proper to be lodged in the national government from an estimate of its immediate necessities. There ought to be a CAPACITY to provide for future contingencies as they may happen; and as these are illimitable in their nature, so it is impossible safely to limit that capacity. It is true, perhaps, that a computation might be made with sufficient accuracy to answer the purpose of the quantity of revenue requisite to discharge the subsisting engagements of the Union, and to maintain those establishments which, for some time to come, would suffice in time of peace. But would it be wise, or would it not rather be the extreme of folly to stop at this point, and to leave the government intrusted with the care of the national defense in a state of absolute incapacity to provide for the protection of the community against future invasions of the public peace by foreign war or domestic convulsions? If we must be obliged to exceed this point, where can we stop, short of an indefinite power of providing for emergencies as they may arise? Though it be easy to assert in general terms the possibility of forming a rational judgment of a due provision against probable dangers, yet we may safely challenge those who make the assertion to bring forward their data, and may affirm that they would be found as vague and uncertain as any that could be produced to establish the probable duration of the world. Observations confined to the mere prospects of internal attacks can deserve no weight; though even these will admit of no satisfactory calculation: but if we mean to be a commercial people, it must form a part of our policy to be able one day to defend that commerce. The support of a navy and of naval wars would involve contingencies that must baffle all the efforts of political arithmetic.

Admitting that we ought to try the novel and absurd experiment in politics of tying up the hands of government from offensive war founded upon reasons of state, yet certainly we ought not to disable it from guarding the community against the ambition or enmity of other nations. A cloud has been for some time hanging over the European world. If it should break forth into a storm, who can insure us that in its progress a part of its fury would not be spent upon us? No reasonable man would hastily pronounce that we are entirely out of its reach. Or if the combustible materials that now seem to be collecting should be dissipated without coming to maturity, or if a flame should be kindled without extending to us, what security can we have that our tranquillity will long remain undisturbed from some other cause or from some other quarter? Let us recollect that peace or war will not always be left to our option; that however moderate or unambitious we may be, we cannot count upon the moderation, or hope to extinguish the ambition of others. Who could have imagined at the conclusion of the last war that France and Britain, wearied and exhausted as they both were, would so soon have looked with so hostile an aspect upon each other? To judge from the history of mankind, we shall be compelled to conclude that the fiery and destructive passions of war reign in the human breast with much more powerful sway than the mild and beneficent sentiments of peace; and that to model our political systems upon speculations of lasting tranquillity would be to calculate on the weaker springs of the human character.

What are the chief sources of expense in every government? What has occasioned that enormous accumulation of debts with which several of the European nations are oppressed? The answer plainly is, wars and rebellions; the support of those institutions which are necessary to guard the body politic against these two most mortal diseases of society. The expenses arising from those institutions which are relative to the mere domestic police of a state, to the support of its legislative, executive, and judiciary departments, with their different appendages, and to the encouragement of agriculture and manufactures (which will comprehend almost all the subjects of state expenditures) are insignificant in comparison with those which relate to the national defense.

In the kingdom of Great Britain, where all the ostentatious apparatus of monarchy is to be provided for, not above a fifteenth part of the annual income of the nation is appropriated to the class of expenses last mentioned; the other fourteen fifteenths are absorbed in the payment of the interest of debts contracted for carrying on the wars in which that country has been engaged, and in the maintenance of fleets and armies. If, on the one hand, it should be observed that the expenses incurred in the prosecution of the ambitious enterprises and vainglorious pursuits of a monarchy are not a proper standard by which to judge of those which might be necessary in a republic, it ought, on the other hand, to be remarked that there should be as great a disproportion between the profusion and extravagance of a wealthy kingdom in its domestic administration, and the frugality and economy which in that particular become the modest simplicity of republican government. If we balance a proper deduction from one side against that which it is supposed ought to be made from the other, the proportion may still be considered as holding good.

But let us take a view of the large debt which we have ourselves contracted in a single war, and let us only calculate on a common share of the events which disturb the peace of nations, and we shall instantly perceive, without the aid of any elaborate illustration, that there must always be an immense disproportion between the objects of federal and state expenditure. It is true that several of the States, separately, are encumbered with considerable debts, which are an excrescence of the late war. But this cannot happen again, if the proposed system be adopted; and when these debts are discharged, the only call for revenue of any consequence which the

State governments will continue to experience will be for the mere support of their respective civil lists; to which, if we add all contingencies, the total amount in every State ought not to exceed two hundred thousand pounds.

If it cannot be denied to be a just principle that in framing a constitution of government for a nation we ought, in those provisions which are designed to be permanent, to calculate, not on temporary, but on permanent causes of expense; our attention would be directed to a provision in favor of the State governments for an annual sum of about 200,000 pounds; while the exigencies of the Union could be susceptible of no limits, even in imagination. In this view of the subject, by what logic can it be maintained that the local governments ought to command, in perpetuity, an *exclusive* source of revenue for any sum beyond the extent of 200,000 pounds? To extend its power further, in *exclusion* of the authority of the Union, would be to take the resources of the community out of those hands which stood in need of them for the public welfare in order to put them into other hands which could have no just or proper occasion for them.

Suppose, then, the convention had been inclined to proceed upon the principle of a repartition of the objects of revenue between the Union and its members in *proportion* to their comparative necessities; what particular fund could have been selected for the use of the States that would not either have been too much or too little—too little for their present, too much for their future wants? As to the line of separation between external and internal taxes, this would leave to the States, at a rough computation, the command of two thirds of the resources of the community to defray from a tenth to a twentieth part of its expenses; and to the Union, one third of the resources of the community to defray from nine tenths to nineteen twentieths of its expenses. If we desert this boundary and content ourselves with leaving to the States an exclusive power of taxing houses and lands, there would still be a great disproportion between the *means* and the *end;* the possession of one third of the resources of the community to supply, at most, one tenth of its wants. If any fund could have been selected and appropriated, equal to and not greater than the object, it would have been inadequate to the discharge of the existing debts of the particular States, and would have left them dependent on the Union for a provision for this purpose.

The preceding train of observations will justify the position which has been elsewhere laid down that "A CONCURRENT JURISDICTION in the article of taxation was the only admissible substitute for an entire subordination, in respect to this branch of power, of State authority to that of the Union." Any separation of the objects of revenue that could have been fallen upon would have amounted to a sacrifice of the great INTERESTS of the Union to the POWER of the individual States. The convention thought the concurrent jurisdiction preferable to that subordination; and it is evident that it has at least the merit of reconciling an indefinite constitutional power of taxation in the federal government with an adequate and independent power in the States to provide for their own necessities. There remain a few other lights in which this important subject of taxation will claim a further consideration. PUBLIUS

No. 35: Hamilton

BEFORE we proceed to examine any other objections to an indefinite power of taxation in the Union, I shall make one general remark; which is that if the jurisdiction of the national government in the article of revenue should be restricted to particular objects, it would naturally occasion an undue proportion of the public burdens to fall upon those objects. Two evils would spring from this source: the oppression of particular branches of industry; and an unequal distribution of the taxes, as well among the several States as among the citizens of the same State.

Suppose, as has been contended for, the federal power of taxation were to be confined to duties on imports, it is evident that the government, for want of being able to command other resources, would frequently be tempted to extend these duties to an injurious excess.

There are persons who imagine that it can never be the case; since the higher they are, the more it is alleged they will tend to discourage an extravagant consumption to produce a favorable balance of trade and to promote domestic manufactures. But all extremes are pernicious in various ways. Exorbitant duties on imported articles would serve to beget a general spirit of smuggling; which is always prejudicial to the fair trader, and eventually to the revenue itself: they tend to render other classes of the community tributary in an improper degree to the manufacturing classes, to whom they give a premature monopoly of the markets; they sometimes force industry out of its more natural channels into others in which it flows with less advantage; and in the last place, they oppress the merchant, who is often obliged to pay them himself without any retribution from the consumer. When the demand is equal to the quantity of goods at market, the consumer generally pays the duty; but when the markets happen to be overstocked, a great proportion falls upon the merchant, and sometimes not only exhausts his profits, but breaks in upon his capital. I am apt to think that a division of the duty, between the seller and the buyer, more often happens than is commonly imagined. It is not always possible to raise the price of a commodity in exact proportion to every additional imposition laid upon it. The merchant especially, in a country of small commercial capital, is often under a necessity of keeping prices down in order to make a more expeditious sale.

The maxim that the consumer is the payer is so much oftener true than the reverse of the proposition, that it is far more equitable that the duties on imports should go into a common stock than that they should redound to the exclusive benefit of the importing States. But it is not so generally true as to render it equitable that those duties should form the only national fund. When they are paid by the merchant they operate as an additional tax upon the importing State, whose citizens pay their proportion of them in the character of consumers. In this view they are productive of inequality among the States; which inequality would be increased with the increased extent of the duties. The confinement of the national revenues to this species of imposts would be attended with inequality, from a different cause, between the manufacturing and the non-manufacturing States. The States which can go furthest towards the supply of their own wants by their own manufactures will not, according to their numbers or wealth, consume so great a proportion of imported articles as those States which are not in the same favorable situation. They would not, therefore, in this mode alone contribute to the public treasury in a ratio to their abilities. To make them do this it is necessary that recourse be had to excises, the proper objects of which are particular kinds of manufactures. New York is more deeply interested in these considerations than such of her citizens as contend for limiting the power of the Union to external taxation may be aware of. New York is an importing State, and from a greater disproportion between her population and territory is less likely, than some other States, speedily to become in any considerable degree a manufacturing State. She would, of course, suffer in a double light from restraining the jurisdiction of the Union to commercial imposts.

So fas as these observations tend to inculcate a danger of the import duties being extended to an injurious extreme it may be observed, conformably to a remark made in another part of these papers, that the interest of the revenue itself would be a sufficient guard against such an extreme. I readily admit that this would be the case as long as other resources were open; but if the avenues to them were closed, HOPE, stimulated by necessity, might beget experiments, fortified by rigorous precautions and additional penalties, which, for a time, might have the intended effect, till there had been leisure to contrive expedients to elude these new precautions. The first success would be apt to inspire false opinions, which it might require a long course of subsequent experience to correct. Necessity, especially in politics, often occasions false hopes, false reasonings, and a system of measures correspondingly erroneous. But even if this supposed excess should not be a consequence of the limitation of the federal power of taxation, the inequalities spoken of would still ensue, though not in the same degree, from the other causes that have been noticed. Let us now return to the examination of objections.

One which, if we may judge from the frequency of its

repetition, seems most to be relied on, is that the House of Representatives is not sufficiently numerous for the reception of all the different classes of citizens in order to combine the interests and feelings of every part of the community, and to produce a true sympathy between the representative body and its constituents. This argument presents itself under a very specious and seducing form; and is well calculated to lay hold of the prejudices of those to whom it is addressed. But when we come to dissect it with attention, it will appear to be made up of nothing but fair-sounding words. The object it seems to aim at is, in the first place, impracticable, and in the sense in which it is contended for, is unnecessary. I reserve for another place the discussion of the question which relates to the sufficiency of the representative body in respect to numbers, and shall content myself with examining here the particular use which has been made of a contrary supposition in reference to the immediate subject of our inquiries.

The idea of an actual representation of all classes of the people by persons of each class is altogether visionary. Unless it were expressly provided in the Constitution that each different occupation should send one or more members, the thing would never take place in practice. Mechanics and manufacturers will always be inclined, with few exceptions, to give their votes to merchants in preference to persons of their own professions or trades. Those discerning citizens are well aware that the mechanic and manufacturing arts furnish the materials of mercantile enterprise and industry. Many of them, indeed, are immediately connected with the operations of commerce. They know that the merchant is their natural patron and friend; and they are aware that however great the confidence they may justly feel in their own good sense, their interests can be more effectually promoted by the merchant than by themselves. They are sensible that their habits in life have not been such as to give them those acquired endowments, without which in a deliberative assembly the greatest natural abilities are for the most part useless; and that the influence and weight and superior acquirements of the merchants render them more equal to a contest with any spirit which might happen to infuse itself into the public councils, unfriendly to the manufacturing and trading interests. These considerations and many others that might be mentioned prove, and experience confirms it, that artisans and manufacturers will commonly be disposed to bestow their votes upon merchants and those whom they recommend. We must therefore consider merchants as the natural representatives of all these classes of the community.

With regard to the learned professions, little need be observed; they truly form no distinct interest in society, and according to their situation and talents, will be indiscriminately the objects of the confidence and choice of each other and of other parts of the community.

Nothing remains but the landed interest; and this in a political view, and particularly in relation to taxes, I take to be perfectly united from the wealthiest landlord to the poorest tenant. No tax can be laid on land which will not affect the proprietor of millions of acres as well as the proprietor of a single acre. Every landholder will therefore have a common interest to keep the taxes on land as low as possible; and common interest may always be reckoned upon as the surest bond of sympathy. But if we even could suppose a distinction of interest between the opulent landholder and the middling farmer, what reason is there to conclude that the first would stand a better chance of being deputed to the national legislature than the last? If we take fact as our guide, and look into our own senate and assembly, we shall find that moderate proprietors of land prevail in both; nor is this less the case in the senate, which consists of a smaller number than in the assembly, which is composed of a greater number. Where the qualifications of the electors are the same, whether they have to choose a small or a large number, their votes will fall upon those in whom they have most confidence; whether these happen to be men of large fortunes, or of moderate property, or of no property at all.

It is said to be necessary that all classes of citizens should have some of their own number in the representative body in order that their feelings and interests may be the better understood and attended to. But we have seen that this will never happen under any arrangement that leaves the votes of the people free. Where this is the case, the representative body, with too few exceptions to have any influence on the spirit of the government, will be composed of landholders, merchants, and men of the learned professions. But where is the danger that the interests and feelings of the different classes of citizens will not be understood or attended to by these three descriptions of men? Will not the landholder know and feel whatever will promote or injure the interest of landed property? And will he not, from his own interest in that species of property, be sufficiently prone to resist every attempt to prejudice or encumber it? Will not the merchant understand and be disposed to cultivate, as far as may be proper, the interests of the mechanic and manufacturing arts to which his commerce is so nearly allied? Will not the man of the learned profession, who will feel a neutrality to the rivalships between the different branches of industry, be likely to prove an impartial arbiter between them, ready to promote either, so far as it shall appear to him conducive to the general interests of the society?

If we take into the account the momentary humors or dispositions which may happen to prevail in particular parts of the society, and to which a wise administration will never be inattentive, is the man whose situation leads to extensive inquiry and information less likely to be a competent judge of their nature, extent, and foundation than one whose observation does not travel beyond the circle of his neighbors and acquaintances? Is it not natural that a man who is a candidate for the favor of the people, and who is dependent on the suffrages of his fellow-citizens for the continuance of his public honors, should take care to inform himself of their dispositions and inclinations and should be willing to allow them their proper degree of influence upon his conduct? This dependence, and the necessity of being bound, himself and his posterity, by the laws to which he gives his assent are the true and they are the strong chords of sympathy between the representative and the constituent.

There is no part of the administration of government that requires extensive information and a thorough knowledge of the principles of political economy so much as the business of taxation. The man who understands those principles best will be least likely to resort to oppressive expedients, or to sacrifice any particular class of citizens to the procurement of revenue. It might be demonstrated that the most productive system of finance will always be the least burdensome. There can be no doubt that in order to a judicious exercise of the power of taxation, it is necessary that the person in whose hands it is should be acquainted with the general genius, habits, and modes of thinking of the people at large and with the resources of the country. And this is all that can be reasonably meant by a knowledge of the interests and feelings of the people. In any other sense the proposition has either no meaning, or an absurd one. And in that sense let every considerate citizen judge for himself where the requisite qualification is most likely to be found.

PUBLIUS

No. 36: Hamilton

WE HAVE seen that the result of the observations to which the foregoing number has been principally devoted is that from the natural operation of the different interests and views of the various classes of the community, whether the representation of the people be more or less numerous, it will consist almost entirely of proprietors of land, of merchants, and of members of the learned professions, who will truly represent all those different interests and views. If it should be objected that we have seen other descriptions of men in the local legislatures, I answer that it is admitted there are exceptions to the rule, but not in sufficient number to influence the general complexion or character of the government. There are strong minds in every walk of life that will rise superior to the disadvantages of situation and will command the tribute due to their merit, not only from the classes to which they particularly belong, but from the society in general. The door ought to be equally open to all; and I trust, for the credit of human nature, that we shall see examples of such vigorous plants flourishing in the soil of federal as well as of State legislation; but occasional instances of this sort will not render the reasoning, founded upon the general course of things, less conclusive.

The subject might be placed in several other lights that would all lead to the same result; and in particular it might be asked, What greater affinity or relation of interest can be conceived between the carpenter and blacksmith, and the linen manufacturer or stocking-weaver, than between the merchant and either of them? It is notorious that there are often as great rivalships between different branches of the mechanic or manufacturing arts as there are between any of the departments of labor and industry; so that unless the representative body were to be far more numerous than would be consistent with any idea of regularity or wisdom in its deliberations, it is impossible that what seems to be the spirit of the objection we have been considering should ever be realized in practice. But I forbear to dwell longer on a matter which has hitherto worn too loose a garb to admit even of an accurate inspection of its real shape or tendency.

There is another objection of a somewhat more precise nature which claims our attention. It has been asserted that a power of internal taxation in the national legislature could never be exercised with advantage, as well from the want of a sufficient knowledge of local circumstances as from an interference between the revenue laws of the Union and of the particular States. The supposition of a want of proper knowledge seems to be entirely destitute of foundation. If any question is depending in a State legislature respecting one of the counties, which demands a knowledge of local details, how is it acquired? No doubt from the information of the members of the county. Cannot the like knowledge be obtained in the national legislature from the representatives of each State? And is it not to be presumed that the men who will generally be sent there will be possessed of the necessary degree of intelligence to be able to communicate that information? Is the knowledge of local circumstances, as applied to taxation, a minute topographical acquaintance with all the mountains, rivers, streams, highways, and bypaths in each State; or is it a general acquaintance with its situation and resources, with the state of its agriculture, commerce, manufactures, with the nature of its products and consumptions, with the different degrees and kinds of its wealth, property, and industry?

Nations in general, even under governments of the more

popular kind, usually commit the administration of their finances to single men or to boards composed of a few individuals, who digest and prepare, in the first instance, the plans of taxation, which are afterwards passed into law by the authority of the sovereign or legislature.

Inquisitive and enlightened statesmen are everywhere deemed best qualified to make a judicious selection of the objects proper for revenue; which is a clear indication, as far as the sense of mankind can have weight in the question, of the species of knowledge of local circumstances requisite to the purposes of taxation.

The taxes intended to be comprised under the general denomination of internal taxes may be subdivided into those of the *direct* and those of the *indirect* kind. Though the objection be made to both, yet the reasoning upon it seems to be confined to the former branch. And indeed, as to the latter, by which must be understood duties and excises on articles of consumption, one is at a loss to conceive what can be the nature of the difficulties apprehended. The knowledge relating to them must evidently be of a kind that will either be suggested by the nature of the article itself, or can easily be procured from any well-informed man, especially of the mercantile class. The circumstances that may distinguish its situation in one State from its situation in another must be few, simple, and easy to be comprehended. The principal thing to be attended to would be to avoid those articles which had been previously appropriated to the use of a particular State; and there could be no difficulty in ascertaining the revenue system of each. This could always be known from the respective codes of laws, as well as from the information of the members of the several States.

The objection, when applied to real property or to houses and lands, appears to have, at first sight, more foundation, but even in this view it will not bear a close examination. Land taxes are commonly laid in one of two modes, either by *actual* valuations, permanent or periodical, or by occasional assessments, at the discretion, or according to the best judgment, of certain officers whose duty it is to make them. In either case, the EXECUTION of the business, which alone requires the knowledge of local details, must be developed upon discreet persons in the character of commissioners or assessors, elected by the people or appointed by the government for the purpose. All that the law can do must be to name the persons or to prescribe the manner of their election or appointment, to fix their numbers and qualifications, and to draw the general outlines of their powers and duties. And what is there in all this that cannot as well be performed by the national legislature as by a State legislature? The attention of either can only reach to general principles; local details, as already observed, must be referred to those who are to execute the plan.

But there is a simple point of view in which this matter may be placed that must be altogether satisfactory. The national legislature can make use of the *system of each State within that State*. The method of laying and collecting this species of taxes in each State can, in all its parts, be adopted and employed by the federal government.

Let it be recollected that the proportion of these taxes is not to be left to the discretion of the national legislature, but is to be determined by the numbers of each State, as described in the second section of the first article. An actual census or enumeration of the people must furnish the rule, a circumstance which effectually shuts the door to partiality or oppression. The abuse of this power of taxation seems to have been provided against with guarded circumspection. In addition to the precaution just mentioned, there is a provision that "all duties, imposts, and excises shall be UNIFORM throughout the United States."

It has been very properly observed by different speakers and writers on the side of the Constitution that if the exercise of the power of internal taxation by the Union should be judged beforehand upon mature consideration, or should be discovered on experiment to be really inconvenient, the federal government may forbear the use of it, and have recourse to requisitions in its stead. By way of answer to this, it has been triumphantly asked, Why not in the first instance omit that ambiguous power and rely upon the latter resource? Two solid answers may be given. The first is that the actual exercise of the power may be found both convenient and necessary; for it is impossible to prove in theory, or otherwise than by the experiment, that it cannot be advantageously exercised. The contrary, indeed, appears most probable. The second answer is that the existence of such a power in the Constitution will have a strong influence in giving efficacy to requisitions. When the States know that the Union can supply itself without their agency, it will be a powerful motive for exertion on their part.

As to the interference of the revenue laws of the Union and of its members, we have already seen that there can be no clashing or repugnancy of authority. The laws cannot, therefore, in a legal sense, interfere with each other; and it is far from impossible to avoid an interference even in the policy of their different systems. An effectual expedient for this purpose will be mutually to abstain from those objects which either side may have first had recourse to. As neither can *control* the other, each will have an obvious and sensible interest in this reciprocal forbearance. And where there is an *immediate* common interest, we may safely count upon its operation. When the particular debts of the States are done away and their expenses come to be limited within their natural compass, the possibility almost of interference will vanish. A small land tax will answer the purposes of the States, and will be their most simple and most fit resource.

Many specters have been raised out of this power of internal taxation to excite the apprehensions of the people: double sets of revenue officers, a duplication of their burdens by double taxations, and the frightful forms of odious and oppressive poll taxes have been played off with all the ingenious dexterity of political legerdemain.

As to the first point, there are two cases in which there can be no room for double sets of officers: one, where the right of imposing the tax is exclusively vested in the Union, which applies to the duties on imports; the other, where the object has not fallen under any State regulation or provision, which may be applicable to a variety of objects. In other cases, the probability is that the United States will either wholly abstain from the objects preoccupied for local purposes, or will make use of the State officers and State regulations for collecting the additional imposition. This will best answer the views of revenue, because it will save expense in the collection, and will best avoid any occasion of disgust to the State governments and to the people. At all events, here is a practicable expedient for avoiding such an inconvenience; and nothing more can be required than to show that evils predicted do not necessarily result from the plan.

As to any argument derived from a supposed system of influence, it is a sufficient answer to say that it ought not to be presumed; but the supposition is susceptible of a more precise answer. If such a spirit should infest the councils of the Union, the most certain road to the accomplishment of its aim would be to employ the State officers as much as possible, and to attach them to the Union by an accumulation of their emoluments. This would serve to turn the tide of State influence into the channels of the national government, instead of making federal influence flow in an opposite and adverse current. But all suppositions of this kind are invidious, and ought to be banished from the consideration of the great question before the people. They can answer no other end than to cast a mist over the truth.

As to the suggestion of double taxation, the answer is plain. The wants of the Union are to be supplied in one way or another; if to be done by the authority of the federal government, it will not need to be done by that of the State governments. The quantity of taxes to be paid by the community must be the same in either case; with this advantage—if the provision is to be made by the Union—that the capital resource of commercial imposts, which is the most convenient branch of revenue, can be prudently improved to a much greater extent under federal than under State regulation, and of course will render it less necessary to recur to more inconvenient methods; and with this further advantage, that as far as there may be any real difficulty in the exercise of the power of internal taxation, it will impose a disposition to greater care in the choice and arrangement of the means; and must naturally tend to make it a fixed point of policy in the national administration to go as far as may be practicable in making the luxury of the rich tributary to the public treasury in order to diminish the necessity of those impositions which might create dissatisfaction in the poorer and most numerous classes of the society. Happy it is when the interest which the government has in the preservation of its own power coincides with a proper distribution of the public burdens and tends to guard the least wealthy part of the community from oppression!

As to poll taxes, I, without scruple, confess my disapprobation of them; and though they have prevailed from an early period in those States * which have uniformly been the most tenacious of their rights, I should lament to see them introduced into practice under the national government. But does it follow because there is a power to lay them that they will actually be laid? Every State in the Union has power to impose taxes of this kind; and yet in several of them they are unknown in practice. Are the State governments to be stigmatized as tyrannies because they possess this power? If they are not, with what propriety can the like power justify such a charge against the national government, or even be urged as an obstacle to its adoption? As little friendly as I am to the species of imposition, I still feel a thorough conviction that the power of having recourse to it ought to exist in the federal government. There are certain emergencies of nations in which expedients that in the ordinary state of things ought to be forborne become essential to the public weal. And the government, from the possibility of such emergencies, ought ever to have the option of making use of them. The real scarcity of objects in this country, which may be considered as productive sources of revenue, is a reason peculiar to itself for not abridging the discretion of the national councils in this respect. There may exist certain critical and tempestuous conjunctures of the State, in which a poll tax may become an inestimable resource. And as I know nothing to exempt this portion of the globe from the common calamities that have befallen other parts of it, I acknowledge my aversion to every project that is calculated to disarm the government of a single weapon, which in any possible contingency might be usefully employed for the general defense and security.

I have now gone through the examination of those powers proposed to be conferred upon the federal government which relate more peculiarly to its energy, and to its efficiency for answering the great and primary

* The New England States.

objects of union. There are others which, though omitted here, will, in order to render the view of the subject more complete, be taken notice of under the next head of our inquiries. I flatter myself the progress already made will have sufficed to satisfy the candid and judicious part of the community that some of the objections which have been most strenuously urged against the Constitution, and which were most formidable in their first appearance, are not only destitute of substance, but if they had operated in the formation of the plan, would have rendered it incompetent to the great ends of public happiness and national prosperity. I equally flatter myself that a further and more critical investigation of the system will serve to recommend it still more to every sincere and disinterested advocate for good government and will leave no doubt with men of this character of the propriety and expediency of adopting it. Happy will it be for ourselves, and most honorable for human nature, if we have wisdom and virtue enough to set so glorious an example to mankind! PUBLIUS

No. 37: Madison

IN REVIEWING the defects of the existing Confederation, and showing that they cannot be supplied by a government of less energy than that before the public, several of the most important principles of the latter fell of course under consideration. But as the ultimate object of these papers is to determine clearly and fully the merits of this Constitution, and the expediency of adopting it, our plan cannot be completed without taking a more critical and thorough survey of the work of the convention, without examining it on all its sides, comparing it in all its parts, and calculating its probable effects. That this remaining task may be executed under impressions conducive to a just and fair result, some reflections must in this place be indulged, which candor previously suggests.

It is a misfortune, inseparable from human affairs, that public measures are rarely investigated with that spirit of moderation which is essential to a just estimate of their real tendency to advance or obstruct the public good; and that this spirit is more apt to be diminished than promoted by those occasions which require an unusual exercise of it. To those who have been led by experience to attend to this consideration, it could not appear surprising that the act of the convention, which recommends so many important changes and innovations, which may be viewed in so many lights and relations, and which touches the springs of so many passions and interests, should find or excite dispositions unfriendly, both on one side and on the other, to a fair discussion and accurate judgment of its merits. In some, it has been too evident from their own publications that they have scanned the proposed Constitution, not only with a predisposition to censure, but with a predetermination to condemn; as the language held by others betrays an opposite predetermination or bias, which must render their opinions also of little moment in the question. In placing, however, these different characters on a level with respect to the weight of their opinions I wish not to insinuate that there may not be a material difference in the purity of their intentions. It is but just to remark in favor of the latter description that as our situation is universally admitted to be peculiarly critical, and to require indispensably that something should be done for our relief, the pedetermined patron of what has been actually done may have taken his bias from the weight of these considerations, as well as from considerations of a sinister nature. The predetermined adversary, on the other hand, can have been governed by no venial motive whatever. The intentions of the first may be upright, as they may on the contrary be culpable. The views of the last cannot be upright, and must be culpable. But the truth is that these papers are not addressed to persons falling under either of these characters. They solicit the attention of those only who add to a sincere zeal for the happiness of their country, a temper favorable to a just estimate of the means of promoting it.

Persons of this character will proceed to an examination of the plan submitted by the convention, not only without a disposition to find or to magnify faults; but will see the propriety of reflecting that a faultless plan was not to be expected. Nor will they barely make allowances for the errors which may be chargeable on the fallibility to which the convention, as a body of men, were liable; but will keep in mind that they themselves also are but men and ought not to assume an infallibility in rejudging the fallible opinions of others.

With equal readiness will it be perceived that besides these inducements to candor, many allowances ought to be made for the difficulties inherent in the very nature of the undertaking referred to the convention.

The novelty of the undertaking immediately strikes us. It has been shown in the course of these papers that the existing Confederation is founded on principles which are fallacious; that we must consequently change this first foundation, and with it the superstructure resting upon it. It has been shown that the other confederacies which could be consulted as precedents have been vitiated by the same erroneous principles, and can therefore furnish no other light than that of beacons, which give warning of the course to be shunned, without pointing out that which ought to be pursued. The most that the convention could do in such a situation was to avoid the errors suggested by the past experience of other countries, as well as of our own; and to provide a convenient mode of rectifying their own errors, as future experience may unfold them.

Among the difficulties encountered by the convention, a very important one must have lain in combining the requisite stability and energy in government with the inviolable attention due to liberty and to the republican form. Without substantially accomplishing this part of their undertaking, they would have very imperfectly fulfilled the object of their appointment, or the expectation of the public; yet that it could not be easily accomplished will be denied by no one who is unwilling to betray his ignorance of the subject. Energy in government is essential to that security against external and internal danger and to that prompt and salutary execution of the laws which enter into the very definition of good government. Stability in government is essential to national character and to the advantages annexed to it, as well as to that repose and confidence in the minds of the people, which are among the chief blessings of civil society. An irregular and mutable legislation is not more an evil in itself than it is odious to the people; and it may be pronounced with assurance that the people of this country, enlightened as they are with regard to the nature, and interested, as the great body of them are, in the effects of good government, will never be satisfied till some remedy be applied to the vicissitudes and uncertainties which characterize the State administrations. On comparing, however, these valuable ingredients with the vital principles of liberty, we must perceive at once the difficulty of mingling them together in their due proportions. The genius of republican liberty seems to demand on one side not only that all power should be derived from the people, but that those intrusted with it should be kept in dependence on the people by a short duration of their appointments; and that even during this short period the trust should be placed not in a few, but a number of hands. Stability, on the contrary, requires that the hands in which power is lodged should continue for a length of time the same. A frequent change of men will result from a frequent return of elections; and a frequent change of measures from a frequent change of men: whilst energy in government requires not only a certain duration of power, but the execution of it by a single hand.

How far the convention may have succeeded in this part of their work will better appear on a more accurate view of it. From the cursory view here taken, it must clearly appear to have been an arduous part.

Not less arduous must have been the task of marking the proper line of partition between the authority of the general and that of the State governments. Every man will be sensible of this difficulty in proportion as he has been accustomed to contemplate and discriminate objects extensive and complicated in their nature. The faculties of the mind itself have never yet been distinguished and defined with satisfactory precision by all the efforts of the most acute and metaphysical philosophers. Sense, perception, judgment, desire, volition, memory, imagination are found to be separated by such delicate shades and minute gradations that their boundaries have eluded the most subtle investigations, and remain a pregnant source of ingenious disquisition and controversy. The boundaries between the great kingdom of nature, and, still more, between the various provinces and lesser portions into which they are subdivided afford another illustration of the same important truth. The most sagacious and laborious naturalists have never yet succeeded in tracing with certainty the line which separates the district of vegetable life from the neighboring region of unorganized matter, or which marks the termination of the former and the commencement of the animal empire. A still greater obscurity lies in the distinctive characters by which the objects in each of these great departments of nature have been arranged and assorted.

When we pass from the works of nature, in which all the delineations are perfectly accurate and appear to be otherwise only from the imperfection of the eye which surveys them, to the institutions of man, in which the obscurity arises as well from the object itself as from the organ by which it is contemplated, we must perceive the necessity of moderating still further our expectations and hopes from the efforts of human sagacity. Experience has instructed us that no skill in the science of government has yet been able to discriminate and define, with sufficient certainty, its three great provinces—the legislative, executive, and judiciary; or even the privileges and powers of the different legislative branches. Questions daily occur in the course of practice which prove the obscurity which reigns in these subjects, and which puzzle the greatest adepts in political science.

The experience of ages, with the continued and combined labors of the most enlightened legislators and jurists, has been equally unsuccessful in delineating the several objects and limits of different codes of laws and different tribunals of justice. The precise extent of the common law, and the statute law, the maritime law, the ecclesiastical law, the law of corporations, and other local laws and customs, remains still to be clearly and finally established in Great Britain, where accuracy in such subjects has been more industriously pursued than in any other part of the world. The jurisdiction of her several courts, general and local, of law, of equity, of admiralty, etc., is not less a source of frequent and intricate discussions, sufficiently denoting the indeterminate limits by which they are respectively circumscribed.

All new laws, though penned with the greatest technical skill and passed on the fullest and most mature deliberation, are considered as more or less obscure and equivocal, until their meaning be liquidated and ascertained by a series of particular discussions and adjudications. Besides the obscurity arising from the complexity of objects and the imperfection of the human faculties, the medium through which the conceptions of men are conveyed to each other adds a fresh embarrassment. The use of words is to express ideas. Perspicuity, therefore, requires not only that the ideas should be distinctly formed, but that they should be expressed by words distinctly and exclusively appropriate to them. But no language is so copious as to supply words and phrases for every complex idea, or so correct as not to include many equivocally denoting different ideas. Hence it must happen that however accurately objects may be discriminated in themselves, and however accurately the discrimination may be considered, the definition of them may be rendered inaccurate by the inaccuracy of the terms in which it is delivered. And this unavoidable inaccuracy must be greater or less, according to the complexity and novelty of the objects defined. When the Almighty himself condescends to address mankind in their own language, his meaning, luminous as it must be, is rendered dim and doubtful by the cloudy medium through which it is communicated.

Here, then, are three sources of vague and incorrect definitions: indistinctness of the object, imperfection of the organ of conception, inadequateness of the vehicle of ideas. Any one of these must produce a certain degree of obscurity. The convention, in delineating the boundary between the federal and State jurisdictions, must have experienced the full effect of them all.

To the difficulties already mentioned may be added the interfering pretensions of the larger and smaller States. We cannot err in supposing that the former would contend for a participation in the government, fully proportioned to their superior wealth and importance; and that the latter would not be less tenacious of the equality at present enjoyed by them. We may well suppose that neither side would entirely yield to the other, and consequently that the struggle could be terminated only by compromise. It is extremely probable, also, that after the ratio of representation had been adjusted, this very compromise must have produced a fresh struggle between the same parties to give such a turn to the organization of the government and to the distribution of its powers as would increase the importance of the branches, in forming which they had respectively obtained the greatest share of influence. There are features in the Constitution which warrant each of these suppositions; and as far as either of them is well founded, it shows that the convention must have been compelled to sacrifice theoretical propriety to the force of extraneous considerations.

Nor could it have been the large and small States only which would marshal themselves in opposition to each other on various points. Other combinations, resulting from a difference of local position and policy, must have created additional difficulties. As every State may be divided into different districts, and its citizens into different classes, which give birth to contending interests and local jealousies, so the different parts of the United States are distinguished from each other by a variety of circumstances, which produce a like effect on a larger scale. And although this variety of interests, for reasons sufficiently explained in a former paper, may have a salutary influence on the administration of the government when formed, yet every one must be sensible of the contrary influence which must have been experienced in the task of forming it.

Would it be wonderful if, under the pressure of all these difficulties, the convention should have been forced into some deviations from that artificial structure and regular symmetry which an abstract view of the subject might lead an ingenious theorist to bestow on a Constitution planned in his closet or in his imagination? The real wonder is that so many difficulties should have been surmounted, and surmounted with a unanimity almost as unprecedented as it must have been unexpected. It is impossible for any man of candor to reflect on this circumstance without partaking of the astonishment. It is impossible for the man of pious reflection not to perceive in it a finger of that Almighty hand which has been so frequently and signally extended to our relief in the critical stages of the revolution.

We had occasion in a former paper to take notice of the repeated trials which have been unsuccessfully made in the United Netherlands for reforming the baneful and notorious vices of their constitution. The history of almost all the great councils and consultations held among mankind for reconciling their discordant opinions, assuaging their mutual jealousies and adjusting their respective interests, is a history of factions, contentions, and disappointments, and may be classed among the most dark and degrading pictures which display the infirmities and depravities of the human character. If in a few scattered instances a brighter aspect is presented, they serve only as exceptions to admonish us of the general truth; and by their luster to darken the gloom of the adverse prospect to which they are contrasted. In resolving the causes from which these exceptions result, and applying them to the particular instances before us, we are necessarily led to two important conclusions. The first is that the convention must have enjoyed, in a very singular degree, an exemption from the pestilential influence of party animosities—the disease most incident to deliberative bodies and most apt to contaminate their proceedings. The second conclusion is that all the deputations composing the convention were either satisfactorily accommodated by the final act, or were induced to accede to it by a deep conviction of the necessity of sacrificing private opinions and partial interests to the public good, and by a despair of seeing this necessity diminished by delays or by new experiments.

PUBLIUS

No. 38: Madison

IT IS not a little remarkable that in every case reported by ancient history in which government has been established with deliberation and consent, the task of framing it has not been committed to an assembly of men, but has been performed by some individual citizen of preeminent wisdom and approved integrity.

Minos, we learn, was the primitive founder of the government of Crete, as Zaleucus was of that of the Locrians. Theseus first, and after him Draco and Solon, instituted the government of Athens. Lycurgus was the lawgiver of Sparta. The foundation of the original government of Rome was laid by Romulus, and the work completed by two of his elective successors, Numa and Tullius Hostilius. On the abolition of royalty the consular administration was substituted by Brutus, who stepped forward with a project for such a reform, which, he alleged, had been prepared by Servius Tullius, and to which his address obtained the assent and ratification of the senate and people. This remark is applicable to confederate governments also. Amphictyon, we are told, was the author of that which bore his name. The Achæan league received its first birth from Achæus, and its second from Aratus.

What degree of agency these reputed lawgivers might have in their respective establishments, or how far they might be clothed with the legitimate authority of the people, cannot in every instance be ascertained. In some, however, the proceeding was strictly regular. Draco appears to have been intrusted by the people of Athens with indefinite powers to reform its government and laws. And Solon, according to Plutarch, was in a manner compelled by the universal suffrage of his fellow-citizens to take upon him the sole and absolute power of new-modeling the constitution. The proceedings under Lycurgus were less regular; but as far as the advocates for a regular reform could prevail, they all turned their eyes towards the single efforts of that celebrated patriot and sage, instead of seeking to bring about a revolution by the intervention of a deliberative body of citizens.

Whence could it have proceeded that a people, jealous as the Greeks were of their liberty, should so far abandon the rules of caution as to place their destiny in the hands of a single citizen? Whence could it have proceeded that the Athenians, a people who would not suffer an army to be commanded by fewer than ten generals, and who required no other proof of danger to their liberties than the illustrious merit of a fellow-citizen, should consider one illustrious citizen as a more eligible depositary of the fortunes of themselves and their posterity than a select body of citizens, from whose common deliberations more wisdom, as well as more safety, might have been expected? These questions cannot be fully answered without supposing that the fears of discord and disunion among a number of counselors exceeded the apprehension of treachery or incapacity in a single individual. History informs us, likewise, of the difficulties with which these celebrated reformers had to contend, as well as of the expedients which thev were obliged to employ in order to carry their reforms into effect. Solon, who seems to have indulged a more temporizing policy, confessed that he had not given to his countrymen the government best suited to their happiness, but most tolerable to their prejudices. And Lycurgus, more true to his object, was under the necessity of mixing a portion of violence with the authority of superstition, and of securing his final success by a voluntary renunciation, first of his country and then of his life. If these lessons teach us, on one hand, to admire the improvement made by America on the ancient mode of preparing and establishing regular plans of government, they serve not less, on the other, to admonish us of the hazards and difficulties incident to such experiments, and of the great imprudence of unnecessarily multiplying them.

Is it an unreasonable conjecture that the errors which may be contained in the plan of the convention are such as have resulted rather from the defect of antecedent experience on this complicated and difficult subject, than from a want of accuracy or care in the investigation of it; and, consequently, such as will not be ascertained until an actual trial shall have pointed them out? This conjecture is rendered probable, not only by many considerations of a general nature, but by the particular case of the Articles of Confederation. It is observable that among the numerous objections and amendments suggested by the several States, when these articles were submitted for their ratification, not one is found which alludes to the great and radical error which on actual trial has discovered itself. And if we except the observations which New Jersey was led to make, rather by her local situation than by her peculiar foresight, it may be questioned whether a single suggestion was of sufficient moment to justify a revision of the system.

There is abundant reason, nevertheless, to suppose that immaterial as these objections were, they would have been adhered to with a very dangerous inflexibility in some States, had not a zeal for their opinions and supposed interests been stifled by the more powerful sentiment of self-preservation. One State, we may remember, persisted for several years in refusing her concurrence, although the enemy remained the whole period at our gates, or rather in the very bowels of our country. Nor was her pliancy in the end effected by a lesser motive than the fear of being chargeable with protracting the public calamities and endangering the event of the contest. Every candid reader will make the proper reflections on these important facts.

A patient who finds his disorder daily growing worse, and that an efficacious remedy can no longer be delayed without extreme danger, after coolly revolving his situation and the characters of different physicians, selects and calls in such of them as he judges most capable of administering relief, and best entitled to his confidence. The physicians attend; the case of the patient is carefully examined; a consultation is held; they are unanimously agreed that the symptoms are critical, but that the case, with proper and timely relief, so far from being desperate that it may be made to issue in an improvement of his constitution. They are equally unanimous in prescribing the remedy by which this happy effect is to be produced. The prescription is no sooner made known, however, than a number of persons interpose, and, without denying the reality or danger of the disorder, assure the patient that the prescription will be poison to his constitution, and forbid him, under pain of certain death, to make use of it. Might not the patient reasonably demand, before he ventured to follow this advice, that the authors of it should at least agree among themselves on some other remedy to be substituted? And if he found them differing as much from one another as from his first counselors, would he not act prudently in trying the experiment unanimously recommended by the latter, rather than be hearkening to those who could neither deny the necessity of a speedy remedy, nor agree in proposing one?

Such a patient and in such a situation is America at

this moment. She has been sensible of her malady. She has obtained a regular and unanimous advice from men of her own deliberate choice. And she is warned by others against following this advice under pain of the most fatal consequences. Do the monitors deny the reality of her danger? No. Do they deny the necessity of some speedy and powerful remedy? No. Are they agreed, are any two of them agreed, in their objections to the remedy proposed, or in the proper one to be substituted? Let them speak for themselves. This one tells us that the proposed Constitution ought to be rejected because it is not a confederation of the States, but a government over individuals. Another admits that it ought to be a government over individuals to a certain extent, but by no means to the extent proposed. A third does not object to the government over individuals, or to the extent proposed, but to the want of a bill of rights. A fourth concurs in the absolute necessity of a bill of rights, but contends that it ought to be declaratory, not of the personal rights of individuals, but of the rights reserved to the States in their political capacity. A fifth is of opinion that a bill of rights of any sort would be superfluous and misplaced, and that the plan would be unexceptionable but for the fatal power of regulating the times and places of election. An objector in a large State exclaims loudly against the unreasonable equality of representation in the Senate. An objector in a small State is equally loud against the dangerous inequality in the House of Representatives. From this quarter we are alarmed with the amazing expense from the number of persons who are to administer the new government. From another quarter, and sometimes from the same quarter, on another occasion, the cry is that the Congress will be but a shadow of a representation, and that the government would be far less objectionable if the number and the expense were doubled. A patriot in a State that does not import or export discerns insuperable objections against the power of direct taxation. The patriotic adversary in a State of great exports and imports is not less dissatisfied that the whole burden of taxes may be thrown on consumption. This politician discovers in the Constitution a direct and irresistible tendency to monarchy; that is equally sure it will end in aristocracy. Another is puzzled to say which of these shapes it will ultimately assume, but sees clearly it must be one or other of them; whilst a fourth is not wanting, who with no less confidence affirms that the Constitution is so far from having a bias towards either of these dangers, that the weight on that side will not be sufficient to keep it upright and firm against its opposite propensities. With another class of adversaries to the Constitution the language is that the legislative, executive, and judiciary departments are intermixed in such a manner as to contradict all the ideas of regular government and all the requisite precautions in favor of liberty. Whilst this objection circulates in vague and general expressions, there are but a few who lend their sanction to it. Let each one come forward with his particular explanation, and scarce any two are exactly agreed upon the subject. In the eyes of one the junction of the Senate with the President in the responsible function of appointing to offices, instead of vesting this executive power in the Executive alone, is the vicious part of the organization. To another, the exclusion of the House of Representatives, whose numbers alone could be a due security against corruption and partiality in the exercise of such a power, is equally obnoxious. With another the admission of the President into any share of a power which must ever be a dangerous engine in the hands of the executive magistrate is an unpardonable violation of the maxims of republican jealousy. No part of the arrangement, according to some, is more inadmissible than the trial of impeachments by the Senate, which is alternately a member both of the legislative and executive departments, when this power so evidently belonged to the judiciary department. "We concur fully," reply others, "in the objection to this part of the plan, but we can never agree that a reference of impeachments to the judiciary authority would be an amendment of the error. Our principal dislike to the organization arises from the extensive powers already lodged in that department." Even among the zealous patrons of a council of state the most irreconcilable variance is discovered concerning the mode in which it ought to be constituted. The demand of one gentleman is that the council should consist of a small number to be appointed by the most numerous branch of the legislature. Another would prefer a larger number, and considers it as a fundamental condition that the appointment should be made by the President himself.

As it can give no umbrage to the writers against the plan of the federal Constitution, let us suppose that as they are the most zealous, so they are also the most sagacious, of those who think the late convention were unequal to the task assigned them, and that a wiser and better plan might and ought to be substituted. Let us further suppose that their country should concur, both in this favorable opinion of their merits, and in their unfavorable opinion of the convention; and should accordingly proceed to form them into a second convention, with full powers, and for the express purpose of revising and remolding the work of the first. Were the experiment to be seriously made, though it requires some effort to view it seriously even in fiction, I leave it to be decided by the sample of opinions just exhibited whether, with all their enmity to their predecessors, they would, in any one point, depart so widely from their example as in the discord and ferment that would mark their own deliberations; and whether the Constitution now before the public would not stand as fair a chance for immortality as Lycurgus gave to that of Sparta by making its change to depend on his own return from exile and death, if it were to be immediately adopted and were to continue in force, not until a BETTER, but until ANOTHER, should be agreed upon by this new assembly of lawgivers.

It is a matter both of wonder and regret that those who raise so many objections against the new Constitution should never call to mind the defects of that which is to be exchanged for it. It is not necessary that the former should be perfect: it is sufficient that the latter is more imperfect. No man would refuse to give brass for silver or gold, because the latter had some alloy in it. No man would refuse to quit a shattered and tottering habitation for a firm and commodious building because the latter had not a porch to it, or because some of the rooms might be a little larger or smaller, or the ceiling a little higher or lower than his fancy would have planned them. But waiving illustrations of this sort, is it not manifest that most of the capital objections urged against the new system lie with tenfold weight against the existing Confederation? Is an indefinite power to raise money dangerous in the hands of the federal government? The present Congress can make requisitions to any amount they please, and the States are constitutionally bound to furnish them; they can emit bills of credit as long as they will pay for the paper; they can borrow, both abroad and at home, as long as a shilling will be lent. Is an indefinite power to raise troops dangerous? The Confederation gives to Congress that power also; and they have already begun to make use of it. Is it improper and unsafe to intermix the different powers of government in the same body of men? Congress, a single body of men, are the sole depositary of all the federal powers. Is it particularly dangerous to give the keys of the treasury, and the command of the army, into the same hands? The Confederation places them both in the hands of Congress. Is a bill of rights essential to liberty? The Confederation has no bill of rights. Is it an objection against the new Constitution that it empowers the Senate, with the concurrence of the executive, to make treaties which are to be the laws of the land? The existing Congress, without any such control, can make treaties which they themselves have declared and most of the States have recognized, to be the supreme law of the land. Is the importation of slaves permitted by the new Constitution for twenty years? By the old it is permitted forever.

I shall be told that however dangerous this mixture of powers may be in theory, it is rendered harmless by the dependence of Congress on the States for the means of carrying them into practice; that however large the mass of powers may be, it is in fact a lifeless mass. Then, say I, in the first place, that the Confederation is chargeable with the still greater folly of declaring certain powers in the federal government to be absolutely necessary, and at the same time rendering them absolutely nugatory; and, in the next place, that if the Union is to continue, and no better government be substituted, effective powers must either be granted to, or assumed by, the existing Congress; in either of which events, the contrast just stated will hold good. But this is not all. Out of this lifeless mass has already grown an excrescent power, which tends to realize all the dangers that can be apprehended from a defective construction of the supreme government of the Union. It is now no longer a point of speculation and hope that the Western territory is a mine of vast wealth to the United States; and although it is not of such a nature as to extricate them from their present distresses, or for some time to come to yield any regular supplies for the public expenses, yet must it hereafter be able, under proper management, both to effect a gradual discharge of the domestic debt and to furnish, for a certain period, liberal tributes to the federal treasury. A very large proportion of this fund has been already surrendered by individual States; and it may with reason be expected that the remaining States will not persist in withholding similar proofs of their equity and generosity. We may calculate, therefore, that a rich and fertile country of an area equal to the inhabited extent of the United States will soon become a national stock. Congress have assumed the administration of this stock. They have begun to render it productive. Congress have undertaken to do more: they have proceeded to form new States, to erect temporary governments, to appoint officers for them, and to prescribe the conditions on which such States shall be admitted into the Confederacy. All this has been done; and done without the least color of constitutional authority. Yet no blame has been whispered; no alarm has been sounded. A GREAT and INDEPENDENT fund of revenue is passing into the hands of a SINGLE BODY of men, who can RAISE TROOPS to an INDEFINITE NUMBER and appropriate money to their support for an INDEFINITE PERIOD OF TIME. And yet there are men, who have not only been silent spectators of this prospect, but who are advocates for the system which exhibits it; and at the same time urge against the new system the objections which we have heard. Would they not act with more consistency in urging the establishment of the latter as no less necessary to guard the Union against the future powers and resources of a body constructed like the existing Congress, than to save it from the dangers threatened by the present impotency of that assembly?

I mean not by anything here said to throw censure on the measures which have been pursued by Congress.

I am sensible they could not have done otherwise. The public interest, the necessity of the case, imposed upon them the task of overleaping their constitutional limits. But is not the fact an alarming proof of the danger resulting from a government which does not possess regular powers commensurate to its objects? A dissolution or usurpation is the dreadful dilemma to which it is continually exposed. PUBLIUS

No. 39: Madison

THE last paper having concluded the observations which were meant to introduce a candid survey of the plan of government reported by the convention, we now proceed to the execution of that part of our undertaking.

The first question that offers itself is whether the general form and aspect of the government be strictly republican. It is evident that no other form would be reconcilable with the genius of the people of America; with the fundamental principles of the Revolution; or with that honorable determination which animates every votary of freedom to rest all our political experiments on the capacity of mankind for self-government. If the plan of the convention, therefore, be found to depart from the republican character, its advocates must abandon it as no longer defensible.

What, then, are the distinctive characters of the republican form? Were an answer to this question to be sought, not by recurring to principles but in the application of the term by political writers to the constitutions of different States, no satisfactory one would ever be found. Holland, in which no particle of the supreme authority is derived from the people, has passed almost universally under the denomination of a republic. The same title has been bestowed on Venice, where absolute power over the great body of the people is exercised in the most absolute manner by a small body of hereditary nobles. Poland, which is a mixture of aristocracy and of monarchy in their worst forms, has been dignified with the same appellation. The government of England, which has one republican branch only, combined with an hereditary aristocracy and monarchy, has with equal impropriety been frequently placed on the list of republics. These examples, which are nearly as dissimilar to each other as to a genuine republic, show the extreme inaccuracy with which the term has been used in political disquisitions.

If we resort for a criterion to the different principles on which different forms of government are established, we may define a republic to be, or at least may bestow that name on, a government which derives all its powers directly or indirectly from the great body of the people, and is administered by persons holding their offices during pleasure for a limited period, or during good behavior. It is *essential* to such a government that it be derived from the great body of the society, not from an inconsiderable proportion or a favored class of it; otherwise a handful of tyrannical nobles, exercising their oppressions by a delegation of their powers, might aspire to the rank of republicans and claim for their government the honorable title of republic. It is *sufficient* for such a government that the persons administering it be appointed, either directly or indirectly, by the people; and that they hold their appointments by either of the tenures just specified; otherwise every government in the United States, as well as every other popular government that has been or can be well organized or well executed, would be degraded from the republican character. According to the constitution of every State in the Union, some or other of the officers of government are appointed indirectly only by the people. According to most of them, the chief magistrate himself is so appointed. And according to one, this mode of appointment is extended to one of the co-ordinate branches of the legislature. According to all the constitutions, also, the tenure of the highest offices is extended to a definite period, and in many instances, both within the legislative and executive departments, to a period of years. According to the provisions of most of the constitutions, again, as well as according to the most respectable and received opinions on the subject, the members of the judiciary department are to retain their offices by the firm tenure of good behavior.

On comparing the Constitution planned by the convention with the standard here fixed, we perceived at once that it is, in the most rigid sense, conformable to it. The House of Representatives, like that of one branch at least of all the State legislatures, is elected immediately by the great body of the people. The Senate, like the present Congress and the Senate of Maryland, derives its appointment indirectly from the people. The President is indirectly derived from the choice of the people, according to the example in most of the States. Even the judges, with all other officers of the Union, will, as in the several States, be the choice, though a remote choice, of the people themselves. The duration of the appointments is equally conformable to the republican standard and to the model of State constitutions. The House of Representatives is periodically elective, as in all the States; and for the period of two years, as in the State of South Carolina. The Senate is elective for the period of six years, which is but one year more than the period of the Senate of Maryland, and but two more than that of the Senates of New York and Virginia. The President is to continue in office for the period of four years; as in New York and Delaware the chief magistrate is elected for three years, and in South Carolina for two years. In the other States the election is annual. In several of the States, however, no explicit provision is made for the impeachment of the chief magistrate. And in Delaware and Virginia he is not impeachable till out of office. The President of the United States is impeachable at any time during his continuance in office. The tenure by which the judges are to hold their places is, as it unquestionably ought to be, that of good behavior. The tenure of the ministerial offices generally will be a subject of legal regulation, conformably to the reason of the case and the example of the State constitutions.

Could any further proof be required of the republican complexion of this system, the most decisive one might be found in its absolute prohibition of titles of nobility, both under the federal and the State governments; and in its express guaranty of the republican form to each of the latter.

"But it was not sufficient," say the adversaries of the proposed Constitution, "for the convention to adhere to the republican form. They ought with equal care to have preserved the *federal* form, which regards the Union as a *Confederacy* of sovereign states; instead of which they have framed a *national* government, which regards the Union as a *consolidation* of the States." And it is asked by what authority this bold and radical innovation was undertaken? The handle which has been made of this objection requires that it should be examined with some precision.

Without inquiring into the accuracy of the distinction on which the objection is founded, it will be necessary to a just estimate of its force, first, to ascertain the real character of the government in question; secondly, to inquire how far the convention were authorized to propose such a government; and thirdly, how far the duty they owed to their country could supply any defect of regular authority.

First.—In order to ascertain the real character of the government, it may be considered in relation to the foundation on which it is to be established; to the sources from which its ordinary powers are to be drawn; to the operation of those powers; to the extent of them; and to the authority by which future changes in the government are to be introduced.

On examining the first relation, it appears, on one hand, that the Constitution is to be founded on the assent and ratification of the people of America, given by deputies elected for the special purpose; but, on the other, that this assent and ratification is to be given by the people, not as individuals composing one entire nation, but as composing the distinct and independent States to which they respectively belong. It is to be the assent and ratification of the several States, derived from the supreme authority in each State—the authority of the people themselves. The act, therefore, establishing the Constitution will not be a *national* but a *federal* act.

That it will be a federal and not a national act, as these terms are understood by the objectors—the act of the people, as forming so many independent States, not as forming one aggregate nation—is obvious from this single consideration: that it is to result neither from the decision of a *majority* of the people of the Union, nor from that of a *majority* of the States. It must result from the *unanimous* assent of the several States that are parties to it, differing no otherwise from their ordinary assent than in its being expressed, not by the legislative authority, but by that of the people themselves. Were the people regarded in this transaction as forming one nation, the will of the majority of the whole people of the United States would bind the minority, in the same manner as the majority in each State must bind the minority; and the will of the majority must be determined either by a comparison of the individual votes, or by considering the will of the majority of the States as evidence of the will of a majority of the people of the United States. Neither of these rules has been adopted. Each State, in ratifying the Constitution, is considered as a sovereign body independent of all others, and only to be bound by its own voluntary act. In this relation, then, the new Constitution will, if established, be a *federal* and not a *national* constitution.

The next relation is to the sources from which the ordinary powers of government are to be derived. The House of Representatives will derive its powers from the people of America; and the people will be represented in the same proportion and on the same principle as they are in the legislature of a particular State. So far the government is *national,* not *federal.* The Senate, on the other hand, will derive its powers from the States as political and coequal societies; and these will be represented on the principle of equality in the Senate, as they now are in the existing Congress. So far the government is *federal,* not *national.* The executive power will be derived from a very compound source. The immediate election of the President is to be made by the States in their political characters. The votes allotted to them are in a compound ratio, which considers them partly as distinct and coequal societies, partly as unequal members of the same society. The eventual election, again, is to be made by that branch of the legislature which consists of the national representatives; but in this particular act they are to be thrown into the form of individual delegations from so many distinct and coequal bodies politic. From this aspect of the government it appears to be of a mixed character, presenting at least as many *federal* as *national* features.

The difference between a federal and national government, as it relates to the *operation of the government*, is by the adversaries of the plan of the convention supposed to consist in this, that in the former the powers operate on the political bodies composing the Confederacy in their political capacities; in the latter, on the individual citizens composing the nation in their individual capacities. On trying the Constitution by this criterion, it falls under the *national* not the *federal* character; though perhaps not so completely as has been understood. In several cases, and particularly in the trial of controversies to which States may be parties, they must be viewed and proceeded against in their collective and political capacities only. But the operation of the government on the people in their individual capacities, in its ordinary and most essential proceedings, will, in the sense of its opponents, on the whole, designate it, in this relation, a *national* government.

But if the government be national with regard to the *operation* of its powers, it changes its aspect again when we contemplate it in relation to the extent of its powers. The idea of a national government involves in it not only an authority over the individual citizens, but an indefinite supremacy over all persons and things, so far as they are objects of lawful government. Among a people consolidated into one nation, this supremacy is completely vested in the national legislature. Among communities united for particular purposes, it is vested partly in the general and partly in the municipal legislatures. In the former case, all local authorities are subordinate to the supreme; and may be controlled, directed, or abolished by it at pleasure. In the latter, the local or municipal authorities form distinct and independent portions of the supremacy, no more subject, within their respective spheres, to the general authority than the general authority is subject to them, within its own sphere. In this relation, then, the proposed government cannot be deemed a *national* one; since its jurisdiction extends to certain enumerated objects only, and leaves to the several States a residuary and inviolable sovereignty over all other objects. It is true that in controversies relating to the boundary between the two jurisdictions, the tribunal which is ultimately to decide is to be established under the general government. But this does not change the principle of the case. The decision is to be impartially made, according to the rules of the Constitution; and all the usual and most effectual precautions are taken to secure this impartiality. Some such tribunal is clearly essential to prevent an appeal to the sword and a dissolution of the compact; and that it ought to be established under the general rather than under the local governments, or, to speak more properly, that it could be safely established under the first alone, is a position not likely to be combated.

If we try the Constitution by its last relation to the authority by which amendments are to be made, we find it neither wholly *national* nor wholly *federal*. Were it wholly national, the supreme and ultimate authority would reside in the *majority* of the people of the Union; and this authority would be competent at all times, like that of a majority of every national society to alter or abolish its established government. Were it wholly federal, on the other hand, the concurrence of each State in the Union would be essential to every alteration that would be binding on all. The mode provided by the plan of the convention is not founded on either of these principles. In requiring more than a majority, and particularly in computing the proportion by *States*, not by *citizens*, it departs from the national and advances towards the *federal* character; in rendering the concurrence of less than the whole number of States sufficient, it loses again the *federal* and partakes of the *national* character.

The proposed Constitution, therefore, even when tested by the rules laid down by its antagonists, is, in strictness, neither a national nor a federal Constitution, but a composition of both. In its foundation it is federal, not national; in the sources from which the ordinary powers of the government are drawn, it is partly federal and partly national; in the operation of these powers, it is national, not federal; in the extent of them, again, it is federal, not national; and, finally in the authoritative mode of introducing amendments, it is neither wholly federal nor wholly national.

PUBLIUS

No. 40: Madison

THE *second* point to be examined is whether the convention were authorized to frame and propose this mixed Constitution.

The powers of the convention ought, in strictness, to be determined by an inspection of the commissions given to the members by their respective constituents. As all of these, however, had reference either to the recommendation from the meeting at Annapolis, in September, 1786, or to that from Congress, in February, 1787, it will be sufficient to recur to these particular acts.

The act from Annapolis recommends the "appointment of commissioners to take into consideration the situation of the United States; to devise *such further provisions* as shall appear to them necessary to render the Constitution of the federal government *adequate to the exigencies of the Union;* and to report such an act for that purpose to the United States in Congress assembled, as when agreed to by them, and afterwards confirmed by the legislature of every State, will effectually provide for the same."

The recommendatory act of a Congress is in the words following: "Whereas there is provision in the articles of Confederation and perpetual Union for making alterations therein, by the assent of a Congress of the United States and of the legislatures of the several States; and whereas experience hath evinced that there are defects in the present Confederation; as a means to remedy which, several of the States, and *particularly the State of New York,* by express instructions to their delegates in Congress, have suggested a convention for the purposes expressed in the following resolution; and such convention appearing to be the most probable mean of establishing in these States *a firm national government:*

"*Resolved*—That in the opinion of Congress it is expedient that on the second Monday in May next a convention of delegates, who shall have been appointed by the several States, be held at Philadelphia for the sole and express purpose *of revising the articles of Confedera-*

tion and reporting to Congress and the several legislatures such *alterations and provisions therein* as shall, when agreed to in Congress and confirmed by the States, render the federal Constitution *adequate to the exigencies of government and the preservation of the Union.*"

From these two acts, it appears, 1st, that the object of the convention was to establish in these States a *firm national government;* 2nd, that this government was to be such as would be *adequate to the exigencies of government* and *the preservation of the Union;* 3rd, that these purposes were to be effected by *alterations and provisions in the Articles of Confederation*, as it is expressed in the act of Congress, or by *such further provisions as should appear necessary,* as it stands in the recommendatory act from Annapolis; 4th, that the alterations and provisions were to be reported to Congress and to the States in order to be agreed to by the former and confirmed by the latter.

From a comparison and fair construction of these several modes of expression is to be deduced the authority under which the convention acted. They were to frame a *national government,* adequate to the *exigencies of government* and *of the Union;* and to reduce the articles of Confederation into such form as to accomplish these purposes.

There are two rules of construction, dictated by plain reason as well as founded on legal axioms. The one is that every part of the expression ought, if possible, to be allowed some meaning, and be made to conspire to some common end. The other is that where the several parts cannot be made to coincide, the less important should give way to the more important part; the means should be sacrificed to the end, rather than the end to the means.

Suppose, then, that the expressions defining the authority of the convention were irreconcilably at variance with each other; that a *national* and *adequate government* could not possibly, in the judgment of the convention, be effected by *alterations* and *provisions* in the *Articles of Confederation;* which part of the definition ought to have been embraced and which rejected? Which was the more important, which the less important part? Which the end; which the means? Let the most scrupulous expositors of delegated powers, let the most inveterate objectors against those exercised by the convention answer these questions. Let them declare whether it was of most importance to the happiness of the people of America that the Articles of Confederation should be disregarded, and an adequate government be provided, and the Union preserved; or that an adequate government should be omitted, and the Articles of Confederation preserved. Let them declare whether the preservation of these articles was the end for securing which a reform of the government was to be introduced as the means; or whether the establishment of a government adequate to the national happiness was the end at which these articles themselves originally aimed, and to which they ought, as insufficient means, to have been sacrificed.

But is it necessary to suppose that these expressions are absolutely irreconcilable to each other; that no *alterations* or *provisions* in *the Articles of the Confederation* could possibly mold them into a national and adequate government; into such a government as has been proposed by the convention?

No stress, it is presumed, will, in this case, be laid on the *title;* a change of that could never be deemed an exercise of ungranted power. *Alterations* in the body of the instrument are expressly authorized. *New provisions* therein are also expressly authorized. Here then is a power to change the title; to insert new articles; to alter old ones. Must it of necessity be admitted that this power is infringed, so long as a part of the old articles remain? Those who maintain the affirmative ought at least to mark the boundary between authorized and usurped innovations; between that degree of change which lies within the compass of *alterations and further provisions* and that which amounts to a *transmutation* of the government. Will it be said that the alterations ought not to have touched the substances of the Confederation? The States would never have appointed a convention with so much solemnity, nor described its objects with so much latitude, if some *substantial* reform had not been in contemplation. Will it be said that the *fundamental principles* of the Confederation were not within the purview of the convention, and ought not to have been varied? I ask, What are these principles? Do they require that in the establishment of the Constitution the States should be regarded as distinct and independent sovereigns? They are so regarded by the Constitution proposed. Do they require that the members of the government should derive their appointment from the legislatures, not from the people of the States? One branch of the new government is to be appointed by these legislatures; and under the Confederation the delegates to Congress *may all* be appointed immediately by the people, and in two States * are actually so appointed. Do they require that the powers of the government should act on the States and not immediately on individuals? In some instances, as has been shown, the powers of the new government will act on the States in their collective characters. In some instances, also, those of the existing government act immediately on individuals. In cases of capture; of piracy; of the post office; of coins, weights, and measures; of trade with the Indians; of claims under grants of land by different States; and, above all, in the case of trials by courts-martial in the army and navy, by which death may be inflicted without the intervention of a jury, or even of a civil magistrate—in all these cases the powers of the Confederation operate immediately on the persons and interests of individual citizens. Do these fundamental principles require, particularly, that no tax should be levied without the intermediate agency of the States? The Confederation itself authorizes a direct tax, to a certain extent, on the post office. The power of coinage has been so construed by Congress as to levy a tribute immediately from that source also. But pretermitting these instances, was it not an acknowledged object of the convention and the universal expectation of the people that the regulation of trade should be submitted to the general government in such a form as would render it an immediate source of general revenue? Had not Congress repeatedly recommended this measure as not inconsistent with the fundamental principles of the Confederation? Had not every State but one, had not New York herself, so far complied with the plan of Congress as to recognize the *principle* of the innovation? Do these principles, in fine, require that the powers of the general government should be limited, and that, beyond this limit, the

* Connecticut and Rhode Island

States should be left in possession of their sovereignty and independence? We have seen that in the new government, as in the old, the general powers are limited; and that the States, in all unenumerated cases, are left in the enjoyment of their soverign and independent jurisdiction.

The truth is that the great principles of the Constitution proposed by the convention may be considered less as absolutely new than as the expansion of principles which are found in the Articles of Confederation. The misfortune under the latter system has been that these principles are so feeble and confined as to justify all the charges of inefficiency which have been urged against it, and to require a degree of enlargement which gives to the new system the aspect of an entire transformation of the old.

In one particular it is admitted that the convention have departed from the tenor of their commission. Instead of reporting a plan requiring the confirmation *of all the States,* they have reported a plan which is to be confirmed and may be carried into effect by *nine States only*. It is worthy of remark that this objection, though the most plausible, has been the least urged in the publications which have swarmed against the convention. The forbearance can only have proceeded from an irresistible conviction of the absurdity of subjecting the fate of twelve States to the perverseness or corruption of a thirteenth; from the example of inflexible opposition given by *a majority* of one sixtieth of the people of America to a measure approved and called for by the voice of twelve States, comprising fifty-nine sixtieths of the people—an example still fresh in the memory and indignation of every citizen who has felt for the wounded honor and prosperity of his country. As this objection, therefore, has been in a manner waived by those who have criticized the powers of the convention, I dismiss it without further observation.

The *third* point to be inquired into is how far considerations of duty arising out of the case itself could have supplied any defect of regular authority.

In the preceding inquiries the powers of the convention have been analyzed and tried with the same rigor, and by the same rules, as if they had been real and final powers for the establishment of a Constitution for the United

States. We have seen in what manner they have borne the trial even on that supposition. It is time now to recollect that the powers were merely advisory and recommendatory; that they were so meant by the States and so understood by the convention; and that the latter have accordingly planned and proposed a Constitution which is to be of no more consequence than the paper on which it is written, unless it be stamped with the approbation of those to whom it is addressed. This reflection places the subject in a point of view altogether different, and will enable us to judge with propriety of the course taken by the convention.

Let us view the ground on which the convention stood. It may be collected from their proceedings that they were deeply and unanimously impressed with the crisis, which had led their country almost with one voice to make so singular and solemn an experiment for correcting the errors of a system by which this crisis had been produced; that they were no less deeply and unanimously convinced that such a reform as they have proposed was absolutely necessary to effect the purposes of their appointment. It could not be unknown to them that the hopes and expectations of the great body of citizens, throughout this great empire, were turned with the keenest anxiety to the event of their deliberations. They had every reason to believe that the contrary sentiments agitated the minds and bosoms of every external and internal foe to the liberty and prosperity of the United States. They had seen in the origin and progress of the experiment the alacrity with which the *proposition,* made by a single State (Virginia) towards a partial amendment of the Confederation, had been attended to and promoted. They had seen the *liberty assumed* by a *very few* deputies from a *very few* States, convened at Annapolis, of recommending a great and critical object, wholly foreign to their commission, not only justified by the public opinion, but actually carried into effect by twelve out of the thirteen States. They had seen, in a variety of instances, assumptions by Congress, not only of recommendatory, but of operative, powers, warranted, in the public estimation, by occasions and objects infinitely less urgent than those by which their conduct was to be governed. They must have reflected that in all great changes of established governments forms ought to give way to substance; that a rigid adherence in such cases to the former would render nominal and nugatory the transcendent and precious right of the people to "abolish or alter their governments as to them shall seem most likely to effect their safety and happiness," * since it is impossible for the people spontaneously and universally to move in concert towards their object; and it is therefore essential that such changes be instituted by some *informal and unauthorized propositions,* made by some patriotic and respectable citizen or number of citizens. They must have recollected that it was by this irregular and assumed privilege of proposing to the people plans for their safety and happiness that the States were first united against the danger with which they were threatened by their ancient government; that committees and congresses were formed for concentrating their efforts and defending their rights; and that *conventions* were *elected* in *the several States* for establishing the constitutions under which they are now governed; nor could it have been forgotten that no little ill-timed scruples, no zeal for adhering to ordinary forms, were anywhere seen, except in those who wished to indulge, under these masks, their secret enmity to the substance contended for. They must have borne in mind that as the plan to be framed and proposed was to be submitted to *the people themselves,* the disapprobation of this supreme authority would destroy it forever; its approbation blot out antecedent errors and irregularities. It might even have occurred to them that where a disposition to cavil prevailed, their neglect to execute the degree of power vested in them, and still more their recommendation of any measure whatever not warranted by their commission, would not less excite animadversion than a recommendation at once of a measure fully commensurate to the national exigencies.

Had the convention, under all these impressions and in the midst of all these considerations, instead of exercising a manly confidence in their country, by whose confidence they had been so peculiarly distinguished, and of pointing out a system capable, in their judgment, of se-

* Declaration of Independence.

curing its happiness, taken the cold and sullen resolution of disappointing its ardent hopes, of sacrificing substance to forms, of committing the dearest interests of their country to the uncertainties of delay and the hazard of events, let me ask the man who can raise his mind to one elevated conception, who can awaken in his bosom one patriotic emotion, what judgment ought to have been pronounced by the impartial world, by the friends of mankind, by every virtuous citizen, on the conduct and character of this assembly? Or if there be a man whose propensity to condemn is susceptible of no control, let me then ask what sentence he has in reserve for the twelve States who *usurped the power* of sending deputies to the convention, a body utterly unknown to their constitutions; for Congress, who recommended the appointment of this body, equally unknown to the Confederation; and for the State of New York, in particular, which first urged and then complied with this unauthorized interposition?

But that the objectors may be disarmed of every pretext, it shall be granted for a moment that the convention were neither authorized by their commission, nor justified by circumstances in proposing a Constitution for their country: does it follow that the Constitution ought, for that reason alone, to be rejected? If, according to the noble precept, it be lawful to accept good advice even from an enemy, shall we set the ignoble example of refusing such advice even when it is offered by our friends? The prudent inquiry, in all cases, ought surely to be not so much *from whom* the advice comes, as whether the advice be *good*.

The sum of what has been here advanced and proved is that the charge against the convention of exceeding their powers, except in one instance little urged by the objectors, has no foundation to support it; that if they had exceeded their powers, they were not only warranted, but required as the confidential servants of their country, by the circumstances in which they were placed to exercise the liberty which they assumed; and that finally, if they had violated both their powers and their obligations in proposing a Constitution, this ought nevertheless to be embraced, if it be calculated to accomplish the views and happiness of the people of America. How far this character is due to the Constitution is the subject under investigation. PUBLIUS

No. 41: Madison

THE Constitution proposed by the convention may be considered under two general points of view. The FIRST relates to the sum or quantity of power which it vests in the government, including the restraints imposed on the States. The SECOND, to the particular structure of the government and the distribution of this power among its several branches.

Under the first view of the subject, two important questions arise: 1. Whether any part of the powers transferred to the general government be unnecessary or improper? 2. Whether the entire mass of them be dangerous to the portion of jurisdiction left in the several States?

Is the aggregate power of the general government greater than ought to have been vested in it? This is the first question.

It cannot have escaped those who have attended with candor to the arguments employed against the extensive powers of the government that the authors of them have very little considered how far these powers were necessary means of attaining a necessary end. They have chosen rather to dwell on the inconveniences which must be unavoidably blended with all political advantages; and on the possible abuses which must be incident to every power or trust of which a beneficial use can be made. This method of handling the subject cannot impose on the good sense of the people of America. It may display the subtlety of the writer; it may open a boundless field for rhetoric and declamation; it may inflame the passions of the unthinking and may confirm the prejudices of the misthinking: but cool and candid people will at once reflect that the purest of human blessings must have a portion of alloy in them; that the choice must always be made, if not of the lesser evil, at least of the GREATER, not the PERFECT, good; and that in every political institution, a power to advance the public happiness involves a discretion which may be misapplied and abused. They will see, therefore, that in all cases where power is to be conferred, the point first to be decided is whether such a power be necessary to the public good; as the next will be, in case of an affirmative decision, to guard as effectually as possible against a perversion of the power to the public detriment.

That we may form a correct judgment on this subject, it will be proper to review the several powers conferred on the government of the Union; and that this may be the more conveniently done they may be reduced into different classes as they relate to the following different objects: 1. Security against foreign danger; 2. Regulation of the intercourse with foreign nations; 3. Maintenance of harmony and proper intercourse among the States; 4. Certain miscellaneous objects of general utility; 5. Restraint of the States from certain injurious acts; 6. Provisions for giving due efficacy to all these powers.

The powers falling within the first class are those of declaring war and granting letters of marque; of providing armies and fleets; of regulating and calling forth the militia; of levying and borrowing money.

Security against foreign danger is one of the primitive objects of civil society. It is an avowed and essential object of the American Union. The powers requisite for attaining it must be effectually confided to the federal councils.

Is the power of declaring war necessary? No man will answer this question in the negative. It would be superfluous, therefore, to enter into a proof of the affirmative. The existing Confederation establishes this power in the most ample form.

Is the power of raising armies and equipping fleets necessary? This is involved in the foregoing power. It is involved in the power of self-defense.

But was it necessary to give an INDEFINITE POWER of raising TROOPS, as well as providing fleets; and of maintaining both in PEACE as well as in WAR?

The answer to these questions has been too far anticipated in another place to admit an extensive discussion of them in this place. The answer indeed seems to be so obvious and conclusive as scarcely to justify such a discussion in any place. With what color of propriety could the force necessary for defense be limited by those who cannot limit the force of offense? If a federal Constitution could chain the ambition or set bounds to the exertions of all other nations, then indeed might it prudently chain the discretion of its own government and set bounds to the exertions for its own safety.

How could a readiness for war in time of peace be safely prohibited, unless we could prohibit in like manner the preparations and establishments of every hostile nation? The means of security can only be regulated by the means and the danger of attack. They will, in fact, be ever determined by these rules and by no others. It is in vain to oppose constitutional barriers to the impulse of self-preservation. It is worse than in vain; because it plants in the Constitution itself necessary usurpations of power, every precedent of which is a germ of unnecessary and multiplied repetitions. If one nation maintains constantly a disciplined army, ready for the service of ambition or revenge, it obliges the most pacific nations who may be within the reach of its enterprises to take corresponding precautions. The fifteenth century was the unhappy epoch of military establishments in time of peace. They were introduced by Charles VII of France. All Europe has followed, or been forced into, the example. Had the example not been followed by other nations, all Europe must long ago have worn the chains of a universal monarch. Were every nation except France now to disband its peace establishment, the same event might follow. The veteran legions of Rome were an over-match for the undisciplined valor of all other nations, and rendered her mistress of the world.

Not the less true is it that the liberties of Rome proved the final victim to her military triumphs; and that the liberties of Europe, as far as they ever existed, have, with few exceptions, been the price of her military establishments. A standing force, therefore, is a dangerous, at the same time that it may be a necessary, provision. On the smallest scale it has its inconveniences. On an extensive scale its consequences may be fatal. On any scale it is an object of laudable circumspection and precaution. A wise nation will combine all these considerations; and, whilst it does not rashly preclude itself from any resource which may become essential to its safety, will exert all its prudence in diminishing both the necessity and the danger of resorting to one which may be inauspicious to its liberties.

The clearest marks of this prudence are stamped on the proposed Constitution. The Union itself, which it cements and secures, destroys every pretext for a military establishment which could be dangerous. America united, with a handful of troops, or without a single soldier, exhibits a more forbidding posture to foreign ambition than America disunited, with a hundred thousand veterans ready for combat. It was remarked on a former occasion that the want of this pretext had saved the liberties of one nation in Europe. Being rendered by her insular situation and her maritime resources impregnable to the armies of her neighbors, the rulers of Great Britain have never been able, by real or artificial dangers, to cheat the public into an extensive peace establishment. The distance of the United States from the powerful nations of the world gives them the same happy security. A dangerous establishment can never be necessary or plausible, so long as they continue a united people. But let it never for a moment be forgotten that they are indebted for this advantage to their Union alone. The moment of its dissolution will be the date of a new order of things. The fears of the weaker, or the ambition of the stronger States, or Confederacies, will set the same example in the new as Charles VII did in the old world. The example will be followed here from the same motives which produced universal imitation there. Instead of deriving from our situation the precious advantage which Great Britain has derived from hers, the face of America will be but a copy of that of the continent of Europe. It will present liberty everywhere crushed between standing armies and perpetual taxes. The fortunes of disunited America will be even more disastrous than those of Europe. The sources of evil in the latter are confined to her own limits. No superior powers of another quarter of the globe intrigue among her rival nations, inflame their mutual animosities, and render them the instruments of foreign ambition, jealousy, and revenge. In America the miseries springing from her internal jealousies, contentions, and wars would form a part only of her lot. A plentiful addition of evils would have their source in that relation in which Europe stands to this quarter of the earth, and which no other quarter of the earth bears to Europe.

This picture of the consequences of disunion cannot be too highly colored, or too often exhibited. Every man who loves peace, every man who loves his country, every man who loves liberty ought to have it ever before his eyes that he may cherish in his heart a due attachment to the Union of America and be able to set a due value on the means of preserving it.

Next to the effectual establishment of the Union, the best possible precaution against danger from standing armies is a limitation of the term for which revenue may be appropriated to their support. This precaution the Constitution has prudently added. I will not repeat here the observations which I flatter myself have placed this subject in a just and satisfactory light. But it may not be improper to take notice of an argument against this part of the Constitution, which has been drawn from the policy and practice of Great Britain. It is said that the continuance of an army in that kingdom requires an annual vote of the legislature; whereas the American Constitution has lengthened this critical period to two years. This is the form in which the comparison is usually stated to the public: but is it a just form? Is it a fair comparison? Does the British Constitution restrain the parliamentary discretion to one year? Does the American impose on the Congress appropriations for two years? On the contrary, it cannot be unknown to the authors of the fallacy themselves that the British Constitution fixes no limit whatever to the discretion of the legislature, and that the American ties down the legislature to two years as the longest admissible term.

Had the argument from the British example been truly stated, it would have stood thus: The term for which supplies may be appropriated to the army establishment, though unlimited by the British Constitution, has nevertheless, in practice, been limited by parliamentary discretion to a single year. Now, if in Great Britain, where the House of Commons is elected for seven years; where so great a proportion of the members are elected by so small a proportion of the people; where the electors are so corrupted by the representatives, and the representatives so corrupted by the Crown, the representative body can possess a power to make appropriations to the army for an indefinite term, without desiring, or without daring, to extend the term beyond a single year, ought not suspicion herself to blush, in pretending that the representatives of the United States, elected FREELY by the WHOLE BODY of the people every SECOND YEAR, cannot be safely intrusted with the discretion over such appropriations, expressly limited to the short period of TWO YEARS?

A bad cause seldom fails to betray itself. Of this truth the management of the opposition to the federal government is an unvaried exemplification. But among all the blunders which have been committed, none is more striking than the attempt to enlist on that side the prudent jealousy entertained by the people of standing armies. The attempt has awakened fully the public attention to that important subject; and has led to investigations which must terminate in a thorough and universal conviction, not only that the Constitution has provided the most effectual guards against danger from that quarter, but that nothing short of a Constitution fully adequate to the national defense and the preservation of the Union can save America from as many standing armies as it may be split into States or Confederacies, and from such a progressive augmentation of these establishments in each as will render them as burdensome to the properties and ominous to the liberties of the people as any establishment that can become necessary under a united and efficient government must be tolerable to the former and safe to the latter.

The palpable necessity of the power to provide and maintain a navy has protected that part of the Constitution against a spirit of censure which has spared few other parts. It must, indeed, be numbered among the greatest blessings of America that as her Union will be the only source of her maritime strength, so this will be a principal source of her security against danger from abroad. In this respect our situation bears another likeness to the insular advantage of Great Britain. The batteries most capable of repelling foreign enterprises on our safety are happily such as can never be turned by a perfidious government against our liberties.

The inhabitants of the Atlantic frontier are all of them deeply interested in this provision for naval protection, and if they have hitherto been suffered to sleep quietly in their beds; if their property has remained safe against the predatory spirit of licentious adventurers; if their maritime towns have not yet been compelled to ransom themselves from the terrors of a conflagration by yielding to the exactions of daring and sudden invaders, these instances of good fortune are not to be ascribed to the capacity of the existing government for the protection of those from whom it claims allegiance, but to causes that are fugitive and fallacious. If we except perhaps Virginia and Maryland, which are peculiarly vulnerable on their eastern frontiers, no part of the Union ought to feel more anxiety on this subject than New York. Her seacoast is extensive. A very important district of the State is an island. The State itself is penetrated by a large navigable river for more than fifty leagues. The great emporium of its commerce, the great reservoir of its wealth, lies every moment at the mercy of events, and may also be regarded as a hostage for ignominious compliances with the dictates of a foreign enemy, or even with the rapacious demands of pirates and barbarians. Should a war be the result of the precarious situation of European affairs, and all the unruly passions attending it be let loose on the ocean, our escape from insults and depredations, not only on that element, but every part of the other bordering on it, will be truly miraculous. In the present condition of America, the States more immediately exposed to these calamities have nothing to hope from the phantom of a general government which now exists; and if their single resources were equal to the task of fortifying themselves against the danger, the object to be protected would be almost consumed by the means of protecting them.

The power of regulating and calling forth the militia has been already sufficiently vindicated and explained.

The power of levying and borrowing money, being the sinew of that which is to be exerted in the national defense, is properly thrown into the same class with it. This power, also, has been examined already with such attention, and has, I trust, been clearly shown to be necessary, both in the extent and form given to it by the Constitution. I will address one additional reflection only to those who contend that the power ought to have been restrained to external taxation — by which they mean taxes on articles imported from other countries. It cannot be doubted that this will always be a valuable source of revenue; that for a considerable time it must be a principal source; that at this moment it is an essential one. But we may form very mistaken ideas on this subject, if we do not call to mind in our calculations that the extent of revenue drawn from foreign commerce must vary with the variations, both in the extent and the kind of imports; and that these variations do not correspond with the progress of population, which must be the general measure of the public wants. As long as agriculture continues the sole field of labor, the importation of manufactures must increase as the consumers multiply. As soon as domestic manufactures are begun by the hands not called for by agriculture, the imported manufactures will decrease as the numbers of people increase. In a more remote stage, the imports may consist in a considerable part of raw materials, which will be wrought into articles for exportation, and will, therefore, require rather the encouragement of bounties than to be loaded with discouraging duties. A system of government meant for duration ought to contemplate these revolutions and be able to accommodate itself to them.

Some who have not denied the necessity of the power of taxation have grounded a very fierce attack against the Constitution, on the language in which it is defined. It has been urged and echoed that the power "to lay and collect taxes, duties, imposts, and excises, to pay the debts, and provide for the common defense and general welfare of the United States," amounts to an unlimited commission to exercise every power which may be alleged to be necessary for the common defense or general welfare. No stronger proof could be given of the distress under which these writers labor for objections, than their stooping to such a misconstruction.

Had no other enumeration or definition of the powers of the Congress been found in the Constitution than the general expressions just cited, the authors of the objection might have had some color for it; though it would have been difficult to find a reason for so awkward a form of describing an authority to legislate in all possible cases. A power to destroy the freedom of the press, the trial by jury, or even to regulate the course of descents, or the forms of conveyances, must be very singularly expressed by the terms "to raise money for the general welfare."

But what color can the objection have, when a specification of the objects alluded to by these general terms immediately follows and is not even separated by a longer pause than a semicolon? If the different parts of the same instrument ought to be so expounded as to give meaning to every part which will bear it, shall one part of the same sentence be excluded altogether from a share in the meaning; and shall the more doubtful and indefinite terms be retained in their full extent, and the clear and precise expressions be denied any signification whatsoever? For what purpose could the enumeration of particular powers be inserted, if these and all others were meant to be included in the preceding general power? Nothing is more natural nor common than first to use a general phrase, and then to explain and qualify it by a recital of particulars. But the idea of an enumeration of particulars which neither explain nor qualify the general meaning, and can have no other effect than to confound and mislead, is an absurdity, which, as we are reduced to the dilemma of charging either on the authors of the objection or on the authors of the Constitution, we must take the liberty of supposing had not its origin with the latter.

The objection here is the more extraordinary, as it appears that the language used by the convention is a copy from the Articles of Confederation. The objects of the Union among the States, as described in article third, are "their common defense, security of their liberties, and mutual and general welfare." The terms of article eighth are still more identical: "All charges of war and all other expenses that shall be incurred for the common defense or general welfare and allowed by the United States in Congress shall be defrayed out of a common treasury," etc. A similar language again occurs in article ninth. Construe either of these articles by the rules which would justify the construction put on the new Constitution, and they vest in the existing Congress a power to legislate in all cases whatsoever. But what would have been thought of that assembly, if, attaching themselves to these general expressions and disregarding the specifications which ascertain and limit their import, they had exercised an unlimited power of providing for the common defense and general welfare? I appeal to the objectors themselves, whether they would in that case have employed the same reasoning in justification of Congress as they now make use of against the convention. How difficult it is for error to escape its own condemnation.

PUBLIUS

No. 42: Madison

THE *second* class of powers lodged in the general government consist of those which regulate the intercourse with foreign nations, to wit: to make treaties; to send and receive ambassadors, other public ministers, and consuls; to define and punish piracies and felonies committed on the high seas, and offenses against the law of nations; to regulate foreign commerce, including a power to prohibit, after the year 1808, the importation of slaves, and to lay an intermediate duty of ten dollars per head, as a discouragement to such importations.

This class of powers forms an obvious and essential branch of the federal administration. If we are to be one nation in any respect, it clearly ought to be in respect to other nations.

The powers to make treaties and to send and receive ambassadors speak their own propriety. Both of them are comprised in the Articles of Confederation, with this difference only, that the former is disembarrassed by the plan of the convention, of an exception under which treaties might be substantially frustrated by regulations of the States; and that a power of appointing and receiving "other public ministers and consuls" is expressly and very properly added to the former provision concerning ambassadors. The term ambassador, if taken strictly, as seems to be required by the second of the

Articles of Confederation, comprehends the highest grade only of public ministers, and excludes the grades which the United States will be most likely to prefer, where foreign embassies may be necessary. And under no latitude of construction will the term comprehend consuls. Yet it has been found expedient, and has been the practice of Congress, to employ the inferior grades of public ministers and to send and receive consuls.

It is true that where treaties of commerce stipulate for the mutual appointment of consuls, whose functions are connected with commerce, the admission of foreign consuls may fall within the power of making commercial treaties; and that where no such treaties exist, the mission of American consuls into foreign countries may *perhaps* be covered under the authority, given by the ninth article of the Confederation, to appoint all such civil officers as may be necessary for managing the general affairs of the United States. But the admission of consuls into the United States, where no previous treaty has stipulated it, seems to have been nowhere provided for. A supply of the omission is one of the lesser instances in which the convention have improved on the model before them. But the most minute provisions become important when they tend to obviate the necessity or the pretext for gradual and unobserved usurpations of power. A list of the cases in which Congress have been betrayed, or forced by the defects of the Confederation, into violations of their chartered authorities would not a little surprise those who have paid no attention to the subject; and would be no inconsiderable argument in favor of the new Constitution, which seems to have provided no less studiously for the lesser than the more obvious and striking defects of the old.

The power to define and punish piracies and felonies committed on the high seas and offenses against the law of nations belongs with equal propriety to the general government, and is a still greater improvement on the Articles of Confederation. These articles contain no provision for the case of offenses against the law of nations; and consequently leave it in the power of any indiscreet member to embroil the Confederacy with foreign nations. The provision of the federal articles on the subject of piracies and felonies extends no further than to the establishment of courts for the trial of these offenses. The definition of piracies might, perhaps, without inconveniency, be left to the law of nations; though a legislative definition of them is found in most municipal codes. A definition of felonies on the high seas is evidently requisite. Felony is a term of loose signification even in the common law of England; and of various import in the statute law of that kingdom. But neither the common nor the statute law of that, or of any other nation, ought to be a standard for the proceedings of this, unless previously made its own by legislative adoption. The meaning of the term, as defined in the codes of the several States, would be as impracticable as the former would be a dishonorable and illegitimate guide. It is not precisely the same in any two of the States; and varies in each with every revision of its criminal laws. For the sake of certainty and uniformity, therefore, the power of defining felonies in this case was in every respect necessary and proper.

The regulation of foreign commerce, having fallen within several views which have been taken of this subject, has been too fully discussed to need additional proofs here of its being properly submitted to the federal administration.

It were doubtless to be wished that the power of prohibiting the importation of slaves had not been postponed until the year 1808, or rather that it had been suffered to have immediate operation. But it is not difficult to account either for this restriction on the general government, or for the manner in which the whole clause is expressed. It ought to be considered as a great point gained in favor of humanity that a period of twenty years may terminate forever, within these States, a traffic which has so long and so loudly upbraided the barbarism of modern policy; that within that period it will receive a considerable discouragement from the federal government, and may be totally abolished, by a concurrence of the few States which continue the unnatural traffic in the prohibitory example which has been given by so great a majority of the Union. Happy would it be for the unfortunate Africans if an equal prospect lay before them of being redeemed from the oppressions of their European brethren!

Attempts have been made to pervert this clause into an objection against the Constitution by representing it on one side as a criminal toleration of an illicit practice, and on another as calculated to prevent voluntary and beneficial emigrations from Europe to America. I mention these misconstructions not with a view to give them an answer, for they deserve none, but as specimens of the manner and spirit in which some have thought fit to conduct their opposition to the proposed government.

The powers included in the *third* class are those which provide for the harmony and proper intercourse among the States.

Under this head might be included the particular restraints imposed on the authority of the States and certain powers of the judicial department; for the former are reserved for a distinct class and the latter will be particularly examined when we arrive at the structure and organization of the government. I shall confine myself to a cursory review of the remaining powers comprehended under this third description, to wit: to regulate commerce among the several States and the Indian tribes; to coin money, regulate the value thereof and of foreign coin; to provide for the punishment of counterfeiting the current coin and securities of the United States; to fix the standard of weights and measures; to establish a uniform rule of naturalization, and uniform laws of bankruptcy; to prescribe the manner in which the public acts, records, and judicial proceedings of each State shall be proved, and the effect they shall have in other States; and to establish post offices and post roads.

The defect of power in the existing Confederacy to regulate the commerce between its several members is in the number of those which have been clearly pointed out by experience. To the proofs and remarks which former papers have brought into view on this subject, it may be added that without this supplemental provision, the great and essential power of regulating foreign commerce would have been incomplete and ineffectual. A very material object of this power was the relief of the States which import and export through other States from the improper contributions levied on them by the latter. Were these at liberty to regulate the trade between State and State, it must be foreseen that ways would be found out to load the articles of import and export, during the passage through their jurisdiction, with duties which would fall on the makers of the latter and the consumers of the former. We may be assured by past experience that such a practice would be introduced by future contrivances; and both by that and a common knowledge of human affairs that it would nourish unceasing animosities, and not improbably terminate in serious interruptions of the public tranquillity. To those who do not view the question through the medium of passion or of interest, the desire of the commercial States to collect, in any form, an indirect revenue from their uncommercial neighbors must appear not less impolitic than it is unfair; since it would stimulate the injured party by resentment as well as interest to resort to less convenient channels for their foreign trade. But the mild voice of reason, pleading the cause of an enlarged and permanent interest, is but too often drowned, before public bodies as well as individuals, by the clamors of an impatient avidity for immediate and immoderate gain.

The necessity of a superintending authority over the reciprocal trade of confederated States has been illustrated by other examples as well as our own. In Switzerland, where the Union is so very slight, each canton is obliged to allow to merchandises a passage through its jurisdiction into other cantons, without an augmentation of the tolls. In Germany it is a law of the empire that the princes and states shall not lay tolls or customs on bridges, rivers, or passages, without the consent of the emperor and the diet; though it appears from a quotation in an antecedent paper that the practice in this, as in many other instances in that confederacy, has not followed the law, and has produced there the mischiefs which have been foreseen here. Among the restraints imposed by the Union of the Netherlands on its members, one is that they shall not establish imposts disadvantageous to their neighbors without the general permission.

The regulation of commerce with the Indian tribes is very properly unfettered from two limitations in the Articles of Confederation, which render the provision obscure and contradictory. The power is there restrained to Indians, not members of any of the States, and is not to violate or infringe the legislative right of any State within its own limits. What description of Indians are to be deemed members of a State is not yet settled, and has been a question of frequent perplexity and contention in the federal councils. And how the trade with Indians, though not members of a State, yet residing within its legislative jurisdiction can be regulated by an external authority, without so far intruding on the internal rights of legislation, is absolutely incomprehensible. This is not the only case in which the Articles of Confederation have inconsiderately endeavored to accomplish impossibilities; to reconcile a partial sovereignty in the Union, with complete sovereignty in the States; to subvert a mathematical axiom by taking away a part and letting the whole remain.

All that need be remarked on the power to coin money, regulate the value thereof, and of foreign coin, is that by providing for this last case, the Constitution has supplied a material omission in the Articles of Confederation. The authority of the existing Congress is restrained to the regulation of coin *struck* by their own authority, or that of the respective States. It must be seen at once that the proposed uniformity in the *value* of the current coin might be destroyed by subjecting that of foreign coin to the different regulations of the different States.

The punishment of counterfeiting the public securities, as well as the current coin, is submitted of course to that authority which is to secure the value of both.

The regulation of weights and measures is transferred from the Articles of Confederation, and is founded on like considerations with the preceding power of regulating coin.

The dissimilarity in the rules of naturalization has long been remarked as a fault in our system, and as laying a foundation for intricate and delicate questions. In the fourth article of the Confederation, it is declared "that the *free inhabitants* of each of these States, paupers, vagabonds, and fugitives from justice excepted, shall be entitled to all privileges and immunities of *free citizens* in the several States; and *the people* of each State shall, in every other, enjoy all the privileges of trade and commerce," etc. There is a confusion of language here which is remarkable. Why the terms *free inhabitants* are used in one part of the article, *free citizens* in another, and *people* in another; or what was meant by superadding to "all privileges and immunities of free citizens," "all the privileges of trade and commerce," cannot easily be determined. It seems to be a construction scarcely avoidable, however, that those who come under the denomination of *free inhabitants* of a State, although not citizens of such State, are entitled, in every other State, to all the privileges of *free citizens* of the latter; that is, to greater privileges than they may be entitled to in their own State: so that it may be in the power of a particular State, or rather every State is laid under a necessity not only to confer the rights of citizenship in other States upon any whom it may admit to such rights within itself, but upon any whom it may allow to become inhabitants within its jurisdiction. But were an exposition of the term "inhabitants" to be admitted which would confine the stipulated privileges to citizens alone, the difficulty is diminished only, not removed. The very improper power would still be retained by each State of naturalizing aliens in every other State. In one State, residence for a short term confirms all the rights of citizenship: in another, qualifications of greater importance are required. An alien, therefore, legally incapacitated for certain rights in the latter, may, by previous residence only in the former, elude his incapacity; and thus the law of one State be preposterously rendered paramount to the law of another, within the jurisdiction of the other. We owe it to mere casualty that very serious embarrassments on this subject have been hitherto escaped. By the laws of several States, certain descriptions of aliens, who had rendered themselves obnoxious, were laid under interdicts inconsistent not only with the rights of citizenship but with the privilege of residence. What would have been the consequence if such persons, by residence or otherwise, had acquired the character of citizens under the laws of another State, and then asserted their rights as such, both to residence and citizenship, within the State proscribing them? Whatever the legal consequences might have been, other consequences would probably have resulted of too serious a nature not to be provided against. The new Constitution has accordingly, with great propriety, made provision against them, and all others proceeding from the defect of the Confederation on this head, by authorizing the general government to establish a uniform rule of naturalization throughout the United States.

The power of establishing uniform laws of bankruptcy is so intimately connected with the regulation of commerce, and will prevent so many frauds where the parties or their property may lie or be removed into different States, that the expediency of it seems not likely to be drawn into question.

The power of prescribing by general laws the manner in which the public acts, records, and judicial proceedings of each State shall be proved, and the effect they shall have in other States, is an evident and valuable improvement on the clause relating to this subject in the Articles of Confederation. The meaning of the latter is extremely indeterminate, and can be of little importance under any interpretation which it will bear. The power here established may be rendered a very convenient instrument of justice, and be particularly beneficial on the borders of contiguous States, where the effects liable to justice may be suddenly and secretly translated in any stage of the process within a foreign jurisdiction.

The power of establishing post roads must, in every view, be a harmless power and may, perhaps, by judicious management become productive of great public conveniency. Nothing which tends to facilitate the intercourse between the States can be deemed unworthy of the public care.

PUBLIUS

No. 43: Madison

THE *fourth* class comprises the following miscellaneous powers:

1. A power "to promote the progress of science and useful arts by securing, for a limited time, to authors and inventors the exclusive right to their respective writings and discoveries."

The utility of this power will scarcely be questioned. The copyright of authors has been solemnly adjudged in Great Britain to be a right of common law. The right to useful inventions seems with equal reason to belong to the inventors. The public good fully coincides in both cases with the claims of individuals. The States cannot separately make effectual provision for either of the cases, and most of them have anticipated the decision of this point by laws passed at the instance of Congress.

2. "To exercise exclusive legislation, in all cases whatsoever, over such district (not exceeding ten miles square) as may, by cession of particular States and the acceptance of Congress, become the seat of the government of the United States; and to exercise like authority over all places purchased by the consent of the legislatures of the States in which the same shall be, for the erection of forts, magazines, arsenals, dockyards, and other needful buildings."

The indispensable necessity of complete authority at the seat of government carries its own evidence with it. It is a power exercised by every legislature of the Union, I might say of the world, by virtue of its general supremacy. Without it not only the public authority might be insulted and its proceedings interrupted with impunity, but a dependence of the members of the general government on the State comprehending the seat of the government for protection in the exercise of their duty might bring on the national councils an imputation of awe or influence equally dishonorable to the government and dissatisfactory to the other members of the Confederacy. This consideration has the more weight as the gradual accumulation of public improvements at the stationary residence of the government would be both too great a public pledge to be left in the hands of a single State, and would create so many obstacles to a removal of the government, as still further to abridge its necessary independence. The extent of this federal district is sufficiently circumscribed to satisfy every jealousy of an opposite nature. And as it is to be appropriated to this use with the consent of the State ceding it; as the State will no doubt provide in the compact for the rights and the consent of the citizens inhabiting it; as the inhabitants will find sufficient inducements of interest to become willing parties to the cession; as they will have had their voice in the election of the government which is to exercise authority over them; as a municipal legislature for local purposes, derived from their own suffrages, will of course be allowed them; and as the authority of the legislature of the State, and of the inhabitants of the ceded part of it, to concur in the cession will be derived from the whole people of the State in their adoption of the Constitution, every imaginable objection seems to be obviated.

The necessity of a like authority over forts, magazines, etc., established by the general government, is not less evident. The public money expended on such places, and the public property deposited in them, require that they should be exempt from the authority of the particular State. Nor would it be proper for the places on which the security of the entire Union may depend to be in any degree dependent on a particular member of it. All objections and scruples are here also obviated by requiring the concurrence of the States concerned in every such establishment.

3. "To declare the punishment of treason, but no attainder of treason shall work corruption of blood, or forfeiture, except during the life of the person attainted."

As treason may be committed against the United States, the authority of the United States ought to be enabled to punish it. But as new-fangled and artificial treasons have been the great engines by which violent factions, the natural offspring of free government, have usually wreaked their alternate malignity on each other, the convention have, with great judgment, opposed a barrier to this peculiar danger, by inserting a constitutional definition of the crime, fixing the proof necessary for conviction of it, and restraining the Congress, even in punishing it, from extending the consequences of guilt beyond the person of its author.

4. "To admit new States into the Union; but no new State shall be formed or erected within the jurisdiction of any other State; nor any State be formed by the junction of two or more States, or parts of States, without the consent of the legislatures of the States concerned, as well as of the Congress."

In the Articles of Confederation, no provision is found on this important subject. Canada was to be admitted of right, on her joining in the measures of the United States; and the other *colonies,* by which were evidently meant the other British colonies, at the discretion of nine States. The eventual establishment of *new States* seems to have been overlooked by the compilers of that instrument. We have seen the inconvenience of this omission, and the assumption of power into which Congress have been led by it. With great propriety, therefore, has the new system supplied the defect. The general precaution that no new States shall be formed without the concurrence of the federal authority and that of the States concerned is consonant to the principles which ought to govern such transactions. The particular precaution against the erection of new States, by the partition of a State without its consent, quiets the jealousy of the larger States; as that of the smaller is quieted by a like precaution against a junction of States without their consent.

5. "To dispose of and make all needful rules and regulations respecting the territory or other property belonging to the United States, with a proviso that nothing in the Constitution shall be so construed as to prejudice any claims of the United States, or of any particular State."

This is a power of very great importance, and required by considerations similar to those which show the propriety of the former. The proviso annexed is proper in itself, and was probably rendered absolutely necessary by jealousies and questions concerning the Western territory sufficiently known to the public.

6. "To guarantee to every State in the Union a republican form of government; to protect each of them against invasion; and on application of the legislature, or of the executive (when the legislature cannot be convened), against domestic violence."

In a confederacy founded on republican principles, and composed of republican members, the superintending government ought clearly to possess authority to defend the system against aristocratic or monarchical innovations. The more intimate the nature of such a union may be, the greater interest have the members in the political institutions of each other; and the greater right to insist that the forms of government under which the compact was entered into should be *substantially* maintained. But a right implies a remedy; and where else could the remedy be deposited than where it is deposited by the Constitution? Governments of dissimilar principles and forms have been found less adapted to a federal coalition of any sort than those of a kindred nature. "As the confederate republic of Germany," says Montesquieu, "consists of free cities and petty states, subject to different princes, experience shows us that it is more imperfect than that of Holland and Switzerland." "Greece was undone," he adds, "as soon as the king of Macedon obtained a seat among the Amphictyons." In the latter case, no doubt, the disproportionate force, as well as the monarchical form of the new confederate, had its share of influence on the events. It may possibly be asked what need there could be of such a precaution, and whether it may not become a pretext for alterations in the State governments, without the concurrence of the States themselves. These questions admit of ready answers. If the interposition of the general government should not be needed, the provision for such an event will be a harmless superfluity only in the Constitution. But who can say what experiments may be produced by the caprice of particular States, by the ambition of enterprising leaders, or by the intrigues and influence of foreign powers? To the second question it may be answered that if the general government should interpose by virtue of this constitutional authority, it will be, of course, bound to pursue the authority. But the authority extends no further than to a *guaranty* of a republican form of government, which supposes a pre-existing government of the form which is to be guaranteed. As long, therefore, as the existing republican forms are continued by the States, they are guaranteed by the federal Constitution. Whenever the States may choose to substitute other republican forms, they have a right to do so and to claim the federal guaranty for the latter. The only restriction imposed on them is that they shall not exchange republican for anti-republican Constitutions; a restriction which, it is presumed, will hardly be considered as a grievance.

A protection against invasion is due from every society to the parts composing it. The latitude of the expression here used seems to secure each State not only against foreign hostility, but against ambitious or vindictive enterprises of its more powerful neighbors. The history both of ancient and modern confederacies proves that the weaker members of the Union ought not to be insensible to the policy of this article.

Protection against domestic violence is added with equal propriety. It has been remarked that even among the Swiss cantons, which, properly speaking, are not under one government, provision is made for this object; and the history of that league informs us that mutual aid is frequently claimed and afforded; and as well by the most democratic as the other cantons. A recent and well-known event among ourselves has warned us to be prepared for emergencies of a like nature.

At first view, it might seem not to square with the republican theory to suppose either that a majority have not the right, or that a minority will have the force, to subvert a government; and consequently that the federal interposition can never be required but when it would be improper. But theoretic reasoning, in this as in most other cases, must be qualified by the lessons of practice. Why may not illicit combinations, for purposes of violence, be formed as well by a majority of a State, especially a small State, as by a majority of a county, or a district of the same State; and if the authority of the State ought, in the latter case, to protect the local magistracy, ought not the federal authority, in the former, to support the State authority? Besides, there are certain parts of the State constitutions which are so interwoven with the federal Constitution that a violent blow cannot be given to the one without communicating the wound to the other. Insurrections in a State will rarely induce a federal interposition, unless the number concerned in them bear some proportion to the friends of government. It will be much better that the violence in such cases should be repressed by the superintending power, than that the majority should be left to maintain their cause by a bloody and obstinate contest. The existence of a right to interpose will generally prevent the necessity of exerting it.

Is it true that force and right are necessarily on the same side in republican governments? May not the minor party possess such a superiority of pecuniary resources, of military talents and experience, or of secret succors from foreign powers, as will render it superior also in an appeal to the sword? May not a more compact and advantageous position turn the scale on the same side against a superior number so situated as to be less capable of a prompt and collected exertion of its strength? Nothing can be more chimerical than to imagine that in a trial of actual force victory may be calculated by the rules which prevail in a census of the inhabitants, or which determine the event of an election! May it not happen, in fine, that the minority of *citizens* may become a majority of *persons,* by the accession of alien residents, of a casual concourse of adventurers, or of those whom the constitution of the State has not admitted to the rights of suffrage? I take no notice of an unhappy species of population abounding in some of the States, who, during the calm of regular government, are sunk below the level of men; but who, in the tempestuous scenes of civil violence, may emerge into the human character and give a superiority of strength to any party with which they may associate themselves.

In cases where it may be doubtful on which side justice lies, what better umpires could be desired by two violent factions, flying to arms and tearing a State to pieces, than the representatives of confederate States, not heated by the local flame? To the impartiality of judges, they would unite the affection of friends. Happy would it be if such a remedy for its infirmities could be enjoyed by all free governments; if a project equally effectual could be established for the universal peace of mankind!

Should it be asked what is to be the redress for an insurrection pervading all the States, and comprising a superiority of the entire force, though not a constitutional right? the answer must be that such a case, as it would be without the compass of human remedies, so it is fortunately not within the compass of human probability; and that it is a sufficient recommendation of the federal Constitution that it diminishes the risk of a calamity for which no possible constitution can provide a cure.

Among the advantages of a confederate republic enumerated by Montesquieu, an important one is "that should a popular insurrection happen in one of the States, the others are able to quell it. Should abuses creep into one part, they are reformed by those that remain sound."

7. "To consider all debts contracted and engagements entered into before the adoption of this Constitution as being no less valid against the United States under this Constitution than under the Confederation."

This can only be considered as a declaratory proposition; and may have been inserted, among other reasons, for the satisfaction of the foreign creditors of the United States, who cannot be strangers to the pretended doctrine that a change in the political form of civil society has the magical effect of dissolving its moral obligations.

Among the lesser criticisms which have been exercised on the Constitution, it has been remarked that the validity of engagements ought to have been asserted in favor of the United States, as well as against them; and in the spirit which usually characterizes little critics, the omission has been transformed and magnified into a plot against the national rights. The authors of this discovery may be told what few others need to be informed of, that as engagements are in their nature reciprocal, an assertion of their validity on one side necessarily involves a validity on the other side; and that as the article is merely declaratory, the establishment of the principle in one case is sufficient for every case. They may be further told that every constitution must limit its precautions to dangers that are not altogether imaginary; and that no real danger can exist that the government would *dare,* with or even without this constitutional declaration before it, to remit the debts justly due to the public on the pretext here condemned.

8. "To provide for amendments to be ratified by three fourths of the States under two exceptions only."

That useful alterations will be suggested by experience could not but be foreseen. It was requisite, therefore, that a mode for introducing them should be provided. The mode preferred by the convention seems to be stamped with every mark of propriety. It guards equally against that extreme facility, which would render the Constitution too mutable; and that extreme difficulty, which might perpetuate its discovered faults. It, moreover, equally enables the general and the State governments to originate the amendment of errors, as they may be pointed out by the experience on one side, or on the other. The exception in favor of the equality of suffrage in the Senate was probably meant as a palladium to the residuary sovereignty of the States, implied and secured by that principle of representation in one branch of the legislature; and was probably insisted on by the States particularly attached to that equality. The other exception must have been admitted on the same considerations which produced the privilege defended by it.

9. "The ratification of the conventions of nine States shall be sufficient for the establishment of this Constitution between the States, ratifying the same."

This article speaks for itself. The express authority of the people alone could give due validity to the Constitution. To have required the unanimous ratification of the thirteen States would have subjected the essential interests of the whole to the caprice or corruption of a single member. It would have marked a want of foresight in the convention, which our own experience would have rendered inexcusable.

Two questions of a very delicate nature present themselves on this occasion: 1. On what principle the Confederation, which stands in the solemn form of a compact among the States, can be superseded without the unanimous consent of the parties to it? 2. What relation is to subsist between the nine or more States ratifying the Constitution, and the remaining few who do not become parties to it?

The first question is answered at once by recurring to the absolute necessity of the case; to the great principle of self-preservation; to the transcendent law of nature and of nature's God, which declares that the safety and happiness of society are the objects at which all political institutions aim and to which all such institutions must be sacrificed. *Perhaps,* also, an answer may be found without searching beyond the principles of the compact itself. It has been heretofore noted among the defects of the Confederation that in many of the States it had received no higher sanction than a mere legislative ratification. The principle of reciprocality seems to require that its obligation on the other States should be reduced to the same standard. A compact between independent sovereigns, founded on ordinary acts of legislative authority, can pretend to no higher validity than a league or treaty between the parties. It is an established doctrine on the subject of treaties that all the articles are mutually conditions of each other; that a breach of any one article is a breach of the whole treaty; and that a breach, committed by either of the parties, absolves the others, and authorizes them, if they please, to pronounce the compact violated and void. Should it unhappily be necessary to appeal to these delicate truths for a justification for dispensing with the consent of particular States to a dissolution of the federal pact, will not the complaining parties find it a difficult task to answer the *multiplied* and *important* infractions with which they may be confronted? The time has been when it was incumbent on us all to veil the ideas which this paragraph exhibits. The scene is now changed, and with it the part which the same motives dictate.

The second question is not less delicate; and the flattering prospect of its being merely hypothetical forbids an over-curious discussion of it. It is one of those cases which must be left to provide for itself. In general, it may be observed that although no political relation can subsist between the assenting and dissenting States, yet the moral relations will remain uncanceled. The claims of justice, both on one side and on the other, will be in force, and must be fulfilled; the rights of humanity must in all cases be duly and mutually respected; whilst considerations of a common interest, and, above all, the remembrance of the endearing scenes which are past, and the anticipation of a speedy triumph over the obstacles to reunion, will, it is hoped, not urge in vain *moderation* on one side, and *prudence* on the other. PUBLIUS

No. 44: Madison

A *fifth* class of provisions in favor of the federal authority consists of the following restrictions on the authority of the several States.

1. "No State shall enter into any treaty, alliance, or confederation; grant letters of marque and reprisal; coin money; emit bills of credit; make anything but gold and silver a legal tender in payment of debts; pass any bill of

attainder, *ex post facto* law, or law impairing the obligation of contracts; or grant any title of nobility."

The prohibition against treaties, alliances, and confederations makes a part of the existing articles of Union; and for reasons which need no explanation, is copied into the new Constitution. The prohibition of letters of marque is another part of the old system, but is somewhat extended in the new. According to the former, letters of marque could be granted by the States after a declaration of war; according to the latter, these licenses must be obtained, as well during war as previous to its declaration, from the government of the United States. This alteration is fully justified by the advantage of uniformity in all points which relate to foreign powers; and of immediate responsibility to the nation in all those for whose conduct the nation itself is to be responsible.

The right of coining money, which is here taken from the States, was left in their hands by the Confederation as a concurrent right with that of Congress, under an exception in favor of the exclusive right of Congress to regulate the alloy and value. In this instance, also, the new provision is an improvement on the old. Whilst the alloy and value depended on the general authority, a right of coinage in the particular States could have no other effect than to multiply expensive mints and diversify the forms and weights of the circulating pieces. The latter inconveniency defeats one purpose for which the power was originally submitted to the federal head; and as far as the former might prevent an inconvenient remittance of gold and silver to the central mint for recoinage, the end can be as well attained by local mints established under the general authority.

The extension of the prohibition to bills of credit must give pleasure to every citizen in proportion to his love of justice and his knowledge of the true springs of public prosperity. The loss which America has sustained since the peace, from the pestilent effects of paper money on the necessary confidence between man and man, on the necessary confidence in the public councils, on the industry and morals of the people, and on the character of republican government, constitutes an enormous debt against the States chargeable with this unadvised measure, which must long remain unsatisfied; or rather an accumulation of guilt, which can be expiated no otherwise than by a voluntary sacrifice on the altar of justice of the power which has been the instrument of it. In addition to these persuasive considerations, it may be observed that the same reasons which show the necessity of denying to the States the power of regulating coin prove with equal force that they ought not to be at liberty to substitute a paper medium in the place of coin. Had every State a right to regulate the value of its coin, there might be as many different currencies as States, and thus the intercourse among them would be impeded; retrospective alterations in its value might be made, and thus the citizens of other States be injured, and animosities be kindled among the States themselves. The subjects of foreign powers might suffer from the same cause, and hence the Union be discredited and embroiled by the indiscretion of a single member. No one of these mischiefs is less incident to a power in the States to emit paper money than to coin gold or silver. The power to make anything but gold and silver a tender in payment of debts is withdrawn from the States on the same principle with that of issuing a paper currency.

Bills of attainder, *ex post facto* laws, and laws impairing the obligation of contracts, are contrary to the first principles of the social compact and to every principle of sound legislation. The two former are expressly prohibited by the declarations prefixed to some of the State constitutions, and all of them are prohibited by the spirit and scope of these fundamental charters. Our own experience has taught us, nevertheless, that additional fences against these dangers ought not to be omitted. Very properly, therefore, have the convention added this constitutional bulwark in favor of personal security and private rights; and I am much deceived if they have not, in so doing, as faithfully consulted the genuine sentiments as the undoubted interests of their constituents. The sober people of America are weary of the fluctuating policy which has directed the public councils. They have seen with regret and indignation that sudden changes and legislative interferences, in cases affecting personal rights, become jobs in the hands of enterprising and influential speculators, and snares to the more industrious and less informed part of the community. They have seen, too, that one legislative interference is but the first link of a long chain of repetitions, every subsequent interference being naturally produced by the effects of the preceding. They very rightly infer, therefore, that some thorough reform is wanting, which will banish speculations on public measures, inspire a general prudence and industry, and give a regular course to the business of society. The prohibition with respect to titles of nobility is copied from the Articles of Confederation and needs no comment.

2. "No State shall, without the consent of the Congress, lay any imposts or duties on imports or exports, except what may be absolutely necessary for executing its inspection laws, and the net produce of all duties and imposts laid by any State on imports or exports shall be for the use of the treasury of the United States; and all such laws shall be subject to the revision and control of the Congress. No State shall, without the consent of Congress, lay any duty on tonnage, keep troops or ships of war in time of peace, enter into any agreement or compact with another State, or with a foreign power, or engage in war unless actually invaded, or in such imminent danger as will not admit of delay."

The restraint on the power of the States over imports and exports is enforced by all the arguments which prove the necessity of submitting the regulation of trade to the federal councils. It is needless, therefore, to remark further on this head, than that the manner in which the restraint is qualified seems well calculated at once to secure to the States a reasonable discretion in providing for the conveniency of their imports and exports, and to the United States a reasonable check against the abuse of this discretion. The remaining particulars of this clause fall within reasonings which are either so obvious, or have been so fully developed, that they may be passed over without remark.

The *sixth* and last class consists of the several powers and provisions by which efficacy is given to all the rest.

1. Of these the first is the "power to make all laws which shall be necessary and proper for carrying into execution the foregoing powers, and all other powers vested by this Constitution in the government of the United States, or in any department or office thereof."

Few parts of the Constitution have been assailed with more intemperance than this; yet on a fair investigation of it, as has been elsewhere shown, no part can appear more completely invulnerable. Without the *substance* of this power, the whole Constitution would be a dead letter. Those who object to the article, therefore, as a part of the Constitution, can only mean that the *form* of the provision is improper. But have they considered whether a better form could have been substituted?

There are four other possible methods which the Convention might have taken on this subject. They might have copied the second article of the existing Confederation, which would have prohibited the exercise of any power not *expressly* delegated; they might have attempted a positive enumeration of the powers comprehended under the general terms "necessary and proper"; they might have attempted a negative enumeration of them by specifying the powers excepted from the general definition; they might have been altogether silent on the subject, leaving these necessary and proper powers to construction and inference.

Had the convention taken the first method of adopting the second article of Confederation, it is evident that the new Congress would be continually exposed, as their predecessors have been, to the alternative of construing the term *"expressly"* with so much rigor as to disarm the government of all real authority whatever, or with so much latitude as to destroy altogether the force of the restriction. It would be easy to show, if it were necessary, that no important power delegated by the Articles of Confederation has been or can be executed by Congress, without recurring more or less to the doctrine of *construction* or *implication*. As the powers delegated under the new system are more extensive, the government which is to administer it would find itself still more distressed with the alternative of betraying the public interests by doing nothing, or of violating the Constitution by exercising powers indispensably necessary and proper, but, at the same time, not *expressly* granted.

Had the convention attempted a positive enumeration of the powers necessary and proper for carrying their other powers into effect, the attempt would have involved a complete digest of laws on every subject to which the

Constitution relates; accommodated too not only to the existing state of things, but to all the possible changes which futurity may produce; for in every new application of a general power, the *particular powers,* which are the means of attaining the *object* of the general power, must always necessarily vary with that object, and be often properly varied whilst the object remains the same.

Had they attempted to enumerate the particular powers or means not necessary or proper for carrying the general powers into execution, the task would have been no less chimerical; and would have been liable to this further objection, that every defect in the enumeration would have been equivalent to a positive grant of authority. If, to avoid this consequence, they had attempted a partial enumeration of the exceptions, and described the residue by the general terms *not necessary or proper,* it must have happened that the enumeration would comprehend a few of the excepted powers only; that these would be such as would be least likely to be assumed or tolerated, because the enumeration would of course select such as would be least necessary or proper; and that the unnecessary and improper powers included in the residuum would be less forcibly excepted than if no partial enumeration had been made.

Had the Constitution been silent on this head, there can be no doubt that all the particular powers requisite as means of executing the general powers would have resulted to the government by unavoidable implication. No axiom is more clearly established in law, or in reason, than that wherever the end is required, the means are authorized; wherever a general power to do a thing is given, every particular power necessary for doing it is included. Had this last method, therefore, been pursued by the convention, every objection now urged against their plan would remain in all its plausibility; and the real inconveniency would be incurred of not removing a pretext which may be seized on critical occasions for drawing into question the essential powers of the Union.

If it be asked what is to be the consequence, in case the Congress shall misconstrue this part of the Constitution and exercise powers not warranted by its true meaning, I answer the same as if they should misconstrue or enlarge any other power vested in them; as if the general power had been reduced to particulars, and any one of these were to be violated; the same, in short, as if the State legislatures should violate their respective constitutional authorities. In the first instance, the success of the usurpation will depend on the executive and judiciary departments, which are to expound and give effect to the legislative acts; and in the last resort a remedy must be obtained from the people, who can, by the election of more faithful representatives, annul the acts of the usurpers. The truth is that this ultimate redress may be more confided in against unconstitutional acts of the federal than of the State legislatures, for this plain reason that as every such act of the former will be an invasion of the rights of the latter, these will be ever ready to mark the innovation, to sound the alarm to the people, and to exert their local influence in effecting a change of federal representatives. There being no such intermediate body between the State legislatures and the people interested in watching the conduct of the former, violations of the State constitutions are more likely to remain unnoticed and unredressed.

2. "This Constitution and the laws of the United States which shall be made in pursuance thereof, and all treaties made, or which shall be made, under the authority of the United States, shall be the supreme law of the land, and the judges in every State shall be bound thereby, anything in the constitution or laws of any State to the contrary notwithstanding."

The indiscreet zeal of the adversaries to the Constitution has betrayed them into an attack on this part of it also, without which it would have been evidently and radically defective. To be fully sensible of this, we need only suppose for a moment that the supremacy of the State constitutions had been left complete by a saving clause in their favor.

In the first place, as these constitutions invest the State legislatures with absolute sovereignty in all cases not excepted by the existing Articles of Confederation, all the authorities contained in the proposed Constitution, so far as they exceed those enumerated in the Confederation, would have been annulled, and the new Congress would have been reduced to the same impotent condition with their predecessors.

In the next place, as the constitutions of some of the States do not even expressly and fully recognize the existing powers of the Confederacy, an express saving of the supremacy of the former would, in such States, have brought into question every power contained in the proposed Constitution.

In the third place, as the constitutions of the States differ much from each other, it might happen that a treaty or national law of great and equal importance to the States would interfere with some and not with other constitutions, and would consequently be valid in some of the States at the same time that it would have no effect in others.

In fine, the world would have seen, for the first time, a system of government founded on an inversion of the fundamental principles of all government; it would have seen the authority of the whole society everywhere subordinate to the authority of the parts; it would have seen a monster, in which the head was under the direction of the members.

3. "The senators and representatives, and the members of the several State legislatures, and all executive and judicial officers, both of the United States and the several States, shall be bound by oath or affirmation to support this Constitution."

It has been asked why it was thought necessary that the State magistracy should be bound to support the federal Constitution, and unnecessary that a like oath should be imposed on the officers of the United States in favor of the State constitutions.

Several reasons might be assigned for the distinction. I content myself with one, which is obvious and conclusive. The members of the federal government will have no agency in carrying the State constitutions into effect. The members and officers of the State governments, on the contrary, will have an essential agency in giving effect to the federal Constitution. The election of the President and Senate will depend, in all cases, on the legislatures of the several States. And the election of the House of Representatives will equally depend on the same authority in the first instance; and will, probably, forever be conducted by the officers and according to the laws of the States.

4. Among the provisions for giving efficacy to the federal powers might be added those which belong to the executive and judiciary departments: but as these are reserved for particular examination in another place, I pass them over in this.

We have now reviewed, in detail, all the articles composing the sum or quantity of power delegated by the proposed Constitution to the federal government, and are brought to this undeniable conclusion that no part of the power is unnecessary or improper for accomplishing the necessary objects of the Union. The question, therefore, whether this amount of power shall be granted or not resolves itself into another question, whether or not a government commensurate to the exigencies of the Union shall be established; or, in other words, whether the Union itself shall be preserved. PUBLIUS

No. 45: Madison

HAVING shown that no one of the powers transferred to the federal government is unnecessary or improper, the next question to be considered is whether the whole mass of them will be dangerous to the portion of authority left in the several States.

The adversaries to the plan of the convention, instead of considering in the first place what degree of power was absolutely necessary for the purposes of the federal government, have exhausted themselves in a secondary inquiry into the possible consequences of the proposed degree of power to the governments of the particular States. But if the Union, as has been shown, be essential to the security of the people of America against foreign danger; if it be essential to their security against contentions and wars among the different States; if it be essential to guard them against those violent and oppressive factions which embitter the blessings of liberty and against those military establishments which must gradually poison its very fountain; if, in a word, the Union be essential to the happiness of the people of America, is it not preposterous to urge as an objection to a government, without which the objects of the Union cannot be attained, that such a government may derogate from the importance of the governments of the individual States? Was, then, the American Revolution effected, was the American Confederacy formed, was the precious blood of thousands spilt, and the hard-earned substance of millions lavished, not that the people of America should enjoy peace, liberty, and safety, but that the governments of the individual States, that particular municipal establishments, might enjoy a certain extent of power and be arrayed with certain dignities and attributes of sovereignty? We have heard of the impious doctrine in the old world, that the people were made for kings, not kings for the people. Is the same doctrine to be revived in the new, in another shape—that the solid happiness of the people is to be sacrificed to the views of political institutions of a different form? It is too early for politicians to presume on our forgetting that the public good, the real welfare of the great body of the people, is the supreme object to be pursued; and that no form of government whatever has any other value than as it may be fitted for the attainment of this object. Were the plan of the convention adverse to the public happiness, my voice would be, Reject the plan. Were the Union itself inconsistent with the public happiness, it would be, Abolish the Union. In like manner, as far as the sovereignty of the States cannot be reconciled to the happiness of the people, the voice of every good citizen must be, Let the former be sacrificed to the latter. How far the sacrifice is necessary has been shown. How far the unsacrificed residue will be endangered is the question before us.

Several important considerations have been touched in the course of these papers, which discountenance the supposition that the operation of the federal government will by degrees prove fatal to the State governments. The more I revolve the subject, the more fully I am persuaded that the balance is much more likely to be disturbed by the preponderancy of the last than of the first scale.

We have seen, in all the examples of ancient and modern confederacies, the strongest tendency continually betraying itself in the members to despoil the general government of its authorities, with a very ineffectual capacity in the latter to defend itself against the encroachments. Although, in most of these examples, the system has been so dissimilar from that under consideration as greatly to weaken any inference concerning the latter from the fate of the former, yet, as the States will retain under the proposed Constitution a very extensive portion of active sovereignty, the inference ought not to be wholly disregarded. In the Achæan league it is probable that the federal head had a degree and species of power which gave it a considerable likeness to the government framed by the convention. The Lycian Confederacy, as far as its principles and form are transmitted, must have borne a still greater analogy to it. Yet history does not inform us that either of them ever degenerated, or tended to degenerate, into one consolidated government. On the contrary, we know that the ruin of one of them proceeded from the incapacity of the federal authority to prevent the dissensions, and finally the disunion, of the subordinate authorities. These cases are the more worthy of our attention as the external causes by which the component parts were pressed together were much more numerous and powerful than in our case; and consequently less powerful ligaments within would be sufficient to bind the members to the head and to each other.

In the feudal system, we have seen a similar propensity exemplified. Notwithstanding the want of proper sympathy in every instance between the local sovereigns and the people, and the sympathy in some instances between the general sovereign and the latter, it usually happened that the local sovereigns prevailed in the rivalship for encroachments. Had no external dangers enforced internal harmony and subordination, and particularly, had the local sovereigns possessed the affections of the people, the great kingdoms in Europe would at this time consist of as many independent princes as there were formerly feudatory barons.

The State governments will have the advantage of the federal government, whether we compare them in respect to the immediate dependence of the one on the other; to the weight of personal influence which each side will possess; to the powers respectively vested in them; to the predilection and probable support of the people;

to the disposition and faculty of resisting and frustrating the measures of each other.

The State governments may be regarded as constituent and essential parts of the federal government; whilst the latter is nowise essential to the operation or organization of the former. Without the intervention of the State legislatures, the President of the United States cannot be elected at all. They must in all cases have a great share in his appointment, and will, perhaps, in most cases, of themselves determine it. The Senate will be elected absolutely and exclusively by the State legislatures. Even the House of Representatives, though drawn immediately from the people, will be chosen very much under the influence of that class of men whose influence over the people obtains for themselves an election into the State legislatures. Thus, each of the principal branches of the federal government will owe its existence more or less to the favor of the State governments, and must consequently feel a dependence, which is much more likely to beget a disposition too obsequious than too overbearing towards them. On the other side, the component parts of the State governments will in no instance be indebted for their appointment to the direct agency of the federal government, and very little, if at all, to the local influence of its members.

The number of individuals employed under the Constitution of the United States will be much smaller than the number employed under the particular States. There will consequently be less of personal influence on the side of the former than of the latter. The members of the legislative, executive, and judiciary departments of thirteen and more States, the justices of peace, officers of militia, ministerial officers of justice, with all the county, corporation, and town officers, for three millions and more of people, intermixed and having particular acquaintance with every class and circle of people must exceed, beyond all proportion, both in number and influence, those of every description who will be employed in the administration of the federal system. Compare the members of the three great departments of the thirteen States, excluding from the judiciary department the justices of peace, with the members of the corresponding departments of the single government of the Union; compare the militia officers of three millions of people with the military and marine officers of any establishment which is within the compass of probability, or, I may add, of possibility, and in this view alone, we may pronounce the advantage of the States to be decisive. If the federal government is to have collectors of revenue, the State governments will have theirs also. And as those of the former will be principally on the seacoast, and not very numerous, whilst those of the latter will be spread over the face of the country, and will be very numerous, the advantage in this view also lies on the same side. It is true that the Confederacy is to possess, and may exercise, the power of collecting internal as well as external taxes throughout the States; but it is probable that this power will not be resorted to, except for supplemental purposes of revenue; that an option will then be given to the States to supply their quotas by previous collections of their own; and that the eventual collection, under the immediate authority of the Union, will generally be made by the officers, and according to the rules, appointed by the several States. Indeed it is extremely probable that in other instances, particularly in the organization of the judicial power, the officers of the States will be clothed with the correspondent authority of the Union. Should it happen, however, that separate collectors of internal revenue should be appointed under the federal government, the influence of the whole number would not bear a comparison with that of the multitude of State officers in the opposite scale. Within every district to which a federal collector would be allotted, there would not be less than thirty or forty, or even more, officers of different descriptions, and many of them persons of character and weight whose influence would lie on the side of the State.

The powers delegated by the proposed Constitution to the federal government are few and defined. Those which are to remain in the State governments are numerous and indefinite. The former will be exercised principally on external objects, as war, peace, negotiation, and foreign commerce; with which last the power of taxation will, for the most part, be connected. The powers reserved to the several States will extend to all the objects which, in the ordinary course of affairs, concern the lives, liberties, and properties of the people, and the internal order, improvement, and prosperity of the State.

The operations of the federal government will be most extensive and important in times of war and danger; those of the State governments in times of peace and security. As the former periods will probably bear a small proportion to the latter, the State governments will here enjoy another advantage over the federal government. The more adequate, indeed, the federal powers may be rendered to the national defense, the less frequent will be those scenes of danger which might favor their ascendancy over the governments of the particular States.

If the new Constitution be examined with accuracy and candor, it will be found that the change which it proposes consists much less in the addition of NEW POWERS to the Union than in the invigoration of its ORIGINAL POWERS. The regulation of commerce, it is true, is a new power; but that seems to be an addition which few oppose and from which no apprehensions are entertained. The powers relating to war and peace, armies and fleets, treaties and finance, with the other more considerable powers, are all vested in the existing Congress by the Articles of Confederation. The proposed change does not enlarge these powers; it only substitutes a more effectual mode of administering them. The change relating to taxation may be regarded as the most important; and yet the present Congress have as complete authority to REQUIRE of the States indefinite supplies of money for the common defense and general welfare as the future Congress will have to require them of individual citizens; and the latter will be no more bound than the States themselves have been to pay the quotas respectively taxed on them. Had the States complied punctually with the Articles of Confederation, or could their compliance have been enforced by as peaceable means as may be used with success towards single persons, our past experience is very far from countenancing an opinion that the State governments would have lost their constitutional powers, and have gradually undergone an entire consolidation. To maintain that such an event would have ensued would be to say at once that the existence of the State governments is incompatible with any system whatever that accomplishes the essential purposes of the Union.

PUBLIUS

No. 46: Madison

RESUMING the subject of the last paper, I proceed to inquire whether the federal government or the State governments will have the advantage with regard to the predilection and support of the people. Notwithstanding the different modes in which they are appointed, we must consider both of them as substantially dependent on the great body of the citizens of the United States. I assume this position here as it respects the first, reserving the proofs for another place. The federal and State governments are in fact but different agents and trustees of the people, constituted with different powers and designed for different purposes. The adversaries of the Constitution seem to have lost sight of the people altogether in their reasonings on this subject; and to have viewed these different establishments not only as mutual rivals and enemies, but as uncontrolled by any common superior in their efforts to usurp the authorities of each other. These gentlemen must here be reminded of their error. They must be told that the ultimate authority, wherever the derivative may be found, resides in the people alone, and that it will not depend merely on the comparative ambition or address of the different governments whether either, or which of them, will be able to enlarge its sphere of jurisdiction at the expense of the other. Truth, no less than decency, requires that the event in every case should be supposed to depend on the sentiments and sanction of their common constituents.

Many considerations, besides those suggested on a former occasion, seem to place it beyond doubt that the first and most natural attachment of the people will be to the governments of their respective States. Into the administration of these a greater number of individuals will expect to rise. From the gift of these a greater number of offices and emoluments will flow. By the superintending care of these, all the more domestic and personal interests of the people will be regulated and provided for. With the affairs of these, the people will be more familiarly and minutely conversant. And with the members of these will a greater proportion of the people have the ties of personal acquaintance and friendship, and of family and party attachments; on the side of these, therefore, the popular bias may well be expected most strongly to incline.

Experience speaks the same language in this case. The federal administration, though hitherto very defective in comparison with what may be hoped under a better system, had, during the war, and particularly whilst the independent fund of paper emissions was in credit, an activity and importance as great as it can well have in any future circumstances whatever. It was engaged, too, in a course of measures which had for their object the protection of everything that was dear, and the acquisition of everything that could be desirable to the people at large. It was, nevertheless, invariably found, after the transient enthusiasm for the early Congresses was over, that the attention and attachment of the people were turned anew to their own particular governments; that the federal council was at no time the idol of popular favor; and that opposition to proposed enlargements of its powers and importance was the side usually taken by the men who wished to build their political consequence on the prepossessions of their fellow-citizens.

If, therefore, as has been elsewhere remarked, the people should in future become more partial to the federal than to the State governments, the change can only result from such manifest and irresistible proofs of a better administration as will overcome all their antecedent propensities. And in that case, the people ought not surely to be precluded from giving most of their confidence where they may discover it to be most due; but even in that case the State governments could have little to apprehend, because it is only within a certain sphere that the federal power can, in the nature of things, be advantageously administered.

The remaining points on which I propose to compare the federal and State governments are the disposition and the faculty they may respectively possess to resist and frustrate the measures of each other.

It has been already proved that the members of the federal will be more dependent on the members of the State governments than the latter will be on the former. It has appeared also that the prepossessions of the people, on whom both will depend, will be more on the side of the State governments than of the federal government. So far as the disposition of each towards the other may be influenced by these causes, the State governments must clearly have the advantage. But in a distinct and very important point of view, the advantage will lie on the same side. The prepossessions, which the members themselves will carry into the federal government, will generally be favorable to the States; whilst it will rarely happen that the members of the State governments will carry into the public councils a bias in favor of the general government. A local spirit will infallibly prevail much more in the members of Congress than a national spirit will prevail in the legislatures of the particular States. Everyone knows that a great proportion of the errors committed by the State legislatures proceeds from the disposition of the members to sacrifice the comprehensive and permanent interest of the State to the particular and separate views of the counties or districts in which they reside. And if they do not sufficiently enlarge their policy to embrace the collective welfare of their particular State, how can it be imagined that they will make the aggregate prosperity of the Union, and the dignity and respectability of its government, the objects of their affections and consultations? For the same reason that the members of the State legislatures will be unlikely to attach themselves sufficiently to national objects, the members of the federal legislature will be likely to attach themselves too much to local objects. The States will be to the latter what counties and towns are to the former. Measures will too often be decided according to their probable effect, not on the national prosperity and happiness, but on the prejudices, interests, and pursuits of the governments and people of the individual States. What is the spirit that has in general characterized the proceedings of Congress? A perusal of their journals, as well as the candid acknowledgments of such as have had a seat in that assembly, will inform us that the members have but too frequently displayed the character rather of partisans of their respective States than of impartial guardians of a common interest; that where on one occasion improper sacrifices have been made of local considerations to the aggrandizement of the federal government, the great interests of the nation have suffered on a hundred from an undue attention to the local prejudices, interests, and views of the particular States. I mean not by these reflections to insinuate that the new federal government will not embrace a more enlarged plan of policy than the existing government may have pursued; much less that its views will be as confined as those of the State legislatures; but only that it will partake sufficiently of the spirit of both to be disinclined to invade the rights of the individual States, or the prerogatives of their governments. The motives on the part of the State governments to augment their prerogatives by defalcations from the federal government will be overruled by no reciprocal predispositions in the members.

Were it admitted, however, that the federal government may feel an equal disposition with the State governments to extend its power beyond the due limits, the latter would still have the advantage in the means of defeating such encroachments. If an act of a particular State, though unfriendly to the national government, be generally popular in that State, and should not too grossly violate the oaths of the State officers, it is executed immediately and, of course, by means on the spot and depending on the State alone. The opposition of the federal government, or the interposition of federal officers, would but inflame the zeal of all parties on the side of the State, and the evil could not be prevented or repaired, if at all, without the employment of means which must always be resorted to with reluctance and difficulty. On the other hand, should an unwarrantable measure of the federal government be unpopular in particular States, which would seldom fail to be the case, or even a warrantable measure be so, which may sometimes be the case, the means of opposition to it are powerful and at hand. The disquietude of the people; their repugnance and, perhaps, refusal to co-operate with the officers of the Union; the frowns of the executive magistracy of the State; the embarrassments created by legislative devices, which would often be added on such occasions, would oppose, in any State, difficulties not to be despised; would form, in a large State, very serious impediments; and where the sentiments of several adjoining States happened to be in unison, would present obstructions which the federal government would hardly be willing to encounter.

But ambitious encroachments of the federal government on the authority of the State governments would not excite the opposition of a single State, or of a few States only. They would be signals of general alarm. Every government would espouse the common cause. A correspondence would be opened. Plans of resistance would be concerted. One spirit would animate and conduct the whole. The same combinations, in short, would result from an apprehension of the federal, as was produced by the dread of a foreign, yoke; and unless the projected innovations should be voluntarily renounced, the same appeal to a trial of force would be made in the one case as was made in the other. But what degree of madness could ever drive the federal government to such an extremity? In the contest with Great Britain, one part of the empire was employed against the other. The more numerous part invaded the rights of the less numerous part. The attempt was unjust and unwise; but it was not in speculation absolutely chimerical. But what would be the contest in the case we are supposing? Who would be the parties? A few representatives of the people would be opposed to the people themselves; or rather one set of representatives would be contending against thirteen sets of representatives, with the whole body of their common constituents on the side of the latter.

The only refuge left for those who prophesy the downfall of the State governments is the visionary supposition that the federal government may previously accumulate a military force for the projects of ambition. The reasonings contained in these papers must have been employed to little purpose indeed, if it could be necessary now to disprove the reality of this danger. That the people and the States should, for a sufficient period of time, elect an uninterrupted succession of men ready to betray both; that the traitors should, throughout this period, uniformly and systematically pursue some fixed plan for the extension of the military establishment; that the governments and the people of the States should silently and patiently behold the gathering storm and continue to supply the materials until it should be prepared to burst on their own heads must appear to everyone more like the incoherent dreams of a delirious jealousy, or the misjudged exaggerations of a counterfeit zeal, than like the sober apprehensions of genuine patriotism. Extravagant as the supposition is, let it, however, be made. Let a regular army, fully equal to the resources of the country, be formed; and let it be entirely at the devotion of the federal government: still it would not be going too far to say that the State governments with the people on their side would be able to repel the danger. The highest number to which, according to the best computation, a standing army can be carried in any country does not exceed one hundredth part of the whole number of souls; or one twenty-fifth part of the number able to bear arms. This proportion would not yield, in the United States, an army of more than twenty-five or thirty thousand men. To these would be opposed a militia amounting to near half a million of citizens with arms in their hands, officered by men chosen from among themselves, fighting for their common liberties and united and conducted by governments possessing their affections and confidence. It may well be doubted whether a militia thus circumstanced could ever be conquered by such a proportion of regular troops. Those who are best acquainted with the late successful resistance of this country against the British arms will be most inclined to deny the possibility of it. Besides the advantage of being armed, which the Americans possess over the people of almost every other nation, the existence of subordinate governments, to which the people are attached and by which the militia officers are appointed, forms a barrier against the enterprises of ambition, more insurmountable than any which a simple government of any form can admit of. Notwithstanding the military establishments in the several kingdoms of Europe, which are carried as far as the public resources will bear, the governments are afraid to trust the people with arms. And it is not certain that with this aid alone they would not be able to shake off their yokes. But were the people to possess the additional advantages of local governments chosen by themselves, who could collect the national will and direct the national force, and of officers appointed out of the militia by these governments and attached both to them and to the militia, it may be affirmed with the greatest assurance that the throne of every tyranny in Europe would be speedily overturned in spite of the legions which surround it. Let us not insult the free and gallant citizens of America with the suspicion that they would be less able to defend the rights of which they would be in actual possession than the debased subjects of arbitrary power would be to rescue theirs from the hands of their oppressors. Let us rather no longer insult them with the supposition that they can ever reduce themselves to the necessity of making the experiment by a blind and tame submission to the long train of insidious measures which must precede and produce it.

The argument under the present head may be put into a very concise form, which appears altogether conclusive. Either the mode in which the federal government is to be constructed will render it sufficiently dependent on the people, or it will not. On the first supposition, it will be restrained by that dependence from forming schemes obnoxious to their constituents. On the other supposition, it will not possess the confidence of the people, and its schemes of usurpation will be easily defeated by the State governments, who will be supported by the people.

On summing up the considerations stated in this and the last paper, they seem to amount to the most convincing evidence that the powers proposed to be lodged in the federal government are as little formidable to those reserved to the individual States as they are indispensably necessary to accomplish the purposes of the Union; and that all those alarms which have been sounded of a meditated and consequential annihilation of the State governments must, on the most favorable interpretation, be ascribed to the chimerical fears of the authors of them.

PUBLIUS

No. 47: Madison

HAVING reviewed the general form of the proposed government and the general mass of power allotted to it, I proceed to examine the particular structure of this government, and the distribution of this mass of power among its constituent parts.

One of the principal objections inculcated by the more respectable adversaries to the Constitution is its supposed violation of the political maxim that the legislative, executive, and judiciary departments ought to be separate and distinct. In the structure of the federal government no regard, it is said, seems to have been paid to this essential precaution in favor of liberty. The several departments of power are distributed and blended in such a manner as at once to destroy all symmetry and beauty of form, and to expose some of the essential parts of the edifice to the danger of being crushed by the disproportionate weight of other parts.

No political truth is certainly of greater intrinsic value, or is stamped with the authority of more enlightened patrons of liberty than that on which the objection is founded. The accumulation of all powers, legislative, executive, and judiciary, in the same hands, whether of one, a few, or many, and whether hereditary, self-appointed, or elective, may justly be pronounced the very definition of tyranny. Were the federal Constitution, therefore, really chargeable with this accumulation of power, or with a mixture of powers, having a dangerous tendency to such an accumulation, no further arguments would be necessary to inspire a universal reprobation of the system. I persuade myself, however, that it will be made apparent to everyone that the charge cannot be supported, and that the maxim on which it relies has been totally misconceived and misapplied. In order to form correct ideas on this important subject it will be proper to investigate the sense in which the preservation of liberty requires that the three great departments of power should be separate and distinct.

The oracle who is always consulted and cited on this subject is the celebrated Montesquieu. If he be not the author of this invaluable precept in the science of politics, he has the merit at least of displaying and recommending it most effectually to the attention of mankind. Let us endeavor, in the first place, to ascertain his meaning on this point.

The British Constitution was to Montesquieu what

Homer has been to the didactic writers on epic poetry. As the latter have considered the work of the immortal bard as the perfect model from which the principles and rules of the epic art were to be drawn, and by which all similar works were to be judged, so this great political critic appears to have viewed the Constitution of England as the standard, or to use his own expression, as the mirror of political liberty; and to have delivered, in the form of elementary truths, the several characteristic principles of that particular system. That we may be sure, then, not to mistake his meaning in this case, let us recur to the source from which the maxim was drawn.

On the slightest view of the British Constitution, we must perceive that the legislative, executive, and judiciary departments are by no means totally separate and distinct from each other. The executive magistrate forms an integral part of the legislative authority. He alone has the prerogative of making treaties with foreign sovereigns which, when made, have, under certain limitations, the force of legislative acts. All the members of the judiciary department are appointed by him, can be removed by him on the address of the two Houses of Parliament, and form, when he pleases to consult them, one of his constitutional councils. One branch of the legislative department forms also a great constitutional council to the executive chief, as, on another hand, it is the sole depositary of judicial power in cases of impeachment, and is invested with the supreme appellate jurisdiction in all other cases. The judges, again, are so far connected with the legislative department as often to attend and participate in its deliberations, though not admitted to a legislative vote.

From these facts, by which Montesquieu was guided, it may clearly be inferred that in saying "There can be no liberty where the legislative and executive powers are united in the same person, or body of magistrates," or, "if the power of judging be not separated from the legislative and executive powers," he did not mean that these departments ought to have no *partial agency* in, or no *control* over, the acts of each other. His meaning, as his own words import, and still more conclusively as illustrated by the example in his eye, can amount to no more than this, that where the *whole* power of one department is exercised by the same hands which possess the *whole* power of another department, the fundamental principles of a free constitution are subverted. This would have been the case in the constitution examined by him, if the king, who is the sole executive magistrate, had possessed also the complete legislative power, or the supreme administration of justice; or if the entire legislative body had possessed the supreme judiciary, or the supreme executive authority. This, however, is not among the vices of that constitution. The magistrate in whom the whole executive power resides cannot of himself make a law, though he can put a negative on every law; nor administer justice in person, though he has the appointment of those who do administer it. The judges can exercise no executive prerogative, though they are shoots from the executive stock; nor any legislative function, though they may be advised by the legislative councils. The entire legislature can perform no judiciary act, though by the joint act of two of its branches the judges may be removed from their offices, and though one of its branches is possessed of the judicial power in the last resort. The entire legislature, again, can exercise no executive prerogative, though one of its branches constitutes the supreme executive magistracy, and another, on the impeachment of a third, can try and condemn all the subordinate officers in the executive department.

The reasons on which Montesquieu grounds his maxim are a further demonstration of his meaning. "When the legislative and executive powers are united in the same person or body," says he, "there can be no liberty, because apprehensions may arise lest *the same* monarch or senate should *enact* tyrannical laws to *execute* them in a tyrannical manner." Again: "Were the power of judging joined with the legislative, the life and liberty of the subject would be exposed to arbitrary control, for *the judge* would then be *the legislator*. Were it joined to the executive power, *the judge* might behave with all the violence of *an oppressor*." Some of these reasons are more fully explained in other passages; but briefly stated as they are here they sufficiently establish the meaning which we have put on this celebrated maxim of this celebrated author.

If we look into the constitutions of the several States

we find that, notwithstanding the emphatical and, in some instances, the unqualified terms in which this axiom has been laid down, there is not a single instance in which the several departments of power have been kept absolutely separate and distinct. New Hampshire, whose constitution was the last formed, seems to have been fully aware of the impossibility and inexpediency of avoiding any mixture whatever of these departments, and has qualified the doctrine by declaring "that the legislative, executive, and judiciary powers ought to be kept as separate from, and independent of, each other *as the nature of a free government will admit; or as is consistent with that chain of connection that binds the whole fabric of the constitution in one indissoluble bond of unity and amity.*" Her constitution accordingly mixes these departments in several respects. The Senate, which is a branch of the legislative department, is also a judicial tribunal for the trial of impeachments. The President, who is the head of the executive department, is the presiding member also of the Senate; and, besides an equal vote in all cases, has a casting vote in case of a tie. The executive head is himself eventually elective every year by the legislative department, and his council is every year chosen by and from the members of the same department. Several of the officers of state are also appointed by the legislature. And the members of the judiciary department are appointed by the executive department.

The constitution of Massachusetts has observed a sufficient though less pointed caution in expressing this fundamental article of liberty. It declares "that the legislative department shall never exercise the executive and judicial powers, or either of them; the executive shall never exercise the legislative and judicial powers, or either of them; the judicial shall never exercise the legislative and executive powers, or either of them." This declaration corresponds precisely with the doctrine of Montesquieu, as it has been explained, and is not in a single point violated by the plan of the convention. It goes no farther than to prohibit any one of the entire departments from exercising the powers of another department. In the very Constitution to which it is prefixed, a partial mixture of powers has been admitted. The executive magistrate has a qualified negative on the legislative body, and the Senate, which is a part of the legislature, is a court of impeachment for members both of the executive and judiciary departments. The members of the judiciary department, again, are appointable by the executive department, and removable by the same authority on the address of the two legislative branches. Lastly, a number of the officers of government are annually appointed by the legislative department. As the appointment to offices, particularly executive offices, is in its nature an executive function, the compilers of the Constitution have, in this last point at least, violated the rule established by themselves.

I pass over the constitutions of Rhode Island and Connecticut, because they were formed prior to the Revolution and even before the principle under examination had become an object of political attention.

The constitution of New York contains no declaration on this subject, but appears very clearly to have been framed with an eye to the danger of improperly blending the different departments. It gives, nevertheless, to the executive magistrate, a partial control over the legislative department; and, what is more, gives a like control to the judiciary department; and even blends the executive and judiciary departments in the exercise of this control. In its council of appointment members of the legislative are associated with the executive authority, in the appointment of officers, both executive and judiciary. And its court for the trial of impeachments and correction of errors is to consist of one branch of the legislature and the principal members of the judiciary department.

The constitution of New Jersey has blended the different powers of government more than any of the preceding. The governor, who is the executive magistrate, is appointed by the legislature; is chancellor and ordinary, or surrogate of the State; is a member of the Supreme Court of Appeals, and president, with a casting vote, of one of the legislative branches. The same legislative branch acts again as executive council to the governor, and with him constitutes the Court of Appeals. The members of the judiciary department are appointed by the legislative department, and removable by one branch of it, on the impeachment of the other.

According to the constitution of Pennsylvania, the president, who is the head of the executive department, is annually elected by a vote in which the legislative department predominates. In conjunction with an executive council, he appoints the members of the judiciary department and forms a court of impeachment for trial of all officers, judiciary as well as executive. The judges of the Supreme Court and justices of the peace seem also to be removable by the legislature; and the executive power of pardoning, in certain cases, to be referred to the same department. The members of the executive council are made EX OFFICIO justices of peace throughout the State.

In Delaware, the chief executive magistrate is annually elected by the legislative department. The speakers of the two legislative branches are vice-presidents in the executive department. The executive chief, with six others appointed, three by each of the legislative branches, constitutes the Supreme Court of Appeals; he is joined with the legislative department in the appointment of the other judges. Throughout the States it appears that the members of the legislature may at the same time be justices of the peace; in this State, the members of one branch of it are EX OFFICIO justices of the peace; as are also the members of the executive council. The principal officers of the executive department are appointed by the legislative; and one branch of the latter forms a court of impeachments. All officers may be removed on address of the legislature.

Maryland has adopted the maxim in the most unqualified terms; declaring that the legislative, executive, and judicial powers of government ought to be forever separate and distinct from each other. Her constitution, notwithstanding, makes the executive magistrate appointable by the legislative department; and the members of the judiciary by the executive department.

The language of Virginia is still more pointed on this subject. Her constitution declares "that the legislative, executive, and judiciary departments shall be separate and distinct; so that neither exercises the powers properly belonging to the other; nor shall any person exercise the powers of more than one of them at the same time, except that the justices of county courts shall be eligible to either House of Assembly." Yet we find not only this express exception with respect to the members of the inferior courts, but that the chief magistrate, with his executive council, are appointable by the legislature; that two members of the latter are triennially displaced at the pleasure of the legislature; and that all the principal offices, both executive and judiciary, are filled by the same department. The executive prerogative of pardon, also, is in one case vested in the legislative department.

The constitution of North Carolina, which declares "that the legislative, executive, and supreme judicial powers of government ought to be forever separate and distinct from each other," refers, at the same time, to the legislative department, the appointment not only of the executive chief, but all the principal officers within both that and the judiciary department.

In South Carolina, the constitution makes the executive magistracy eligible by the legislative department. It gives to the latter, also, the appointment of the members of the judiciary department, including even justices of the peace and sheriffs; and the appointment of officers in the executive department, down to captains in the army and navy of the State.

In the constitution of Georgia where it is declared "that the legislative, executive, and judiciary departments shall be separate and distinct, so that neither exercise the powers properly belonging to the other," we find that the executive department is to be filled by appointments of the legislature; and the executive prerogative of pardon to be finally exercised by the same authority. Even justices of the peace are to be appointed by the legislature.

In citing these cases, in which the legislative, executive, and judiciary departments have not been kept totally separate and distinct, I wish not to be regarded as an advocate for the particular organizations of the several State governments. I am fully aware that among the many excellent principles which they exemplify they carry strong marks of the haste, and still stronger of the inexperience, under which they were framed. It is but too obvious that in some instances the fundamental principle under consideration has been violated by too great a mixture, and even an actual consolidation of the different powers; and that in no instance has a competent provision been made for maintaining in practice the separation delineated on paper. What I have wished to evince is that the charge brought against the proposed Constitution of violating the sacred maxim of free government is warranted neither by the real meaning annexed to that maxim by its author, nor by the sense in which it has hitherto been understood in America. This interesting subject will be resumed in the ensuing paper. PUBLIUS

No. 48: Madison

IT WAS shown in the last paper that the political apothegm there examined does not require that the legislative, executive, and judiciary departments should be wholly unconnected with each other. I shall undertake, in the next place, to show that unless these departments be so far connected and blended as to give to each a constitutional control over the others, the degree of separation which the maxim requires, as essential to a free government, can never in practice be duly maintained.

It is agreed on all sides that the powers properly belonging to one of the departments ought not to be directly and completely administered by either of the other departments. It is equally evident that none of them ought to possess, directly or indirectly, an overruling influence over the others in the administration of their respective powers. It will not be denied that power is of an encroaching nature and that it ought to be effectually restrained from passing the limits assigned to it. After discriminating, therefore, in theory, the several classes of power, as they may in their nature be legislative, executive, or judiciary, the next and most difficult task is to provide some practical security for each, against the invasion of the others. What this security ought to be is the great problem to be solved.

Will it be sufficient to mark, with precision, the boundaries of these departments in the constitution of the government, and to trust to these parchment barriers against the encroaching spirit of power? This is the security which appears to have been principally relied on by the compilers of most of the American constitutions. But experience assures us that the efficacy of the provision has been greatly overrated; and that some more adequate defense is indispensably necessary for the more feeble against the more powerful members of the government. The legislative department is everywhere extending the sphere of its activity and drawing all power into its impetuous vortex.

The founders of our republics have so much merit for the wisdom which they have displayed that no task can be less pleasing than that of pointing out the errors into which they have fallen. A respect for truth, however, obliges us to remark that they seem never for a moment to have turned their eyes from the danger, to liberty, from the overgrown and all-grasping prerogative of an hereditary magistrate, supported and fortified by an hereditary branch of the legislative authority. They seem never to have recollected the danger from legislative usurpations, which, by assembling all power in the same hands, must lead to the same tyranny as is threatened by executive usurpations.

In a government where numerous and extensive prerogatives are placed in the hands of an hereditary monarch, the executive department is very justly regarded as the source of danger, and watched with all the jealousy which a zeal for liberty ought to inspire. In a democracy, where a multitude of people exercise in person the legislative functions and are continually exposed, by their incapacity for regular deliberation and concerted measures, to the ambitious intrigues of their executive magistrates, tyranny may well be apprehended, on some favorable emergency, to start up in the same quarter. But in a representative republic where the executive magistracy is carefully limited, both in the extent and the duration of its power; and where the legislative power is exercised by an assembly, which is inspired by a supposed influence over the people with an intrepid confidence in its own strength; which is sufficiently numerous to feel all the passions which actuate a multitude, yet not so numerous as to be incapable of pursuing the objects of its passions by means which reason prescribes; it is against the enterprising ambition of this department that the people ought to indulge all their jealousy and exhaust all their precautions.

The legislative department derives a superiority in our governments from other circumstances. Its constitutional powers being at once more extensive, and less susceptible of precise limits, it can, with the greater facility, mask, under complicated and indirect measures, the encroachments which it makes on the co-ordinate departments. It is not unfrequently a question of real nicety in legislative bodies whether the operation of a particular measure will, or will not, extend beyond the legislative sphere. On the other side, the executive power being restrained within a narrower compass and being more simple in its nature, and the judiciary being described by landmarks still less uncertain, projects of usurpation by either of these departments would immediately betray and defeat themselves. Nor is this all: as the legislative department alone has access to the pockets of the people, and has in some constitutions full discretion, and in all a prevailing influence, over the pecuniary rewards of those who fill the other departments, a dependence is thus created in the latter, which gives still greater facility to encroachments of the former.

I have appealed to our own experience for the truth of what I advance on this subject. Were it necessary to verify this experience by particular proofs, they might be multiplied without end. I might collect vouchers in abundance from the records and archives of every State in the Union. But as a more concise and at the same time equally satisfactory evidence, I will refer to the example of two States, attested by two unexceptionable authorities.

The first example is that of Virginia, a State which, as we have seen, has expressly declared in its constitution that the three great departments ought not to be intermixed. The authority in support of it is Mr. Jefferson, who, besides his other advantages for remarking the operation of the government, was himself the chief magistrate of it. In order to convey fully the ideas with which his experience had impressed him on this subject, it will be necessary to quote a passage of some length from his very interesting *Notes on the State of Virginia,* p. 195. "All the powers of government, legislative, executive, and judiciary, result to the legislative body. The concentrating these in the same hands is precisely the definition of despotic government. It will be no alleviation that these powers will be exercised by a plurality of hands, and not by a single one. One hundred and seventy-three despots would surely be as oppressive as one. Let those who doubt it turn their eyes on the republic of Venice. As little will it avail us that they are chosen by ourselves. An *elective despotism* was not the government we fought for; but one which should not only be founded on free principles, but in which the powers of government should be so divided and balanced among several bodies of magistracy as that no one could transcend their legal limits without being effectually checked and restrained by the others. For this reason that convention which passed the ordinance of government laid its foundation on this basis, that the legislative, executive, and judiciary departments should be separate and distinct, so that no person should exercise the powers of more than one of them at the same time. *But no barrier was provided between these several powers.* The judiciary and the executive members were left dependent on the legislative for their subsistence in office, and some of them for their continuance in it. If, therefore, the legislature assumes executive and judiciary powers, no opposition is likely to be made; nor, if made, can be effectual; because in that case they may put their proceedings into the form of acts of Assembly, which will render them obligatory on the other branches. They have accordingly, *in many* instances, *decided rights* which should have been left to *judiciary controversy,* and *the direction of the executive, during the whole time of their session, is becoming habitual and familiar.*"

The other State which I shall have for an example is Pennsylvania; and the other authority, the Council of Censors, which assembled in the years 1783 and 1784. A part of the duty of this body, as marked out by the Constitution, was "to inquire whether the Constitution had been preserved inviolate in every part; and whether the legislative and executive branches of government had performed their duty as guardians of the people, or assumed to themselves, or exercised, other or greater powers than they are entitled to by the Constitution." In the execution of this trust, the council were necessarily led to a comparison of both the legislative and executive proceedings with the constitutional powers of these departments; and from the facts enumerated, and to the truth of most of which both sides in the council subscribed, it appears that the Constitution had been flagrantly violated by the legislature in a variety of important instances.

A great number of laws had been passed violating, without any apparent necessity, the rule requiring that all bills of a public nature shall be previously printed for the consideration of the people; although this is one of the precautions chiefly relied on by the Constitution against improper acts of the legislature.

The constitutional trial by jury had been violated and powers assumed which had not been delegated by the Constitution.

Executive powers had been usurped.

The salaries of the judges, which the Constitution expressly requires to be fixed, had been occasionally varied; and cases belonging to the judiciary department frequently drawn within legislative cognizance and determination.

Those who wish to see the several particulars falling under each of these heads may consult the journals of the council which are in print. Some of them, it will be found, may be imputable to peculiar circumstances connected with the war; but the greater part of them may be considered as the spontaneous shoots of an ill-constituted government.

It appears, also, that the executive department had not been innocent of frequent breaches of the Constitution. There are three observations, however, which ought to be made on this head: *first,* a great proportion of the instances were either immediately produced by the necessities of the war, or recommended by Congress or the commander-in-chief; *second,* in most of the other instances they conformed either to the declared or the known sentiments of the legislative department; *third,* the executive department of Pennsylvania is distinguished from that of the other States by the number of members composing it. In this respect, it has as much affinity to a legislative assembly as to an executive council. And being at once exempt from the restraint of an individual responsibility for the acts of the body, and deriving confidence from mutual example and joint influence, unauthorized measures would, of course, be more freely hazarded, than where the executive department is administered by a single hand, or by a few hands.

The conclusion which I am warranted in drawing from these observations is that a mere demarcation on parchment of the constitutional limits of the several departments is not a sufficient guard against those encroachments which lead to a tyrannical concentration of all the powers of government in the same hands.

PUBLIUS

No. 49: Madison

THE author of the *Notes on the State of Virginia*, quoted in the last paper, has subjoined to that valuable work the draught of a constitution, which had been prepared in order to be laid before a convention expected to be called in 1783, by the legislature, for the establishment of a constitution for that commonwealth. The plan, like everything from the same pen, marks a turn of thinking, original, comprehensive, and accurate; and is the more worthy of attention as it equally displays a fervent attachment to republican government and an enlightened view of the dangerous propensities against which it ought to be guarded. One of the precautions which he proposes, and on which he appears ultimately to rely as a palladium to the weaker departments of power against the invasions of the stronger, is perhaps altogether his own, and as it immediately relates to the subject of our present inquiry, ought not to be overlooked.

His proposition is "that whenever any two of the three branches of government shall concur in opinion, each by the voices of two thirds of their whole number, that a convention is necessary for altering the Constitution, or *correcting breaches of it*, a convention shall be called for the purpose."

As the people are the only legitimate fountain of power, and it is from them that the constitutional charter, under which the several branches of government hold their power, is derived, it seems strictly consonant to the republican theory to recur to the same original authority, not only whenever it may be necessary to enlarge, diminish, or new-model the powers of government, but also whenever any one of the departments may commit encroachments on the chartered authorities of the others. The several departments being perfectly co-ordinate by the terms of their common commission, neither of them, it is evident, can pretend to an exclusive or superior right of settling the boundaries between their respective powers; and how are the encroachments of the stronger to be prevented, or the wrongs of the weaker to be redressed, without an appeal to the people themselves, who, as the grantors of the commission, can alone declare its true meaning, and enforce its observance?

There is certainly great force in this reasoning, and it must be allowed to prove that a constitutional road to the decision of the people ought to be marked out and kept open, for certain great and extraordinary occasions. But there appear to be insuperable objections against the proposed recurrence to the people, as a provision in all cases for keeping the several departments of power within their constitutional limits.

In the first place, the provision does not reach the case of a combination of two of the departments against the third. If the legislative authority, which possesses so many means of operating on the motives of the other departments, should be able to gain to its interest either of the others, or even one third of its members, the remaining department could derive no advantage from this remedial provision. I do not dwell, however, on this objection, because it may be thought to lie rather against the modification of the principle, than against the principle itself.

In the next place, it may be considered as an objection inherent in the principle that as every appeal to the people would carry an implication of some defect in the government, frequent appeals would, in great measure, deprive the government of that veneration which time bestows on everything, and without which perhaps the wisest and freest governments would not possess the requisite stability. If it be true that all governments rest on opinion, it is no less true that the strength of opinion in each individual, and its practical influence on his conduct, depend much on the number which he supposes to have entertained the same opinion. The reason of man, like man himself, is timid and cautious when left alone, and acquires firmness and confidence in proportion to the number with which it is associated. When the examples which fortify opinion are *ancient* as well as *numerous,* they are known to have a double effect. In a nation of philosophers, this consideration ought to be disregarded. A reverence for the laws would be sufficiently inculcated by the voice of an enlightened reason. But a nation of philosophers is as little to be expected as the philosophical race of kings wished for by Plato. And in every other nation, the most rational government will not find it a superfluous advantage to have the prejudices of the community on its side.

The danger of disturbing the public tranquillity by interesting too strongly the public passions is a still more serious objection against a frequent reference of constitutional questions to the decision of the whole society. Notwithstanding the success which has attended the revisions of our established forms of government and which does so much honor to the virtue and intelligence of the people of America, it must be confessed that the experiments are of too ticklish a nature to be unnecessarily multiplied. We are to recollect that all the existing constitutions were formed in the midst of a danger which repressed the passions most unfriendly to order and concord; of an enthusiastic confidence of the people in their patriotic leaders, which stifled the ordinary diversity of opinions on great national questions; of a universal ardor for new and opposite forms, produced by a universal resentment and indignation against the ancient government; and whilst no spirit of party connected with the changes to be made, or the abuses to be reformed, could mingle its leaven in the operation. The future situations in which we must expect to be usually placed do not present any equivalent security against the danger which is apprehended.

But the greatest objection of all is that the decisions which would probably result from such appeals would not answer the purpose of maintaining the constitutional equilibrium of the government. We have seen that the tendency of republican governments is to an aggrandizement of the legislative at the expense of the other departments. The appeals to the people, therefore, would usually be made by the executive and judiciary departments. But whether made by one side or the other, would each side enjoy equal advantages on the trial? Let us view their different situations. The members of the executive and judiciary departments are few in number, and can be personally known to a small part only of the people. The latter, by the mode of their appointment, as well as by the nature and permanency of it, are too far removed from the people to share much in their prepossessions. The former are generally the objects of jealousy and their administration is always liable to be discolored and rendered unpopular. The members of the legislative department, on the other hand, are numerous. They are distributed and dwell among the people at large. Their connections of blood, of friendship, and of acquaintance embrace a great proportion of the most influential part of the society. The nature of their public trust implies a personal influence among the people, and that they are more immediately the confidential guardians of the rights and liberties of the people. With these advantages it can hardly be supposed that the adverse party would have an equal chance for a favorable issue.

But the legislative party would not only be able to plead their cause most successfully with the people. They would probably be constituted themselves the judges. The same influence which had gained them an election into the legislature would gain them a seat in the convention. If this should not be the case with all, it would probably be the case with many, and pretty certainly with those leading characters, on whom everything depends in such bodies. The convention, in short, would be composed chiefly of men who had been, who actually were, or who expected to be, members of the department whose conduct was arraigned. They would consequently be parties to the very question to be decided by them.

It might, however, sometimes happen, that appeals would be made under circumstances less adverse to the executive and judiciary departments. The usurpations of the legislature might be so flagrant and so sudden, as to admit of no specious coloring. A strong party among themselves might take side with the other branches. The executive power might be in the hands of a peculiar favorite of the people. In such a posture of things, the public decision might be less swayed by prepossessions in favor of the legislative party. But still it could never be expected to turn on the true merits of the question. It would inevitably be connected with the spirit of pre-existing parties, or of parties springing out of the question itself. It would be connected with persons of distinguished character and extensive influence in the community. It would be pronounced by the very men who had been agents in, or opponents of, the measures to which the decision would relate. The *passions,* therefore, not the *reason,* of the public would sit in judgment. But it is the reason, alone, of the public, that ought to control and regulate the government. The passions ought to be controlled and regulated by the government.

We found in the last paper that mere declarations in the written Constitution are not sufficient to restrain the several departments within their legal rights. It appears in this that occasional appeals to the people would be neither a proper nor an effectual provision for that purpose. How far the provisions of a different nature contained in the plan above quoted might be adequate I do not examine. Some of them are unquestionably founded on sound political principals, and all of them are framed with singular ingenuity and precision. PUBLIUS

No. 50: Madison

IT MAY be contended, perhaps, that instead of *occasional* appeals to the people, which are liable to the objections urged against them, *periodical* appeals are the proper and adequate means of *preventing and correcting infractions of the Constitution.*

It will be attended to that in the examination of these expedients I confine myself to their aptitude for *enforcing* the Constitution, by keeping the several departments of power within their due bounds without particularly considering them as provisions for *altering* the Constitution itself. In the first view, appeals to the people at fixed periods appear to be nearly as ineligible as appeals on particular occasions as they emerge. If the periods be separated by short intervals, the measures to be reviewed and rectified will have been of recent date, and will be connected with all the circumstances which tend to vitiate and pervert the result of occasional revisions. If the periods be distant from each other, the same remark will be applicable to all recent measures; and in proportion as the remoteness of the others may favor a dispassionate review of them, this advantage is inseparable from inconveniences which seem to counterbalance it. In the first place, a distant prospect of public censure would be a very feeble restraint on power from those excesses to which it might be urged by the force of present motives. Is it to be imagined that a legislative assembly, consisting of a hundred or two hundred members, eagerly bent on some favorite object, and breaking through the restraints of the Constitution in pursuit of it, would be arrested in their career by considerations drawn from a censorial revision of their conduct at the future distance of ten, fifteen, or twenty years? In the next place, the abuses would often have completed their mischievous effects before the remedial provision would be applied. And in the last place, where this might not be the case, they would be of long standing, would have taken deep root, and would not easily be extirpated.

The scheme of revising the Constitution, in order to correct recent breaches of it, as well as for other purposes, has been actually tried in one of the States. One of the objects of the Council of Censors which met in Pennsylvania in 1783 and 1784, was, as we have seen, to inquire, "whether the Constitution had been violated, and whether the legislative and executive departments had encroached on each other." This important and novel experiment in politics merits, in several points of view, very particular attention. In some of them it may, perhaps, as a single experiment, made under circumstances somewhat peculiar, be thought to be not absolutely conclusive. But as applied to the case under consideration it involves some facts which I venture to remark, as a complete and satisfactory illustration of the reasoning which I have employed.

First. It appears, from the names of the gentlemen who composed the council that some, at least, of its most active and leading members had also been active and leading characters in the parties which pre-existed in the State.

Second. It appears that the same active and leading members of the council had been active and influential members of the legislative and executive branches within the period to be reviewed; and even patrons or opponents of the very measures to be thus brought to the test of the Constitution. Two of the members had been vice-presidents of the State, and several others, members of the executive council within the seven preceding years. One of them had been speaker, and a number of others distinguished members of the legislative assembly within the same period.

Third. Every page of their proceedings witnesses the effect of all these circumstances on the temper of their deliberations. Throughout the continuance of the council, it was split into two fixed and violent parties. The fact is acknowledged and lamented by themselves. Had this not been the case, the face of their proceedings exhibits a proof equally satisfactory. In all questions, however unimportant in themselves, or unconnected with each other, the same names stand invariably contrasted on the opposite columns. Every unbiased observer may infer, without danger of mistake, and at the same time without meaning to reflect on either party, or any individuals of either party, that, unfortunately, *passion,* not *reason,* must have presided over their decisions. When men exercise their reason coolly and freely on a variety of distinct questions, they inevitably fall into different opinions on some of them. When they are governed by a common passion, their opinions, if they are so to be called, will be the same.

Fourth. It is at least problematical whether the decisions of this body do not, in several instances, misconstrue the limits prescribed for the legislative and executive departments, instead of reducing and limiting them within their constitutional places.

Fifth. I have never understood that the decisions of the council on constitutional questions, whether rightly or erroneously formed, have had any effect in varying the practice founded on legislative constructions. It even appears, if I mistake not, that in one instance the contemporary legislature denied the constructions of the council, and actually prevailed in the contest.

This censorial body, therefore, proves at the same time, by its researches, the existence of the disease, and by its example, the inefficacy of the remedy.

This conclusion cannot be invalidated by alleging that the State in which the experiment was made was at that crisis, and had been for a long time before, violently heated and distracted by the rage of party. Is it to be presumed that at any future septennial epoch the same State will be free from parties? Is it to be presumed that any other State, at the same or any other given period, will be exempt from them? Such an event ought to be neither presumed nor desired; because an extinction of parties necessarily implies either a universal alarm for the public safety, or an absolute extinction of liberty.

Were the precaution taken of excluding, from the assemblies elected by the people to revise the preceding administration of the government, all persons who should have been concerned with the government within the given period, the difficulties would not be obviated. The important task would probably devolve on men, who, with inferior capacities, would in other respects be little better qualified. Although they might not have been personally concerned in the administration, and therefore not immediately agents in the measures to be examined, they would probably have been involved in the parties connected with these measures and have been elected under their auspices.

PUBLIUS

No. 51: Madison

TO WHAT expedient, then, shall we finally resort, for maintaining in practice the necessary partition of power among the several departments as laid down in the Constitution? The only answer that can be given is that as all these exterior provisions are found to be inadequate the defect must be supplied, by so contriving the interior structure of the government as that its several constituent parts may, by their mutual relations, be the means of keeping each other in their proper places. Without presuming to undertake a full development of this important idea I will hazard a few general observations which may perhaps place it in a clearer light, and enable us to form a more correct judgment of the principles and structure of the government planned by the convention.

In order to lay a due foundation for that separate and distinct exercise of the different powers of government, which to a certain extent is admitted on all hands to be essential to the preservation of liberty, it is evident that each department should have a will of its own; and consequently should be so constituted that the members of each should have as little agency as possible in the appointment of the members of the others. Were this principle rigorously adhered to, it would require that all the appointments for the supreme executive, legislative, and judiciary magistracies should be drawn from the same fountain of authority, the people, through channels having no communication whatever with one another. Perhaps such a plan of constructing the several departments would be less difficult in practice than it may in contemplation appear. Some difficulties, however, and some additional expense would attend the execution of it. Some deviations, therefore, from the principle must be admitted. In the constitution of the judiciary department in particular, it might be inexpedient to insist rigorously on the principle: first, because peculiar qualifications being essential in the members, the primary consideration ought to be to select that mode of choice which best secures these qualifications; second, because the permanent tenure by which the appointments are held in that department must soon destroy all sense of dependence on the authority conferring them.

It is equally evident that the members of each department should be as little dependent as possible on those of the others for the emoluments annexed to their offices. Were the executive magistrate, or the judges, not independent of the legislature in this particular, their independence in every other would be merely nominal.

But the great security against a gradual concentration of the several powers in the same department consists in giving to those who administer each department the necessary constitutional means and personal motives to resist encroachments of the others. The provision for defense must in this, as in all other cases, be made commensurate to the danger of attack. Ambition must be made to counteract ambition. The interest of the man must be connected with the constitutional rights of the place. It may be a reflection on human nature that such devices should be necessary to control the abuses of government. But what is government itself but the greatest of all reflections on human nature? If men were angels, no government would be necessary. If angels were to govern men, neither external nor internal controls on government would be necessary. In framing a government which is to be administered by men over men, the great difficulty lies in this: you must first enable the government to control the governed; and in the next place oblige it to control itself. A dependence on the people is, no doubt, the primary control on the government; but experience has taught mankind the necessity of auxiliary precautions.

This policy of supplying, by opposite and rival interests, the defect of better motives, might be traced through the whole system of human affairs, private as well as public. We see it particularly displayed in all the subordinate distributions of power, where the constant aim is to divide and arrange the several offices in such a manner as that each may be a check on the other—that the private interest of every individual may be a sentinel over the public rights. These inventions of prudence cannot be less requisite in the distribution of the supreme powers of the State.

But it is not possible to give to each department an equal power of self-defense. In republican government, the legislative authority necessarily predominates. The remedy for this inconveniency is to divide the legislature into different branches; and to render them, by different modes of election and different principles of action, as little connected with each other as the nature of their common functions and their common dependence on the society will admit. It may even be necessary to guard against dangerous encroachments by still further precautions. As the weight of the legislative authority requires that it should be thus divided, the weakness of the executive may require, on the other hand, that it should be fortified. An absolute negative on the legislature appears, at first view, to be the natural defense with which the executive magistrate should be armed. But perhaps it would be neither altogether safe nor alone sufficient. On ordinary occasions it might not be exerted with the requisite firmness, and on extraordinary occasions it might be perfidiously abused. May not this defect of an absolute negative be supplied by some qualified connection between this weaker department and the weaker branch of the stronger department, by which the latter may be led to support the constitutional rights of the former, without being too much detached from the rights of its own department?

If the principles on which these observations are founded be just, as I persuade myself they are, and they be applied as a criterion to the several State constitutions, and to the federal Constitution, it will be found that if the latter does not perfectly correspond with them, the former are infinitely less able to bear such a test.

There are, moreover, two considerations particularly applicable to the federal system of America, which place that system in a very interesting point of view.

First. In a single republic, all the power surrendered by the people is submitted to the administration of a single government; and the usurpations are guarded against by a division of the government into distinct and separate departments. In the compound republic of America, the power surrendered by the people is first divided between two distinct governments, and then the portion allotted to each subdivided among distinct and separate departments. Hence a double security arises to the rights of the people. The different governments will control each other, at the same time that each will be controlled by itself.

Second. It is of great importance in a republic not only to guard the society against the oppression of its rulers, but to guard one part of the society against the injustice of the other part. Different interests necessarily exist in different classes of citizens. If a majority be united by a common interest, the rights of the minority will be insecure. There are but two methods of providing against this evil: the one by creating a will in the community independent of the majority—that is, of the society itself; the other, by comprehending in the society so many separate descriptions of citizens as will render an unjust combination of a majority of the whole very improbable, if not impracticable. The first method prevails in all governments possessing an hereditary or self-appointed authority. This, at best, is but a precarious security; because a power independent of the society may as well espouse the unjust views of the major as the rightful interests of the minor party, and may possibly be turned against both parties. The second method will be exemplified in the federal republic of the United States. Whilst all authority in it will be derived from and dependent on the society, the society itself will be broken into so many parts, interests and classes of citizens, that the rights of individuals, or of the minority, will be in little danger from interested combinations of the majority. In a free government the security for civil rights must be the same as that for religious rights. It consists in the one case in the multiplicity of interests, and in the other in the multiplicity of sects. The degree of security in both cases will depend on the number of interests and sects; and this may be presumed to depend on the extent of country and number of people comprehended under the same government. This view of the subject must particularly recommend a proper federal system to all the sincere and considerate friends of republican government, since it shows that in exact proportion as the territory of the Union may be formed into more circumscribed Confederacies, or States, oppressive combinations of a majority will be facilitated; the best security, under the republican forms, for the rights of every class of citizen, will be diminished; and consequently the stability and independence of some member of the government, the only other security, must be proportionally increased. Justice is the end of government. It is the end of civil society. It ever has been and ever will be pursued until it be obtained, or until liberty be lost in the pursuit. In a society under the forms of which the stronger faction can readily unite and oppress the weaker, anarchy may as truly be said to reign as in a state of nature, where the weaker individual is not secured against the violence of the stronger; and as, in the latter state, even the stronger individuals are prompted, by the uncertainty of their condition, to submit to a government which may protect the weak as well as themselves; so, in the former state, will the more powerful factions or parties be gradually induced, by a like motive, to wish for a government which will protect all parties, the weaker as well as the more powerful. It can be little doubted that if the State of Rhode Island was separated from the Confederacy and left to itself, the insecurity of rights under the popular form of government within such narrow limits would be displayed by such reiterated oppressions of factious majorities that some power altogether independent of the people would soon be called for by the voice of the very factions whose misrule had proved the necessity of it. In the extended republic of the United States, and among the great variety of interests, parties, and sects which it embraces, a coalition of a majority of the whole society could seldom take place on any other principles than those of justice and the general good; whilst there being thus less danger to a minor from the will of a major party, there must be less pretext, also, to provide for the security of the former, by introducing into the government a will not dependent on the latter, or, in other words, a will independent of the society itself. It is no less certain than it is important, notwithstanding the contrary opinions which have been entertained, that the larger the society, provided it lie within a practicable sphere, the more duly capable it will be of self-government. And happily for the *republican cause,* the practicable sphere may be carried to a very great extent by a judicious modification and mixture of the *federal principle.*

PUBLIUS

No. 52: Madison

FROM the more general inquiries pursued in the four last papers, I pass on to a more particular examination of the several parts of the government. I shall begin with the House of Representatives.

The first view to be taken of this part of the government relates to the qualifications of the electors and the elected. Those of the former are to be the same with those of the electors of the most numerous branch of the

State legislatures. The definition of the right of suffrage is very justly regarded as a fundamental article of republican government. It was incumbent on the convention, therefore, to define and establish this right in the Constitution. To have left it open for the occasional regulation of the Congress would have been improper for the reason just mentioned. To have submitted it to the legislative discretion of the States would have been improper for the same reason; and for the additional reason that it would have rendered too dependent on the State governments that branch of the federal government which ought to be dependent on the people alone. To have reduced the different qualifications in the different States to one uniform rule would probably have been as dissatisfactory to some of the States as it would have been difficult to the convention. The provision made by the convention appears, therefore, to be the best that lay within their option. It must be satisfactory to every State, because it is comfortable to the standard already established, or which may be established, by the State itself. It will be safe to the United States because, being fixed by the State constitutions, it is not alterable by the State governments, and it cannot be feared that the people of the States will alter this part of their constitutions in such a manner as to abridge the rights secured to them by the federal Constitution.

The qualifications of the elected, being less carefully and properly defined by the State constitutions, and being at the same time more susceptible of uniformity, have been very properly considered and regulated by the convention. A representative of the United States must be of the age of twenty-five years; must have been seven years a citizen of the United States; must, at the time of his election, be an inhabitant of the State he is to represent; and, during the time of his service, must be in no office under the United States. Under these reasonable limitations, the door of this part of the federal government is open to merit of every description, whether native or adoptive, whether young or old, and without regard to poverty or wealth, or to any particular profession of religious faith.

The term for which the representatives are to be elected falls under a second view which may be taken of this branch. In order to decide on the propriety of this article, two questions must be considered: first, whether biennial elections will, in this case, be safe; second, whether they be necessary or useful.

First. As it is essential to liberty that the government in general should have a common interest with the people, so it is particularly essential that the branch of it under consideration should have an immediate dependence on, and an intimate sympathy with, the people. Frequent elections are unquestionably the only policy by which this dependence and sympathy can be effectually secured. But what particular degree of frequency may be absolutely necessary for the purpose does not appear to be susceptible of any precise calculation, and must depend on a variety of circumstances with which it may be connected. Let us consult experience, the guide that ought always to be followed whenever it can be found.

The scheme of representation as a substitute for a meeting of the citizens in person being at most but very imperfectly known to ancient polity, it is in more modern times only that we are to expect instructive examples. And even here, in order to avoid a research too vague and diffusive, it will be proper to confine ourselves to the few examples which are best known, and which bear the greatest analogy to our particular case. The first to which this character ought to be applied is the House of Commons in Great Britain. The history of this branch of the English Constitution, anterior to the date of Magna Charta, is too obscure to yield instruction. The very existence of it has been made a question among political antiquaries. The earliest records of subsequent date prove that parliaments were to *sit* only every year; not that they were to be *elected* every year. And even these annual sessions were left so much at the discretion of the monarch, that, under various pretexts, very long and dangerous intermissions were often contrived by royal ambition. To remedy this grievance, it was provided by a statute in the reign of Charles II that the intermissions should not be protracted beyond a period of three years. On the accession of William III, when a revolution took place in the government, the subject was still more seriously resumed, and it was declared to be among the fundamental rights of the people that parliaments ought to be held *frequently*. By another statute, which passed a few years later in the same reign, the term "frequently," which had alluded to the triennial period settled in the time of Charles II, is reduced to a precise meaning, it being expressly enacted that a new parliament shall be called within three years after the termination of the former. The last change, from three to seven years, is well known to have been introduced pretty early in the present century, under an alarm for the Hanoverian succession. From these facts it appears that the greatest frequency of elections which has been deemed necessary in that kingdom for binding the representatives to their constituents does not exceed a triennial return of them. And if we may argue from the degree of liberty retained even under septennial elections, and all the other vicious ingredients in the parliamentary Constitution, we cannot doubt that a reduction of the period from seven to three years, with the other necessary reforms, would so far extend the influence of the people over their representatives as to satisfy us that biennial elections, under the federal system, cannot possibly be dangerous to the requisite dependence of the House of Representatives on their constituents.

Elections in Ireland, till of late, were regulated entirely by the discretion of the crown, and were seldom repeated, except on the accession of a new prince, or some other contingent event. The Parliament which commenced with George II was continued throughout his whole reign, a period of about thirty-five years. The only dependence of the representatives on the people consisted in the right of the latter to supply occasional vacancies by the election of new members, and in the chance of some event which might produce a general new election. The ability also of the Irish parliament to maintain the rights of their constituents, so far as the disposition might exist, was extremely shackled by the control of the crown over the subjects of their deliberation. Of late, these shackles, if I mistake not, have been broken; and octennial parliaments have besides been established. What effect may be produced by this partial reform must be left to further experience. The example of Ireland, from this view of it, can throw but little light on the subject. As far as we can draw any conclusion from it, it must be that if the people of that country have been able under all these disadvantages to retain any liberty whatever, the advantage of biennial elections would secure to them every degree of liberty, which might depend on a due connection between their representatives and themselves.

Let us bring our inquiries nearer home. The example of these States, when British colonies, claims particular attention, at the same time that it is so well known as to require little to be said on it. The principle of representation, in one branch of the legislature at least, was established in all of them. But the periods of election were different. They varied from one to seven years. Have we any reason to infer, from the spirit and conduct of the representatives of the people, prior to the Revolution, that biennial elections would have been dangerous to the public liberties? The spirit which everywhere displayed itself at the commencement of the struggle, and which vanquished the obstacles to independence, is the best of proofs that a sufficient portion of liberty had been everywhere enjoyed to inspire both a sense of its worth and a zeal for its proper enlargement. This remark holds good as well with regard to the then colonies whose elections were least frequent, as to those whose elections were most frequent. Virginia was the colony which stood first in resisting the parliamentary usurpations of Great Britain; it was the first also in espousing, by public act, the resolution of independence. In Virginia, nevertheless, if I have not been misinformed, elections under the former government were septennial. This particular example is brought into view, not as a proof of any peculiar merit, for the priority in those instances was probably accidental; and still less of any advantage in *septennial* elections, for when compared with a greater frequency they are inadmissible; but merely as a proof, and I conceive it to be a very substantial proof, that the liberties of the people can be in no danger from *biennial* elections.

The conclusion resulting from these examples will be not a little strengthened by recollecting three circumstances. The first is, that the federal legislature will possess a part only of that supreme legislative authority which is vested completely in the British Parliament; and which, with a few exceptions, was exercised by the colonial assemblies and the Irish legislature. It is a received and well-founded maxim that where no other circumstances affect the case, the greater the power is, the shorter ought to be its duration; and, conversely, the smaller the power, the more safely may its duration be protracted. In the second place it has, on another occasion, been shown that the federal legislature will not only be restrained by its dependence on the people, as other legislative bodies are, but that it will be, moreover, watched and controlled by the several collateral legislatures, which other legislative bodies are not. And in the third place, no comparison can be made between the means that will be possessed by the more permanent branches of the federal government for seducing, if they should be disposed to seduce, the House of Representatives from their duty to the people, and the means of influence over the popular branch possessed by the other branches of the government above cited. With less power, therefore, to abuse, the federal representatives can be less tempted on one side, and will be doubly watched on the other.

PUBLIUS

No. 53: Madison

I SHALL here, perhaps, be reminded of a current observation "that where annual elections end, tyranny begins." If it be true, as has often been remarked, that sayings which become proverbial are generally founded in reason, it is not less true that when once established they are often applied to cases to which the reason of them does not extend. I need not look for a proof beyond the case before us. What is the reason on which this proverbial observation is founded? No man will subject himself to the ridicule of pretending that any natural connection subsists between the sun or the seasons, and the period within which human virtue can bear the temptations of power. Happily for mankind, liberty is not, in this respect, confined to any single point of time, but lies within extremes, which afford sufficient latitude for all the variations which may be required by the various situations and circumstances of civil society. The election of magistrates might be, if it were found expedient, as in some instances it actually has been, daily, weekly, or monthly, as well as annual; and if circumstances may require a deviation from the rule on one side, why not also on the other side? Turning our attention to the periods established among ourselves, for the election of the most numerous branches of the State legislatures, we find them by no means coinciding any more in this instance than in the elections of other civil magistrates. In Connecticut and Rhode Island, the periods are half-yearly. In the other States, South Carolina excepted, they are annual. In South Carolina they are biennial—as is proposed in the federal government. Here is a difference, as four to one, between the longest and shortest periods; and yet it would be not easy to show, that Connecticut or Rhode Island is better governed, or enjoys a greater share of rational liberty, than South Carolina; or that either the one or the other of these States is distinguished in these respects, and by these causes, from the States whose elections are different from both.

In searching for the grounds of this doctrine, I can discover but one, and that is wholly inapplicable to our case. The important distinction so well understood in America between a Constitution established by the people and unalterable by the government, and a law established by the government and alterable by the government, seems to have been little understood and less observed in any other country. Wherever the supreme power of legislation has resided, has been supposed to reside also a full power to change the form of the government. Even in Great Britain, where the principles of political and civil liberty have been most discussed, and where we hear most of the rights of the Constitution, it is maintained that the authority of the Parliament is transcendent and uncontrollable as well with regard to the Constitution as the ordinary objects of legislative provision. They have accordingly, in several instances, actually changed, by legislative acts, some of the most fundamental articles of the government. They have in particular, on several occasions, changed the period of election; and, on the last occasion, not only introduced septennial in place of triennial elections, but by the same act, continued themselves in place four years beyond the term for which they were elected by the people. An attention to these dangerous practices has produced a very natural alarm in the votaries of free government, of which frequency of elections is the cornerstone; and has led them to seek for some security to liberty, against the danger to which it is exposed. Where no Constitution, paramount to the government, either existed or could be obtained, no constitutional security, similar to that established in the United States, was to be attempted. Some other security, therefore, was to be sought for; and what better security would the case admit than that of selecting and appealing to some simple and familiar portion of time as a standard for measuring the danger of innovations, for fixing the national sentiment, and for uniting the patriotic exertions? The most simple and familiar portion of time applicable to the subject was that of a year; and hence the doctrine has been inculcated by a laudable zeal to erect some barrier against the gradual innovations of an unlimited government, that the advance towards tyranny was to be calculated by the distance of departure from the fixed point of annual elections. But what necessity can there be of applying this expedient to a government limited, as the federal government will be, by the authority of a paramount Constitution? Or who will pretend that the liberties of the people of America will not be more secure under biennial elections, unalterably fixed by such a Constitution, than those of any other nation would be, where elections were annual, or even more frequent, but subject to alterations by the ordinary power of the government?

The second question stated is whether biennial elections be necessary or useful. The propriety of answering this question in the affirmative will appear from several very obvious considerations.

No man can be a competent legislator who does not add to an upright intention and a sound judgment a certain degree of knowledge of the subjects on which he is to legislate. A part of this knowledge may be acquired by means of information which lie within the compass of men in private as well as public stations. Another part can only be attained, or at least thoroughly attained, by actual experience in the station which requires the use of it. The period of service ought, therefore, in all such cases, to bear some proportion to the extent of practical knowledge requisite to the due performance of the service.

The period of legislative service established in most of the States for the more numerous branch is, as we have seen, one year. The question then may be put into this simple form: does the period of two years bear no greater proportion to the knowledge requisite for federal legislation than one year does to the knowledge requisite for State legislation? The very statement of the question, in this form, suggests the answer that ought to be given to it.

In a single State, the requisite knowledge relates to the existing laws which are uniform throughout the State and with which all the citizens are more or less conversant; and to the general affairs of the State, which lie within a small compass, are not very diversified, and occupy much of the attention and conversation of every class of people. The great theater of the United States presents a very different scene. The laws are so far from being uniform that they vary in every State; whilst the public affairs of the Union are spread throughout a very extensive region and are extremely diversified by the local affairs connected with them, and can with difficulty be correctly learned in any other place than in the central councils, to which a knowledge of them will be brought by the representatives of every part of the empire. Yet some knowledge of the affairs, and even of the laws, of all the States, ought to be possessed by the members from each of the States. How can foreign trade be properly regulated by uniform laws without some acquaintance with the commerce, the ports, the usages, and the regulations of the different States? How can the trade between the different States be duly regulated without some knowledge of their relative situations in these and other points? How can taxes be judiciously imposed and effectually collected if they be not accommodated to the different laws and local circumstances relating to these objects in the different States? How can uniform regulations for the militia be duly provided without a similar knowledge of some internal circumstances by which the States are distinguished from each other? These are the principal objects of federal legislation and suggest most forcibly the extensive information which the representatives ought to acquire. The other inferior objects will require a proportional degree of information with regard to them.

It is true that all these difficulties will, by degrees, be very much diminished. The most laborious task will be the proper inauguration of the government and the primeval formation of a federal code. Improvements on the first draught will every year become both easier and fewer. Past transactions of the government will be a ready and accurate source of information to new members. The affairs of the Union will become more and more objects of curiosity and conversation among the citizens at large. And the increased intercourse among those of different States will contribute not a little to diffuse a mutual knowledge of their affairs, as this again will contribute to a general assimilation of their manners and laws. But with all these abatements, the business of federal legislation must continue so far to exceed, both in novelty and difficulty, the legislative business of a single State, as to justify the longer period of service assigned to those who are to transact it.

A branch of knowledge which belongs to the acquirements of a federal representative and which has not been mentioned is that of foreign affairs. In regulating our own commerce, he ought to be not only acquainted with the treaties between the United States and other nations, but also with the commercial policy and laws of other nations. He ought not to be altogether ignorant of the law of nations; for that, as far as it is a proper object of municipal legislation, is submitted to the federal government. And although the House of Representatives is not immediately to participate in foreign negotiations and arrangements, yet from the necessary connection between the several branches of public affairs, those particular branches will frequently deserve attention in the ordinary course of legislation and will sometimes demand particular legislative sanction and co-operation. Some portion of this knowledge may, no doubt, be acquired in a man's closet; but some of it also can only be derived from the public sources of information; and all of it will be acquired to best effect by a practical attention to the subject during the period of actual service in the legislature.

There are other considerations, of less importance perhaps, but which are not unworthy of notice. The distance which many of the representatives will be obliged to travel and the arrangements rendered necessary by that circumstance might be much more serious objections with fit men to this service, if limited to a single year, than if extended to two years. No argument can be drawn on this subject from the case of the delegates to the existing Congress. They are elected annually, it is true; but their re-election is considered by the legislative assemblies almost as a matter of course. The election of the representatives by the people would not be governed by the same principle.

A few of the members, as happens in all such assemblies, will possess superior talents; will, by frequent reelections, become members of long standing; will be thoroughly masters of the public business, and perhaps not unwilling to avail themselves of those advantages. The greater the proportion of new members and the less the information of the bulk of the members, the more apt will they be to fall into the snares that may be laid for them. This remark is no less applicable to the relation which will subsist between the House of Representatives and the Senate.

It is an inconvenience mingled with the advantages of our frequent elections, even in single States, where they are large, and hold but one legislative session in a year, that spurious elections cannot be investigated and annulled in time for the decision to have its due effect. If a return can be obtained, no matter by what unlawful means, the irregular member, who takes his seat of course, is sure of holding it a sufficient time to answer his purposes. Hence, a very pernicious encouragement is given to the use of unlawful means for obtaining irregular returns. Were elections for the federal legislature to be annual this practice might become a very serious abuse, particularly in the more distant States. Each house is, as it necessarily must be, the judge of the elections, qualifications, and returns of its members; and whatever improvements may be suggested by experience for simplifying and accelerating the process in disputed cases, so great a portion of a year would unavoidably elapse before an illegitimate member could be dispossessed of his seat that the prospect of such an event would be little check to unfair and illicit means of obtaining a seat.

All these considerations taken together warrant us in

affirming that biennial elections will be as useful to the affairs of the public as we have seen that they will be safe to the liberties of the people. PUBLIUS

No. 54: Madison

THE next view which I shall take of the House of Representatives relates to the apportionment of its members to the several States, which is to be determined by the same rule with that of direct taxes.

It is not contended that the number of people in each State ought not to be the standard for regulating the proportion of those who are to represent the people of each State. The establishment of the same rule for the apportionment of taxes will probably be as little contested; though the rule itself, in this case, is by no means founded on the same principle. In the former case, the rule is understood to refer to the personal rights of the people, with which it has a natural and universal connection. In the latter, it has reference to the proportion of wealth of which it is in no case a precise measure, and in ordinary cases a very unfit one. But notwithstanding the imperfection of the rule as applied to the relative wealth and contributions of the States, it is evidently the least exceptionable among the practicable rules, and had too recently obtained the general sanction of America not to have found a ready preference with the convention.

All this is admitted, it will perhaps be said; but does it follow, from an admission of numbers for the measure of representation, or of slaves combined with free citizens as a ratio of taxation, that slaves ought to be included in the numerical rule of representation? Slaves are considered as property, not as persons. They ought therefore to be comprehended in estimates of taxation which are founded on property, and to be excluded from representation which is regulated by a census of persons. This is the objection, as I understand it, stated in its full force. I shall be equally candid in stating the reasoning which may be offered on the opposite side.

"We subscribe to the doctrine," might one of our Southern brethren observe, "that representation relates more immediately to persons, and taxation more immediately to property, and we join in the application of this distinction to the case of our slaves. But we must deny the fact that slaves are considered merely as property, and in no respect whatever as persons. The true state of the case is that they partake of both these qualities: being considered by our laws, in some respects, as persons, and in other respects as property. In being compelled to labor, not for himself, but for a master; in being vendible by one master to another master; and in being subject at all times to be restrained in his liberty and chastised in his body, by the capricious will of another—the slave may appear to be degraded from the human rank, and classed with those irrational animals which fall under the legal denomination of property. In being protected, on the other hand, in his life and in his limbs, against the violence of all others, even the master of his labor and his liberty; and in being punishable himself for all violence committed against others—the slave is no less evidently regarded by the law as a member of the society, not as a part of the irrational creation; as a moral person, not as a mere article of property. The federal Constitution, therefore, decides with great propriety on the case of our slaves, when it views them in the mixed character of persons and of property. This is in fact their true character. It is the character bestowed on them by the laws under which they live; and it will not be denied that these are the proper criterion; because it is only under the pretext that the laws have transformed the Negroes into subjects of property that a place is disputed them in the computation of numbers; and it is admitted that if the laws were to restore the rights which have been taken away, the Negroes could no longer be refused an equal share of representation with the other inhabitants.

"This question may be placed in another light. It is agreed on all sides that numbers are the best scale of wealth and taxation, as they are the only proper scale of representation. Would the convention have been impartial or consistent, if they had rejected the slaves from the list of inhabitants when the shares of representation were to be calculated, and inserted them on the lists when the tariff of contributions was to be adjusted? Could it be reasonably expected that the Southern States would concur in a system which considered their slaves in some degree as men when burdens were to be imposed, but refused to consider them in the same light when advantages were to be conferred? Might not some surprise also be expressed that those who reproach the Southern States with the barbarous policy of considering as property a part of their human brethren should themselves contend that the government to which all the States are to be parties ought to consider this unfortunate race more completely in the unnatural light of property than the very laws of which they complain?

"It may be replied, perhaps, that slaves are not included in the estimate of representatives in any of the States possessing them. They neither vote themselves nor increase the votes of their masters. Upon what principle, then, ought they to be taken into the federal estimate of representation? In rejecting them altogether, the Constitution would, in this respect, have followed the very laws which have been appealed to as the proper guide.

"This objection is repelled by a single observation. It is a fundamental principle of the proposed Constitution that as the aggregate number of representatives allotted to the several States is to be determined by a federal rule founded on the aggregate number of inhabitants, so the right of choosing this allotted number in each State is to be exercised by such part of the inhabitants as the State itself may designate. The qualifications on which the right of suffrage depend are not, perhaps, the same in any two States. In some of the States the difference is very material. In every State, a certain proportion of inhabitants are deprived of this right by the constitution of the State, who will be included in the census by which the federal Constitution apportions the representatives. In this point of view the Southern States might retort the complaint by insisting that the principle laid down by the convention required that no regard should be had to the policy of particular States towards their own inhabitants; and consequently that the slaves, as inhabitants, should have been admitted into the census according to their full number, in like manner with other inhabitants, who, by the policy of other States, are not admitted to all the rights of citizens. A rigorous adherence, however, to this principle is waived by those who would be gainers by it.

All that they ask is that equal moderation be shown on the other side. Let the case of the slaves be considered, as it is in truth a peculiar one. Let the compromising expedient of the Constitution be mutually adopted which regards them as inhabitants, but as debased by servitude below the equal level of free inhabitants; which regards the *slave* as divested of two fifths of the *man.*

"After all, may not another ground be taken on which this article of the Constitution will admit of a still more ready defense? We have hitherto proceeded on the idea that representation related to persons only, and not at all to property. But is it a just idea? Government is instituted no less for protection of the property than of the persons of individuals. The one as well as the other, therefore, may be considered as represented by those who are charged with the government. Upon this principle it is that in several of the States, and particularly in the State of New York, one branch of the government is intended more especially to be the guardian of property and is accordingly elected by that part of the society which is most interested in this object of government. In the federal Constitution, this policy does not prevail. The rights of property are committed into the same hands with the personal rights. Some attention ought, therefore, to be paid to property in the choice of those hands.

"For another reason, the votes allowed in the federal legislature to the people of each State ought to bear some proportion to the comparative wealth of the States. States have not, like individuals, an influence over each other, arising from superior advantages of fortune. If the law allows an opulent citizen but a single vote in the choice of his representative, the respect and consequence which he derives from his fortunate situation very frequently guide the votes of others to the objects of his choice; and through this imperceptible channel the rights of property are conveyed into the public representation. A State possesses no such influence over other States. It is not probable that the richest State in the Confederacy will ever influence the choice of a single representative in any other State. Nor will the representatives of the larger and richer States possess any other advantage in the federal legislature over the representatives of other States than what may result from their superior number alone. As far, therefore, as their superior wealth and weight may justly entitle them to any advantage, it ought to be secured to them by a superior share of representation. The new Constitution is, in this respect, materially different from the existing Confederation, as well as from that of the United Netherlands, and other similar confederacies. In each of the latter, the efficacy of the federal resolutions depends on the subsequent and voluntary resolutions of the States composing the union. Hence the States, though possessing an equal vote in the public councils, have an unequal influence, corresponding with the unequal importance of these subsequent and voluntary resolutions. Under the proposed Constitution, the federal acts will take effect without the necessary intervention of the individual States. They will depend merely on the majority of votes in the federal legislature, and consequently each vote, whether proceeding from a larger or a smaller State, or a State more or less wealthy or powerful, will have an equal weight and efficacy: in the same manner as the votes individually given in a State legislature, by the representatives of unequal counties or other districts, have each a precise equality of value and effect; or if there be any difference in the case, it proceeds from the difference in the personal character of the individual representative, rather than from any regard to the extent of the district from which he comes."

Such is the reasoning which an advocate for the Southern interests might employ on this subject; and although it may appear to be a little strained in some points, yet on the whole, I must confess that it fully reconciles me to the scale of representation which the convention have established.

In one respect, the establishment of a common measure for representation and taxation will have a very salutary effect. As the accuracy of the census to be obtained by the Congress will necessarily depend, in a considerable degree, on the disposition, if not on the co-operation of the States, it is of great importance that the States should feel as little bias as possible to swell or to reduce the amount of their numbers. Were their share of representation alone to be governed by this rule, they would have an interest in exaggerating their inhabitants. Were the rule to decide their share of taxation alone, a contrary temptation would prevail. By extending the rule to both objects, the States will have opposite interests which will control and balance each other and produce the requisite impartiality. PUBLIUS

No. 55: Madison

THE number of which the House of Representatives is to consist forms another and a very interesting point of view under which this branch of the federal legislature may be contemplated. Scarce any article, indeed, in the whole Constitution seems to be rendered more worthy of attention by the weight of character and the apparent force of argument with which it has been assailed. The charges exhibited against it are, first, that so small a number of representatives will be an unsafe depositary of the public interests; second, that they will not possess a proper knowledge of the local circumstances of their numerous constituents; third, that they will be taken from that class of citizens which will sympathize least with the feelings of the mass of the people and be most likely to aim at a permanent elevation of the few on the depression of the many; fourth, that defective as the number will be in the first instance, it will be more and more disproportionate, by the increase of the people and the obstacles which will prevent a correspondent increase of the representatives.

In general it may be remarked on this subject that no political problem is less susceptible of a precise solution than that which relates to the number most convenient for a representative legislature; nor is there any point on which the policy of the several States is more at variance, whether we compare their legislative assemblies directly with each other, or consider the proportions which they respectively bear to the number of their constituents. Passing over the difference between the smallest and largest States, as Delaware, whose most numerous branch consists of twenty-one representatives, and Massachusetts, where it amounts to between three and four hundred, a very considerable difference is observable among States nearly equal in population. The number of representatives in Pennsylvania is not more than one fifth of that in the State last mentioned. New York, whose population is to that of South Carolina as six to five, has little more than one third of the number of representatives. As great a disparity prevails between the States of Georgia and Delaware or Rhode Island. In Pennsylvania, the representatives do not bear a greater proportion to their constituents than of one for every four or five thousand. In Rhode Island, they bear a proportion of at least one for every thousand. And according to the constitution of Georgia, the proportion may be carried to one to every ten electors; and must unavoidably far exceed the proportion in any of the other States.

Another general remark to be made is that the ratio between the representatives and the people ought not to be the same where the latter are very numerous as where they are very few. Were the representatives in Virginia to be regulated by the standard in Rhode Island, they would, at this time, amount to between four and five hundred; and twenty or thirty years hence, to a thousand. On the other hand, the ratio of Pennsylvania, if applied to the State of Delaware, would reduce the representative assembly of the latter to seven or eight members. Nothing can be more fallacious than to found our political calculations on arithmetical principles. Sixty or seventy men may be more properly trusted with a given degree of power than six or seven. But it does not follow that six or seven hundred would be proportionably a better depositary. And if we carry on the supposition to six or seven thousand, the whole reasoning ought to be reversed. The truth is that in all cases a certain number at least seems to be necessary to secure the benefits of free consultation and discussion, and to guard against too easy a combination for improper purposes; as, on the other hand, the number ought at most to be kept within a certain limit, in order to avoid the confusion and intemperance of a multitude. In all very numerous assemblies, of whatever characters composed, passion never fails to wrest the scepter from reason. Had every Athenian citizen been a Socrates, every Athenian assembly would still have been a mob.

It is necessary also to recollect here the observations which were applied to the case of biennial elections. For the same reason that the limited powers of the Congress, and the control of the State legislatures, justify less frequent election than the public safety might otherwise require, the members of the Congress need be less numerous than if they possessed the whole power of legislation, and were under no other than the ordinary restraints of other legislative bodies.

With these general ideas in our minds, let us weigh the objections which have been stated against the number of members proposed for the House of Representatives. It is said, in the first place, that so small a number cannot be safely trusted with so much power.

The number of which this branch of the legislature is to consist, at the outset of the government, will be sixty-five. Within three years a census is to be taken, when the number may be augmented to one for every thirty thousand inhabitants; and within every successive period of ten years the census is to be renewed, and augmentations may continue to be made under the above limitation. It will not be thought an extravagant conjecture that the first census will, at the rate of one for every thirty thousand, raise the number of representatives to at least one hundred. Estimating the Negroes in the proportion of three fifths, it can scarcely be doubted that the population of the United States will by that time, if it does not already, amount to three millions. At the expiration of twenty-five years, according to the computed rate of increase, the number of representatives will amount to two hundred; and of fifty years, to four hundred. This is a number which, I presume, will put an end to all fears arising from the smallness of the body. I take for granted here what I shall, in answering the fourth objection, hereafter show, that the number of representatives will be augmented from time to time in the manner provided by the Constitution. On a contrary supposition, I should admit the objection to have very great weight indeed.

The true question to be decided, then, is whether the smallness of the number, as a temporary regulation, be dangerous to the public liberty? Whether sixty-five members for a few years, and a hundred or two hundred for a few more, be a safe depositary for a limited and well-guarded power of legislating for the United States? I must own that I could not give a negative answer to this question, without first obliterating every impression which I have received with regard to the present genius of the people of America, the spirit which actuates the State legislatures, and the principles which are incorporated with the political character of every class of citizens. I am unable to conceive that the people of America, in their present temper, or under any circumstances which can speedily happen, will choose, and every second year repeat the choice of, sixty-five or a hundred men who would be disposed to form and pursue a scheme of tyranny or treachery. I am unable to conceive that the State legislatures, which must feel so many motives to watch and which possess so many means of counteracting the federal legislature, would fail either to detect or to defeat a conspiracy of the latter against the liberties of their common constituents. I am equally unable to conceive that there are at this time, or can be in any short time, in the United States, any sixty-five or a hundred men capable of recommending themselves to the choice of the people at large, who would either desire or dare, within the short space of two years, to betray the solemn trust committed to them. What change of circumstances time, and a fuller population of our country may produce requires a prophetic spirit to declare, which makes no part of my pretensions. But judging from the circumstances now before us, and from the probable state of them within a moderate period of time, I must pronounce that the liberties of America cannot be unsafe in the number of hands proposed by the federal Constitution.

From what quarter can the danger proceed? Are we afraid of foreign gold? If foreign gold could so easily corrupt our federal rulers and enable them to ensnare and betray their constituents, how has it happened that we are at this time a free and independent nation? The Congress which conducted us through the Revolution was a less numerous body than their successors will be; they were not chosen by, nor responsible to, their fellow-citizens at large; though appointed from year to year, and recallable at pleasure, they were generally continued for three years, and, prior to the ratification of the federal articles, for a still longer term. They held their consultations always under the veil of secrecy; they had the sole transaction of our affairs with foreign nations; though the whole course of the war they had the fate of their country more in their hands than it is to be hoped will ever be the case with our future representatives; and from the greatness of the prize at stake, and the eagerness of the party which lost it, it may well be supposed that the use of other means than force would not have been scrupled. Yet we know by happy experience that the public trust was not betrayed; nor has the purity of our public councils in this particular ever suffered, even from the whispers of calumny.

Is the danger apprehended from the other branches of the federal government? But where are the means to be found by the President, or the Senate, or both? Their emoluments of office, it is to be presumed, will not, and without a previous corruption of the House of Representatives cannot, more than suffice for very different purposes; their private fortunes, as they must all be American citizens, cannot possibly be sources of danger. The only means, then, which they can possess, will be in the dispensation of appointments. Is it here that suspicion rests her charge? Sometimes we are told that this fund of corruption is to be exhausted by the President in subduing the virtue of the Senate. Now, the fidelity of the other House is to be the victim. The improbability of such a mercenary and perfidious combination of the several members of government, standing on as different foundations as republican principles will well admit, and at the same time accountable to the society over which they are placed, ought alone to quiet this apprehension. But, fortunately, the Constitution has provided a still further safeguard. The members of the Congress are rendered ineligible to any civil offices that may be created, or of which the emoluments may be increased, during the term of their election. No offices therefore can be dealt out to the existing members but such as may become vacant by ordinary casualties: and to suppose that these would be sufficient to purchase the guardians of the people, selected by the people themselves, is to renounce every rule by which events ought to be calculated, and to substitute an indiscriminate and unbounded jealousy, with which all reasoning must be vain. The sincere friends of liberty who give themselves up to the extravagancies of this passion are not aware of the injury they do their own cause. As there is a degree of depravity in mankind which requires a certain degree of circumspection and distrust, so there are other qualities in human nature which justify a certain portion of esteem and confidence. Republican government presupposes the existence of these qualities in a higher degree than any other form. Were the pictures which have been drawn by the political jealousy of some among us faithful likenesses of the human character, the inference would be that there is not sufficient virtue among men for self-government; and that nothing less than the chains of despotism can restrain them from destroying and devouring one another.

PUBLIUS

No. 56: Madison

THE *second* charge against the House of Representatives is that it will be too small to possess a due knowledge of the interests of its constituents.

As this objection evidently proceeds from a comparison of the proposed number of representatives with the great extent of the United States, the number of their inhabitants, and the diversity of their interests, without taking into view at the same time the circumstances which will distinguish the Congress from other legislative bodies, the best answer that can be given to it will be a brief explanation of these peculiarities.

It is a sound and important principle that the representative ought to be acquainted with the interests and circumstances of his constituents. But this principle can extend no further than to those circumstances and interests to which the authority and care of the representative relate. An ignorance of a variety of minute and particular objects which do not lie within the compass of legislation is consistent with every attribute necessary to a due performance of the legislative trust. In determining the extent of information required in the exercise of a particular authority, recourse then must be had to the objects within the purview of that authority.

What are to be the objects of federal legislation? Those which are of most importance, and which seem most to require local knowledge, are commerce, taxation, and the militia.

A proper regulation of commerce requires much information, as has been elsewhere remarked; but as far as this information relates to the laws and local situation of each individual State, a very few representatives would be very sufficient vehicles of it to the federal councils.

Taxation will consist, in a great measure, of duties which will be involved in the regulation of commerce. So far the preceding remark is applicable to this object. As far as it may consist of internal collections, a more diffusive knowledge of the circumstances of the State may be necessary. But will not this also be possessed in sufficient degree by a very few intelligent men, diffusively elected within the State? Divide the largest State into ten or twelve districts and it will be found that there will be no peculiar local interests in either which will not be within the knowledge of the representative of the district. Besides this source of information, the laws of the State, framed by representatives from every part of it, will be almost of themselves a sufficient guide. In every State there have been made, and must continue to be made, regulations on this subject which will, in many cases, leave little more to be done by the federal legislature than to review the different laws and reduce them in one general act. A skilful individual in his closet, with all the local codes before him, might compile a law on some subjects of taxation for the whole Union, without any aid from oral information, and it may be expected that whenever internal taxes may be necessary, and particularly in cases requiring uniformity throughout the States, the more simple objects will be preferred. To be fully sensible of the facility which will be given to this branch of federal legislation by the assistance of the State codes, we need only suppose for a moment that this or any other State were divided into a number of parts, each having and exercising within itself a power of local legislation. Is it not evident that a degree of local information and preparatory labor would be found in the several volumes of their proceedings, which would very much shorten the labors of the general legislature, and render a much smaller number of members sufficient for it? The federal councils will derive great advantage from another circumstance. The representatives of each State will not only bring with them a considerable knowledge of its laws, and a local knowledge of their respective districts, but will probably in all cases have been members, and may even at the very time be members, of the State legislature, where all the local information and interests of the State are assembled, and from whence they may easily be conveyed by a very few hands into the legislature of the United States.

With regard to the regulation of the militia, there are scarcely any circumstances in reference to which local knowledge can be said to be necessary. The general face of the country, whether mountainous or level, most fit for the operations of infantry or cavalry, is almost the only consideration of this nature that can occur. The art of war teaches general principles of organization, movement, and discipline, which apply universally.

The attentive reader will discern that the reasoning here used to prove the sufficiency of a moderate number of representatives does not in any respect contradict what was urged on another occasion with regard to the extensive information which the representatives ought to possess, and the time that might be necessary for acquiring it. This information, so far as it may relate to local objects, is rendered necessary and difficult, not by a difference of laws and local circumstances within a single State, but of those among different States. Taking each State by itself, its laws are the same, and its interests but little diversified. A few men, therefore, will possess all the knowledge requisite for a proper representation of them. Were the interests and affairs of each individual State perfectly simple and uniform, a knowledge of them in one part would involve a knowledge of them in every other, and the whole State might be competently represented by a single member taken from any part of it. On a comparison of the different States together, we find a great dissimilarity in their laws, and in many other circumstances connected with the objects of federal legislation, with all of which the federal representatives ought to have some acquaintance. Whilst a few representatives, therefore, from each State may bring with them a due knowledge of their own State, every representative will have much information to acquire concerning all the other States. The changes of time, as was formerly remarked, on the comparative situation of the different States, will have an assimilating effect. The effect of time on the internal affairs of the States, taken singly, will be just the contrary. At present some of the States are little more than a society of husbandmen. Few of them have made much progress in those branches of industry which give a variety and complexity to the affairs of a nation. These, however, will in all of them be the fruits of a more advanced population; and will require, on the part of each State, a fuller representation. The foresight of the convention has accordingly taken care that the progress of population may be accompanied with a proper increase of the representative branch of the government.

The experience of Great Britain, which presents to mankind so many political lessons, both of the monitory and exemplary kind, and which has been frequently consulted in the course of these inquiries, corroborates the result of the reflections which we have just made. The number of inhabitants in the two kingdoms of England and Scotland cannot be stated at less than eight millions. The representatives of these eight millions in the House of Commons amount to five hundred and fifty-eight. Of this number, one ninth are elected by three hundred and sixty-four persons, and one half, by five thousand seven hundred and twenty-three persons.* It cannot be supposed that the half thus elected, and who do not even reside among the people at large, can add anything either to the security of the people against the government, or to the knowledge of their circumstances and interests in the legislative councils. On the contrary, it is notorious that they are more frequently the representatives and instruments of the executive magistrate than the guardians and advocates of the popular rights. They might therefore, with great propriety, be considered as something more than a mere deduction from the real representatives of the nation. We will, however, consider them in this light alone, and will not extend the deduction to a considerable number of others who do not reside among their constituents, are very faintly connected with them, and have very little particular knowledge of their affairs.

* Burgh's *Political Disquisitions*.

With all these concessions, two hundred and seventy-nine persons only will be the depositary of the safety, interest, and happiness of eight millions—that is to say, there will be one representative only to maintain the rights and explain the situation *of twenty-eight thousand six hundred and seventy* constituents, in an assembly exposed to the whole force of executive influence and extending its authority to every object of legislation within a nation whose affairs are in the highest degree diversified and complicated. Yet it is very certain, not only that a valuable portion of freedom has been preserved under all these circumstances, but that the defects in the British code are chargeable, in a very small proportion, on the ignorance of the legislature concerning the circumstances of the people. Allowing to this case the weight which is due to it, and comparing it with that of the House of Representatives as above explained, it seems to give the fullest assurance that a representative for every *thirty thousand inhabitants* will render the latter both a safe and competent guardian of the interests which will be confided to it.

PUBLIUS

No. 57: Madison

THE *third* charge against the House of Representatives is that it will be taken from that class of citizens which will have least sympathy with the mass of the people, and be most likely to aim at an ambitious sacrifice of the many to the aggrandizement of the few.

Of all the objections which have been framed against the federal Constitution, this is perhaps the most extraordinary. Whilst the objection itself is leveled against a pretended oligarchy, the principle of it strikes at the very root of republican government.

The aim of every political constitution is, or ought to be, first to obtain for rulers men who possess most wisdom to discern, and most virtue to pursue, the common good of the society; and in the next place, to take the most effectual precautions for keeping them virtuous whilst they continue to hold their public trust. The elective mode of obtaining rulers is the characteristic policy of republican government. The means relied on in this form of government for preventing their degeneracy are numerous and various. The most effectual one is such a limitation of the term of appointments as will maintain a proper responsibility to the people.

Let me now ask what circumstance there is in the constitution of the House of Representatives that violates the principles of republican government, or favors the elevation of the few on the ruins of the many? Let me ask whether every circumstance is not, on the contrary, strictly conformable to these principles, and scrupulously impartial to the rights and pretensions of every class and description of citizens?

Who are to be the electors of the federal representatives? Not the rich, more than the poor; not the learned, more than the ignorant; not the haughty heirs of distinguished names, more than the humble sons of obscure and unpropitious fortune. The electors are to be the great body of the people of the United States. They are to be the same who exercise the right in every State of electing the corresponding branch of the legislature of the State.

Who are to be the objects of popular choice? Every citizen whose merit may recommend him to the esteem and confidence of his country. No qualification of wealth, of birth, of religious faith, or of civil profession is permitted to fetter the judgment or disappoint the inclination of the people.

If we consider the situation of the men on whom the free suffrages of their fellow-citizens may confer the representative trust, we shall find it involving every security which can be devised or desired for their fidelity to their constituents.

In the first place, as they will have been distinguished by the preference of their fellow-citizens, we are to presume that in general they will be somewhat distinguished also by those qualities which entitle them to it, and which promise a sincere and scrupulous regard to the nature of their engagements.

In the second place, they will enter into the public service under circumstances which cannot fail to produce a temporary affection at least to their constituents. There is in every breast a sensibility to marks of honor, of favor, of esteem, and of confidence, which, apart from all considerations of interests, is some pledge for grateful and benevolent returns. Ingratitude is a common topic of declamation against human nature; and it must be confessed that instances of it are but too frequent and flagrant, both in public and in private life. But the universal and extreme indignation which it inspires is itself a proof of the energy and prevalence of the contrary sentiment.

In the third place, those ties which bind the representative to his constituents are strengthened by motives of a more selfish nature. His pride and vanity attach him to a form of government which favors his pretensions and gives him a share in its honors and distinctions. Whatever hopes or projects might be entertained by a few aspiring characters, it must generally happen that a great proportion of the men deriving their advancement from their influence with the people would have more to hope from a preservation of the favor than from innovations in the government subversive of the authority of the people.

All these securities, however, would be found very insufficient without the restraint of frequent elections. Hence, in the fourth place, the House of Representatives is so constituted as to support in the members an habitual recollection of their dependence on the people. Before the sentiments impressed on their minds by the mode of their elevation can be effaced by the exercise of power, they will be compelled to anticipate the moment when their power is to cease, when their exercise of it is to be reviewed, and when they must descend to the level from which they were raised; there forever to remain unless a faithful discharge of their trust shall have established their title to a renewal of it.

I will add, as a fifth circumstance in the situation of the House of Representatives, restraining them from oppressive measures, that they can make no law which will not have its full operation on themselves and their friends, as well as on the great mass of the society. This has always been deemed one of the strongest bonds by which human policy can connect the rulers and the people together. It creates between them that communion of interests and sympathy of sentiments of which few governments have furnished examples; but without which every government degenerates into tyranny. If it be asked, what is to restrain the House of Representatives from making legal discriminations in favor of themselves and a particular class of the society? I answer: the genius of the whole system; the nature of just and constitutional laws; and, above all, the vigilant and manly spirit which actuates the people of America—a spirit which nourishes freedom, and in return is nourished by it.

If this spirit shall ever be so far debased as to tolerate a law not obligatory on the legislature, as well as on the people, the people will be prepared to tolerate anything but liberty.

Such will be the relation between the House of Representatives and their constituents. Duty, gratitude, interest, ambition itself, are the cords by which they will be bound to fidelity and sympathy with the great mass of the people. It is possible that these may all be insufficient to control the caprice and wickedness of men. But are they not all that government will admit, and that human prudence can devise? Are they not the genuine and the characteristic means by which republican government provides for the liberty and happiness of the people? Are they not the identical means on which every State government in the Union relies for the attainment of these important ends? What, then, are we to understand by the objection which this paper has combated? What are we to say to the men who profess the most flaming zeal for republican government, yet boldly impeach the fundamental principle of it; who pretend to be champions for the right and the capacity of the people to choose their own rulers, yet maintain that they will prefer those only who will immediately and infallibly betray the trust committed to them?

Were the objection to be read by one who had not seen the mode prescribed by the Constitution for the choice of representatives, he could suppose nothing less than that some unreasonable qualification of property was annexed to the right of suffrage; or that the right of eligibility was limited to persons of particular families or fortunes; or at least that the mode prescribed by the State constitutions was, in some respect or other, very grossly departed from. We have seen how far such a supposition would err, as to the two first points. Nor would it, in fact, be less erroneous as to the last. The only difference discoverable between the two cases is that each representative of the United States will be elected by five or six thousand citizens; whilst in the individual States, the election of a representative is left to about as many hundreds. Will it be pretended that this difference is sufficient to justify an attachment to the State governments and an abhorrence to the federal government? If this be the point on which the objection turns, it deserves to be examined.

Is it supported by *reason?* This cannot be said, without maintaining that five or six thousand citizens are less capable of choosing a fit representative, or more liable to be corrupted by an unfit one, than five or six hundred. Reason, on the contrary, assures us that as in so great a number a fit representative would be most likely to be found, so the choice would be less likely to be diverted from him by the intrigues of the ambitious or the bribes of the rich.

Is the *consequence* from this doctrine admissible? If we say that five or six hundred citizens are as many as can jointly exercise their right of suffrage, must we not deprive the people of the immediate choice of their public servants in every instance where the administration of the government does not require as many of them as will amount to one for that number of citizens?

Is the doctrine warranted by *facts?* It was shown in the last paper that the real representation in the British House of Commons very little exceeds the proportion of one for every thirty thousand inhabitants. Besides a variety of powerful causes not existing here, and which favor in that country the pretensions of rank and wealth, no person is eligible as a representative of a county unless he possess real estate of the clear value of six hundred pounds sterling per year; nor of a city or borough, unless he possess a like estate of half that annual value. To this qualification on the part of the county representatives is added another on the part of the county electors, which restrains the right of suffrage to persons having a freehold estate of the annual value of more than twenty pounds sterling, according to the present rate of money. Notwithstanding these unfavorable circumstances, and notwithstanding some very unequal laws in the British code, it cannot be said that the representatives of the nation have elevated the few on the ruins of the many.

But we need not resort to foreign experience on this subject. Our own is explicit and decisive. The districts in New Hampshire in which the senators are chosen immediately by the people are nearly as large as will be necessary for her representatives in the Congress. Those of Massachusetts are larger than will be necessary for that purpose; and those of New York still more so. In the last State the members of Assembly for the cities and counties of New York and Albany are elected by very nearly as many voters as will be entitled to a representative in the Congress, calculating on the number of sixty-five representatives only. It makes no difference that in these senatorial districts and counties a number of representatives are voted for by each elector at the same time. If the same electors at the same time are capable of choosing four or five representatives, they cannot be incapable of choosing one. Pennsylvania is an additional example. Some of her counties, which elect her State representatives, are almost as large as her districts will be by which her federal representatives will be elected. The city of Philadelphia is supposed to contain between fifty and sixty thousand souls. It will therefore form nearly two districts for the choice of federal representatives. It forms, however, but one county, in which every elector votes for each of its representatives in the State legislature. And what may appear to be still more directly to our purpose, the whole city actually elects a *single member* for the executive council. This is the case in all the other counties of the State.

Are not these facts the most satisfactory proofs of the fallacy which has been employed against the branch of the federal government under consideration? Has it appeared on trial that the senators of New Hampshire, Massachusetts, and New York, or the executive council of Pennsylvania, or the members of the Assembly in the two last States, have betrayed any peculiar disposition to sacrifice the many to the few, or are in any respect less worthy of their places than the representatives and magistrates appointed in other States by very small divisions of the people?

But there are cases of a stronger complexion than any which I have yet quoted. One branch of the legislature of Connecticut is so constituted that each member of it is elected by the whole State. So is the governor of that State, of Massachusetts, and of this State, and the president of New Hampshire. I leave every man to decide whether the result of any one of these experiments can be said to countenance a suspicion that a diffusive mode of choosing representatives of the people tends to elevate traitors and to undermine the public liberty. PUBLIUS

No. 58: Madison

THE remaining charge against the House of Representatives, which I am to examine, is grounded on a supposition that the number of members will not be augmented from time to time, as the progress of population may demand.

It has been admitted that this objection, if well supported, would have great weight. The following observations will show that, like most other objections against the Constitution, it can only proceed from a partial view of the subject, or from a jealousy which discolors and disfigures every object which is beheld.

1. Those who urge the objection seem not to have recollected that the federal Constitution will not suffer by a comparison with the State constitutions, in the security provided for a gradual augmentation of the number of representatives. The number which is to prevail in the first instance is declared to be temporary. Its duration is limited to the short term of three years.

Within every successive term of ten years a census of inhabitants is to be repeated. The unequivocal objects of these regulations are, first, to readjust, from time to time, the apportionment of representatives to the number of inhabitants, under the single exception that each State shall have one representative at least; secondly, to augment the number of representatives at the same periods, under the sole limitation that the whole number shall not exceed one for every thirty thousand inhabitants. If we review the constitutions of the several States we shall find that some of them contain no determinate regulations on this subject, that others correspond pretty much on this point with the federal Constitution, and that the most effectual security in any of them is resolvable into a mere directory provision.

2. As far as experience has taken place on this subject, a gradual increase of representatives under the State constitutions has at least kept pace with that of the constituents, and it appears that the former have been as ready to concur in such measures as the latter have been to call for them.

3. There is a peculiarity in the federal Constitution which insures a watchful attention in a majority both of the people and of their representatives to a constitutional augmentation of the latter. The peculiarity lies in this, that one branch of the legislature is a representation of citizens, the other of the States: in the former, consequently, the larger States will have most weight; in the latter, the advantage will be in favor of the smaller States. From this circumstance it may with certainty be inferred that the larger States will be strenuous advocates for increasing the number and weight of that part of the legislature in which their influence predominates. And it so happens that four only of the largest will have a majority of the whole votes in the House of Representatives. Should the representatives or people, therefore, of the smaller States oppose at any time a reasonable addition of members, a coalition of a very few States will be sufficient to overrule the opposition; a coalition which, notwithstanding the rivalship and local prejudices which might prevent it on ordinary occasions, would not fail to take place when not merely prompted by common interest, but justified by equity and the principles of the Constitution.

It may be alleged, perhaps, that the Senate would be prompted by like motives to an adverse coalition; and as their concurrence would be indispensable, the just and constitutional views of the other branch might be defeated. This is the difficulty which has probably created the most serious apprehensions in the jealous friends of a numerous representation. Fortunately it is among the difficulties which, existing only in appearance, vanish on a close and accurate inspection. The following reflections will, if I mistake not, be admitted to be conclusive and satisfactory on this point.

Notwithstanding the equal authority which will subsist between the two houses on all legislative subjects, except the originating of money bills, it cannot be doubted that the House, composed of the greater number of members, when supported by the more powerful States, and speaking the known and determined sense of a majority of the people, will have no small advantage in a question depending on the comparative firmness of the two houses.

This advantage must be increased by the consciousness, felt by the same side, of being supported in its demands by right, by reason, and by the Constitution; and the consciousness, on the opposite side, of contending against the force of all these solemn considerations.

It is farther to be considered that in the gradation between the smallest and largest States there are several which, though most likely in general to arrange themselves among the former, are too little removed in extent and population from the latter to second an opposition to their just and legitimate pretensions. Hence it is by no means certain that a majority of votes, even in the Senate, would be unfriendly to proper augmentations in the number of representatives.

It will not be looking too far to add that the senators from all the new States may be gained over to the just views of the House of Representatives by an expedient too obvious to be overlooked. As these States will, for a great length of time, advance in population with peculiar rapidity, they will be interested in frequent reapportionments of the representatives to the number of inhabitants. The large States, therefore, who will prevail in the House of Representatives, will have nothing to do but to make reapportionments and augmentations mutually conditions of each other; and the senators from all the most growing States will be bound to contend for the latter, by the interest which their States will feel in the former.

These considerations seem to afford ample security on this subject, and ought alone to satisfy all the doubts and fears which have been indulged with regard to it. Admitting, however, that they should all be insufficient to subdue the unjust policy of the smaller States, or their predominant influence in the councils of the Senate, a constitutional and infallible resource still remains with the larger States by which they will be able at all times to accomplish their just purposes. The House of Representatives cannot only refuse, but they alone can propose the supplies requisite for the support of government. They, in a word, hold the purse—that powerful instrument by which we behold, in the history of the British Constitution, an infant and humble representation of the people gradually enlarging the sphere of its activity and importance, and finally reducing, as far as it seems to have wished, all the overgrown prerogatives of the other branches of the government. This power over the purse may, in fact, be regarded as the most complete and effectual weapon with which any constitution can arm the immediate representatives of the people, for obtaining a redress of every grievance, and for carrying into effect every just and salutary measure.

But will not the House of Representatives be as much interested as the Senate in maintaining the government in its proper functions, and will they not therefore be unwilling to stake its existence or its reputation on the pliancy of the Senate? For, if such a trial of firmness between the two branches were hazarded, would not the one be as likely first to yield as the other? These questions will create no difficulty with those who reflect that in all cases the smaller the number, and the more permanent and conspicuous the station of men in power, the stronger must be the interest which they will individually feel in whatever concerns the government. Those who represent the dignity of their country in the eyes of other nations will be particularly sensible to every prospect of public danger, or of a dishonorable stagnation in public affairs. To those causes we are to ascribe the continual triumph of the British House of Commons over the other branches of the government, whenever the engine of a money bill has been employed. An absolute inflexibility on the side of the latter, although it could not have failed to involve every department of the state in the general confusion, has neither been apprehended nor experienced. The utmost degree of firmness that can be displayed by the federal Senate or President will not be more than equal to a resistance in which they will be supported by constitutional and patriotic principles.

In this review of the Constitution of the House of Representatives, I have passed over the circumstances of economy which, in the present state of affairs, might have had some effect in lessening the temporary number of representatives, and a disregard of which would probably have been as rich a theme of declamation against the Constitution as has been furnished by the smallness of the number proposed. I omit also any remarks on the difficulty which might be found, under present circumstances, in engaging in the federal service a large number of such characters as the people will probably elect. One observation, however, I must be permitted to add on this subject as claiming, in my judgment, a very serious attention. It is that in all legislative assemblies the greater the number composing them may be, the fewer will be the men who will in fact direct their proceedings. In the first place, the more numerous any assembly may be, of whatever characters composed, the greater is known to be the ascendancy of passion over reason. In the next place, the larger the number, the greater will be the proportion of members of limited information and of weak capacities. Now, it is precisely on characters of this description that the eloquence and address of the few are known to act with all their force. In the ancient republics, where the whole body of the people assembled in person, a single orator, or an artful statesman, was generally seen to rule with as complete a sway as if a scepter had been placed in his single hand. On the same principle, the more multitudinous a representative assembly may be rendered, the more it will partake of the infirmities incident to collective meetings of the people. Ignorance will be the dupe of cunning, and passion the slave of sophistry and declamation. The people can never err more than in supposing that by multiplying their representatives beyond a certain limit they strengthen the barrier against the government of a few. Experience will forever admonish them that, on the contrary, *after securing a sufficient number for the purposes of safety, of local information, and of diffusive sympathy with the whole society,* they will counteract their own views by every addition to their representatives. The countenance of the government may become more democratic, but the soul that animates it will be more oligarchic. The machine will be enlarged, but the fewer, and often the more secret, will be the springs by which its motions are directed.

As connected with the objection against the number of representatives may properly be here noticed that which has been suggested against the number made competent for legislative business. It has been said that more than a majority ought to have been required for a quorum; and in particular cases, if not in all, more than a majority of a quorum for a decision. That some advantages might have resulted from such a precaution cannot be denied. It might have been an additional shield to some particular interests, and another obstacle generally to hasty and partial measures. But these considerations are outweighed by the inconveniences in the opposite scale. In all cases where justice or the general good might require new laws to be passed, or active measures to be pursued, the fundamental principle of free government would be reversed. It would be no longer the majority that would rule: the power would be transferred to the minority. Were the defensive privilege limited to particular cases, an interested minority might take advantage of it to screen themselves from equitable sacrifices to the general weal, or, in particular emergencies, to extort unreasonable indulgences. Lastly, it would facilitate and foster the baneful practice of secessions, a practice which has shown itself even in States where a majority only is required; a practice subversive of all the principles of order and regular government; a practice which leads more directly to public convulsions and the ruin of popular governments than any other which has yet been displayed among us.

PUBLIUS

No. 59: Hamilton

THE natural order of the subject leads us to consider, in this place, that provision of the Constitution which authorizes the national legislature to regulate, in the last resort, the election of its own members. It is in these words: "The *times, places,* and *manner* of holding elections for senators and representatives shall be prescribed in each State by the legislature thereof; but the Congress may, at any time, by law, make or alter *such regulations,* except as to the *places* of choosing senators." * This provision has not only been declaimed against by those who condemn the Constitution in the gross; but it has been censured by those who have objected with less latitude and greater moderation; and, in one instance, it has been thought exceptionable by a gentleman who had declared himself the advocate of every other part of the system.

I am greatly mistaken, notwithstanding, if there be any article in the whole plan more completely defensible than this. Its propriety rests upon the evidence of this plain proposition, that *every government ought to contain in itself the means of its own preservation.* Every just reasoner will, at first sight, approve an adherence to this rule, in the work of the convention; and will disapprove every deviation from it which may not appear to have been dictated by the necessity of incorporating into the work some particular ingredient with which a rigid conformity to the rule was incompatible. Even in this case, though he may acquiesce in the necessity, yet he will not cease to regard a departure from so fundamental a principle as a portion of imperfection in the system which may prove the seed of future weakness, and perhaps anarchy.

It will not be alleged that an election law could have been framed and inserted in the Constitution which would have been applicable to every probable change in the situation of the country; and it will therefore not be denied that a discretionary power over elections ought to exist somewhere. It will, I presume, be as readily conceded that there were only three ways in which this power could have been reasonably modified and disposed: that it must either have been lodged wholly in the national legislature, or wholly in the State legislatures, or primarily in the latter and ultimately in the former. The last mode has, with reason, been preferred by the convention. They have submitted the regulation of elections for the federal

* 1st clause, 4th section, of the 1st article.

government, in the first instance, to the local administrations; which, in ordinary cases, and when no improper views prevail, may be both more convenient and more satisfactory; but they have reserved to the national authority a right to interpose, whenever extraordinary circumstances might render that interposition necessary to its safety.

Nothing can be more evident than that an exclusive power of regulating elections for the national government, in the hands of the State legislatures, would leave the existence of the Union entirely at their mercy. They could at any moment annihilate it by neglecting to provide for the choice of persons to administer its affairs. It is to little purpose to say that a neglect or omission of this kind would not be likely to take place. The constitutional possibility of the thing, without an equivalent for the risk, is an unanswerable objection. Nor has any satisfactory reason been yet assigned for incurring that risk. The extravagant surmises of a distempered jealousy can never be dignified with that character. If we are in a humor to presume abuses of power, it is as fair to presume them on the part of the State governments as on the part of the general government. And as it is more consonant to the rules of a just theory to trust the Union with the care of its own existence than to transfer that care to any other hands, if abuses of power are to be hazarded on the one side or on the other, it is more rational to hazard them where the power would naturally be placed than where it would unnaturally be placed.

Suppose an article had been introduced into the Constitution empowering the United States to regulate the elections for the particular States, would any man have hesitated to condemn it, both as an unwarrantable transposition of power and as a premeditated engine for the destruction of the State governments? The violation of principle, in this case, would have required no comment; and, to an unbiased observer, it will not be less apparent in the project of subjecting the existence of the national government, in a similar respect, to the pleasure of the State governments. An impartial view of the matter cannot fail to result in a conviction that each, as far as possible, ought to depend on itself for its own preservation.

As an objection to this position, it may be remarked that the constitution of the national Senate would involve, in its full extent, the danger which it is suggested might flow from an exclusive power in the State legislatures to regulate the federal elections. It may be alleged that by declining the appointment of senators they might at any time give a fatal blow to the Union; and from this it may be inferred that as its existence would be thus rendered dependent upon them in so essential a point, there can be no objection to intrusting them with it in the particular case under consideration. The interest of each State, it may be added, to maintain its representation in the national councils, would be a complete security against an abuse of the trust.

This argument, though specious, will not, upon examination, be found solid. It is certainly true that the State legislatures, by forbearing the appointment of senators, may destroy the national government. But it will not follow that, because they have the power to do this in one instance, they ought to have it in every other. There are cases in which the pernicious tendency of such a power may be far more decisive, without any motive equally cogent with that which must have regulated the conduct of the convention in respect to the construction of the Senate to recommend their admission into the system. So far as that construction may expose the Union to the possibility of injury from the State legislatures, it is an evil; but it is an evil which could not have been avoided without excluding the States, in their political capacities, wholly from a place in the organization of the national government. If this had been done it would doubtless have been interpreted into an entire dereliction of the federal principle, and would certainly have deprived the State governments of that absolute safeguard which they will enjoy under this provision. But however wise it may have been to have submitted in this instance to an inconvenience, for the attainment of a necessary advantage or a greater good, no inference can be drawn from thence to favor an accumulation of the evil, where no necessity urges, nor any greater good invites.

It may easily be discerned also that the national government would run a much greater risk from a power in the State legislatures over the elections of its House of

Representatives than from their power of appointing the members of its Senate. The senators are to be chosen for the period of six years; there is to be a rotation, by which the seats of a third part of them are to be vacated and replenished every two years; and no State is to be entitled to more than two senators; a quorum of the body is to consist of sixteen members. The joint result of these circumstances would be that a temporary combination of a few States to intermit the appointment of senators could neither annul the existence nor impair the activity of the body; and it is not from a general or permanent combination of the States that we can have anything to fear. The first might proceed from sinister designs in the leading members of a few of the State legislatures; the last would suppose a fixed and rooted disaffection in the great body of the people which will either never exist at all, or will, in all probability, proceed from an experience of the inaptitude of the general government to the advancement of their happiness—in which event no good citizen could desire its continuance.

But with regard to the federal House of Representatives, there is intended to be a general election of members once in two years. If the State legislatures were to be invested with an exclusive power of regulating these elections, every period of making them would be a delicate crisis in the national situation, which might issue in a dissolution of the Union, if the leaders of a few of the most important States should have entered into a previous conspiracy to prevent an election.

I shall not deny that there is a degree of weight in the observation that the interests of each State, to be represented in the federal councils, will be a security against the abuse of a power over its elections in the hands of the State legislatures. But the security will not be considered as complete by those who attend to the force of an obvious distinction between the interest of the people in the public felicity and the interest of their local rulers in the power and consequence of their offices. The people of America may be warmly attached to the government of the Union, at times when the particular rulers of particular States, stimulated by the natural rivalship of power, and by the hopes of personal aggrandizement, and supported by a strong faction in each of those States, may be in a very opposite temper. This diversity of sentiment between a majority of the people and the individuals who have the greatest credit in their councils is exemplified in some of the States at the present moment, on the present question. The scheme of separate confederacies, which will always multiply the chances of ambition, will be a never-failing bait to all such influential characters in the State administrations as are capable of preferring their own emolument and advancement to the public weal. With so effectual a weapon in their hands as the exclusive power of regulating elections for the national government, a combination of a few such men, in a few of the most considerable States, where the temptation will always be the strongest, might accomplish the destruction of the Union by seizing the opportunity of some casual dissatisfaction among the people (and which perhaps they may themselves have excited) to discontinue the choice of members for the federal House of Representatives. It ought never to be forgotten that a firm union of this country, under an efficient government, will probably be an increasing object of jealousy to more than one nation of Europe; and that enterprises to subvert it will sometimes originate in the intrigues of foreign powers and will seldom fail to be patronized and abetted by some of them. Its preservation, therefore, ought in no case that can be avoided to be committed to the guardianship of any but those whose situation will uniformly beget an immediate interest in the faithful and vigilant performance of the trust. PUBLIUS

No. 60: Hamilton

WE HAVE seen that an uncontrollable power over the elections to the federal government could not, without hazard, be committed to the State legislatures. Let us now see what would be the danger on the other side; that is, from confiding the ultimate right of regulating its own elections to the Union itself. It is not pretended that this right would ever be used for the exclusion of any State from its share in the representation. The interest of all would, in this respect at least, be the security of all. But it is alleged that it might be employed in such a manner as to promote the election of some favorite class of men in exclusion of others by confining the places of election to particular districts and rendering it impracticable to the citizens at large to partake in the choice. Of all chimerical suppositions, this seems to be the most chimerical. On the one hand, no rational calculation of probabilities would lead us to imagine that the disposition which a conduct so violent and extraordinary would imply could ever find its way into the national councils; and on the other it may be concluded with certainty that if so improper a spirit should ever gain admittance into them, it would display itself in a form altogether different and far more decisive.

The improbability of the attempt may be satisfactorily inferred from this single reflection, that it could never be made without causing an immediate revolt of the great body of the people, headed and directed by the State governments. It is not difficult to conceive that this characteristic right of freedom may, in certain turbulent and factious seasons, be violated, in respect to a particular class of citizens, by a victorious majority; but that so fundamental a privilege, in a country so situated and enlightened, should be invaded to the prejudice of the great mass of the people by the deliberate policy of the government without occasioning a popular revolution, is altogether inconceivable and incredible.

In addition to this general reflection, there are considerations of a more precise nature which forbid all apprehension on the subject. The dissimilarity in the ingredients which will compose the national government, and still more in the manner in which they will be brought into action in its various branches, must form a powerful obstacle to a concert of views in any partial scheme of elections. There is sufficient diversity in the state of property, in the genius, manners, and habits of the people of the different parts of the Union to occasion a material diversity of disposition in their representatives towards the different ranks and conditions in society. And though an intimate intercourse under the same government will promote a gradual assimilation of temper and sentiments, yet there are causes, as well physical as moral, which may, in a greater or less degree, permanently nourish different propensities and inclinations in this particular. But the circumstance which will be likely to have the greatest influence in the matter will be the dissimilar modes of constituting the several component parts of the government. The House of Representatives' being to be elected immediately by the people, the Senate by the State legislatures, the President by electors chosen for that purpose by the people, there would be little probability of a common interest to cement these different branches in a predilection for any particular class of electors.

As to the Senate, it is impossible that any regulation of "time and manner," which is all that is proposed to be submitted to the national government in respect to that body, can affect the spirit which will direct the choice of its members. The collective sense of the State legislatures can never be influenced by extraneous circumstances of that sort; a consideration which alone ought to satisfy us that the discrimination apprehended would never be attempted. For what inducement could the Senate have to concur in a preference in which itself would not be included? Or to what purpose would it be established, in reference to one branch of the legislature, if it could not be extended to the other? The composition of the one would in this case counteract that of the other. And we can never suppose that it would embrace the appointments to the Senate unless we can at the same time suppose the voluntary co-operation of the State legislatures. If we make the latter supposition, it then becomes immaterial where the power in question is placed—whether in their hands or in those of the Union.

But what is to be the object of this capricious partiality in the national councils? Is it to be exercised in a discrimination between the different departments of industry, or between the different kinds of property, or between the different degrees of property? Will it lean in favor of the landed interest, or the moneyed interest, or the mercantile interest, or the manufacturing interest? Or, to speak in the fashionable language of the adversaries to the Constitution, will it court the elevation of the "wealthy and the well-born," to the exclusion and debasement of all the rest of the society?

If this partiality is to be exerted in favor of those who

are concerned in any particular description of industry or property, I presume it will readily be admitted that the competition for it will lie between landed men and merchants. And I scruple not to affirm that it is infinitely less likely that either of them should gain an ascendant in the national councils, than that the one or the other of them should predominate in all the local councils. The inference will be that a conduct tending to give an undue preference to either is much less to be dreaded from the former than from the latter.

The several States are in various degrees addicted to agriculture and commerce. In most, if not all of them, agriculture is predominant. In a few of them, however, commerce nearly divides its empire, and in most of them has a considerable share of influence. In proportion as either prevails, it will be conveyed into the national representation; and for the very reason that this will be an emanation from a greater variety of interests and in much more various proportions than are to be found in any single State, it will be much less apt to espouse either of them with a decided partiality than the representation of any single State.

In a country consisting chiefly of the cultivators of land, where the rules of an equal representation obtain, the landed interest must, upon the whole, preponderate in the government. As long as this interest prevails in most of the State legislatures, so long it must maintain a correspondent superiority in the national Senate, which will generally be a faithful copy of the majorities of those assemblies. It cannot therefore be presumed that a sacrifice of the landed to the mercantile class will ever be a favorite object of this branch of the federal legislature. In applying thus particularly to the Senate a general observation suggested by the situation of the country, I am governed by the consideration that the credulous votaries of State power cannot, upon their own principles, suspect that the State legislatures would be warped from their duty by any external influence. But in reality the same situation must have the same effect, in the primitive composition at least of the federal House of Representatives: an improper bias towards the mercantile class is as little to be expected from this quarter as from the other.

In order, perhaps, to give countenance to the objection, at any rate, it may be asked, is there not danger of an opposite bias in the national government, which may dispose it to endeavor to secure a monopoly of the federal administration to the landed class? As there is little likelihood that the supposition of such a bias will have any terrors for those who would be immediately injured by it, a labored answer to this question will be dispensed with. It will be sufficient to remark, first, that for the reasons elsewhere assigned it is less likely that any decided partiality should prevail in the councils of the Union than in those of any of its members. Secondly, that there would be no temptation to violate the Constitution in favor of the landed class, because that class would, in the natural course of things, enjoy as great a preponderancy as itself could desire. And thirdly, that men accustomed to investigate the sources of public prosperity upon a large scale must be too well convinced of the utility of commerce to be inclined to inflict upon it so deep a wound as would be occasioned by the entire exclusion of those who would best understand its interest from a share in the management of them. The importance of commerce, in the view of revenue alone, must effectually guard it against the enmity of a body which would be continually importuned in its favor by the urgent calls of public necessity.

I rather consult brevity in discussing the probability of a preference founded upon a discrimination between the different kinds of industry and property, because, as far as I understand the meaning of the objectors, they contemplate a discrimination of another kind. They appear to have in view, as the objects of the preference with which they endeavor to alarm us, those whom they designate by the description of the "wealthy and the well-born." These, it seems, are to be exalted to an odious pre-eminence over the rest of their fellow-citizens. At one time, however, their elevation is to be a necessary consequence of the smallness of the representative body; at another time it is to be effected by depriving the people at large of the opportunity of exercising their right of suffrage in the choice of that body.

But upon what principle is the discrimination of the places of election to be made, in order to answer the purpose of the meditated preference? Are the wealthy and the well-born, as they are called, confined to particular spots in the several States? Have they, by some miraculous instinct or foresight, set apart in each of them a common place of residence? Are they only to be met with in the towns or cities? Or are they, on the contrary, scattered over the face of the country as avarice or chance may have happened to cast their own lot or that of their predecessors? If the latter is the case (as every intelligent man knows it to be *) is it not evident that the policy of confining the places of elections to particular districts would be as subversive of its own aim as it would be exceptionable on every other account? The truth is that there is no method of securing to the rich the preference apprehended but by prescribing qualifications of property either for those who may elect or be elected. But this forms no part of the power to be conferred upon the national government. Its authority would be expressly restricted to the regulation of the *times*, the *places*, and the *manner* of elections. The qualifications of the persons who may choose or be chosen, as has been remarked upon other occasions, are defined and fixed in the Constitution, and are unalterable by the legislature.

Let it, however, be admitted, for argument sake, that the expedient suggested might be successful; and let it at the same time be equally taken for granted that all the scruples which a sense of duty or an apprehension of the danger of the experiment might inspire were overcome in the breasts of the national rulers, still I imagine it will hardly be pretended that they could ever hope to carry such an enterprise into execution without the aid of a military force sufficient to subdue the resistance of the great body of the people. The improbability of the existence of a force equal to that object has been discussed and demonstrated in different parts of these papers; but that the futility of the objection under consideration may appear in the strongest light, it shall be conceded for a moment that such a force might exist and the national government shall be supposed to be in the actual possession of it. What will be the conclusion? With a disposition to invade the essential rights of the community and with the means of gratifying that disposition, is it pre-

* Particularly in the Southern States and in this State.

sumable that the persons who were actuated by it would amuse themselves in the ridiculous task of fabricating election laws for securing a preference to a favorite class of men? Would they not be likely to prefer a conduct better adapted to their own immediate aggrandizement? Would they not rather boldly resolve to perpetuate themselves in office by one decisive act of usurpation, than to trust to precarious expedients which, in spite of all the precautions that might accompany them, might terminate in the dismission, disgrace, and ruin of their authors? Would they not fear that citizens, not less tenacious than conscious of their rights, would flock from the remotest extremes of their respective States to the places of election, to overthrow their tyrants and to substitute men who would be disposed to avenge the violated majesty of the people?

PUBLIUS

No. 61: Hamilton

THE more candid opposers of the provisions respecting elections contained in the plan of the convention, when pressed in argument, will sometimes concede the propriety of that provision; with this qualification, however, that it ought to have been accompanied with a declaration that all elections should be had in the counties where the electors resided. This, say they, was a necessary precaution against an abuse of the power. A declaration of this nature would certainly have been harmless; so far as it would have had the effect of quieting apprehensions it might not have been undesirable. But it would, in fact, have afforded little or no additional security against the danger apprehended; and the want of it will never be considered by an impartial and judicious examiner as a serious, still less as an insuperable, objection to the plan. The different views taken of the subject in the two preceding papers must be sufficient to satisfy all dispassionate and discerning men, that if the public liberty should ever be the victim of the ambition of the national rulers, the power under examination, at least, will be guiltless of the sacrifice.

If those who are inclined to consult their jealousy only

would exercise it in a careful inspection of the several State constitutions, they would find little less room for disquietude and alarm from the latitude which most of them allow in respect to elections than from the latitude which is proposed to be allowed to the national government in the same respect. A review of their situation, in this particular, would tend greatly to remove any ill impressions which may remain in regard to this matter. But as that view would lead into long and tedious details, I shall content myself with the single example of the State in which I write. The constitution of New York makes no other provision for *locality* of elections than that the members of the Assembly shall be elected in the *counties;* those of the Senate, in the great districts into which the State is or may be divided: these at present are four in number and comprehend each from two to six counties. It may readily be perceived that it would not be more difficult to the legislature of New York to defeat the suffrages of the citizens of New York by confining elections to particular places than for the legislature of the United States to defeat the suffrages of the citizens of the Union by the like expedient. Suppose, for instance, the city of Albany was to be appointed the sole place of election for the county and district of which it is a part, would not the inhabitants of that city speedily become the only electors of the members both of the Senate and Assembly for that county and district? Can we imagine that the electors who reside in the remote subdivisions of the counties of Albany, Saratoga, Cambridge, etc., or in any part of the county of Montgomery, would take the trouble to come to the city of Albany to give their votes for members of the Assembly or Senate sooner than they would repair to the city of New York to participate in the choice of the members of the federal House of Representatives? The alarming indifference discoverable in the exercise of so invaluable a privilege under the existing laws, which afford every facility to it, furnishes a ready answer to this question. And, abstracted from any experience on the subject, we can be at no loss to determine that when the place of election is at an *inconvenient distance* from the elector, the effect upon his conduct will be the same whether that distance be twenty miles or twenty thousand miles. Hence it must appear that objections to the particular modification of the federal power of regulating elections will, in substance, apply with equal force to the modification of the like power in the constitution of this State; and for this reason it will be impossible to acquit the one and to condemn the other. A similar comparison would lead to the same conclusion in respect to the constitutions of most of the other States.

If it should be said that defects in the State constitutions furnish no apology for those which are to be found in the plan proposed, I answer that as the former have never been thought chargeable with inattention to the security of liberty, where the imputations thrown on the latter can be shown to be applicable to them also, the presumption is that they are rather the cavilling refinements of a predetermined opposition than the well-founded inferences of a candid research after truth. To those who are disposed to consider, as innocent omissions in the State constitutions, what they regard as unpardonable blemishes in the plan of the convention, nothing can be said; or at most, they can only be asked to assign some substantial reason why the representatives of the people in a single State should be more impregnable to the lust of power, or other sinister motives, than the representatives of the people of the United States? If they cannot do this, they ought at least to prove to us that it is easier to subvert the liberties of three millions of people, with the advantage of local governments to head their opposition, than of two hundred thousand people who are destitute of that advantage. And in relation to the point immediately under consideration, they ought to convince us that it is less probable that a predominant faction in a single State should, in order to maintain its superiority, incline to a preference of a particular class of electors, than that a similar spirit should take possession of the representatives of thirteen States, spread over a vast region, and in several respects distinguishable from each other by a diversity of local circumstances, prejudices, and interests.

Hitherto my observations have only aimed at a vindication of the provision in question on the ground of theoretic propriety, on that of the danger of placing the power elsewhere, and on that of the safety of placing it in the manner proposed. But there remains to be mentioned a positive advantage which will result from this disposition and which could not as well have been obtained from any other: I allude to the circumstance of uniformity in the time of elections for the federal House of Representatives. It is more than possible that this uniformity may be found by experience to be of great importance to the public welfare, both as a security against the perpetuation of the same spirit in the body, and as a cure for the diseases of faction. If each State may choose its own time of election it is possible there may be at least as many different periods as there are months in the year. The times of election in the several States, as they are now established for local purposes, vary between extremes as wide as March and November. The consequence of this diversity would be that there could never happen a total dissolution or renovation of the body at one time. If an improper spirit of any kind should happen to prevail in it, that spirit would be apt to infuse itself into the new members, as they come forward in succession. The mass would be likely to remain nearly the same, assimilating constantly to itself its gradual accretions. There is a contagion in example which few men have sufficient force of mind to resist. I am inclined to think that treble the duration in office, with the condition of a total dissolution of the body at the same time, might be less formidable to liberty than one third of that duration subject to gradual and successive alterations.

Uniformity in the time of elections seems not less requisite for executing the idea of a regular rotation in the Senate, and for conveniently assembling the legislature at a stated period in each year.

It may be asked, Why, then, could not a time have been fixed in the Constitution? As the most zealous adversaries of the plan of the convention in this State are, in general, not less zealous admirers of the constitution of the State, the question may be retorted, and it may be asked, Why was not a time for the like purpose fixed in the constitution of this State? No better answer can be given than that it was a matter which might safely be intrusted to legislative discretion; and that if a time had been appointed, it might, upon experiment, have been found less convenient than some other time. The same answer may be given to the question put on the other side.

And it may be added that the supposed danger of a gradual change being merely speculative, it would have been hardly advisable upon that speculation to establish, as a fundamental point, what would deprive several States of the convenience of having the elections for their own governments and for the national government at the same epoch.

PUBLIUS

No. 62: Probably Madison

HAVING examined the constitution of the House of Representatives, and answered such of the objections against it as seemed to merit notice, I enter next on the examination of the Senate. The heads into which this member of the government may be considered are: I. The qualifications of senators; II. The appointment of them by the State legislatures; III. The equality of representation in the Senate; IV. The number of senators, and the term for which they are to be elected; V. The powers vested in the Senate.

I. The qualifications proposed for senators, as distinguished from those of representatives, consist in a more advanced age and a longer period of citizenship. A senator must be thirty years of age at least; as a representative must be twenty-five. And the former must have been a citizen nine years; as seven years are required for the latter. The propriety of these distinctions is explained by the nature of the senatorial trust, which, requiring greater extent of information and stability of character, requires at the same time that the senator should have reached a period of life most likely to supply these advantages; and which, participating immediately in transactions with foreign nations, ought to be exercised by none who are not thoroughly weaned from the prepossessions and habits incident to foreign birth and education. The term of nine years appears to be a prudent mediocrity between a total exclusion of adopted citizens, whose merits and talents may claim a share in the public confidence, and an indiscriminate and hasty admission of them, which might create a channel for foreign influence on the national councils.

II. It is equally unnecessary to dilate on the appointment of senators by the State legislatures. Among the various modes which might have been devised for constituting this branch of the government, that which has been proposed by the convention is probably the most congenial with the public opinion. It is recommended by the double advantage of favoring a select appointment, and of giving to the State governments such an agency in the formation of the federal government as must secure the authority of the former, and may form a convenient link between the two systems.

III. The equality of representation in the Senate is another point which, being evidently the result of compromise between the opposite pretensions of the large and the small States, does not call for much discussion. If indeed it be right that among a people thoroughly incorporated into one nation every district ought to have a *proportional* share in the government and that among independent and sovereign States, bound together by a simple league, the parties, however unequal in size, ought to have an *equal* share in the common councils, it does not appear to be without some reason that in a compound republic, partaking both of the national and federal character, the government ought to be founded on a mixture of the principles of proportional and equal representation. But it is superfluous to try, by the standard of theory, a part of the Constitution which is allowed on all hands to be the result, not of theory, but "of a spirit of amity, and that mutual deference and concession which the peculiarity of our political situation rendered indispensable." A common government, with powers equal to its objects, is called for by the voice, and still more loudly by the political situation, of America. A government founded on principles more consonant to the wishes of the larger States is not likely to be obtained from the smaller States. The only option, then, for the former lies between the proposed government and a government still more objectionable. Under this alternative, the advice of prudence must be to embrace the lesser evil; and instead of indulging a fruitless anticipation of the possible mischiefs which may ensue, to contemplate rather the advantageous consequences which may qualify the sacrifice.

In this spirit it may be remarked that the equal vote allowed to each State is at once a constitutional recognition of the portion of sovereignty remaining in the individual States and an instrument for preserving that residuary sovereignty. So far the equality ought to be no less acceptable to the large than to the small States; since they are not less solicitous to guard, by every possible expedient, against an improper consolidation of the States into one simple republic.

Another advantage accruing from this ingredient in the constitution of the Senate is the additional impediment it must prove against improper acts of legislation. No law or resolution can now be passed without the concurrence, first, of a majority of the people, and then of a majority of the States. It must be acknowledged that this complicated check on legislation may in some instances be injurious as well as beneficial; and that the peculiar defense which it involves in favor of the smaller States would be more rational if any interests common to them and distinct from those of the other States would otherwise be exposed to peculiar danger. But as the larger States will always be able, by their power over the supplies, to defeat unreasonable exertions of this prerogative of the lesser States, and as the facility and excess of law-making seem to be the diseases to which our governments are most liable, it is not impossible that this part of the Constitution may be more convenient in practice than it appears to many in contemplation.

IV. The number of senators and the duration of their appointment come next to be considered. In order to form an accurate judgment on both these points it will be proper to inquire into the purposes which are to be answered by a senate; and in order to ascertain these it will be necessary to review the inconveniences which a republic must suffer from the want of such an institution.

First. It is a misfortune incident to republican government, though in a less degree than to other governments, that those who administer it may forget their obligations to their constituents and prove unfaithful to their important trust. In this point of view a senate, as a second branch of the legislative assembly distinct from and dividing the power with a first, must be in all cases a salutary check on the government. It doubles the security to the people by requiring the concurrence of two distinct bodies in schemes of usurpation or perfidy, where the ambition or corruption of one would otherwise be sufficient. This is a precaution founded on such clear principles, and now so well understood in the United States, that it would be more than superfluous to enlarge on it. I will barely remark that as the improbability of sinister combinations will be in proportion to the dissimilarity in the genius of the two bodies, it must be politic to distinguish them from each other by every circumstance which will consist with a due harmony in all proper measures, and with the genuine principles of republican government.

Second. The necessity of a senate is not less indicated by the propensity of all single and numerous assemblies to yield to the impulse of sudden and violent passions, and to be seduced by factious leaders into intemperate and pernicious resolutions. Examples on this subject might be cited without number; and from proceedings within the United States, as well as from the history of other nations. But a position that will not be contradicted need not be proved. All that need be remarked is that a body which is to correct this infirmity ought itself to be free from it, and consequently ought to be less numerous. It ought, moreover, to possess great firmness, and consequently ought to hold its authority by a tenure of considerable duration.

Third. Another defect to be supplied by a senate lies in a want of due acquaintance with the objects and principles of legislation. It is not possible that an assembly of men called for the most part from pursuits of a private nature continued in appointment for a short time and led by no permanent motive to devote the intervals of public occupation to a study of the laws, the affairs, and the comprehensive interests of their country, should, if left wholly to themselves, escape a variety of important errors in the exercise of their legislative trust. It may be affirmed, on the best grounds, that no small share of the present embarrassments of America is to be charged on the blunders of our governments; and that these have proceeded from the heads rather than the hearts of most of the authors of them. What indeed are all the repealing, explaining, and amending laws, which fill and disgrace our voluminous codes, but so many monuments of deficient wisdom; so many impeachments exhibited by each succeeding against each preceding session; so many admonitions to the people of the value of those aids which may be expected from a well-constituted senate?

A good government implies two things: first, fidelity to the object of government, which is the happiness of the people; secondly, a knowledge of the means by which that object can be best attained. Some governments are deficient in both these qualities; most governments are deficient in the first. I scruple not to assert that in American governments too little attention has been paid to the last. The federal Constitution avoids this error; and what merits particular notice, it provides for the last in a mode which increases the security for the first.

Fourth. The mutability in the public councils arising from a rapid succession of new members, however qualified they may be, points out, in the strongest manner, the necessity of some stable institution in the government. Every new election in the States is found to change one half of the representatives. From this change of men must proceed a change of opinions; and from a change of opinions, a change of measures. But a continual change even of good measures is inconsistent with every rule of prudence and every prospect of success. The remark is verified in private life, and becomes more just, as well as more important, in national transactions.

To trace the mischievous effects of a mutable government would fill a volume. I will hint a few only, each of which will be perceived to be a source of innumerable others.

In the first place, it forfeits the respect and confidence of other nations, and all the advantages connected with national character. An individual who is observed to be inconstant to his plans, or perhaps to carry on his affairs without any plan at all, is marked at once by all prudent people as a speedy victim to his own unsteadiness and folly. His more friendly neighbors may pity him, but all will decline to connect their fortunes with his; and not a few will seize the opportunity of making their fortunes out of his. One nation is to another what one individual is to another; with this melancholy distinction, perhaps, that the former, with fewer of the benevolent emotions than the latter, are under fewer restraints also from taking undue advantage of the indiscretions of each other. Every nation, consequently, whose affairs betray a want of wisdom and stability, may calculate on every loss which can be sustained from the more systematic policy of its wiser neighbors. But the best instruction on this subject is unhappily conveyed to America by the example of her own situation. She finds that she is held in no respect by her friends; that she is the derision of her enemies; and that she is a prey to every nation which has an interest in speculating on her fluctuating councils and embarrassed affairs.

The internal effects of a mutable policy are still more calamitous. It poisons the blessings of liberty itself. It will be of little avail to the people that the laws are made by men of their own choice if the laws be so voluminous that they cannot be read, or so incoherent that they cannot be understood; if they be repealed or revised before they are promulgated, or undergo such incessant changes that no man, who knows what the law is today, can guess what it will be tomorrow. Law is defined to be a rule of action; but how can that be a rule, which is little known, and less fixed?

Another effect of public instability is the unreasonable advantage it gives to the sagacious, the enterprising, and the moneyed few over the industrious and uniformed mass of the people. Every new regulation concerning commerce or revenue, or in any manner affecting the value of the different species of property, presents a new harvest to those who watch the change, and can trace its consequences; a harvest, reared not by themselves, but by the toils and cares of the great body of their fellow-citizens. This is a state of things in which it may be said with some truth that laws are made for the *few,* not for the *many.*

In another point of view, great injury results from an unstable government. The want of confidence in the public councils damps every useful undertaking, the success and profit of which may depend on a continuance of existing arrangements. What prudent merchant will hazard his fortunes in any new branch of commerce when he knows not but that his plans may be rendered unlawful before they can be executed? What farmer or manufacturer will lay himself out for the encouragement given to any particular cultivation or establishment, when he can have no assurance that his preparatory labors and advances will not render him a victim to an inconstant government? In a word, no great improvement or laudable enterprise can go forward which requires the auspices of a steady system of national policy.

But the most deplorable effect of all is that diminution of attachment and reverence which steals into the hearts of the people towards a political system which betrays so many marks of infirmity, and disappoints so many of their flattering hopes. No government, any more than an individual, will long be respected without being truly respectable; nor be truly respectable without possessing a certain portion of order and stability. PUBLIUS

No. 63: Probably Madison

A *fifth* desideratum, illustrating the utility of a senate, is the want of a due sense of national character. Without a select and stable member of the government, the esteem of foreign powers will not only be forfeited by an unenlightened and variable policy, proceeding from the causes already mentioned, but the national councils will not possess that sensibility to the opinion of the world which is perhaps not less necessary in order to merit than it is to obtain its respect and confidence.

An attention to the judgment of other nations is important to every government for two reasons: the one is that independently of the merits of any particular plan or measure, it is desirable, on various accounts, that it should appear to other nations as the offspring of a wise and honorable policy; the second is that in doubtful cases, particularly where the national councils may be warped by some strong passion or momentary interest, the presumed or known opinion of the impartial world may be the best guide that can be followed. What has not America lost by her want of character with foreign nations; and how many errors and follies would she not have avoided, if the justice and propriety of her measures had, in every instance, been previously tried by the light in which they would probably appear to the unbiased part of mankind?

Yet however requisite a sense of national character may be, it is evident that it can never be sufficiently possessed by a numerous and changeable body. It can only be found in a number so small that a sensible degree of the praise and blame of public measures may be the portion of each individual; or in an assembly so durably invested with public trust that the pride and consequence of its members may be sensibly incorporated with the reputation and prosperity of the community. The half-yearly representatives of Rhode Island would probably have been little affected in their deliberations on the iniquitous measures of that State by arguments drawn from the light in which such measures would be viewed by foreign nations, or even by the sister States; whilst it can scarcely be doubted that if the concurrence of a select and stable body had been necessary, a regard to national character alone would have prevented the calamities under which that misguided people is now laboring.

I add, as a *sixth* defect, the want, in some important cases, of a due responsibility in the government to the people, arising from that frequency of elections which in other cases produces this responsibility. This remark will, perhaps, appear not only new, but paradoxical. It must nevertheless be acknowledged, when explained, to be as undeniable as it is important.

Responsibility, in order to be reasonable, must be limited to objects within the power of the responsible party, and in order to be effectual, must relate to operations of that power, of which a ready and proper judgment can be formed by the constituents. The objects of government may be divided into two general classes: the one depending on measures which have singly an immediate and sensible operation; the other depending on a succession of well-chosen and well-connected measures, which have a gradual and perhaps unobserved operation. The importance of the latter description to the collective and permanent welfare of every country needs no explanation. And yet it is evident that an assembly elected for so short a term as to be unable to provide more than one or two links in a chain of measures, on which the general welfare may essentially depend, ought not to be answerable for the final result any more than a steward or tenant, engaged for one year, could be justly made to answer for places or improvements which could not be accomplished in less than half a dozen years. Nor is it possible for the people to estimate the *share* of influence which their annual assemblies may respectively have on events resulting from the mixed transactions of several years. It is sufficiently difficult, at any rate, to preserve a personal responsibility in the members of a *numerous* body, for such acts of the body as have an immediate, detached, and palpable operation on its constituents.

The proper remedy for this defect must be an additional body in the legislative department, which, having sufficient permanency to provide for such objects as require a continued attention, and a train of measures, may be justly and effectually answerable for the attainment of those objects.

Thus far I have considered the circumstances which point out the necessity of a well-constructed Senate only as they relate to the representatives of the people. To a people as little blinded by prejudice or corrupted by flattery as those whom I address, I shall not scruple to add that such an institution may be sometimes necessary as a defense to the people against their own temporary errors and delusions. As the cool and deliberate sense of the community ought, in all governments, and actually will, in all free governments, ultimately prevail over the views of its rulers; so there are particular moments in public affairs when the people, stimulated by some irregular passion, or some illicit advantage, or misled by the artful misrepresentations of interested men, may call for measures which they themselves will afterwards be the most ready to lament and condemn. In these critical moments, how salutary will be the interference of some temperate and respectable body of citizens, in order to check the misguided career and to suspend the blow meditated by the people against themselves, until reason, justice, and truth can regain their authority over the public mind? What bitter anguish would not the people of Athens have often escaped if their government had contained so provident a safeguard against the tyranny of their own passions? Popular liberty might then have escaped the indelible reproach of decreeing to the same citizens the hemlock on one day and statues on the next.

It may be suggested that a people spread over an extensive region cannot, like the crowded inhabitants of a small district, be subject to the infection of violent passions or to the danger of combining in pursuit of unjust measures. I am far from denying that this is a distinction of peculiar importance. I have, on the contrary, endeavored in a former paper to show that it is one of the principal recommendations of a confederated republic. At the same time, this advantage ought not to be considered as superseding the use of auxiliary precautions. It may even be remarked that the same extended situation which will exempt the people of America from some of the dangers incident to lesser republics will expose them to the inconveniency of remaining for a longer time under the influence of those misrepresentations which the combined industry of interested men may succeed in distributing among them.

It adds no small weight to all these considerations to recollect that history informs us of no long-lived republic which had not a senate. Sparta, Rome, and Carthage are, in fact, the only states to whom that character can be applied. In each of the two first there was a senate for life. The constitution of the senate in the last is less known. Circumstantial evidence makes it probable that it was not different in this particular from the two others. It is at least certain that it had some quality or other which rendered it an anchor against popular fluctuations; and that a smaller council, drawn out of the senate, was appointed not only for life, but filled up vacancies itself. These examples, though as unfit for the imitation as they are repugnant to the genius of America, are, notwithstanding, when compared with the fugitive and turbulent existence of other ancient republics, very instructive proofs of the necessity of some institution that will blend stability with liberty. I am not unaware of the circumstances which distinguish the American from other popular governments, as well ancient as modern; and which render extreme circumspection necessary, in reasoning from one case to the other. But after allowing due weight to this consideration it may still be maintained that there are many points of similitude which render these examples not unworthy of our attention. Many of the defects, as we have seen, which can only be supplied by a senatorial institution, are common to a numerous assembly frequently elected by the people, and to the people themselves. There are others peculiar to the former which require the control of such an institution. The people can never wilfully betray their own interests; but they may possibly be betrayed by the representatives of the people; and the danger will be evidently greater where the whole legislative trust is lodged in the hands of one body of men than where the concurrence of separate and dissimilar bodies is required in every public act.

The difference most relied on between the American and other republics consists in the principle of representation, which is the pivot on which the former move, and which is supposed to have been unknown to the latter, or at least to the ancient part of them. The use which has been made of this difference, in reasonings contained in former papers, will have shown that I am disposed neither to deny its existence nor to undervalue its importance. I feel the less restraint, therefore, in observing that the position concerning the ignorance of the ancient governments on the subject of representation is by no means precisely true in the latitude commonly given to it. Without entering into a disquisition which here would be misplaced, I will refer to a few known facts in support of what I advance.

In the most pure democracies of Greece, many of the executive functions were performed, not by the people themselves, but by officers elected by the people, and *representing* the people in their *executive* capacity.

Prior to the reform of Solon, Athens was governed by nine Archons, annually *elected by the people at large*. The degree of power delegated to them seems to be left in great obscurity. Subsequent to that period we find an assembly, first of four, and afterwards of six hundred members, annually *elected by the people;* and *partially* representing them in their *legislative* capacity, since they were not only associated with the people in the function of making laws, but had the exclusive right of originating legislative propositions to the people. The senate of Carthage, also, whatever might be its power or the duration of its appointment, appears to have been elective by the suffrages of the people. Similar instances might be traced in most, if not all, the popular governments of antiquity.

Lastly, in Sparta we meet with the Ephori, and in Rome with the Tribunes; two bodies, small indeed in number, but annually *elected by the whole body of the people,* and considered as the *representatives* of the people, almost in their *plenipotentiary* capacity. The Cosmi of Crete were also annually *elected by the people,* and have been considered by some authors as an institution analogous to those of Sparta and Rome, with this difference only, that in the election of that representative body the right of suffrage was communicated to a part only of the people.

From these facts, to which many others might be added, it is clear that the principle of representation was neither unknown to the ancients nor wholly overlooked in their political constitutions. The true distinction between these and the American governments lies *in the total exclusion of the people in their collective capacity,* from any share in the *latter,* and not in the *total exclusion of the representatives of the people* from the administration of the *former.* The distinction, however, thus qualified, must be admitted to leave a most advantageous superiority in favor of the United States. But to insure to this advantage its full effect, we must be careful not to separate it from the other advantage, of an extensive territory. For it cannot be believed that any form of representative government could have succeeded within the narrow limits occupied by the democracies of Greece.

In answer to all these arguments, suggested by reason, illustrated by examples, and enforced by our own experience, the jealous adversary of the Constitution will probably content himself with repeating that a senate appointed not immediately by the people, and for the term of six years, must gradually acquire a dangerous pre-eminence in the government and finally transform it into a tyrannical aristocracy.

To this general answer the general reply ought to be sufficient, that liberty may be endangered by the abuses of liberty as well as by the abuses of power; that there are numerous instances of the former as well as of the latter; and that the former, rather than the latter, is apparently most to be apprehended by the United States. But a more particular reply may be given.

Before such a revolution can be effected, the Senate, it is to be observed, must in the first place corrupt itself; must next corrupt the State legislatures, must then corrupt the House of Representatives, and must finally corrupt the people at large. It is evident that the Senate must be first corrupted before it can attempt an establishment of tyranny. Without corrupting the State legislatures it cannot prosecute the attempt because the periodical change of members would otherwise regenerate the whole body. Without exerting the means of corruption with equal success on the House of Representatives, the opposition of that co-equal branch of the government would inevitably defeat the attempt; and without corrupting the people themselves, a succession of new representatives would speedily restore all things to their pristine order. Is there any man who can seriously persuade himself that the proposed Senate can, by any possible means within the compass of human address, arrive at the object of a lawless ambition through all these obstructions?

If reason condemns the suspicion, the same sentence is pronounced by experience. The constitution of Maryland furnishes the most apposite example. The Senate of that State is elected, as the federal Senate will be, indirectly by the people, and for a term less by one year only than the federal Senate. It is distinguished, also, by the remarkable prerogative of filling up its own vacancies within the term of its appointment, and at the same time is not under the control of any such rotation as is provided for the federal Senate. There are some other lesser distinctions which would expose the former to colorable objections that do not lie against the latter. If the federal Senate, therefore, really contained the danger which has been so loudly proclaimed, some symptoms at least of a like danger ought by this time to have been betrayed by the Senate of Maryland, but no such symptoms have appeared. On the contrary, the jealousies at first entertained by men of the same description with those who view with terror the correspondent part of the federal Constitution have been gradually extinguished by the progress of the experiment; and the Maryland constitution is daily deriving, from the salutary operation of this part of it, a reputation in which it will probably not be rivaled by that of any State in the Union.

But if anything could silence the jealousies on this subject, it ought to be the British example. The Senate there, instead of being elected for a term of six years, and of being unconfined to particular families or fortunes, is an hereditary assembly of opulent nobles. The House of Representatives, instead of being elected for two years, and by the whole body of the people, is elected for seven years, and, in very great proportion, by a very small proportion of the people. Here, unquestionably, ought to be seen in full display the aristocratic usurpations and tyranny which are at some future period to be exemplified in the United States. Unfortunately, however, for the anti-federal argument, the British history informs us that this hereditary assembly has not been able to defend itself against the continual encroachments of the House of Representatives, and that it no sooner lost the support of the monarch than it was actually crushed by the weight of the popular branch.

As far as antiquity can instruct us on this subject, its examples support the reasoning which we have employed. In Sparta, the Ephori, the annual representatives of the people, were found an overmatch for the senate for life, continually gained on its authority and finally drew all power into their own hands. The Tribunes of Rome who were the representatives of the people prevailed, it is well known, in almost every contest with the senate for life, and in the end gained the most complete triumph over it. The fact is the more remarkable as unanimity was required in every act of the Tribunes, even after their number was augmented to ten. It proves the irresistible force possessed by that branch of a free government, which has the people on its side. To these examples might be added that of Carthage, whose senate, according to the testimony of Polybius, instead of drawing all power into its vortex had, at the commencement of the second Punic War, lost almost the whole of its original portion.

Besides the conclusive evidence resulting from this assemblage of facts that the federal Senate will never be able to transform itself, by gradual usurpations, into an independent and aristocratic body, we are warranted in believing that if such a revolution should ever happen from causes which the foresight of man cannot guard against, the House of Representatives, with the people on their side, will at all times be able to bring back the Constitution to its primitive form and principles. Against the force of the immediate representatives of the people nothing will be able to maintain even the constitutional authority of the Senate, but such a display of enlightened policy, and attachment to the public good, as will divide with that branch of the legislature the affections and support of the entire body of the people themselves.

PUBLIUS

No. 64: Jay

IT IS a just and not a new observation that enemies to particular persons, and opponents to particular measures, seldom confine their censures to such things only, in either, as are worthy of blame. Unless, on this principle, it is difficult to explain the motives of their conduct, who condemn the proposed Constitution in the aggregate and treat with severity some of the most unexceptionable articles in it.

The second section gives power to the President, *"by and with the advice and consent of the Senate, to make treaties,* PROVIDED TWO THIRDS OF THE SENATORS PRESENT CONCUR."

The power of making treaties is an important one, especially as it relates to war, peace, and commerce; and it should not be delegated but in such a mode, and with such precautions, as will afford the highest security that it will be exercised by men the best qualified for the purpose, and in the manner most conducive to the public good. The convention appears to have been attentive to both these points; they have directed the President to be chosen by select bodies of electors to be deputed by the people for that express purpose; and they have committed the appointment of senators to the State legislatures. This mode has, in such cases, vastly the advantage of elections by the people in their collective capacity where the activity of party zeal, taking advantage of the supineness, the ignorance, and the hopes and fears of the unwary and interested, often places men in office by the votes of a small proportion of the electors.

As the select assemblies for choosing the President, as well as the State legislatures who appoint the senators, will in general be composed of the most enlightened and respectable citizens, there is reason to presume that their attention and their votes will be directed to those men only who have become the most distinguished by their abilities and virtue, and in whom the people perceive just grounds for confidence. The Constitution manifests very particular attention to this object. By excluding men under thirty-five from the first office, and those under thirty from the second, it confines the electors to men of whom the people have had time to form a judgment, and with respect to whom they will not be liable to be deceived by those brilliant appearances of genius and patriotism which, like transient meteors, sometimes mislead as well as dazzle. If the observation be well founded that wise kings will always be served by able ministers it is fair to argue that as an assembly of select electors possess, in a greater degree than kings, the means of extensive and accurate information relative to men and characters, so will their appointments bear at least equal marks of discretion and discernment. The inference which naturally results from these considerations is this, that the President and senators so chosen will always be of the number of those who best understand our national interests, whether considered in relation to the several States or to foreign nations, who are best able to promote those interests, and whose reputation for integrity inspires and merits confidence. With such men the power of making treaties may be safely lodged.

Although the absolute necessity of system, in the conduct of any business, is universally known and acknowledged, yet the high importance of it in national affairs has not yet become sufficiently impressed on the public mind. They who wish to commit the power under consideration to a popular assembly composed of members constantly coming and going in quick succession seem not to recollect that such a body must necessarily be inadequate to the attainment of those great objects which require to be steadily contemplated in all their relations and circumstances, and which can only be approached and achieved by measures which not only talents, but also exact information, and often much time, are necessary to concert and to execute. It was wise, therefore, in the convention, to provide not only that the power of making treaties should be committed to able and honest men, but also that they should continue in place a sufficient time to become perfectly acquainted with our national concerns, and to form and introduce a system for the management of them. The duration prescribed is such as will give them an opportunity of greatly extending their political informations, and of rendering their accumulating experience more and more beneficial to their country. Nor has the convention discovered less prudence in providing for the frequent elections of senators in such a way as to obviate the inconvenience of periodically transferring those great affairs entirely to new men; for by leaving a considerable residue of the old ones in place, uniformity and order, as well as a constant succession of official information, will be preserved.

There are few who will not admit that the affairs of trade and navigation should be regulated by a system cautiously formed and steadily pursued; and that both our treaties and our laws should correspond with and be made to promote it. It is of much consequence that this correspondence and conformity be carefully maintained; and they who assent to the truth of this position will see and confess that it is well provided for by making the concurrence of the Senate necessary both to treaties and to laws.

It seldom happens in the negotiation of treaties, of whatever nature, but that perfect *secrecy* and immediate *dispatch* are sometimes requisite. There are cases where the most useful intelligence may be obtained, if the persons possessing it can be relieved from apprehensions of discovery. Those apprehensions will operate on those persons whether they are actuated by mercenary or friendly motives; and there doubtless are many of both descriptions who would rely on the secrecy of the President, but who would not confide in that of the Senate, and still less in that of a large popular assembly. The convention have done well, therefore, in so disposing of the power of making treaties that although the President must, in forming them, act by the advice and consent of the Senate, yet he will be able to manage the business of intelligence in such manner as prudence may suggest.

They who have turned their attention to the affairs of men must have perceived that there are tides in them; tides very irregular in their duration, strength, and direction, and seldom found to run twice exactly in the same manner or measure. To discern and to profit by these tides in national affairs is the business of those who preside over them; and they who have had much experience on this head inform us that there frequently are occasions when days, nay, even when hours, are precious. The loss of a battle, the death of a prince, the removal of a minister, or other circumstances intervening to change the present posture and aspect of affairs may turn the most favorable tide into a course opposite to our wishes. As in the field, so in the cabinet, there are moments to be seized as they pass, and they who preside in either should be left in capacity to improve them. So often and so essentially have we heretofore suffered from the want of secrecy and dispatch that the Constitution would have been inexcusably defective if no attention had been paid to those objects. Those matters which in negotiations usually require the most secrecy and the most dispatch are those preparatory and auxiliary measures which are not otherwise important in a national view, than as they tend to facilitate the attainment of the objects of the negotiation. For these the President will find no difficulty to provide; and should any circumstance occur which requires the advice and consent of the Senate, he may at any time convene them. Thus we see that the Constitution provides that our negotiations for treaties shall have every advantage which can be derived from talents, information, integrity, and deliberate investigations, on the one hand, and from secrecy and dispatch on the other.

But to this plan, as to most others that have ever appeared, objections are contrived and urged.

Some are displeased with it, not on account of any errors or defects in it, but because, as the treaties, when made, are to have the force of laws, they should be made only by men invested with legislative authority. These gentlemen seem not to consider that the judgments of our courts, and the commissions constitutionally given by our governor, are as valid and as binding on all persons whom they concern as the laws passed by our legislature. All constitutional acts of power, whether in the executive or in the judicial department, have as much legal validity and obligation as if they proceeded from the legislature; and therefore, whatever name be given to the power of making treaties, or however obligatory they may be when made, certain it is that the people may, with much propriety, commit the power to a distinct body from the legislature, the executive, or the judicial. It surely does not follow that because they have given the power of making laws to the legislature, that therefore they should likewise give them power to do every other act of sovereignty by which the citizens are to be bound and affected.

Others, though content that treaties should be made in the mode proposed, are averse to their being the *supreme* laws of the land. They insist, and profess to believe, that treaties, like acts of assembly, should be repealable at pleasure. This idea seems to be new and peculiar to this country, but new errors, as well as new truths, often appear. These gentlemen would do well to reflect that a treaty is only another name for a bargain, and that it would be impossible to find a nation who would make any bargain with us, which should be binding on them *absolutely,* but on us only so long and so far as we may think proper to be bound by it. They who make laws may, without doubt, amend or repeal them; and it will not be disputed that they who make treaties may alter or cancel them; but still let us not forget that treaties are made, not by only one of the contracting parties, but by both, and consequently, that as the consent of both was essential to their formation at first, so must it ever afterwards be to alter or cancel them. The proposed Constitution, therefore, has not in the least extended the obligation of treaties. They are just as binding and just as far beyond the lawful reach of legislative acts now as they will be at any future period, or under any form of government.

However useful jealousy may be in republics, yet when like bile in the natural it abounds too much in the body politic, the eyes of both become very liable to be deceived by the delusive appearances which that malady casts on surrounding objects. From this cause, probably, proceed the fears and apprehensions of some, that the President and Senate may make treaties without an equal eye to the interests of all the States. Others suspect that the two thirds will oppress the remaining third, and ask whether those gentlemen are made sufficiently responsible for their conduct; whether, if they act corruptly, they can be punished; and if they make disadvantageous treaties, how are we to get rid of those treaties?

As all the States are equally represented in the Senate, and by men the most able and the most willing to promote the interests of their constituents, they will all have an equal degree of influence in that body, especially while they continue to be careful in appointing proper persons, and to insist on their punctual attendance. In proportion as the United States assume a national form and a national character, so will the good of the whole be more and more an object of attention, and the government must be a weak one indeed if it should forget that the good of the whole can only be promoted by advancing the good of each of the parts or members which compose the whole. It will not be in the power of the President and Senate to make any treaties by which they and their families and estates will not be equally bound and affected with the rest of the community; and, having no private interests distinct from that of the nation, they will be under no temptations to neglect the latter.

As to corruption, the case is not supposable. He must either have been very unfortunate in his intercourse with the world, or possess a heart very susceptible of such impressions, who can think it probable that the President and two thirds of the Senate will ever be capable of such unworthy conduct. The idea is too gross and too invidious to be entertained. But in such a case, if it should ever happen, the treaty so obtained from us would, like all other fraudulent contracts, be null and void by the laws of nations.

With respect to their responsibility, it is difficult to

conceive how it could be increased. Every consideration that can influence the human mind, such as honor, oaths, reputations, conscience, the love of country, and family affections and attachments, afford security for their fidelity. In short, as the Constitution has taken the utmost care that they shall be men of talents, and integrity, we have reason to be persuaded that the treaties they make will be as advantageous as, all circumstances considered, could be made; and so far as the fear of punishment and disgrace can operate, that motive to good behavior is amply afforded by the article on the subject of impeachments.

PUBLIUS

No. 65: Hamilton

THE remaining powers which the plan of the convention allots to the Senate, in a distinct capacity, are comprised in their participation with the executive in the appointment to offices, and in their judicial character as a court for the trial of impeachments. As in the business of appointments the executive will be the principal agent, the provisions relating to it will most properly be discussed in the examination of that department. We will, therefore, conclude this head with a view of the judicial character of the Senate.

A well-constituted court for the trial of impeachments is an object not more to be desired than difficult to be obtained in a government wholly elective. The subjects of its jurisdiction are those offenses which proceed from the misconduct of public men, or, in other words, from the abuse or violation of some public trust. They are of a nature which may with peculiar propriety be denominated POLITICAL, as they relate chiefly to injuries done immediately to the society itself. The prosecution of them, for this reason, will seldom fail to agitate the passions of the whole community, and to divide it into parties more or less friendly or inimical to the accused. In many cases it will connect itself with the pre-existing factions, and will enlist all their animosities, partialities, influence, and interest on one side or on the other; and in such cases there will always be the greatest danger that the decision will be regulated more by the comparative strength of parties than by the real demonstrations of innocence or guilt.

The delicacy and magnitude of a trust which so deeply concerns the political reputation and existence of every man engaged in the administration of public affairs speak for themselves. The difficulty of placing it rightly in a government resting entirely on the basis of periodical elections will as readily be perceived, when it is considered that the most conspicuous characters in it will, from that circumstance, be too often the leaders or the tools of the most cunning or the most numerous faction, and on this account can hardly be expected to possess the requisite neutrality towards those whose conduct may be the subject of scrutiny.

The convention, it appears, thought the Senate the most fit depositary of this important trust. Those who can best discern the intrinsic difficulty of the thing will be the least hasty in condemning that opinion, and will be most inclined to allow due weight to the arguments which may be supposed to have produced it.

What, it may be asked, is the true spirit of the institution itself? Is it not designed as a method of NATIONAL INQUEST into the conduct of public men? If this be the design of it, who can so properly be the inquisitors for the nation as the representatives of the nation themselves? It is not disputed that the power of originating the inquiry, or, in other words, of preferring the impeachment, ought to be lodged in the hands of one branch of the legislative body. Will not the reasons which indicate the propriety of this arrangement strongly plead for an admission of the other branch of that body to a share of the inquiry? The model from which the idea of this institution has been borrowed pointed out that course to the convention. In Great Britain it is the province of the House of Commons to prefer the impeachment, and of the House of Lords to decide upon it. Several of the State constitutions have followed the example. As well the latter as the former seem to have regarded the practice of impeachments as a bridle in the hands of the legislative body upon the executive servants of the government. Is not this the true light in which it ought to be regarded?

Where else than in the Senate could have been found a tribunal sufficiently dignified, or sufficiently independent? What other body would be likely to feel *confidence enough in its own situation* to preserve, unawed and uninfluenced, the necessary impartiality between an *individual* accused and the *representatives of the people, his accusers?*

Could the Supreme Court have been relied upon as answering this description? It is much to be doubted whether the members of that tribunal would at all times be endowed with so eminent a portion of fortitude as would be called for in the execution of so difficult a task; and it is still more to be doubted whether they would possess the degree of credit and authority which might, on certain occasions, be indispensable towards reconciling the people to a decision that should happen to clash with an accusation brought by their immediate representatives. A deficiency in the first would be fatal to the accused; in the last, dangerous to the public tranquillity. The hazard, in both these respects, could only be avoided, if at all, by rendering that tribunal more numerous than would consist with a reasonable attention to economy. The necessity of a numerous court for the trial of impeachments is equally dictated by the nature of the proceeding. This can never be tied down by such strict rules, either in the delineation of the offense by the prosecutors or in the construction of it by the judges, as in common cases serve to limit the discretion of courts in favor of personal security. There will be no jury to stand between the judges who are to pronounce the sentence of the law and the party who is to receive or suffer it. The awful discretion which a court of impeachments must necessarily have to doom to honor or to infamy the most confidential and the most distinguished characters of the community forbids the commitment of the trust to a small number of persons.

These considerations seem alone sufficient to authorize a conclusion, that the Supreme Court would have been an improper substitute for the Senate, as a court of impeachments. There remains a further consideration, which will not a little strengthen this conclusion. It is this: the punishment which may be the consequence of conviction upon impeachment is not to terminate the chastisement of the offender. After having been sentenced to a perpetual ostracism from the esteem and confidence and honors and emoluments of his country, he will still be liable to prosecution and punishment in the ordinary course of law. Would it be proper that the persons who had disposed of his fame, and his most valuable rights as a citizen, in one trial, should, in another trial, for the same offense, be also the disposers of his life and his fortune? Would there not be the greatest reason to apprehend that error, in the first sentence, would be the parent of error in the second sentence? That the strong bias of one decision would be apt to overrule the influence of any new lights which might be brought to vary the complexion of another decision? Those who know anything of human nature will not hesitate to answer these questions in the affirmative; and will be at no loss to perceive that by making the same persons judges in both cases, those who might happen to be the objects of prosecution would, in a great measure, be deprived of the double security intended them by a double trial. The loss of life and estate would often be virtually included in a sentence which, in its terms, imported nothing more than dismission from a present and disqualification for a future office. It may be said that the intervention of a jury, in the second instance, would obviate the danger. But juries are frequently influenced by the opinions of judges. They are sometimes induced to find special verdicts, which refer the main question to the decision of the court. Who would be willing to stake his life and his estate upon the verdict of a jury acting under the auspices of judges who had predetermined his guilt?

Would it have been an improvement of the plan to have united the Supreme Court with the Senate in the formation of the court of impeachments? This union would certainly have been attended with several advantages; but would they not have been overbalanced by the signal disadvantage, already stated, arising from the agency of the same judges in the double prosecution to which the offender would be liable? To a certain extent, the benefits of that union will be obtained from making the chief justice of the Supreme Court the president of the court of impeachments, as is proposed to be done in the plan of the convention; while the inconveniences of an entire incorporation of the former into the latter will be substantially avoided. This was perhaps the prudent mean. I forbear to remark upon the additional pretext for clamor against the judiciary, which so considerable an augmentation of its authority would have afforded.

Would it have been desirable to have composed the court for the trial of impeachments of persons wholly distinct from the other departments of the government? There are weighty arguments, as well against as in favor of such a plan. To some minds it will not appear a trivial objection that it would tend to increase the complexity of the political machine, and to add a new spring to the government, the utility of which would at best be questionable. But an objection which will not be thought by any unworthy of attention is this: a court formed upon such a plan would either be attended with heavy expense, or might in practice be subject to a variety of casualties and inconveniences. It must either consist of permanent officers, stationary at the seat of goverment, and of course entitled to fixed and regular stipends, or of certain officers of the State governments, to be called upon whenever an impeachment was actually depending. It will not be easy to imagine any third mode materially different which could rationally be proposed. As the court, for reasons already given, ought to be numerous, the first scheme will be reprobated by every man who can compare the extent of the public wants with the means of supplying them. The second will be espoused with caution by those who will seriously consider the difficulty of collecting men dispersed over the whole Union; the injury to the innocent, from the procrastinated determination of the charges which might be brought against them; the advantage to the guilty, from the opportunities which delay would afford to intrigue and corruption; and in some cases the detriment to the State, from the prolonged inaction of men whose firm and faithful execution of their duty might have exposed them to the persecution of an intemperate or designing majority in the House of Representatives. Though this latter supposition may seem harsh and might not be likely often to be verified, yet it ought not to be forgotten that the demon of faction will, at certain seasons, extend his scepter over all numerous bodies of men.

But, though one or the other of the substitutes which have been examined or some other that might be devised should be thought preferable to the plan, in this respect reported by the convention, it will not follow that the Constitution ought for this reason to be rejected. If mankind were to resolve to agree in no institution of government, until every part of it had been adjusted to the most exact standard of perfection, society would soon become a general scene of anarchy, and the world a desert. Where is the standard of perfection to be found? Who will undertake to unite the discordant opinions of a whole community in the same judgment of it; and to prevail upon one conceited projector to renounce his *infallible* criterion for the *fallible* criterion of his more *conceited neighbor?* To answer the purpose of the adversaries of the Constitution, they ought to prove, not merely that particular provisions in it are not the best which might have been imagined, but that the plan upon the whole is bad and pernicious. PUBLIUS

No. 66: Hamilton

A REVIEW of the principal objections that have appeared against the proposed court for the trial of impeachments will not improbably eradicate the remains of any unfavorable impressions which may still exist in regard to this matter.

The *first* of these objections is that the provision in question confounds legislative and judiciary authorities in the same body in violation of that important and well-established maxim which requires a separation between the different departments of power. The true meaning of this maxim has been discussed and ascertained in another place, and has been shown to be entirely compatible with a partial intermixture of those departments for special purposes, preserving them, in the main, distinct and unconnected. This partial intermixture is even, in some cases, not only proper but necessary to the mutual defense of the several members of the government against each other. An absolute or qualified negative in the executive upon the acts of the legislative body is admitted, by the ablest adepts in political science, to be an indispensable barrier against the encroachments of the latter upon the former. And it may, perhaps, with no less reason, be contended that the powers relating to impeachments are, as before intimated, an essential check in the hands of that body upon the encroachments of the executive. The division of them between the two branches of the legislature, assigning to one the right of accusing, to the other the right of judging, avoids the inconvenience of making the same persons both accusers and judges; and guards against the danger of persecution, from the prevalency of a factious spirit in either of those branches. As the concurrence of two thirds of the Senate will be requisite to a condemnation, the security to innocence, from this additional circumstance, will be as complete as itself can desire.

It is curious to observe with what vehemence this part of the plan is assailed, on the principle here taken notice of, by men who profess to admire without exception the constitution of this State; while that constitution makes the Senate, together with the chancellor and judges of the Supreme Court, not only a court of impeachments, but the highest judicatory in the State, in all causes, civil and criminal. The proportion, in point of numbers, of the chancellor and judges to the senators, is so inconsiderable that the judiciary authority of New York in the last resort may with truth be said to reside in its Senate. If the plan of the convention be, in this respect, chargeable with a departure from the celebrated maxim which has been so often mentioned, and seems to be so little understood, how much more culpable must be the constitution of New York? *

A *second* objection to the Senate, as a court of impeachments, is that it contributes to an undue accumulation of power in that body, tending to give to the government a countenance too aristocratic. The Senate, it is

* In that of New Jersey, also, the final judiciary authority is in a branch of the legislature. In New Hampshire, Massachusetts, Pennsylvania, and South Carolina, one branch of the legislature is the court for the trial of impeachments.

observed, is to have concurrent authority with the executive in the formation of treaties and in the appointment to offices: if, say the objectors, to these prerogatives is added that of determining in all cases of impeachment, it will give a decided predominancy to senatorial influence. To an objection so little precise in itself it is not easy to find a very precise answer. Where is the measure or criterion to which we can appeal for estimating what will give the Senate too much, too little, or barely the proper degree of influence? Will it not be more safe, as well as more simple, to dismiss such vague and uncertain calculations, to examine each power by itself, and to decide, on general principles, where it may be deposited with most advantage and least inconvenience?

If we take this course, it will lead to a more intelligible if not to a more certain result. The disposition of the power of making treaties which has obtained in the plan of the convention will then, if I mistake not, appear to be fully justified by the consideration stated in a former number, and by others which will occur under the next head of our inquiries. The expediency of the junction of the Senate with the executive, in the power of appointing to offices, will, I trust, be placed in a light not less satisfactory in the disquisitions under the same head. And I flatter myself the observations in my last paper must have gone no inconsiderable way towards proving that it was not easy, if practicable, to find a more fit receptacle for the power of determining impeachments than that which has been chosen. If this be truly the case, the hypothetical danger of the too great weight of the Senate ought to be discarded from our reasonings.

But this hypothesis, such as it is, has already been refuted in the remarks applied to the duration in office prescribed for the senators. It was by them shown, as well on the credit of historical examples as from the reason of the thing, that the most *popular* branch of every government partaking of the republican genius, by being generally the favorite of the people, will be as generally a full match, if not an overmatch, for every other member of the government.

But independent of this most active and operative principle, to secure the equilibrium of the national House of Representatives, the plan of the convention has provided in its favor several important counterpoises to the additional authorities to be conferred upon the Senate. The exclusive privilege of originating money bills will belong to the House of Representatives. The same house will possess the sole right of instituting impeachments; is not this a complete counterbalance to that of determining them? The same house will be the umpire in all elections of the President which do not unite the suffrages of a majority of the whole number of electors; a case which it cannot be doubted will sometimes, if not frequently, happen. The constant possibility of the thing must be a fruitful source of influence to that body. The more it is contemplated, the more important will appear this ultimate though contingent power of deciding the competitions of the most illustrious citizens of the Union, for the first office in it. It would not perhaps be rash to predict, that as a mean influence it will be found to outweigh all the peculiar attributes of the Senate.

A *third* objection to the Senate as a court of impeachments is drawn from the agency they are to have in the appointments to office. It is imagined that they would be too indulgent judges of the conduct of men, in whose official creation they had participated. The principle of this objection would condemn a practice which is to be seen in all the State governments, if not in all the governments with which we are acquainted: I mean that of rendering those who hold office during pleasure dependent on the pleasure of those who appoint them. With equal plausibility might it be alleged in this case that the favoritism of the latter would always be an asylum for the misbehavior of the former. But that practice, in contradiction to this principle, proceeds upon the presumption that the responsibility of those who appoint, for the fitness and competency of the persons on whom they bestow their choice, and the interest they have in the respectable and prosperous administration of affairs, will inspire a sufficient disposition to dismiss from a share in it all such who, by their conduct, may have proved themselves unworthy of the confidence reposed in them. Though facts may not always correspond with this presumption, yet if it be, in the main, just, it must destroy the supposition that the Senate, who will merely sanction the choice of the Executive, should feel a bias towards the objects of that choice strong enough to blind them to the evidences of guilt so extraordinary as to have induced the representatives of the nation to become its accusers.

If any further argument were necessary to evince the improbability of such a bias, it might be found in the nature of the agency of the Senate in the business of appointments. It will be the office of the President to *nominate,* and, with the advice and consent of the Senate, to *appoint.* There will, of course, be no exertion of *choice* on the part of the Senate. They may defeat one choice of the Executive, and oblige him to make another; but they cannot themselves *choose*—they can only ratify or reject the choice he may have made. They might even entertain a preference to some other person at the very moment they were assenting to the one proposed, because there might be no positive ground of opposition to him; and they could not be sure, if they withheld their assent, that the subsequent nomination would fall upon their own favorite, or upon any other person in their estimation more meritorious than the one rejected. Thus it could hardly happen that the majority of the Senate would feel any other complacency towards the object of an appointment than such as the appearances of merit might inspire and the proofs of the want of it destroy.

A *fourth* objection to the Senate, in the capacity of a court of impeachments, is derived from its union with the executive in the power of making treaties. This, it has been said, would constitute the senators their own judges in every case of a corrupt or perfidious execution of that trust. After having combined with the Executive in betraying the interests of the nation in a ruinous treaty, what prospect, it is asked, would there be of their being made to suffer the punishment they would deserve when they were themselves to decide upon the accusation brought against them for the treachery of which they had been guilty?

This objection has been circulated with more earnestness and with greater show of reason than any other which has appeared against this part of the plan; and yet I am deceived if it does not rest upon an erroneous foundation.

The security essentially intended by the Constitution against corruption and treachery in the formation of treaties is to be sought for in the numbers and characters of those who are to make them. The JOINT AGENCY of the Chief Magistrate of the Union, and of two thirds of the members of a body selected by the collective wisdom of the legislatures of the several States, is designed to be the pledge for the fidelity of the national councils in this particular. The convention might with propriety have meditated the punishment of the executive for a deviation from the instructions of the Senate, or a want of integrity in the conduct of the negotiations committed to him; they might also have had in view the punishment of a few leading individuals in the Senate who should have prostituted their influence in that body as the mercenary instruments of foreign corruption: but they could not, with more or with equal propriety, have contemplated the impeachment and punishment of two thirds of the Senate, consenting to an improper treaty, than of a majority of that or of the other branch of the national legislature, consenting to a pernicious or unconstitutional law—a principle which, I believe, has never been admitted into any government. How, in fact, could a majority in the House of Representatives impeach themselves? Not better, it is evident, than two thirds of the Senate might try themselves. And yet what reason is there that a majority of the House of Representatives, sacrificing the interests of the society by an unjust and tyrannical act of legislation, should escape with impunity, more than two thirds of the Senate sacrificing the same interests in an injurious treaty with a foreign power? The truth is that in all such cases it is essential to the freedom and to the necessary independence of the deliberations of the body that the members of it should be exempt from punishment for acts done in a collective capacity; and the security to the society must depend on the care which is taken to confide the trust to proper hands, to make it their interest to execute it with fidelity, and to make it as difficult as possible for them to combine in any interest opposite to that of the public good.

So far as might concern the misbehavior of the executive in perverting the instructions or contravening the views of the Senate, we need not be apprehensive of the want of a disposition in that body to punish the abuse of their confidence or to vindicate their own authority. We may thus far count upon their pride, if not upon their virtue. And so far even as might concern the corruption of leading members by whose arts and influence the majority may have been inveigled into measures odious to the community, if the proofs of that corruption should be satisfactory, the usual propensity of human nature will warrant us in concluding that there would be commonly no defect of inclination in the body to divert the public resentment from themselves by a ready sacrifice of the authors of their mismanagement and disgrace.

PUBLIUS

No. 67: Hamilton

THE constitution of the executive department of the proposed government claims next our attention.

There is hardly any part of the system which could have been attended with greater difficulty in the arrangement of it than this; and there is, perhaps, none which has been inveighed against with less candor or criticized with less judgment.

Here the writers against the Constitution seem to have taken pains to signalize their talent of misrepresentation. Calculating upon the aversion of the people to monarchy, they have endeavored to enlist all their jealousies and apprehensions in opposition to the intended President of the United States; not merely as the embryo, but as the full-grown progeny of that detested parent. To establish the pretended affinity, they have not scrupled to draw resources even from the regions of fiction. The authorities of a magistrate, in few instances greater, in some instances less, than those of a governor of New York, have been magnified into more than royal prerogatives. He has been decorated with attributes superior in dignity and splendor to those of a king of Great Britain. He has been shown to us with the diadem sparkling on his brow and the imperial purple flowing in his train. He has been seated on a throne surrounded with minions and mistresses, giving audience to the envoys of foreign potentates in all the supercilious pomp of majesty. The images of Asiatic despotism and voluptuousness have scarcely been wanting to crown the exaggerated scene. We have been almost taught to tremble at the terrific visages of murdering janizaries, and to blush at the unveiled mysteries of a future seraglio.

Attempts so extravagant as these to disfigure or, it might rather be said, to metamorphose the object, render it necessary to take an accurate view of its real nature and form: in order as well to ascertain its true aspect and genuine appearance, as to unmask the disingenuity and expose the fallacy of the counterfeit resemblances which have been so insidiously, as well as industriously, propagated.

In the execution of this task there is no man who would not find it an arduous effort either to behold with moderation or to treat with seriousness the devices, not less weak than wicked, which have been contrived to pervert the public opinion in relation to the subject. They so far exceed the usual though unjustifiable licenses of party artifice that even in a disposition the most candid and tolerant they must force the sentiments which favor an indulgent construction of the conduct of political adversaries to give place to a voluntary and unreserved indignation. It is impossible not to bestow the imputation of deliberate imposture and deception upon the gross pretense of a similitude between a king of Great Britain and a magistrate of the character marked out for that of the President of the United States. It is still more impossible to withhold that imputation from the rash and barefaced expedients which have been employed to give success to the attempted imposition.

In one instance, which I cite as a sample of the general spirit, the temerity has proceeded so far as to ascribe to the President of the United States a power which by the instrument reported is *expressly* alloted to the executives of the individual States. I mean the power of filling casual vacancies in the Senate.

This bold experiment upon the discernment of his countrymen has been hazarded by a writer who (whatever may be his real merit) has had no inconsiderable share in the applauses of his party;* and who, upon his false and unfounded suggestion, has built a series of

* See CATO, No. V.

observations equally false and unfounded. Let him now be confronted with the evidence of the fact, and let him, if he be able, justify or extenuate the shameful outrage he has offered to the dictates of truth and to the rules of fair dealing.

The second clause of the second section of the second article empowers the President of the United States "to nominate, and by and with the advice and consent of the Senate, to appoint ambassadors, other public ministers and consuls, judges of the Supreme Court, and all other *officers* of the United States whose appointments are *not* in the Constitution *otherwise provided for,* and *which shall be established by law.*" Immediately after this clause follows another in these words: "The President shall have power to fill up all *vacancies* that may happen *during the recess of the Senate,* by granting commissions which shall *expire at the end of their next session.*" It is from this last provision that the pretended power of the President to fill vacancies in the Senate has been deduced. A slight attention to the connection of the clauses and to the obvious meaning of the terms will satisfy us that the deduction is not even colorable.

The first of these two clauses, it is clear, only provides a mode for appointing such officers "whose appointments are *not otherwise provided for* in the Constitution, and which *shall be established by law*"; of course it cannot extend to the appointment of senators, whose appointments are *otherwise provided for* in the Constitution,* and who are *established by the Constitution,* and will not require a future establishment by law. This position will hardly be contested.

The last of these two clauses, it is equally clear, cannot be understood to comprehend the power of filling vacancies in the Senate, for the following reasons:—*First.* The relation in which that clause stands to the other, which declares the general mode of appointing officers of the United States, denotes it to be nothing more than a supplement to the other for the purpose of establishing an auxiliary method of appointment, in cases to which the general method was inadequate. The ordinary power of appointment is confided to the President and Senate

* Article 1, Section 3, Clause 1.

jointly, and can therefore only be exercised during the session of the Senate; but as it would have been improper to oblige this body to be continually in session for the appointment of officers, and as vacancies might happen *in their recess,* which it might be necessary for the public service to fill without delay, the succeeding clause is evidently intended to authorize the President, *singly,* to make temporary appointments "during the recess of the Senate, by granting commissions which shall expire at the end of their next session." *Second.* If this clause is to be considered as supplementary to the one which precedes, the *vacancies* of which it speaks must be construed to relate to the "officers" described in the preceding one; and this, we have seen, excludes from its description the members of the Senate. *Third.* The time within which the power is to operate "during the recess of the Senate," and the duration of the appointments "to the end of the next session" of that body, conspire to elucidate the sense of the provision which, if it had been intended to comprehend senators, would naturally have referred the temporary power of filling vacancies to the recess of the State legislatures, who are to make the permanent appointments, and not to the recess of the national Senate, who are to have no concern in those appointments; and would have extended the duration in office of the temporary senators to the next session of the legislature of the State, in whose representation the vacancies had happened, instead of making it to expire at the end of the ensuing session of the national Senate. The circumstances of the body authorized to make the permanent appointments would, of course, have governed the modification of a power which related to the temporary appointments; and as the national Senate is the body whose situation is alone contemplated in the clause upon which the suggestion under examination has been founded, the vacancies to which it alludes can only be deemed to respect those officers in whose appointment that body has a concurrent agency with the President. But *lastly,* the first and second clauses of the third section of the first article not only obviate all possibility of doubt, but destroy the pretext of misconception. The former provides that "the Senate of the United States shall be composed of two senators from each State, chosen *by the legislature thereof* for six years"; and the latter directs that "if vacancies in that body should happen by resignation or otherwise, *during the recess of the legislature of* ANY STATE, the executive THEREOF may make temporary appointments until the *next meeting of the legislature,* which shall then fill such vacancies." Here is an express power given, in clear and unambiguous terms, to the State executives to fill casual vacancies in the Senate by temporary appointments; which not only invalidates the supposition that the clause before considered could have been intended to confer that power upon the President of the United States, but proves that this supposition, destitute as it is even of the merit of plausibility, must have originated in an intention to deceive the people, too palpable to be obscured by sophistry, too atrocious to be palliated by hypocrisy.

I have taken the pains to select this instance of misrepresentation and to place it in a clear and strong light, as an unequivocal proof of the unwarrantable arts which are practised to prevent a fair and impartial judgment of the real merits of the Constitution submitted to the consideration of the people. Nor have I scrupled, in so flagrant a case, to allow myself a severity of animadversion little congenial with the general spirit of these papers. I hesitate not to submit it to the decision of any candid and honest adversary of the proposed government whether language can furnish epithets of too much asperity for so shameless and so prostitute an attempt to impose on the citizens of America. PUBLIUS

No. 68: Hamilton

THE mode of appointment of the Chief Magistrate of the United States is almost the only part of the system, of any consequence, which has escaped without severe censure or which has received the slightest mark of approbation from its opponents. The most plausible of these, who has appeared in print, has even deigned to admit that the election of the President is pretty well guarded.* I venture somewhat further, and hesitate not to affirm that if the

* *Vide Federal Farmer.*

manner of it be not perfect, it is at least excellent. It unites in an eminent degree all the advantages the union of which was to be desired.

It was desirable that the sense of the people should operate in the choice of the person to whom so important a trust was to be confided. This end will be answered by committing the right of making it, not to any pre-established body, but to men chosen by the people for the special purpose, and at the particular conjuncture.

It was equally desirable that the immediate election should be made by men most capable of analyzing the qualities adapted to the station and acting under circumstances favorable to deliberation, and to a judicious combination of all the reasons and inducements which were proper to govern their choice. A small number of persons, selected by their fellow-citizens from the general mass, will be most likely to possess the information and discernment requisite to so complicated an investigation.

It was also peculiarly desirable to afford as little opportunity as possible to tumult and disorder. This evil was not least to be dreaded in the election of a magistrate who was to have so important an agency in the administration of the government as the President of the United States. But the precautions which have been so happily concerted in the system under consideration promise an effectual security against this mischief. The choice of *several* to form an intermediate body of electors will be much less apt to convulse the community with any extraordinary or violent movements than the choice of *one* who was himself to be the final object of the public wishes. And as the electors, chosen in each State, are to assemble and vote in the State in which they are chosen, this detached and divided situation will expose them much less to heats and ferments, which might be communicated from them to the people, than if they were all to be convened at one time, in one place.

Nothing was more to be desired than that every practicable obstacle should be opposed to cabal, intrigue, and corruption. These most deadly adversaries of republican government might naturally have been expected to make their approaches from more than one quarter, but chiefly from the desire in foreign powers to gain an improper ascendant in our councils. How could they better gratify this than by raising a creature of their own to the chief magistracy of the Union? But the convention have guarded against all danger of this sort with the most provident and judicious attention. They have not made the appointment of the President to depend on any pre-existing bodies of men who might be tampered with beforehand to prostitute their votes; but they have referred it in the first instance to an immediate act of the people of America, to be exerted in the choice of persons for the temporary and sole purpose of making the appointment. And they have excluded from eligibility to this trust all those who from situation might be suspected of too great devotion to the President in office. No senator, representative, or other person holding a place of trust or profit under the United States can be of the number of the electors. Thus without corrupting the body of the people, the immediate agents in the election will at least enter upon the task free from any sinister bias. Their transient existence and their detached situation, already taken notice of, afford a satisfactory prospect of their continuing so, to the conclusion of it. The business of corruption, when it is to embrace so considerable a number of men, requires time as well as means. Nor would it be found easy suddenly to embark them, dispersed as they would be over thirteen States, in any combinations founded upon motives which, though they could not properly be denominated corrupt, might yet be of a nature to mislead them from their duty.

Another and no less important desideratum was that the executive should be independent for his continuance in office on all but the people themselves. He might otherwise be tempted to sacrifice his duty to his complaisance for those whose favor was necessary to the duration of his official consequence. This advantage will also be secured, by making his re-election to depend on a special body of representatives, deputed by the society for the single purpose of making the important choice.

All these advantages will be happily combined in the plan devised by the convention; which is, that the people of each State shall choose a number of persons as electors, equal to the number of senators and representatives of such State in the national government who shall assemble within the State, and vote for some fit person as President.

Their votes, thus given, are to be transmitted to the seat of the national government, and the person who may happen to have a majority of the whole number of votes will be the President. But as a majority of the votes might not always happen to center on one man, and as it might be unsafe to permit less than a majority to be conclusive, it is provided that, in such a contingency, the House of Representatives shall elect out of the candidates who shall have the five highest number of votes the man who in their opinion may be best qualified for the office.

This process of election affords a moral certainty that the office of President will seldom fall to the lot of any man who is not in an eminent degree endowed with the requisite qualifications. Talents for low intrigue, and the little arts of popularity, may alone suffice to elevate a man to the first honors in a single State; but it will require other talents, and a different kind of merit, to establish him in the esteem and confidence of the whole Union, or of so considerable a portion of it as would be necessary to make him a successful candidate for the distinguished office of President of the United States. It will not be too strong to say that there will be a constant probability of seeing the station filled by characters pre-eminent for ability and virtue. And this will be thought no inconsiderable recommendation of the Constitution by those who are able to estimate the share which the executive in every government must necessarily have in its good or ill administration. Though we cannot acquiesce in the political heresy of the poet who says:

> "For forms of government let fools contest—
> That which is best administered is best,"—

yet we may safely pronounce that the true test of a good government is its aptitude and tendency to produce a good administration.

The Vice-President is to be chosen in the same manner with the President; with this difference, that the Senate is to do, in respect to the former, what is to be done by the House of Representatives, in respect to the latter.

The appointment of an extraordinary person, as Vice-President, has been objected to as superfluous, if not mischievous. It has been alleged that it would have been preferable to have authorized the Senate to elect out of their own body an officer answering to that description. But two considerations seem to justify the ideas of the convention in this respect. One is that to secure at all times the possibility of a definitive resolution of the body, it is necessary that the President should have only a casting vote. And to take the senator of any State from his seat as senator, to place him in that of President of the Senate, would be to exchange, in regard to the State from which he came, a constant for a contingent vote. The other consideration is that as the Vice-President may occasionally become a substitute for the President, in the supreme executive magistracy, all the reasons which recommend the mode of election prescribed for the one apply with great if not with equal force to the manner of appointing the other. It is remarkable that in this, as in most other instances, the objection which is made would lie against the constitution of this State. We have a Lieutenant-Governor, chosen by the people at large, who presides in the Senate, and is the constitutional substitute for the Governor, in casualties similar to those which would authorize the Vice-President to exercise the authorities and discharge the duties of the President.

PUBLIUS

No. 69: Hamilton

I PROCEED now to trace the real characters of the proposed executive, as they are marked out in the plan of the convention. This will serve to place in a strong light the unfairness of the representations which have been made in regard to it.

The first thing which strikes our attention is that the executive authority, with few exceptions, is to be vested in a single magistrate. This will scarcely, however, be considered as a point upon which any comparison can be grounded; for if, in this particular, there be a resemblance to the king of Great Britain, there is not less a resemblance to the Grand Seignior, to the khan of Tartary, to the Man of the Seven Mountains, or to the governor of New York.

That magistrate is to be elected for *four* years; and is to be re-eligible as often as the people of the United States shall think him worthy of their confidence. In these circumstances there is a total dissimilitude between *him* and a king of Great Britain, who is an *hereditary* monarch, possessing the crown as a patrimony descendible to his heirs forever; but there is a close analogy between *him* and a governor of New York, who is elected for *three* years, and is re-eligible without limitation or intermission. If we consider how much less time would be requisite for establishing a dangerous influence in a single State than for establishing a like influence throughout the United States, we must conclude that a duration of *four* years for the Chief Magistrate of the Union is a degree of permanency far less to be dreaded in that office, than a duration of *three* years for a corresponding office in a single State.

The President of the United States would be liable to be impeached, tried, and, upon conviction of treason, bribery, or other high crimes or misdemeanors, removed from office; and would afterwards be liable to prosecution and punishment in the ordinary course of law. The person of the King of Great Britain is sacred and inviolable; there is no constitutional tribunal to which he is amenable; no punishment to which he can be subjected without involving the crisis of a national revolution. In this delicate and important circumstance of personal responsibility, the President of Confederated America would stand upon no better ground than a governor of New York, and upon worse ground than the governors of Virginia and Delaware.

The President of the United States is to have power to return a bill, which shall have passed the two branches of the legislature, for reconsideration; but the bill so returned is not to become a law unless, upon that reconsideration, it be approved by two thirds of both houses. The king of Great Britain, on his part, has an absolute negative upon the acts of the two houses of Parliament. The disuse of that power for a considerable time past does not affect the reality of its existence and is to be ascribed wholly to the crown's having found the means of substituting influence to authority, or the art of gaining a majority in one or the other of the two houses, to the necessity of exerting a prerogative which could seldom be exerted without hazarding some degree of national agitation. The qualified negative of the President differs widely from this absolute negative of the British sovereign and tallies exactly with the revisionary authority of the council of revision of this State, of which the governor is a constituent part. In this respect the power of the President would exceed that of the governor of New York, because the former would possess, singly, what the latter shares with the chancellor and judges; but it would be precisely the same with that of the governor of Massachusetts, whose constitution, as to this article, seems to have been the original from which the convention have copied.

The President is to be the "commander-in-chief of the army and navy of the United States, and of the militia of the several States, when called into the actual service of the United States. He is to have power to grant reprieves and pardons for offenses against the United States, *except in cases of impeachment;* to recommend to the consideration of Congress such measures as he shall judge necessary and expedient; to convene, on extraordinary occasions, both houses of the legislature, or either of them, and, in case of disagreement between them *with respect to the time of adjournment,* to adjourn them to such time as he shall think proper; to take care that the laws be faithfully executed; and to commission all officers of the United States." In most of these particulars, the power of the President will resemble equally that of the king of Great Britain and of the governor of New York. The most material points of difference are these:—*First.* The President will have only the occasional command of such part of the militia of the nation as by legislative provision may be called into the actual service of the Union. The king of Great Britain and the governor of New York have at all times the entire command of all the militia within their several jurisdictions. In this article, therefore, the power of the President would be inferior to that of either the monarch or the governor. *Second.* The President is to be commander-in-chief of the army and navy of the United States. In this respect his authority would be nominally the same with that of the king of Great Britain, but in substance much inferior to it. It would amount to nothing more than the supreme command and direction of the military and naval forces, as first general and admiral of the Confederacy; while that of the British king extends to the *declaring* of war and to the *raising* and *regulating* of fleets and armies—all which, by the Constitution under consideration, would appertain to the legislature.* The governor of New York, on the other hand, is by the constitution of the State vested only with the command of its militia and navy. But the constitutions of several of the States expressly declare their governors to be commanders-in-chief, as well of the army as navy; and it may well be a question whether those of New Hampshire and Massachusetts, in particular, do not, in this instance, confer larger powers upon their respective governors than could be claimed by a President of the United States. *Third*. The power of the President, in respect to pardons, would extend to all cases, *except those of impeachment*. The governor of New York may pardon in all cases, even in those of impeachment, except for treason and murder. Is not the power of the governor, in this article, on a calculation of political consequences, greater than that of the President? All conspiracies and plots against the government which have not been matured into actual treason may be screened from punishment of every kind by the interposition of the prerogative of pardoning. If a governor of New York, therefore, should be at the head of any such conspiracy, until the design had been ripened into actual hostility he could insure his accomplices and adherents an entire impunity.

* A writer in a Pennsylvania paper, under the signature of TAMONY, has asserted that the king of Great Britain owes his prerogative as commander-in-chief to an annual mutiny bill. The truth is, on the contrary, that his prerogative in this respect is immemorial, and was only disputed "contrary to all reason and precedent," as Blackstone, vol. i, page 262, expresses it, by the Long Parliament of Charles I; but by the statute the 13th of Charles II, chap. 6, it was declared to be in the king alone, for that the sole supreme government and command of the militia within his Majesty's realms and dominions, and of all forces by sea and land, and of all forts and places of strength, EVER WAS AND IS the undoubted right of his Majesty and his royal predecessors, kings and queens of England, and that both or either house of Parliament cannot nor ought to pretend to the same.

A President of the Union, on the other hand, though he may even pardon treason, when prosecuted in the ordinary course of law, could shelter no offender, in any degree, from the effects of impeachment and conviction. Would not the prospect of a total indemnity for all the preliminary steps be a greater temptation to undertake and persevere in an enterprise against the public liberty, than the mere prospect of an exemption from death and confiscation, if the final execution of the design, upon an actual appeal to arms, should miscarry? Would this last expectation have any influence at all, when the probability was computed that the person who was to afford that exemption might himself be involved in the consequences of the measure, and might be incapacitated by his agency in it from affording the desired impunity? The better to judge of this matter, it will be necessary to recollect that, by the proposed Constitution, the offense of treason is limited "to levying war upon the United States, and adhering to their enemies, giving them aid and comfort"; and that by the laws of New York it is confined within similar bounds. *Fourth.* The President can only adjourn the national legislature in the single case of disagreement about the time of adjournment. The British monarch may prorogue or even dissolve the Parliament. The governor of New York may also prorogue the legislature of this State for a limited time; a power which, in certain situations, may be employed to very important purposes.

The President is to have power, with the advice and consent of the Senate, to make treaties, provided two thirds of the senators present concur. The king of Great Britain is the sole and absolute representative of the nation in all foreign transactions. He can of his own accord make treaties of peace, commerce, alliance, and of every other description. It has been insinuated that his authority in this respect is not conclusive, and that his conventions with foreign powers are subject to the revision, and stand in need of the ratification, of Parliament. But I believe this doctrine was never heard of until it was broached upon the present occasion. Every jurist * of that kingdom, and every other man acquainted with its

* *Vide* Blackstone's *Commentaries,* Vol. I., p. 257.

Constitution knows, as an established fact, that the prerogative of making treaties exists in the crown in its utmost plenitude; and that the compacts entered into by the royal authority have the most complete legal validity and perfection, independent of any other sanction. The Parliament, it is true, is sometimes seen employing itself in altering the existing laws to conform them to the stipulations in a new treaty; and this may have possibly given birth to the imagination that its co-operation was necessary to the obligatory efficacy of the treaty. But this parliamentary interposition proceeds from a different cause: from the necessity of adjusting a most artificial and intricate system of revenue and commercial laws, to the changes made in them by the operation of the treaty; and of adapting new provisions and precautions to the new state of things, to keep the machine from running into disorder. In this respect, therefore, there is no comparison between the intended power of the President and the actual power of the British sovereign. The one can perform alone what the other can only do with the concurrence of a branch of the legislature. It must be admitted that in this instance the power of the federal executive would exceed that of any State executive. But this arises naturally from the exclusive possession by the Union of that part of the sovereign power which relates to treaties. If the Confederacy were to be dissolved, it would become a question whether the executives of the several States were not solely invested with that delicate and important prerogative.

The President is also to be authorized to receive ambassadors and other public ministers. This, though it has been a rich theme of declamation, is more a matter of dignity than of authority. It is a circumstance which will be without consequence in the administration of the government; and it was far more convenient that it should be arranged in this manner than that there should be a necessity of convening the legislature, or one of its branches, upon every arrival of a foreign minister, though it were merely to take the place of a departed predecessor.

The President is to nominate, and, *with the advice and consent of the Senate*, to appoint ambassadors and other public ministers, judges of the Supreme Court, and in general all officers of the United States established by law, and whose appointments are not otherwise provided for by the Constitution. The king of Great Britain is emphatically and truly styled the fountain of honor. He not only appoints to all offices, but can create offices. He can confer titles of nobility at pleasure, and has the disposal of an immense number of church preferments. There is evidently a great inferiority in the power of the President, in this particular, to that of the British king; nor is it equal to that of the governor of New York, if we are to interpret the meaning of the constitution of the State by the practice which has obtained under it. The power of appointment is with us lodged in a council, composed of the governor and four members of the Senate, chosen by the Assembly. The governor *claims,* and has frequently *exercised,* the right of nomination, and is *entitled* to a casting vote in the appointment. If he really has the right of nominating, his authority is in this respect equal to that of the President, and exceeds it in the article of the casting vote. In the national government, if the Senate should be divided, no appointment could be made; in the government of New York, if the council should be divided, the governor can turn the scale and confirm his own nomination.* If we compare the publicity which must necessarily attend the mode of appointment by the President and an entire branch of the national legislature, with the privacy in the mode of appointment by the governor of New York, closeted in a secret apartment with at most four, and frequently with only two persons; and if we at the same time consider how much more easy it must be to influence the small number of which a council of appointment consists than the considerable number of which the national Senate would consist, we cannot hesitate to pronounce that the power of the chief magistrate of this State, in the disposition of offices, must, in practice, be greatly

* Candor, however, demands an acknowledgment that I do not think the claim of the governor to a right of nomination well founded. Yet it is always justifiable to reason from the practice of a government till its propriety has been constitutionally questioned. And independent of this claim, when we take into view the other considerations and pursue them through all their consequences, we shall be inclined to draw much the same conclusion.

superior to that of the Chief Magistrate of the Union.

Hence it appears that, except as to the concurrent authority of the President in the article of treaties, it would be difficult to determine whether that magistrate would, in the aggregate, possess more or less power than the governor of New York. And it appears yet more unequivocally that there is no pretense for the parallel which has been attempted between him and the king of Great Britain. But to render the contrast in this respect still more striking, it may be of use to throw the principal circumstances of dissimilitude into a closer group.

The President of the United States would be an officer elected by the people for *four* years; the king of Great Britain is a perpetual and *hereditary* prince. The one would be amenable to personal punishment and disgrace; the person of the other is sacred and inviolable. The one would have a *qualified* negative upon the acts of the legislative body; the other has an *absolute* negative. The one would have a right to command the military and naval forces of the nation; the other, in addition to this right, possesses that of *declaring* war, and of *raising* and *regulating* fleets and armies by his own authority. The one would have a concurrent power with a branch of the legislature in the formation of treaties; the other is the *sole possessor* of the power of making treaties. The one would have a like concurrent authority in appointing to offices; the other is the sole author of all appointments. The one can confer no privileges whatever; the other can make denizens of aliens, noblemen of commoners; can erect corporations with all the rights incident to corporate bodies. The one can prescribe no rules concerning the commerce or currency of the nation; the other is in several respects the arbiter of commerce, and in this capacity can establish markets and fairs, can regulate weights and measures, can lay embargoes for a limited time, can coin money, can authorize or prohibit the circulation of foreign coin. The one has no particle of spiritual jurisdiction; the other is the supreme head and governor of the national church! What answer shall we give to those who would persuade us that things so unlike resemble each other? The same that ought to be given to those who tell us that a government, the whole power of which would be in the hands of the elective and periodical servants of the people, is an aristocracy, a monarchy, and a despotism. PUBLIUS

No. 70: Hamilton

THERE is an idea, which is not without its advocates, that a vigorous executive is inconsistent with the genius of republican government. The enlightened well-wishers to this species of government must at least hope that the supposition is destitute of foundation; since they can never admit its truth, without at the same time admitting the condemnation of their own principles. Energy in the executive is a leading character in the definition of good government. It is essential to the protection of the community against foreign attacks; it is not less essential to the steady administration of the laws; to the protection of property against those irregular and high-handed combinations which sometimes interrupt the ordinary course of justice; to the security of liberty against the enterprises and assaults of ambition, of faction, and of anarchy. Every man the least conversant in Roman history knows how often that republic was obliged to take refuge in the absolute power of a single man, under the formidable title of dictator, as well against the intrigues of ambitious individuals who aspired to the tyranny, and the seditions of whole classes of the community whose conduct threatened the existence of all government, as against the invasions of external enemies who menaced the conquest and destruction of Rome.

There can be no need, however, to multiply arguments or examples on this head. A feeble executive implies a feeble execution of the government. A feeble execution is but another phrase for a bad execution; and a government ill executed, whatever it may be in theory, must be, in practice, a bad government.

Taking it for granted, therefore, that all men of sense will agree in the necessity of an energetic executive, it will only remain to inquire, what are the ingredients which constitute this energy? How far can they be combined with those other ingredients which constitute safety in the republican sense? And how far does this combination characterize the plan which has been reported by the convention?

The ingredients which constitute energy in the executive are unity; duration; an adequate provision for its support; and competent powers.

The ingredients which constitute safety in the republican sense are a due dependence on the people, and a due responsibility.

Those politicians and statesmen who have been the most celebrated for the soundness of their principles and for the justness of their views have declared in favor of a single executive and a numerous legislature. They have, with great propriety, considered energy as the most necessary qualification of the former, and have regarded this as most applicable to power in a single hand; while they have, with equal propriety, considered the latter as best adapted to deliberation and wisdom, and best calculated to conciliate the confidence of the people and to secure their privileges and interests.

That unity is conducive to energy will not be disputed. Decision, activity, secrecy, and dispatch will generally characterize the proceedings of one man in a much more eminent degree than the proceedings of any greater number; and in proportion as the number is increased, these qualities will be diminished.

This unity may be destroyed in two ways: either by vesting the power in two or more magistrates of equal dignity and authority, or by vesting it ostensibly in one man, subject in whole or in part to the control and cooperation of others, in the capacity of counselors to him. Of the first, the two consuls of Rome may serve as an example; of the last, we shall find examples in the constitutions of several of the States. New York and New Jersey, if I recollect right, are the only States which have intrusted the executive authority wholly to single men.* Both these methods of destroying the unity of the

* New York has no council except for the single purpose of appointing to offices; New Jersey has a council whom the governor may consult. But I think, from the terms of the Constitution, their resolutions do not bind him.

executive have their partisans; but the votaries of an executive council are the most numerous. They are both liable, if not to equal, to similar objections, and may in most lights be examined in conjunction.

The experience of other nations will afford little instruction on this head. As far, however, as it teaches anything, it teaches us not to be enamored of plurality in the executive. We have seen that the Achæans, on an experiment of two Prætors, were induced to abolish one. The Roman history records many instances of mischiefs to the republic from the dissensions between the consuls, and between the military tribunes, who were at times substituted for the consuls. But it gives us no specimens of any peculiar advantages derived to the state from the circumstance of the plurality of those magistrates. That the dissensions between them were not more frequent or more fatal is matter of astonishment, until we advert to the singular position in which the republic was almost continually placed, and to the prudent policy pointed out by the circumstances of the state, and pursued by the consuls, of making a division of the government between them. The patricians engaged in a perpetual struggle with the plebeians for the preservation of their ancient authorities and dignities; the consuls, who were generally chosen out of the former body, were commonly united by the personal interest they had in the defense of the privileges of their order. In addition to this motive of union, after the arms of the republic had considerably expanded the bounds of its empire, it became an established custom with the consuls to divide the administration between themselves by lot—one of them remaining at Rome to govern the city and its environs, the other taking command in the more distant provinces. This expedient must no doubt have had great influence in preventing those collisions and rivalships which might otherwise have embroiled the peace of the republic.

But quitting the dim light of historical research, and attaching ourselves purely to the dictates of reason and good sense, we shall discover much greater cause to reject than to approve the idea of plurality in the executive, under any modification whatever.

Whenever two or more persons are engaged in any

common enterprise or pursuit, there is always danger of difference of opinion. If it be a public trust or office in which they are clothed with equal dignity and authority, there is peculiar danger of personal emulation and even animosity. From either, and especially from all these causes, the most bitter dissensions are apt to spring. Whenever these happen, they lessen the respectability, weaken the authority, and distract the plans and operations of those whom they divide. If they should unfortunately assail the supreme executive magistracy of a country, consisting of a plurality of persons, they might impede or frustrate the most important measures of the government in the most critical emergencies of the state. And what is still worse, they might split the community into the most violent and irreconcilable factions, adhering differently to the different individuals who composed the magistracy.

Men often oppose a thing merely because they have had no agency in planning it, or because it may have been planned by those whom they dislike. But if they have been consulted, and have happened to disapprove, opposition then becomes, in their estimation, an indispensable duty of self-love. They seem to think themselves bound in honor, and by all the motives of personal infallibility, to defeat the success of what has been resolved upon contrary to their sentiments. Men of upright, benevolent tempers have too many opportunities of remarking, with horror, to what desperate lengths this disposition is sometimes carried, and how often the great interests of society are sacrificed to the vanity, to the conceit, and to the obstinacy of individuals, who have credit enough to make their passions and their caprices interesting to mankind. Perhaps the question now before the public may, in its consequences, afford melancholy proofs of the effects of this despicable frailty, or rather detestable vice, in the human character.

Upon the principles of a free government, inconveniences from the source just mentioned must necessarily be submitted to in the formation of the legislature; but it is unnecessary, and therefore unwise, to introduce them into the constitution of the executive. It is here too that they may be most pernicious. In the legislature, promptitude of decision is oftener an evil than a benefit. The differences of opinion, and the jarring of parties in that department of the government, though they may sometimes obstruct salutary plans, yet often promote deliberation and circumspection, and serve to check excesses in the majority. When a resolution too is once taken, the opposition must be at an end. That resolution is a law, and resistance to it punishable. But no favorable circumstances palliate or atone for the disadvantages of dissension in the executive department. Here they are pure and unmixed. There is no point at which they cease to operate. They serve to embarrass and weaken the execution of the plan or measure to which they relate, from the first step to the final conclusion of it. They constantly counteract those qualities in the executive which are the most necessary ingredients in its composition—vigor and expedition, and this without any counterbalancing good. In the conduct of war, in which the energy of the executive is the bulwark of the national security, everything would be to be apprehended from its plurality.

It must be confessed that these observations apply with principal weight to the first case supposed—that is, to a plurality of magistrates of equal dignity and authority, a scheme, the advocates for which are not likely to form a numerous sect; but they apply, though not with equal yet with considerable weight to the project of a council, whose concurrence is made constitutionally necessary to the operations of the ostensible executive. An artful cabal in that council would be able to distract and to enervate the whole system of administration. If no such cabal should exist, the mere diversity of views and opinions would alone be sufficient to tincture the exercise of the executive authority with a spirit of habitual feebleness and dilatoriness.

But one of the weightiest objections to a plurality in the executive, and which lies as much against the last as the first plan is that it tends to conceal faults and destroy responsibility. Responsibility is of two kinds—to censure and to punishment. The first is the more important of the two, especially in an elective office. Men in public trust will much oftener act in such a manner as to render them unworthy of being any longer trusted, than in such a manner as to make them obnoxious to legal punishment. But the multiplication of the executive adds to the difficulty of detection in either case. It often becomes impossible, amidst mutual accusations, to determine on whom the blame or the punishment of a pernicious measure, or series of pernicious measures, ought really to fall. It is shifted from one to another with so much dexterity, and under such plausible appearances, that the public opinion is left in suspense about the real author. The circumstances which may have led to any national miscarriage or misfortune are sometimes so complicated that where there are a number of actors who may have had different degrees and kinds of agency, though we may clearly see upon the whole that there has been mismanagement, yet it may be impracticable to pronounce to whose account the evil which may have been incurred is truly chargeable.

"I was overruled by my council. The council were so divided in their opinions that it was impossible to obtain any better resolution on the point." These and similar pretexts are constantly at hand, whether true or false. And who is there that will either take the trouble or incur the odium of a strict scrutiny into the secret springs of the transaction? Should there be found a citizen zealous enough to undertake the unpromising task, if there happened to be a collusion between the parties concerned, how easy it is to clothe the circumstances with so much ambiguity as to render it uncertain what was the precise conduct of any of those parties.

In the single instance in which the governor of this State is coupled with a council—that is, in the appointment to offices, we have seen the mischiefs of it in the view now under consideration. Scandalous appointments to important offices have been made. Some cases, indeed, have been so flagrant that ALL PARTIES have agreed in the impropriety of the thing. When inquiry has been made, the blame has been laid by the governor on the members of the council, who, on their part, have charged it upon his nomination; while the people remain altogether at a loss to determine by whose influence their interests have been committed to hands so unqualified and so manifestly improper. In tenderness to individuals, I forbear to descend to particulars.

It is evident from these considerations that the plurality of the executive tends to deprive the people of the two greatest securities they can have for the faithful exercise of any delegated power, *first,* the restraints of public opinion, which lose their efficacy, as well on account of the division of the censure attendant on bad measures among a number as on account of the uncertainty on whom it ought to fall; and, *second,* the opportunity of discovering with facility and clearness the misconduct of the persons they trust, in order either to their removal from office or to their actual punishment in cases which admit of it.

In England, the king is a perpetual magistrate; and it is a maxim which has obtained for the sake of the public peace that he is unaccountable for his administration, and his person sacred. Nothing, therefore, can be wiser in that kingdom than to annex to the king a constitutional council, who may be responsible to the nation for the advice they give. Without this, there would be no responsibility whatever in the executive department—an idea inadmissible in a free government. But even there the king is not bound by the resolutions of his council, though they are answerable for the advice they give. He is the absolute master of his own conduct in the exercise of his office and may observe or disregard the counsel given to him at his sole discretion.

But in a republic where every magistrate ought to be personally responsible for his behavior in office, the reason which in the British Constitution dictates the propriety of a council not only ceases to apply, but turns against the institution. In the monarchy of Great Britain, it furnishes a substitute for the prohibited responsibility of the Chief Magistrate, which serves in some degree as a hostage to the national justice for his good behavior. In the American republic, it would serve to destroy, or would greatly diminish, the intended and necessary responsibility of the Chief Magistrate himself.

The idea of a council to the executive, which has so generally obtained in the State constitutions, has been derived from that maxim of republican jealousy which considers power as safer in the hands of a number of men than of a single man. If the maxim should be admitted to be applicable to the case, I should contend that the advantage on that side would not counterbalance the numerous disadvantages on the opposite side. But I do not think the rule at all applicable to the executive power. I clearly concur in opinion, in this particular, with a writer whom the celebrated Junius pronounces to be "deep, solid, and ingenious," that "the executive power is more easily confined when it is one";* that it is far more safe there should be a single object for the jealousy and watchfulness of the people; and, in a word, that all multiplication of the executive is rather dangerous than friendly to liberty.

A little consideration will satisfy us that the species of security sought for in the multiplication of the executive is unattainable. Numbers must be so great as to render combination difficult, or they are rather a source of danger than of security. The united credit and influence of several individuals must be more formidable to liberty than the credit and influence of either of them separately. When power, therefore, is placed in the hands of so small a number of men as to admit of their interests and views being easily combined in a common enterprise, by an artful leader, it becomes more liable to abuse, and more dangerous when abused, than if it be lodged in the hands of one man, who, from the very circumstance of his being alone, will be more narrowly watched and more readily suspected, and who cannot unite so great a mass of influence as when he is associated with others. The decemvirs of Rome, whose name denotes their number,† were more to be dreaded in their usurpation than any ONE of them would have been. No person would think of proposing an executive much more numerous than that body; from six to a dozen have been suggested for the number of the council. The extreme of these numbers is not too great for an easy combination; and from such a combination America would have more to fear than from the ambition of any single individual. A council to a magistrate, who is himself responsible for what he does, are generally nothing better than a clog upon his good intentions, are often the instruments and accomplices of his bad, and are almost always a cloak to his faults.

I forbear to dwell upon the subject of expense; though it be evident that if the council should be numerous enough to answer the principal end aimed at by the insti-

* De Lolme. † Ten

tution, the salaries of the members, who must be drawn from their homes to reside at the seat of government, would form an item in the catalogue of public expenditures too serious to be incurred for an object of equivocal utility.

I will only add that, prior to the appearance of the Constitution, I rarely met with an intelligent man from any of the States who did not admit, as the result of experience, that the UNITY of the executive of this State was one of the best of the distinguishing features of our Constitution. PUBLIUS

No. 71: Hamilton

DURATION in office has been mentioned as the second requisite to the energy of the executive authority. This has relation to two objects: to the personal firmness of the executive magistrate in the employment of his constitutional powers, and to the stability of the system of administration which may have been adopted under his auspices. With regard to the first, it must be evident that the longer the duration in office, the greater will be the probability of obtaining so important an advantage. It is a general principle of human nature that a man will be interested in whatever he possesses, in proportion to the firmness or precariousness of the tenure by which he holds it; will be less attached to what he holds by a momentary or uncertain title, than to what he enjoys by a durable or certain title; and, of course, will be willing to risk more for the sake of the one than for the sake of the other. This remark is not less applicable to a political privilege, or honor, or trust, than to any article of ordinary property. The inference from it is that a man acting in the capacity of chief magistrate, under a consciousness that in a very short time he *must* lay down his office, will be apt to feel himself too little interested in it to hazard any material censure or perplexity from the independent exertion of his powers, or from encountering the ill-humors, however transient, which may happen to prevail, either in a considerable part of the society itself, or even in a predominant faction in the legislative body. If the case should only be that he *might* lay it down, unless continued by a new choice, and if he should be desirious of being continued, his wishes, conspiring with his fears, would tend still more powerfully to corrupt his integrity, or debase his fortitude. In either case, feebleness and irresolution must be the characteristics of the station.

There are some who would be inclined to regard the servile pliancy of the executive to a prevailing current, either in the community or in the legislature, as its best recommendation. But such men entertain very crude notions, as well of the purposes for which government was instituted, as of the true means by which the public happiness may be promoted. The republican principle demands that the deliberate sense of the community should govern the conduct of those to whom they intrust the management of their affairs; but it does not require an unqualified complaisance to every sudden breeze of passion, or to every transient impulse which the people may receive from the arts of men, who flatter their prejudices to betray their interests. It is a just observation that the people commonly *intend* the PUBLIC GOOD. This often applies to their very errors. But their good sense would despise the adulator who should pretend that they always *reason right* about the *means* of promoting it. They know from experience that they sometimes err; and the wonder is that they so seldom err as they do, beset as they continually are by the wiles of parasites and sycophants, by the snares of the ambitious, the avaricious, the desperate, by the artifices of men who possess their confidence more than they deserve it, and of those who seek to possess rather than to deserve it. When occasions present themselves in which the interests of the people are at variance with their inclinations, it is the duty of the persons whom they have appointed to be the guardians of those interests to withstand the temporary delusion in order to give them time and opportunity for more cool and sedate reflection. Instances might be cited in which a conduct of this kind has saved the people from very fatal consequences of their own mistakes, and has procured lasting monuments of their gratitude to the men who had courage and magnanimity enough to serve them at the peril of their displeasure.

But however inclined we might be to insist upon an unbounded complaisance in the executive to the inclinations of the people, we can with no propriety contend for a like complaisance to the humors of the legislature. The latter may sometimes stand in opposition to the former, and at other times the people may be entirely neutral. In either supposition, it is certainly desirable that the executive should be in a situation to dare to act his own opinion with vigor and decision.

The same rule which teaches the propriety of a partition between the various branches of power teaches likewise that this partition ought to be so contrived as to render the one independent of the other. To what purpose separate the executive or the judiciary from the legislative, if both the executive and the judiciary are so constituted as to be at the absolute devotion of the legislative? Such a separation must be merely nominal, and incapable of producing the ends for which it was established. It is one thing to be subordinate to the laws, and another to be dependent on the legislative body. The first comports with, the last violates, the fundamental principles of good government; and, whatever may be the forms of the Constitution, unites all power in the same hands. The tendency of the legislative authority to absorb every other has been fully displayed and illustrated by examples in some preceding numbers. In governments purely republican, this tendency is almost irresistible. The representatives of the people, in a popular assembly, seem sometimes to fancy that they are the people themselves, and betray strong symptoms of impatience and disgust at the least sign of opposition from any other quarter; as if the exercise of its rights, by either the executive or judiciary, were a breach of their privilege and an outrage to their dignity. They often appear disposed to exert an imperious control over the other departments; and as they commonly have the people on their side, they always act with such momentum as to make it very difficult for the other members of the government to maintain the balance of the Constitution.

It may perhaps be asked how the shortness of the duration in office can affect the independence of the executive on the legislature, unless the one were possessed of the power of appointing or displacing the other. One answer to this inquiry may be drawn from the principle already remarked—that is, from the slender interest a man is apt to take in a short-lived advantage, and the little inducement it affords him to expose himself, on account of it, to any considerable inconvenience or hazard. Another answer, perhaps more obvious, though not more conclusive, will result from the consideration of the influence of the legislative body over the people, which might be employed to prevent the re-election of a man who, by an upright resistance to any sinister project of that body, should have made himself obnoxious to its resentment.

It may be asked also whether a duration of four years would answer the end proposed; and if it would not, whether a less period, which would at least be recommended by greater security against ambitious designs, would not, for that reason, be preferable to a longer period which was, at the same time, too short for the purpose of inspiring the desired firmness and independence of the magistrate.

It cannot be affirmed that a duration of four years, or any other limited duration, would completely answer the end proposed; but it would contribute towards it in a degree which would have a material influence upon the spirit and character of the government. Between the commencement and termination of such a period there would always be a considerable interval in which the prospect of annihilation would be sufficiently remote not to have an improper effect upon the conduct of a man endowed with a tolerable portion of fortitude; and in which he might reasonably promise himself that there would be time enough before it arrived to make the community sensible of the propriety of the measures he might incline to pursue. Though it be probable that, as he approached the moment when the public were, by a new election, to signify their sense of his conduct, his confidence, and with it his firmness, would decline; yet both the one and the other would derive support from the opportunities which his previous continuance in the station had afforded him, of establishing himself in the esteem and good-will of his constituents. He might, then, hazard with safety, in proportion to the proofs he had given of his wisdom and integrity, and to the title he had acquired to the respect and attachment of his fellow-citizens. As on the one hand, a duration of four years will contribute to the firmness of the executive in a sufficient degree to render it a very valuable ingredient in the composition, so, on the other, it is not long enough to justify any alarm for the public liberty. If a British House of Commons, from the most feeble beginnings, *from the mere power of assenting or disagreeing to the imposition of a new tax,* have, by rapid strides, reduced the prerogatives of the crown and the privileges of the nobility within the limits they conceived to be compatible with the principles of a free government, while they raised themselves to the rank and consequence of a co-equal branch of the legislature; if they have been able, in one instance, to abolish both the royalty and the aristocracy, and to overturn all the ancient establishments, as well in the Church as State; if they have been able, on a recent occasion, to make the monarch tremble at the prospect of an innovation* attempted by them, what would be to be feared from an elective magistrate of four years' duration with the confined authorities of a President of the United States? What, but that he might be unequal to the task which the Constitution assigns him? I shall only add that if his duration be such as to leave a doubt of his firmness, that doubt is inconsistent with a jealousy of his encroachments.

PUBLIUS

No. 72: Hamilton

THE administration of government, in its largest sense, comprehends all the operations of the body politic, whether legislative, executive, or judiciary; but in its most usual and perhaps in its most precise signification, it is limited to executive details, and falls peculiarly within the province of the executive department. The actual conduct of foreign negotiations, the preparatory plans of finance, the application and disbursement of the

* This was the case with respect to Mr. Fox's India bill, which was carried in the House of Commons and rejected in the House of Lords, to the entire satisfaction, as it is said, of the people.

public moneys in conformity to the general appropriations of the legislature, the arrangement of the army and navy, the direction of the operations of war—these, and other matters of a like nature, constitute what seems to be most properly understood by the administration of government. The persons, therefore, to whose immediate management these different matters are committed ought to be considered as the assistants or deputies of the Chief Magistrate, and on this account they ought to derive their offices from his appointment, at least from his nomination, and ought to be subject to his superintendence. This view of the subject will at once suggest to us the intimate connection between the duration of the executive magistrate in office and the stability of the system of administration. To reverse and undo what has been done by a predecessor is very often considered by a successor as the best proof he can give of his own capacity and desert; and in addition to this propensity, where the alteration has been the result of public choice, the person substituted is warranted in supposing that the dismission of his predecessor has proceeded from a dislike to his measures; and that the less he resembles him, the more he will recommend himself to the favor of his constituents. These considerations, and the influence of personal confidences and attachments, would be likely to induce every new President to promote a change of men to fill the subordinate stations; and these causes together could not fail to occasion a disgraceful and ruinous mutability in the administration of the government.

With a positive duration of considerable extent, I connect the circumstances of re-eligibility. The first is necessary to give the officer himself the inclination and the resolution to act his part well, and to the community time and leisure to observe the tendency of his measures, and thence to form an experimental estimate of their merits. The last is necessary to enable the people, when they see reason to approve of his conduct, to continue him in the station in order to prolong the utility of his talents and virtues, and to secure to the government the advantage of permanency in a wise system of administration.

Nothing appears more plausible at first sight, nor more ill-founded upon close inspection, than a scheme which in relation to the present point has had some respectable advocates—I mean that of continuing the Chief Magistrate in office for a certain time, and then excluding him from it, either for a limited period or forever after. This exclusion, whether temporary or perpetual, would have nearly the same effects, and these effects would be for the most part rather pernicious than salutary.

One ill effect of the exclusion would be a diminution of the inducements to good behavior. There are few men who would not feel much less zeal in the discharge of a duty when they were conscious that the advantage of the station with which it was connected must be relinquished at a determinate period, than when they were permitted to entertain a hope of *obtaining,* by *meriting,* a continuance of them. This position will not be disputed so long as it is admitted that the desire of reward is one of the strongest incentives of human conduct; or that the best security for the fidelity of mankind is to make their interest coincide with their duty. Even the love of fame, the ruling passion of the noblest minds, which would prompt a man to plan and undertake extensive and arduous enterprises for the public benefit, requiring considerable time to mature and perfect them, if he could flatter himself with the prospect of being allowed to finish what he had begun, would, on the contrary, deter him from the undertaking, when he foresaw that he must quit the scene before he could accomplish the work, and must commit that, together with his own reputation, to hands which might be unequal or unfriendly to the task. The most to be expected from the generality of men, in such a situation, is the negative merit of not doing harm, instead of the positive merit of doing good.

Another ill effect of the exclusion would be the temptation to sordid views, to peculation, and, in some instances, to usurpation. An avaricious man who might happen to fill the office, looking forward to a time when he must at all events yield up the advantages he enjoyed, would feel a propensity not easy to be resisted by such a man to make the best use of his opportunities while they lasted, and might not scruple to have recourse to the most corrupt expedients to make the harvest as abundant as it was transitory; though the same man, probably, with a different prospect before him, might content himself with the regular perquisites of his situation, and might even be unwilling to risk the consequences of an abuse of his opportunities. His avarice might be a guard upon his avarice. Add to this that the same man might be vain or ambitious, as well as avaricious. And if he could expect to prolong his honors by his good conduct, he might hesitate to sacrifice his appetite for them to his appetite for gain. But with the prospect before him of approaching and inevitable annihilation, his avarice would be likely to get the victory over his caution, his vanity, or his ambition.

An ambitious man, too, finding himself seated on the summit of his country's honors, looking forward to the time at which he must descend from the exalted eminence forever, and reflecting that no exertion of merit on his part could save him from the unwelcome reverse, would be much more violently tempted to embrace a favorable conjuncture for attempting the prolongation of his power, at every personal hazard, than if he had the probability of answering the same end by doing his duty.

Would it promote the peace of the community, or the stability of the government, to have half a dozen men who had had credit enough to raise themselves to the seat of the supreme magistracy wandering among the people like discontented ghosts and sighing for a place which they were destined never more to possess?

A third ill effect of the exclusion would be the depriving the community of the advantage of the experience gained by the Chief Magistrate in the exercise of his office. That experience is the parent of wisdom is an adage the truth of which is recognized by the wisest as well as the simplest of mankind. What more desirable or more essential than this quality in the governors of nations? Where more desirable or more essential than in the first magistrate of a nation? Can it be wise to put this desirable and essential quality under the ban of the Constitution, and to declare that the moment it is acquired, its possessor shall be compelled to abandon the station in which it was acquired and to which it is adapted? This, nevertheless, is the precise import of all those regulations which exclude men from serving their country, by the choice of their fellow-citizens, after they have by a course of service fitted themselves for doing it with a greater degree of utility.

A fourth ill effect of the exclusion would be the banishing men from stations in which, in certain emergencies of the State, their presence might be of the greatest moment to the public interest or safety. There is no nation which has not, at one period or another, experienced an absolute necessity of the services of particular men in particular situations, perhaps it would not be too strong to say, to the preservation of its political existence. How unwise, therefore, must be every such self-denying ordinance as serves to prohibit a nation from making use of its own citizens in the matter best suited to its exigencies and circumstances! Without supposing the personal essentiality of the man, it is evident that a change of the Chief Magistrate, at the breaking out of a war, or any similar crisis, for another, even of equal merit, would at all times be detrimental to the community, inasmuch as it would substitute inexperience to experience, and would tend to unhinge and set afloat the already settled train of the administration.

A fifth ill effect of the exclusion would be that it would operate as a constitutional interdiction of stability in the administration. By *necessitating* a change of men, in the first office in the nation, it would necessitate a mutability of measures. It is not generally to be expected that men will vary and measures remain uniform. The contrary is the usual course of things. And we need not be apprehensive there will be too much stability, while there is even the option of changing; nor need we desire to prohibit the people from continuing their confidence where they think it may be safely placed, and where, by constancy on their part, they may obviate the fatal inconveniences of fluctuating councils and a variable policy.

These are some of the disadvantages which would flow from the principle of exclusion. They apply most forcibly to the scheme of a perpetual exclusion; but when we consider that even a partial one would always render the readmission of the person a remote and precarious object, the observations which have been made will apply nearly as fully to one case as to the other.

What are the advantages promised to counterbalance these disadvantages? They are represented to be: 1st, greater independence in the magistrate; 2nd, greater security to the people. Unless the exclusion be perpetual, there will be no pretence to infer the first advantage. But even in that case, may he have no object beyond his present station to which he may sacrifice his independence? May he have no connections, no friends, for whom he may sacrifice it? May he not be less willing, by a firm conduct, to make personal enemies, when he acts under the impression that a time is fast approaching, on the arrival of which he not only MAY, but MUST, be exposed to their resentments, upon an equal, perhaps upon an inferior, footing? It is not an easy point to determine whether his independence would be most promoted or impaired by such an arrangement.

As to the second supposed advantage, there is still greater reason to entertain doubts concerning it. If the exclusion were to be perpetual, a man of irregular ambition, of whom alone there could be reason in any case to entertain apprehension, would, with infinite reluctance, yield to the necessity of taking his leave forever of a post in which his passion for power and pre-eminence had acquired the force of habit. And if he had been fortunate or adroit enough to conciliate the good-will of the people, he might induce them to consider as a very odious and unjustifiable restraint upon themselves a provision which was calculated to debar them of the right of giving a fresh proof of their attachment to a favorite. There may be conceived circumstances in which this disgust of the people, seconding the thwarted ambition of such a favorite, might occasion greater danger to liberty than could ever reasonably be dreaded from the possibility of a perpetuation in office by the voluntary suffrages of the community exercising a constitutional privilege.

There is an excess of refinement in the idea of disabling the people to continue in office men who had entitled themselves, in their opinion, to approbation and confidence, the advantages of which are at best speculative and equivocal, and are overbalanced by disadvantages far more certain and decisive. PUBLIUS

No. 73: Hamilton

THE third ingredient towards constituting the vigor of the executive authority is an adequate provision for its support. It is evident that without proper attention to this article, the separation of the executive from the legislative department would be merely nominal and nugatory. The legislature, with a discretionary power over the salary and emoluments of the Chief Magistrate, could render him as obsequious to their will as they might think proper to make him. They might, in most cases, either reduce him by famine, or tempt him by largesses, to surrender at discretion his judgment to their inclinations. These expressions, taken in all the latitude of the terms, would no doubt convey more than is intended. There are men who could neither be distressed nor won into a sacrifice of their duty; but this stern virtue is the growth of few soils; and in the main it will be found that a power over a man's support is a power over his will. If it were necessary to confirm so plain a truth by facts, examples would not be wanting, even in this country, of the intimidation or seduction of the executive by the terrors or allurements of the pecuniary arrangements of the legislative body.

It is not easy, therefore, to commend too highly the judicious attention which has been paid to this subject in the proposed Constitution. It is there provided that "The President of the United States shall, at stated times, receive for his services a compensation *which shall neither be increased nor diminished during the period for which he shall have been elected;* and he *shall not receive within that period any other emolument* from the United States, or any of them." It is impossible to imagine any provision which would have been more eligible than this. The legislature, on the appointment of a President, is once for all to declare what shall be the compensation for his services during the time for which he shall have been elected. This done, they will have no power to alter it, either by increase or diminution, till a new period of service by a new election commences. They can neither weaken his fortitude by operating on his necessities, nor corrupt his integrity by appealing to his avarice. Neither the Union, nor any of its members, will be at liberty to give, nor will he be at liberty to receive, any other emolument than that which may have been determined by the first act. He can, of course, have no pecuniary inducement to renounce or desert the independence intended for him by the Constitution.

The last of the requisites to energy which have been enumerated are competent powers. Let us proceed to consider those which are proposed to be vested in the President of the United States.

The first thing that offers itself to our observation is the qualified negative of the President upon the acts or resolutions of the two houses of the legislature; or, in other words, his power of returning all bills with objections to have the effect of preventing their becoming laws, unless they should afterwards be ratified by two thirds of each of the component members of the legislative body.

The propensity of the legislative department to intrude upon the rights, and to absorb the powers, of the other departments has been already more than once suggested. The insufficiency of a mere parchment delineation of the boundaries of each has also been remarked upon; and the necessity of furnishing each with constitutional arms for its own defense has been inferred and proved. From these clear and indubitable principles results the propriety of a negative, either absolute or qualified, in the executive upon the acts of the legislative branches. Without the one or the other, the former would be absolutely unable to defend himself against the depredations of the latter. He might gradually be stripped of his authorities by successive resolutions or annihilated by a single vote. And in the one mode or the other, the legislative and executive powers might speedily come to be blended in the same hands. If even no propensity had ever discovered itself in the legislative body to invade the rights of the executive, the rules of just reasoning and theoretic propriety would of themselves teach us that the one ought not to be left to the mercy of the other but ought to possess a constitutional and effectual power of self-defense.

But the power in question has a further use. It not only serves as a shield to the executive, but it furnishes an additional security against the enaction of improper laws. It establishes a salutary check upon the legislative body, calculated to guard the community against the effects of faction, precipitancy, or of any impulse unfriendly to the public good, which may happen to influence a majority of that body.

The propriety of a negative has, upon some occasions, been combated by an observation that it was not to be presumed a single man would possess more virtue and wisdom than a number of men; and that unless this presumption should be entertained, it would be improper to give the executive magistrate any species of control over the legislative body.

But this observation, when examined, will appear rather specious than solid. The propriety of the thing does not turn upon the supposition of superior wisdom or virtue in the executive, but upon the supposition that the legislature will not be infallible; that the love of power may sometimes betray it into a disposition to encroach upon the rights of other members of the government; that a spirit of faction may sometimes pervert its deliberations; that impressions of the moment may sometimes hurry it into measures which itself, on maturer reflection, would condemn. The primary inducement to conferring the power in question upon the executive is to enable him to defend himself; the secondary one is to increase the chances in favor of the community against the passing of bad laws, through haste, inadvertence, or design. The oftener the measure is brought under examination, the greater the diversity in the situations of those who are to examine it, the less must be the danger of those errors which flow from want of due deliberation, or of those missteps which proceed from the contagion of some common passion or interest. It is far less probable that culpable views of any kind should infect all the parts of the government at the same moment and in relation to the same object than that they should by turns govern and mislead every one of them.

It may perhaps be said that the power of preventing bad laws includes that of preventing good ones; and may be used to the one purpose as well as to the other. But this objection will have little weight with those who can properly estimate the mischiefs of that inconstancy and mutability in the laws, which form the greatest blemish in the character and genius of our governments. They will consider every institution calculated to restrain the excess of lawmaking, and to keep things in the same state in which they happen to be at any given period as much more likely to do good than harm; because it is favorable to greater stability in the system of legislation. The injury which may possibly be done by defeating a few good laws will be amply compensated by the advantage of preventing a number of bad ones.

Nor is this all. The superior weight and influence of the legislative body in a free government and the hazard to the executive in a trial of strength with that body afford a satisfactory security that the negative would generally be employed with great caution; and that there would oftener be room for a charge of timidity than of rashness in the exercise of it. A king of Great Britain, with all his train of sovereign attributes, and with all the influence he draws from a thousand sources, would, at this day, hesitate to put a negative upon the joint resolutions of the two houses of Parliament. He would not fail to exert the utmost resources of that influence to strangle a measure disagreeable to him, in its progress to the throne, to avoid being reduced to the dilemma of permitting it to take effect, or of risking the displeasure of the nation by an opposition to the sense of the legislative body. Nor is it probable that he would ultimately venture to exert his prerogative, but in a case of manifest propriety, or extreme necessity. All well-informed men in that kingdom will accede to the justness of this remark. A very considerable period has elapsed since the negative of the crown has been exercised.

If a magistrate so powerful and so well fortified as a British monarch would have scruples about the exercise of the power under consideration, how much greater caution may be reasonably expected in a President of the United States, clothed for the short period of four years with the executive authority of a government wholly and purely republican?

It is evident that there would be greater danger of his not using his power when necessary, than of his using it too often, or too much. An argument, indeed, against its expediency, has been drawn from this very source. It has been represented, on this account, as a power odious in appearance, useless in practice. But it will not follow, that because it might be rarely exercised, it would never be exercised. In the case for which it is chiefly designed, that of an immediate attack upon the constitutional rights of the executive, or in a case in which the public good was evidently and palpably sacrificed, a man of tolerable firmness would avail himself of his constitutional means of defense, and would listen to the admonitions of duty and responsibility. In the former supposition, his fortitude would be stimulated by his immediate interest in the power of his office; in the latter, by the probability of the sanction of his constituents who, though they would naturally incline to the legislative body in a doubtful case, would hardly suffer their partiality to delude them in a very plain case. I speak now with an eye to a magistrate possessing only a common share of firmness. There are men who, under any circumstances, will have the courage to do their duty at every hazard.

But the convention have pursued a mean in this business, which will both facilitate the exercise of the power vested in this respect in the executive magistrate, and make its efficacy to depend on the sense of a considerable part of the legislative body. Instead of an absolute negative, it is proposed to give the executive the qualified negative already described. This is a power which would be much more readily exercised than the other. A man who might be afraid to defeat a law by his single VETO might not scruple to return it for reconsideration, subject to being finally rejected only in the event of more than one third of each house concurring in the sufficiency of his objections. He would be encouraged by the reflection that if his opposition should prevail, it would embark in it a very respectable proportion of the legislative body whose influence would be united with his in supporting the propriety of his conduct in the public opinion. A direct and categorical negative has something in the appearance of it more harsh, and more apt to irritate, than the mere suggestion of argumentative objections to be approved or disapproved by those to whom they are addressed. In proportion as it would be less apt to offend, it would be more apt to be exercised; and for this very reason it may in practice be found more effectual. It is to be hoped that it will not often happen that improper views will govern so large a proportion as two thirds of both branches of the legislature at the same time; and this, too, in defiance of the counterpoising weight of the executive. It is at any rate far less probable that this should be the case than that such views should taint the resolutions and conduct of a bare majority. A power of this nature in the executive will often have a silent and unperceived, though forcible, operation. When men, engaged in unjustifiable pursuits, are aware that obstructions may come from a quarter which they cannot control, they will often be restrained by the bare apprehension of opposition from doing what they would with eagerness rush into if no such external impediments were to be feared.

This qualified negative, as has been elsewhere remarked, is in this State vested in a council, consisting of the governor, with the chancellor and judges of the Supreme Court, or any two of them. It has been freely employed upon a variety of occasions, and frequently with success. And its utility has become so apparent, that persons who, in compiling the Constitution, were violent opposers of it, have from experience become its declared admirers.*

I have in another place remarked that the convention, in the formation of this part of their plan, had departed from the model of the constitution of this State in favor of that of Massachusetts. Two strong reasons may be imagined for this preference. One is that the judges, who are to be the interpreters of the law, might receive an improper bias from having given a previous opinion in their revisionary capacities; the other is that by being often associated with the executive, they might be induced to embark too far in the political views of that magistrate, and thus a dangerous combination might by degrees be cemented between the executive and judiciary departments. It is impossible to keep the judges too distinct

* Mr. Abraham Yates, a warm opponent of the plan of the convention, is of this number.

from every other avocation than that of expounding the laws. It is peculiarly dangerous to place them in a situation to be either corrupted or influenced by the executive.

PUBLIUS

No. 74: Hamilton

THE President of the United States is to be "commander-in-chief of the army and navy of the United States, and of the militia of the several States *when called into the actual service* of the United States." The propriety of this provision is so evident in itself and it is at the same time so consonant to the precedents of the State constitutions in general, that little need be said to explain or enforce it. Even those of them which have in other respects coupled the Chief Magistrate with a council have for the most part concentrated the military authority in him alone. Of all the cares or concerns of government, the direction of war most peculiarly demands those qualities which distinguish the exercise of power by a single hand. The direction of war implies the direction of the common strength; and the power of directing and employing the common strength forms a usual and essential part in the definition of the executive authority.

"The President may require the opinion, in writing, of the principal officer in each of the executive departments, upon any subject relating to the duties of their respective offices." This I consider as a mere redundancy in the plan, as the right for which it provides would result of itself from the office.

He is also to be authorized "to grant reprieves and pardons for offenses against the United States, *except in cases of impeachment.*" Humanity and good policy conspire to dictate that the benign prerogative of pardoning should be as little as possible fettered or embarrassed. The criminal code of every country partakes so much of necessary severity that without an easy access to exceptions in favor of unfortunate guilt, justice would wear a countenance too sanguinary and cruel. As the sense of responsibility is always strongest in proportion as it is undivided, it may be inferred that a single man would be most ready to attend to the force of those motives which might plead for a mitigation of the rigor of the law, and least apt to yield to considerations which were calculated to shelter a fit object of its vengeance. The reflection that the fate of a fellow-creature depended on his *sole fiat* would naturally inspire scrupulousness and caution; the dread of being accused of weakness or connivance would beget equal circumspection, though of a different kind. On the other hand, as men generally derive confidence from their numbers, they might often encourage each other in an act of obduracy, and might be less sensible to the apprehension of suspicion or censure for an injudicious or affected clemency. On these accounts, one man appears to be a more eligible dispenser of the mercy of the government than a body of men.

The expediency of vesting the power of pardoning in the President has, if I mistake not, been only contested in relation to the crime of treason. This, it has been urged, ought to have depended upon the assent of one, or both, of the branches of the legislative body. I shall not deny that there are strong reasons to be assigned for requiring in this particular the concurrence of that body or of a part of it. As treason is a crime leveled at the immediate being of the society when the laws have once ascertained the guilt of the offender, there seems a fitness in referring the expediency of an act of mercy towards him to the judgment of the legislature. And this ought the rather to be the case, as the supposition of the connivance of the Chief Magistrate ought not to be entirely excluded. But there are also strong objections to such a plan. It is not to be doubted that a single man of prudence and good sense is better fitted, in delicate conjunctures, to balance the motives which may plead for and against the remission of the punishment than any numerous body whatever. It deserves particular attention that treason will often be connected with seditions which embrace a large proportion of the community, as lately happened in Massachusetts. In every such case we might expect to see the representation of the people tainted with the same spirit which had given birth to the offense. And when parties were pretty equally matched, the secret sympathy of the friends and favorers of the condemned, availing itself of the good nature and weakness of others, might frequently bestow impunity where the terror of an example was necessary. On the other hand, when the sedition had proceeded from causes which had inflamed the resentments of the major party, they might often be found obstinate and inexorable, when policy demanded a conduct of forbearance and clemency. But the principal argument for reposing the power of pardoning in this case in the Chief Magistrate is this: in seasons of insurrection or rebellion, there are often critical moments when a well-timed offer of pardon to the insurgents or rebels may restore the tranquillity of the commonwealth; and which, if suffered to pass unimproved, it may never be possible afterwards to recall. The dilatory process of convening the legislature, or one of its branches, for the purpose of obtaining its sanction to the measure, would frequently be the occasion of letting slip the golden opportunity. The loss of a week, a day, an hour, may sometimes be fatal. If it should be observed that a discretionary power with a view to such contingencies might be occasionally conferred upon the President, it may be answered in the first place that it is questionable, whether, in a limited Constitution, that power could be delegated by law; and in the second place, that it would generally be impolitic beforehand to take any step which might hold out the prospect of impunity. A proceeding of this kind, out of the usual course, would be likely to be construed into an argument of timidity or of weakness, and would have a tendency to embolden guilt.

PUBLIUS

No. 75: Hamilton

THE President is to have power, "by and with the advice and consent of the Senate, to make treaties, provided two thirds of the senators present concur." Though this provision has been assailed, on different grounds, with no small degree of vehemence, I scruple not to declare my firm persuasion that it is one of the best digested and most unexceptionable parts of the plan. One ground of objection is the trite topic of the intermixture of powers: some contending that the President ought alone to possess the power of making treaties; and others, that it ought to have been exclusively deposited in the Senate. Another source of objection is derived from the small number of persons by whom a treaty may be made. Of those who espouse this objection, a part are of opinion that the House of Representatives ought to have been associated in the business, while another part seem to think that nothing more was necessary than to have substituted two thirds of *all* the members of the Senate to two thirds of the members *present*. As I flatter myself the observations made in a preceding number upon this part of the plan must have sufficed to place it, to a discerning eye, in a very favorable light, I shall here content myself with offering only some supplementary remarks, principally with a view to the objections which have been just stated.

With regard to the intermixture of powers, I shall rely upon the explanations already given in other places of the true sense of the rule upon which that objection is founded; and shall take it for granted, as an inference from them, that the union of the executive with the Senate, in the article of treaties, is no infringement of that rule. I venture to add that the particular nature of the power of making treaties indicates a peculiar propriety in that union. Though several writers on the subject of government place that power in the class of executive authorities, yet this is evidently an arbitrary disposition; for if we attend carefully to its operation it will be found to partake more of the legislative than of the executive character, though it does not seem strictly to fall within the definition of either of them. The essence of the legislative authority is to enact laws, or, in other words, to prescribe rules for the regulation of the society; while the execution of the laws and the employment of the common strength, either for this purpose or for the common defense, seem to comprise all the functions of the executive magistrate. The power of making treaties is, plainly, neither the one nor the other. It relates neither to the execution of the subsisting laws nor to the enaction of new ones; and still less to an exertion of the common strength. Its objects are CONTRACTS with foreign nations which have the force of law, but derive it from the obligations of good faith. They are not rules prescribed by the sovereign to the subject, but agreements between sovereign and sovereign. The power in question seems therefore to form a distinct department, and to belong, properly, neither to the legislative nor to the executive. The qualities elsewhere detailed as indispensable in the management of foreign negotiations point out the executive as the most fit agent in those transactions; while the vast importance of the trust and the operation of treaties as laws plead strongly for the participation of the whole or a portion of the legislative body in the office of making them.

However proper or safe it may be in governments where the executive magistrate is an hereditary monarch, to commit to him the entire power of making treaties, it would be utterly unsafe and improper to intrust that power to an elective magistrate of four years' duration. It has been remarked, upon another occasion, and the remark is unquestionably just, that an hereditary monarch, though often the oppressor of his people, has personally too much at stake in the government to be in any material danger of being corrupted by foreign powers. But a man raised from the station of a private citizen to the rank of Chief Magistrate, possessed of but a moderate or slender fortune, and looking forward to a period not very remote when he may probably be obliged to return to the station from which he was taken, might sometimes be under temptations to sacrifice his duty to his interest, which it would require superlative virtue to withstand. An avaricious man might be tempted to betray the interests of the state to the acquisition of wealth. An ambitious man might make his own aggrandizement, by the aid of a foreign power, the price of his treachery to his constituents. The history of human conduct does not warrant that exalted opinion of human virtue which would make it wise in a nation to commit interests of so delicate and momentous a kind, as those which concern its intercourse with the rest of the world, to the sole disposal of a magistrate created and circumstanced as would be a President of the United States.

To have intrusted the power of making treaties to the Senate alone would have been to relinquish the benefits of the constitutional agency of the President in the conduct of foreign negotiations. It is true that the Senate would, in that case, have the option of employing him in this capacity, but they would also have the option of letting it alone and pique or cabal might induce the latter rather than the former. Besides this, the ministerial servant of the Senate could not be expected to enjoy the confidence and respect of foreign powers in the same degree with the constitutional representative of the nation, and, of course, would not be able to act with an equal degree of weight or efficacy. While the Union would, from this cause, lose a considerable advantage in the management of its external concerns, the people would lose the additional security which would result from the co-operation of the executive. Though it would be imprudent to confide in him solely so important a trust, yet it cannot be doubted that his participation in it would materially add to the safety of the society. It must indeed be clear to a demonstration that the joint possession of the power in question, by the President and Senate, would afford a greater prospect of security than the separate possession of it by either of them. And whoever has maturely weighed the circumstances which must concur in the appointment of a President will be satisfied that the office will always bid fair to be filled by men of such characters as to render their concurrence in the formation of treaties peculiarly desirable, as well on the score of wisdom as on that of integrity.

The remarks made in a former number, which have been alluded to in another part of this paper, will apply with conclusive force against the admission of the House of Representatives to a share in the formation of treaties. The fluctuating and, taking its future increase into the account, the multitudinous composition of that body, forbid us to expect in it those qualities which are essential to the proper execution of such a trust. Accurate and comprehensive knowledge of foreign politics; a steady and systematic adherence to the same views; a nice and uniform sensibility to national character; decision, *secrecy,* and dispatch, are imcompatible with the genius of a body so variable and so numerous. The very complication of the business, by introducing a necessity of the concurrence of so many different bodies, would of itself afford a solid objection. The greater frequency of the calls upon the House of Representatives, and the greater length of time which it would often be necessary to keep them together when convened to obtain their sanction in the progressive stages of a treaty would be a source of so great inconvenience and expense as alone ought to condemn the project.

The only objection which remains to be canvassed is that which would substitute the proportion of two thirds of all the members composing the senatorial body to that of two thirds of the members *present.* It has been shown, under the second head of our inquiries, that all provisions which require more than the majority of any body to its resolutions have a direct tendency to embarrass the operations of the government and an indirect one to subject the sense of the majority to that of the minority. This consideration seems sufficient to determine our opinion, that the convention have gone as far in the endeavor to secure the advantage of numbers in the formation of treaties as could have been reconciled either with the activity of the public councils or with a reasonable regard to the major sense of the community. If two thirds of the whole number of members had been required it would, in many cases, from the nonattendance of a part, amount in practice to a necessity of unanimity. And the history of every political establishment in which this principle has prevailed is a history of impotence, perplexity, and disorder. Proofs of this position might be adduced from the examples of the Roman Tribuneship, the Polish Diet, and the States-General of the Netherlands did not an example at home render foreign precedents unnecessary.

To require a fixed proportion of the whole body would not, in all probability, contribute to the advantages of a numerous agency, better than merely to require a proportion of the attending members. The former, by increasing the difficulty of resolutions disagreeable to the minority, diminishes the motives to punctual attendance. The latter, by making the capacity of the body to depend on a *proportion* which may be varied by the absence or presence of a single member, has the contrary effect. And as, by promoting punctuality, it tends to keep the body complete, there is great likelihood that its resolutions would generally be dictated by as great a number in this case as in the other; while there would be much fewer occasions of delay. It ought not to be forgotten that under the existing Confederation two members *may,* and usually *do,* represent a State; whence it happens that Congress, who now are solely invested with *all the powers* of the Union, rarely consists of a greater number of persons than would compose the intended Senate. If we add to this that as the members vote by States, and that where there is only a single member present from a State his vote is lost, it will justify a supposition that the active voices in the Senate, where the members are to vote individually, would rarely fall short in number of the active voices in the existing Congress. When, in addition to these considerations, we take into view the cooperation of the President, we shall not hesitate to infer that the people of America would have greater security against an improper use of the power of making treaties, under the new Constitution, than they now enjoy under the Confederation. And when we proceed still one step further and look forward to the probable augmentation of the Senate, by the erection of new States, we shall not only perceive ample ground of confidence in the sufficiency of the numbers to whose agency that power will be intrusted, but we shall probably be led to conclude that a body more numerous than the Senate would be likely to become, would be very little fit for the proper discharge of the trust. PUBLIUS

No. 76: Hamilton

THE President is "to *nominate,* and, by and with the advice and consent of the Senate, to appoint ambassadors, other public ministers and consuls, judges of the Supreme Court, and all other officers of the United States whose appointments are not otherwise provided for in the Constitution. But the Congress may by law vest the appointment of such inferior officers as they think proper in the President alone, or in the courts of law, or in the heads of departments. The President shall have power to fill up *all vacancies* which may happen *during the recess of the Senate* by granting commissions which shall *expire* at the end of their next session."

It has been observed in a former paper "that the true test of a good government is its aptitude and tendency to produce a good administration." If the justness of this observation be admitted the mode of appointing the officers of the United States contained in the foregoing clauses must, when examined, be allowed to be entitled to particular commendation. It is not easy to conceive a plan better calculated than this to promote a judicious choice of men for filling the offices of the Union; and it will not need proof that on this point must essentially depend the character of its administration.

It will be agreed on all hands that the power of appointment, in ordinary cases can be properly modified only in one of three ways. It ought either to be vested in a single man, or in a *select* assembly of a moderate number, or in a single man with the concurrence of such an assembly. The exercise of it by the people at large will be readily admitted to be impracticable; as waiving every other consideration, it would leave them little time to do anything else. When, therefore, mention is made in the subsequent reasonings of an assembly or body of men, what is said must be understood to relate to a select body or assembly, of the description already given. The people collectively, from their number and from their dispersed situation, cannot be regulated in their movements by that systematic spirit of cabal and intrigue which will be urged as the chief objections to reposing the power in question in a body of men.

Those who have themselves reflected upon the subject, or who have attended to the observations made in other parts of these papers in relation to the appointment of the President will, I presume, agree to the position that there would always be great probability of having the place supplied by a man of abilities, at least respectable. Premising this, I proceed to lay it down as a rule that one man of discernment is better fitted to analyze and estimate the peculiar qualities adapted to particular offices than a body of men of equal or perhaps even of superior discernment.

The sole and undivided responsibility of one man will naturally beget a livelier sense of duty and a more exact regard to reputation. He will, on this account, feel himself under stronger obligations, and more interested to investigate with care the qualities requisite to the stations to be filled, and to prefer with impartiality the persons who may have the fairest pretensions to them. He will have *fewer* personal attachments to gratify than a body of men who may each be supposed to have an equal number; and will be so much the less liable to be misled by the sentiments of friendship and of affection. There is nothing so apt to agitate the passions of mankind as personal considerations, whether they relate to ourselves or to others, who are to be the objects of our choice or preference. Hence, in every exercise of the power of appointing to offices by an assembly of men we must expect to see a full display of all the private and party likings and dislikes, partialities and antipathies, attachments and animosities, which are felt by those who compose the assembly. The choice which may at any time happen to be made under such circumstances will of course be the result either of a victory gained by one party over the other, or of a compromise between the parties. In either case, the intrinsic merit of the candidate will be too often out of sight. In the first, the qualifications best adapted to uniting the suffrages of the party will be more considered than those which fit the person for the station. In the last, the coalition will commonly turn upon some interested equivalent: "Give us the man we wish for this office, and you shall have the one you wish for that." This will be the usual condition of the bargain. And it will rarely happen that the advancement of the public service will be the primary object either of party victories or of party negotiations.

The truth of the principles here advanced seems to have been felt by the most intelligent of those who have found fault with the provision made, in this respect, by the convention. They contend that the President ought solely to have been authorized to make the appointments under the federal government. But it is easy to show that every advantage to be expected from such an arrangement would, in substance, be derived from the power of *nomination* which is proposed to be conferred upon him; while several disadvantages which might attend the absolute power of appointment in the hands of that officer would be avoided. In the act of nomination, his judgment alone would be exercised; and as it would be his sole duty to point out the man who, with the approbation of the Senate, should fill an office, his responsibility would be as complete as if he were to make the final appointment. There can, in this view, be no difference between nominating and appointing. The same motives which would influence a proper discharge of his duty in one case would exist in the other. And as no man could be appointed but on his previous nomination, every man who might be appointed would be, in fact, his choice.

But his nomination may be overruled: this it certainly may, yet it can only be to make place for another nomination by himself. The person ultimately appointed must be the object of his preference, though perhaps not in the first degree. It is also not very probable that his nomination would often be overruled. The Senate could not be tempted by the preference they might feel to another to reject the one proposed; because they could not assure themselves that the person they might wish would be brought forward by a second or by any subsequent nomination. They could not even be certain that a future nomination would present a candidate in any degree more acceptable to them; and as their dissent might cast a kind of stigma upon the individual rejected and might have the appearance of a reflection upon the judgment of the Chief Magistrate, it is not likely that their sanction would often be refused, where there were not special and strong reasons for the refusal.

To what purpose then require the co-operation of the Senate? I answer, that the necessity of their concurrence would have a powerful, though, in general, a silent operation. It would be an excellent check upon a spirit of favoritism in the President, and would tend greatly to prevent the appointment of unfit characters from State prejudice, from family connection, from personal attachment, or from a view to popularity. And, in addition to this, it would be an efficacious source of stability in the administration.

It will readily be comprehended that a man who had himself the sole disposition of offices would be governed much more by his private inclinations and interests than when he was bound to submit the propriety of his choice to the discussion and determination of a different and independent body, and that body an entire branch of the legislature. The possibility of rejection would be a strong motive to care in proposing. The danger to his own reputation, and, in the case of an elective magistrate, to his political existence, from betraying a spirit of favoritism or an unbecoming pursuit of popularity to the observation of a body whose opinion would have great weight in forming that of the public could not fail to operate as a barrier to the one and to the other. He would be both ashamed and afraid to bring forward, for the most distinguished or lucrative stations, candidates who had no other merit than that of coming from the same State to which he particularly belonged, or of being in some way or other personally allied to him, or of possessing the necessary insignificance and pliancy to render them the obsequious instruments of his pleasure.

To this reasoning it has been objected that the President, by the influence of the power of nomination, may secure the complaisance of the Senate to his views. The supposition of universal venality in human nature is little less an error in political reasoning than the supposition of universal rectitude. The institution of delegated power implies that there is a portion of virtue and honor among mankind, which may be a reasonable foundation of confidence. And experience justifies the theory. It has been found to exist in the most corrupt periods of the most corrupt governments. The venality of the British House of Commons has been long a topic of accusation against that body in the country to which they belong, as well as in this; and it cannot be doubted that the charge is, to a considerable extent, well founded. But it is as little to be doubted that there is always a large proportion of the body which consists of independent and public-spirited men who have an influential weight in the councils of the nation. Hence it is (the present reign not excepted) that the sense of that body is often seen to control the inclinations of the monarch, both with regard to men and to measures. Though it might therefore be allowable to suppose that the executive might occasionally influence some individuals in the Senate, yet the supposition that he could in general purchase the integrity of the whole body would be forced and improbable. A man disposed to view human nature as it is, without either flattering its virtues or exaggerating its vices, will see sufficient ground of confidence in the probity of the Senate to rest satisfied, not only that it will be impracticable to the executive to corrupt or seduce a majority of its members, but that the necessity of its co-operation in the business of appointments will be a considerable and salutary restraint upon the conduct of that magistrate. Nor is the integrity of the Senate the only reliance. The Constitution has provided some important guards against the danger of executive influence upon the legislative body. It declares that "No senator or representative shall, during the time *for which he was elected,* be appointed to any civil office under the United States, which shall have been created, or the emoluments whereof shall have been increased, during such time; and no person holding any office under the United States shall be a member of either house during his continuance in office."

PUBLIUS

No. 77: Hamilton

IT HAS been mentioned as one of the advantages to be expected from the co-operation of the Senate, in the business of appointments, that it would contribute to the stability of the administration. The consent of that body would be necessary to displace as well as to appoint. A change of the Chief Magistrate, therefore, would not occasion so violent or so general a revolution in the officers of the government as might be expected if he were the sole disposer of offices. Where a man in any station had given satisfactory evidence of his fitness for it, a new President would be restrained from attempting a change in favor of a person more agreeable to him by the apprehension that a discountenance of the Senate might frustrate the attempt, and bring some degree of discredit upon himself. Those who can best estimate the value of a steady administration will be most disposed to prize a provision which connects the official existence of public men with the approbation or disapprobation of that body which, from the greater permanency of its own composition, will in all probability be less subject to inconstancy than any other member of the government.

To this union of the Senate with the President, in the article of appointments, it has in some cases been suggested that it would serve to give the President an undue influence over the Senate, and in others that it would have an opposite tendency—a strong proof that neither suggestion is true.

To state the first in its proper form is to refute it. It amounts to this: the President would have an improper *influence over* the Senate, because the Senate would have the power of *restraining* him. This is an absurdity in terms. It cannot admit of a doubt that the entire power of appointment would enable him much more effectually to establish a dangerous empire over that body than a mere power of nomination subject to their control.

Let us take a view of the converse of the proposition: "the Senate would influence the executive." As I have had occasion to remark in several other instances, the indistinctness of the objection forbids a precise answer. In what manner is this influence to be exerted? In relation to what objects? The power of influencing a person, in the sense in which it is here used, must imply a power of conferring a benefit upon him. How could the Senate confer a benefit upon the President by the manner of employing their right of negative upon his nominations? If it be said they might sometimes gratify him by an acquiescence in a favorite choice, when public motives might dictate a different conduct, I answer that the instances in which the President could be personally interested in the result would be too few to admit of his being materially affected by the compliances of the Senate. Besides this, it is evident that the POWER which can *originate* the disposition of honors and emoluments is more likely to attract than to be attracted by the POWER which can merely obstruct their course. If by influencing the President be meant *restraining* him, this is precisely what must have been intended. And it has been shown that the restraint would be salutary, at the same time that it would not be such as to destroy a single advantage to be looked for from the uncontrolled agency of that magistrate. The right of nomination would produce all the good, without the ill.

Upon a comparison of the plan for the appointment of the officers of the proposed government with that which is established by the constitution of this State, a decided preference must be given to the former. In that plan the power of nomination is unequivocally vested in the executive. And as there would be a necessity for submitting each nomination to the judgment of an entire branch of the legislature, the circumstances attending an appointment, from the mode of conducting it, would naturally become matters of notoriety, and the public would be at no loss to determine what part had been performed by the different actors. The blame of a bad nomination would fall upon the President singly and absolutely. The censure of rejecting a good one would lie entirely at the door of the Senate, aggravated by the consideration of their having counteracted the good intentions of the executive. If an ill appointment should be made, the executive, for nominating, and the Senate, for approving, would participate, though in different degrees, in the opprobrium and disgrace.

The reverse of all this characterizes the manner of appointment in this State. The council of appointment consists of from three to five persons, of whom the governor is always one. This small body, shut up in a private apartment, impenetrable to the public eye, proceed to the execution of the trust committed to them. It is known that the governor claims the right of nomination upon the strength of some ambiguous expressions in the Constitution; but it is not known to what extent, or in what manner he exercises it; nor upon what occasions he is contradicted or opposed. The censure of a bad appointment, on account of the uncertainty of its author and for want of a determinate object, has neither poignancy nor duration. And while an unbounded field for cabal and intrigue lies open, all idea of responsibility is lost. The most that the public can know is that the governor claims the right of nomination; that *two* out of the inconsiderable number of *four* men can too often be managed without much difficulty; that if some of the members of a particular council should happen to be of an uncomplying character, it is frequently not impossible to get rid of their opposition by regulating the times of meeting in such a manner as to render their attendance inconvenient; and that from whatever cause it may proceed, a great number of very improper appointments are from time to time made. Whether a governor of this State avails himself of the ascendant, he must necessarily have in this delicate and important part of the administration to prefer to offices men who are best qualified for them; or whether he prostitutes that advantage to the advancement of persons whose chief merit is their implicit devotion to his will and to the support of a despicable and dangerous system of personal influence are questions which, unfortunately for the community, can only be the subjects of speculation and conjecture.

Every mere council of appointment, however constituted, will be a conclave in which cabal and intrigue will have their full scope. Their number, without an unwarrantable increase of expense, cannot be large enough to preclude a facility of combination. And as each member will have his friends and connections to provide for, the desire of mutual gratification will beget a scandalous bartering of votes and bargaining for places. The private attachments of one man might easily be satisfied, but to satisfy the private attachments of a dozen, or of twenty men, would occasion a monopoly of all the principal employments of the government in a few families and would lead more directly to an aristocracy or an oligarchy than any measure that could be contrived. If, to avoid an accumulation of offices, there was to be a frequent change in the persons who were to compose the council, this would involve the mischiefs of a mutable administration in their full extent. Such a council would also be more liable to executive influence than the Senate, because they would be fewer in number, and would act less immediately under the public inspection. Such a council, in fine, as a substitute for the plan of the convention, would be productive of an increase of expense, a multiplication of the evils which spring from favoritism and intrigue in the distribution of public honors, a decrease of stability in the administration of the government, and a diminution of the security against an undue influence of the executive. And yet such a council has been warmly contended for as an essential amendment in the proposed Constitution.

I could not with propriety conclude my observations on the subject of appointments without taking notice of a scheme for which there have appeared some, though but a few advocates; I mean that of uniting the House of

Representatives in the power of making them. I shall, however, do little more than mention it, as I cannot imagine that it is likely to gain the countenance of any considerable part of the community. A body so fluctuating and at the same time so numerous can never be deemed proper for the exercise of that power. Its unfitness will appear manifest to all when it is recollected that in half a century it may consist of three or four hundred persons. All the advantages of the stability, both of the Executive and of the Senate, would be defeated by this union, and infinite delays and embarrassments would be occasioned. The example of most of the States in their local constitutions encourages us to reprobate the idea.

The only remaining powers of the executive are comprehended in giving information to Congress of the state of the Union; in recommending to their consideration such measures as he shall judge expedient; in convening them, or either branch, upon extraordinary occasions; in adjourning them when they cannot themselves agree upon the time of adjournment; in receiving ambassadors and other public ministers; in faithfully executing the laws; and in commissioning all the officers of the United States.

Except some cavils about the power of convening *either* house of the legislature, and that of receiving ambassadors, no objection has been made to this class of authorities; nor could they possibly admit of any. It required, indeed, an insatiable avidity for censure to invent exceptions to the parts which have been excepted to. In regard to the power of convening either house of the legislature I shall barely remark that in respect to the Senate, at least, we can readily discover a good reason for it. As this body has a concurrent power with the executive in the article of treaties, it might often be necessary to call it together with a view to this object, when it would be unnecessary and improper to convene the House of Representatives. As to the reception of ambassadors, what I have said in a former paper will furnish a sufficient answer.

We have now completed a survey of the structure and powers of the executive department which, I have endeavored to show, combines, as far as republican principles will admit, all the requisites to energy. The remaining inquiry is: Does it also combine the requisites to safety, in the republican sense—a due dependence on the people, a due responsibility? The answer to this question has been anticipated in the investigation of its other characteristics, and is satisfactorily deducible from these circumstances; the election of the President once in four years by persons immediately chosen by the people for that purpose, and his being at all times liable to impeachment, trial, dismission from office, incapacity to serve in any other, and to the forfeiture of life and estate by subsequent prosecution in the common course of law. But these precautions, great as they are, are not the only ones which the plan of the convention has provided in favor of the public security. In the only instances in which the abuse of the executive authority was materially to be feared, the Chief Magistrate of the United States, would, by that plan, be subjected to the control of a branch of the legislative body. What more can an enlightened and reasonable people desire?

PUBLIUS

No. 78: Hamilton

WE PROCEED now to an examination of the judiciary department of the proposed government.

In unfolding the defects of the existing Confederation, the utility and necessity of a federal judicature have been clearly pointed out. It is the less necessary to recapitulate the considerations there urged as the propriety of the institution in the abstract is not disputed; the only questions which have been raised being relative to the manner of constituting it, and to its extent. To these points, therefore, our observations shall be confined.

The manner of constituting it seems to embrace these several objects: 1st. The mode of appointing the judges. 2nd. The tenure by which they are to hold their places. 3rd. The partition of the judiciary authority between different courts and their relations to each other.

First. As to the mode of appointing the judges: this is the same with that of appointing the officers of the Union in general and has been so fully discussed in the two last numbers that nothing can be said here which would not be useless repetition.

Second. As to the tenure by which the judges are to hold their places: this chiefly concerns their duration in office, the provisions for their support, the precautions for their responsibility.

According to the plan of the convention, all judges who may be appointed by the United States are to hold their offices *during good behavior;* which is conformable to the most approved of the State constitutions, and among the rest, to that of this State. Its propriety having been drawn into question by the adversaries of that plan is no light symptom of the rage for objection which disorders their imaginations and judgments. The standard of good behavior for the continuance in office of the judicial magistracy is certainly one of the most valuable of the modern improvements in the practice of government. In a monarchy it is an excellent barrier to the despotism of the prince; in a republic it is a no less excellent barrier to the encroachments and oppressions of the representative body. And it is the best expedient which can be devised in any government to secure a steady, upright, and impartial administration of the laws.

Whoever attentively considers the different departments of power must perceive that, in a government in which they are separated from each other, the judiciary, from the nature of its functions, will always be the least dangerous to the political rights of the Constitution; because it will be least in a capacity to annoy or injure them. The executive not only dispenses the honors but holds the sword of the community. The legislature not only commands the purse but prescribes the rules by which the duties and rights of every citizen are to be regulated. The judiciary, on the contrary, has no influence over either the sword or the purse; no direction either of the strength or of the wealth of the society, and can take no active resolution whatever. It may truly be said to have neither FORCE nor WILL but merely judgment; and must ultimately depend upon the aid of the executive arm even for the efficacy of its judgments.

This simple view of the matter suggests several important consequences. It proves incontestably that the judiciary is beyond comparison the weakest of the three departments of power;* that it can never attack with success either of the other two; and that all possible care is requisite to enable it to defend itself against their attacks. It equally proves that though individual oppression may now and then proceed from the courts of justice, the general liberty of the people can never be endangered from that quarter; I mean so long as the judiciary remains truly distinct from both the legislature and the executive. For I agree that "there is no liberty if the power of judging be not separated from the legislative and executive powers." † And it proves, in the last place, that as liberty can have nothing to fear from the judiciary alone, but would have everything to fear from its union with either of the other departments; that as all the effects of such a union must ensue from a dependence of the former on the latter, notwithstanding a nominal and apparent separation; that as, from the natural feebleness of the judiciary, it is in continual jeopardy of being overpowered, awed, or influenced by its co-ordinate branches; and that as nothing can contribute so much to its firmness and independence as permanency in office, this quality may therefore be justly regarded as an indispensable ingredient in its constitution, and, in a great measure, as the citadel of the public justice and the public security.

The complete independence of the courts of justice is peculiarly essential in a limited Constitution. By a limited Constitution, I understand one which contains certain specified exceptions to the legislative authority; such, for instance, as that it shall pass no bills of attainder, no *ex post facto* laws, and the like. Limitations of this kind can be preserved in practice no other way than through the medium of courts of justice, whose duty it must be to declare all acts contrary to the manifest tenor of the Constitution void. Without this, all the reservations of particular rights or privileges would amount to nothing.

Some perplexity respecting the rights of the courts to pronounce legislative acts void, because contrary to the

* The celebrated Montesquieu, speaking of them, says: "Of the three powers above mentioned, the JUDICIARY is next to nothing." —*Spirit of Laws,* Vol. I, page 186.

† *Idem,* page 181.

Constitution, has arisen from an imagination that the doctrine would imply a superiority of the judiciary to the legislative power. It is urged that the authority which can declare the acts of another void must necessarily be superior to the one whose acts may be declared void. As this doctrine is of great importance in all the American constitutions, a brief discussion of the grounds on which it rests cannot be unacceptable.

There is no position which depends on clearer principles than that every act of a delegated authority, contrary to the tenor of the commission under which it is exercised, is void. No legislative act, therefore, contrary to the Constitution, can be valid. To deny this would be to affirm that the deputy is greater than his principal; that the servant is above his master; that the representatives of the people are superior to the people themselves; that men acting by virtue of powers may do not only what their powers do not authorize, but what they forbid.

If it be said that the legislative body are themselves the constitutional judges of their own powers and that the construction they put upon them is conclusive upon the other departments it may be answered that this cannot be the natural presumption where it is not to be collected from any particular provisions in the Constitution. It is not otherwise to be supposed that the Constitution could intend to enable the representatives of the people to substitute their *will* to that of their constituents. It is far more rational to suppose that the courts were designed to be an intermediate body between the people and the legislature in order, among other things, to keep the latter within the limits assigned to their authority. The interpretation of the laws is the proper and peculiar province of the courts. A constitution is, in fact, and must be regarded by the judges as, a fundamental law. It therefore belongs to them to ascertain its meaning as well as the meaning of any particular act proceeding from the legislative body. If there should happen to be an irreconcilable variance between the two, that which has the superior obligation and validity ought, of course, to be preferred; or, in other words, the Constitution ought to be preferred to the statute, the intention of the people to the intention of their agents.

Nor does this conclusion by any means suppose a superiority of the judicial to the legislative power. It only supposes that the power of the people is superior to both, and that where the will of the legislature, declared in its statutes, stands in opposition to that of the people, declared in the Constitution, the judges ought to be governed by the latter rather than the former. They ought to regulate their decisions by the fundamental laws rather than by those which are not fundamental.

This exercise of judicial discretion in determining between two contradictory laws is exemplified in a familiar instance. It not uncommonly happens that there are two statutes existing at one time, clashing in whole or in part with each other and neither of them containing any repealing clause or expression. In such a case, it is the province of the courts to liquidate and fix their meaning and operation. So far as they can, by any fair construction, be reconciled to each other, reason and law conspire to dictate that this should be done; where this is impracticable, it becomes a matter of necessity to give effect to one in exclusion of the other. The rule which has obtained in the courts for determining their relative validity is that the last in order of time shall be preferred to the first. But this is a mere rule of construction, not derived from any positive law but from the nature and reason of the thing. It is a rule not enjoined upon the courts by legislative provision but adopted by themselves, as consonant to truth and propriety, for the direction of their conduct as interpreters of the law. They thought it reasonable that between the interfering acts of an *equal* authority that which was the last indication of its will should have the preference.

But in regard to the interfering acts of a superior and subordinate authority of an original and derivative power, the nature and reason of the thing indicate the converse of that rule as proper to be followed. They teach us that the prior act of a superior ought to be preferred to the subsequent act of an inferior and subordinate authority; and that accordingly, whenever a particular statute contravenes the Constitution, it will be the duty of the judicial tribunals to adhere to the latter and disregard the former.

It can be of no weight to say that the courts, on the pretense of a repugnancy, may substitute their own pleasure to the constitutional intentions of the legislature. This might as well happen in the case of two contradictory statutes; or it might as well happen in every adjudication upon any single statute. The courts must declare the sense of the law; and if they should be disposed to exercise WILL instead of JUDGMENT, the consequence would equally be the substitution of their pleasure to that of the legislative body. The observation, if it proved anything, would prove that there ought to be no judges distinct from that body.

If, then, the courts of justice are to be considered as the bulwarks of a limited Constitution against legislative encroachments, this consideration will afford a strong argument for the permanent tenure of judicial offices, since nothing will contribute so much as this to that independent spirit in the judges which must be essential to the faithful performance of so arduous a duty.

This independence of the judges is equally requisite to guard the Constitution and the rights of individuals from the effects of those ill humors which the arts of designing men, or the influence of particular conjunctures, sometimes disseminate among the people themselves, and which, though they speedily give place to better information, and more deliberate reflection, have a tendency, in the meantime, to occasion dangerous innovations in the government, and serious oppressions of the minor party in the community. Though I trust the friends of the proposed Constitution will never concur with its enemies* in questioning that fundamental principle of republican government which admits the right of the people to alter or abolish the established Constitution whenever they find it inconsistent with their happiness; yet it is not to be inferred from this principle that the representatives of the people, whenever a momentary inclination happens to lay hold of a majority of their constituents incompatible with the provisions in the existing Constitution would, on that account, be justifiable in a violation of those provisions; or that the courts would be under a greater obligation to connive at infractions in this shape than when they had proceeded wholly from

* *Vide Protest of the Minority of the Convention of Pennsylvania,* Martin's speech, etc.

the cabals of the representative body. Until the people have, by some solemn and authoritative act, annulled or changed the established form, it is binding upon themselves collectively, as well as individually; and no presumption, or even knowledge of their sentiments, can warrant their representatives in a departure from it prior to such an act. But it is easy to see that it would require an uncommon portion of fortitude in the judges to do their duty as faithful guardians of the Constitution, where legislative invasions of it had been instigated by the major voice of the community.

But it is not with a view to infractions of the Constitution only that the independence of the judges may be an essential safeguard against the effects of occasional ill humors in the society. These sometimes extend no farther than to the injury of the private rights of particular classes of citizens, by unjust and partial laws. Here also the firmness of the judicial magistracy is of vast importance in mitigating the severity and confining the operation of such laws. It not only serves to moderate the immediate mischiefs of those which may have been passed but it operates as a check upon the legislative body in passing them; who, perceiving that obstacles to the success of an iniquitous intention are to be expected from the scruples of the courts, are in a manner compelled, by the very motives of the injustice they meditate, to qualify their attempts. This is a circumstance calculated to have more influence upon the character of our governments than but few may be aware of. The benefits of the integrity and moderation of the judiciary have already been felt in more States than one; and though they may have displeased those whose sinister expectations they may have disappointed, they must have commanded the esteem and applause of all the virtuous and disinterested. Considerate men of every description ought to prize whatever will tend to beget or fortify that temper in the courts; as no man can be sure that he may not be tomorrow the victim of a spirit of injustice, by which he may be a gainer today. And every man must now feel that the inevitable tendency of such a spirit is to sap the foundations of public and private confidence and to introduce in its stead universal distrust and distress.

That inflexible and uniform adherence to the rights

of the Constitution, and of individuals, which we perceive to be indispensable in the courts of justice, can certainly not be expected from judges who hold their offices by a temporary commission. Periodical appointments, however regulated, or by whomsoever made, would, in some way or other, be fatal to their necessary independence. If the power of making them was committed either to the executive or legislature there would be danger of an improper complaisance to the branch which possessed it; if to both, there would be an unwillingness to hazard the displeasure of either; if to the people, or to persons chosen by them for the special purpose, there would be too great a disposition to consult popularity to justify a reliance that nothing would be consulted but the Constitution and the laws.

There is yet a further and a weighty reason for the permanency of the judicial offices which is deducible from the nature of the qualifications they require. It has been frequently remarked with great propriety that a voluminous code of laws is one of the inconveniences necessarily connected with the advantages of a free government. To avoid an arbitrary discretion in the courts, it is indispensable that they should be bound down by strict rules and precedents which serve to define and point out their duty in every particular case that comes before them; and it will readily be conceived from the variety of controversies which grow out of the folly and wickedness of mankind that the records of those precedents must unavoidably swell to a very considerable bulk and must demand long and laborious study to acquire a competent knowledge of them. Hence it is that there can be but few men in the society who will have sufficient skill in the laws to qualify them for the stations of judges. And making the proper deductions for the ordinary depravity of human nature, the number must be still smaller of those who unite the requisite integrity with the requisite knowledge. These considerations apprise us that the government can have no great option between fit characters; and that a temporary duration in office which would naturally discourage such characters from quitting a lucrative line of practice to accept a seat on the bench would have a tendency to throw the administration of justice into hands less able and less well qualified to conduct it with utility and dignity. In the present circumstances of this country and in those in which it is likely to be for a long time to come, the disadvantages on this score would be greater than they may at first sight appear; but it must be confessed that they are far inferior to those which present themselves under the other aspects of the subject.

Upon the whole, there can be no room to doubt that the convention acted wisely in copying from the models of those constitutions which have established *good behavior* as the tenure of their judicial offices, in point of duration; and that so far from being blamable on this account, their plan would have been inexcusably defective if it had wanted this important feature of good government. The experience of Great Britain affords an illustrious comment on the excellence of the institution.

PUBLIUS

No. 79: Hamilton

NEXT to permanency in office, nothing can contribute more to the independence of the judges than a fixed provision for their support. The remark made in relation to the President is equally applicable here. In the general course of human nature, *a power over a man's subsistence amounts to a power over his will.* And we can never hope to see realized in practice the complete separation of the judicial from the legislative power, in any system which leaves the former dependent for pecuniary resources on the occasional grants of the latter. The enlightened friends to good government in every State have seen cause to lament the want of precise and explicit precautions in the State constitutions on this head. Some of these indeed have declared that *permanent* * salaries should be established for the judges; but the experiment has in some instances shown that such expressions are not sufficiently definite to preclude legislative evasions. Something still more positive and unequivocal has been

* *Vide Constitution of Massachusetts,* Chapter 2, Section 1, Article 13.

evinced to be requisite. The plan of the convention accordingly has provided that the judges of the United States "shall at *stated times* receive for their services a compensation which shall not be *diminished* during their continuance in office."

This, all circumstances considered, is the most eligible provision that could have been devised. It will readily be understood that the fluctuations in the value of money and in the state of society rendered a fixed rate of compensation in the Constitution inadmissible. What might be extravagant today might in half a century become penurious and inadequate. It was therefore necessary to leave it to the discretion of the legislature to vary its provisions in conformity to the variations in circumstances, yet under such restrictions as to put it out of the power of that body to change the condition of the individual for the worse. A man may then be sure of the ground upon which he stands, and can never be deterred from his duty by the apprehension of being placed in a less eligible situation. The clause which has been quoted combines both advantages. The salaries of judicial offices may from time to time be altered, as occasion shall require, yet so as never to lessen the allowance with which any particular judge comes into office, in respect to him. It will be observed that a difference has been made by the convention between the compensation of the President and of the judges. That of the former can neither be increased nor diminished; that of the latter can only not be diminished. This probably arose from the difference in the duration of the respective offices. As the President is to be elected for no more than four years, it can rarely happen that an adequate salary, fixed at the commencement of that period, will not continue to be such to the end of it. But with regard to the judges who, if they behave properly, will be secured in the places for life, it may well happen, especially in the early stages of the government, that a stipend which would be very sufficient at their first appointment would become too small in the progress of their service.

This provision for the support of the judges bears every mark of prudence and efficacy; and it may be safely affirmed that, together with the permanent tenure of their offices, it affords a better prospect of their independence than is discoverable in the constitutions of any of the States in regard to their own judges.

The precautions for their responsibility are comprised in the article respecting impeachments. They are liable to be impeached for malconduct by the House of Representatives and tried by the Senate; and, if convicted, may be dismissed from office and disqualified for holding any other. This is the only provision on the point which is consistent with the necessary independence of the judicial character, and is the only one which we find in our own Constitution in respect to our own judges.

The want of a provision for removing the judges on account of inability has been a subject of complaint. But all considerate men will be sensible that such a provision would either not be practiced upon or would be more liable to abuse than calculated to answer any good purpose. The mensuration of the faculties of the mind has, I believe, no place in the catalogue of known arts. An attempt to fix the boundary between the regions of ability and inability would much oftener give scope to personal and party attachments and enmities than advance the interests of justice or the public good. The result, except in the case of insanity, must for the most part be arbitrary; and insanity, without any formal or express provision, may be safely pronounced to be a virtual disqualification.

The constitution of New York, to avoid investigations that must forever be vague and dangerous, has taken a particular age as the criterion of inability. No man can be a judge beyond sixty. I believe there are few at present who do not disapprove of this provision. There is no station in relation to which it is less proper than to that of a judge. The deliberating and comparing faculties generally preserve their strength much beyond that period in men who survive it; and when, in addition to this circumstance, we consider how few there are who outlive the season of intellectual vigor and how improbable it is that any considerable portion of the bench, whether more or less numerous, should be in such a situation at the same time, we shall be ready to conclude that limitations of this sort have little to recommend them. In a republic where fortunes are not affluent and pensions not expedient, the dismission of men from stations in which they have served their country long and usefully, on which they depend for subsistence, and from which it will be too late to resort to any other occupation for a livelihood, ought to have some better apology to humanity than is to be found in the imaginary danger of a superannuated bench.

PUBLIUS

No. 80: Hamilton

TO JUDGE with accuracy of the proper extent of the federal judicature it will be necessary to consider, in the first place, what are its proper objects.

It seems scarcely to admit of controversy that the judiciary authority of the Union ought to extend to these several descriptions of cases: 1st, to all those which arise out of the laws of the United States, passed in pursuance of their just and constitutional powers of legislation; 2nd, to all those which concern the execution of the provisions expressly contained in the articles of Union; 3rd, to all those in which the United States are a party; 4th, to all those which involve the PEACE of the CONFEDERACY, whether they relate to the intercourse between the United States and foreign nations or to that between the States themselves; 5th, to all those which originate on the high seas, and are of admiralty or maritime jurisdiction; and lastly, to all those in which the State tribunals cannot be supposed to be impartial and unbiased.

The first point depends upon this obvious consideration, that there ought always to be a constitutional method of giving efficacy to constitutional provisions. What, for instance, would avail restrictions on the authority of the State legislatures, without some constitutional mode of enforcing the observance of them? The States, by the plan of the convention, are prohibited from doing a variety of things, some of which are incompatible with the interests of the Union and others with the principles of good government. The imposition of duties on imported articles and the emission of paper money are specimens of each kind. No man of sense will believe that such prohibitions would be scrupulously regarded without some effectual power in the government to restrain or correct the infractions of them. This power must either be a direct negative on the State laws, or an authority in the federal courts to overrule such as might be in manifest contravention of the articles of Union. There is no third course that I can imagine. The latter appears to have been thought by the convention preferable to the former, and I presume will be most agreeable to the States.

As to the second point, it is impossible, by any argument or comment, to make it clearer than it is in itself. If there are such things as political axioms, the propriety of the judicial power of a government being coextensive with its legislative may be ranked among the number. The mere necessity of uniformity in the interpretation of the national laws decides the question. Thirteen independent courts of final jurisdiction over the same causes, arising upon the same laws, is a hydra in government from which nothing but contradiction and confusion can proceed.

Still less need be said in regard to the third point. Controversies between the nation and its members or citizens can only be properly referred to the national tribunals. Any other plan would be contrary to reason, to precedent, and to decorum.

The fourth point rests on this plain proposition, that the peace of the WHOLE ought not to be left at the disposal of a PART. The Union will undoubtedly be answerable to foreign powers for the conduct of its members. And the responsibility for an injury ought ever to be accompanied with the faculty of preventing it. As the denial or perversion of justice by the sentences of courts, as well as in any other manner, is with reason classed among the just causes of war, it will follow that the federal judiciary ought to have cognizance of all causes in which the citizens of other countries are concerned. This is not less essential to the preservation of the public faith than to the security of the public tranquillity. A distinction may perhaps be imagined between cases arising upon treaties and the laws of nations and those which may stand merely on the footing of the municipal law. The former kind may be supposed proper for the federal jurisdiction, the latter for that of the States. But it is at least problematical whether an unjust sentence against a foreigner, where the subject of controversy was wholly relative to the *lex loci,* would not, if unredressed, be an aggression upon his sovereign, as well as one which violated the stipulations in a treaty or the general law of nations. And a still greater objection to the distinction would result from the immense difficulty, if not impossibility, of a practical discrimination between the cases of one complexion and those of the other. So great a proportion of the cases in which foreigners are parties involve national questions that it is by far most safe and most expedient to refer all those in which they are concerned to the national tribunals.

The power of determining causes between two States, between one State and the citizens of another, and between the citizens of different States, is perhaps not less essential to the peace of the Union than that which has been just examined. History gives us a horrid picture of the dissensions and private wars which distracted and desolated Germany prior to the institution of the IMPERIAL CHAMBER by Maximilian towards the close of the fifteenth century, and informs us, at the same time, of the vast influence of that institution in appeasing the disorders and establishing the tranquillity of the empire. This was a court invested with authority to decide finally all differences among the members of the Germanic body.

A method of terminating territorial disputes between the States, under the authority of the federal head, was not unattended to, even in the imperfect system by which they have been hitherto held together. But there are many other sources, besides interfering claims of boundary, from which bickerings and animosities may spring up among the members of the Union. To some of these we have been witnesses in the course of our past experience. It will readily be conjectured that I allude to the fraudulent laws which have been passed in too many of the States. And though the proposed Constitution establishes particular guards against the repetition of those instances which have heretofore made their appearance, yet it is warrantable to apprehend that the spirit which produced them will assume new shapes that could not be foreseen nor specifically provided against. Whatever practices may have a tendency to disturb the harmony between the States are proper objects of federal superintendence and control.

It may be esteemed the basis of the Union that "the citizens of each State shall be entitled to all the privileges and immunities of citizens of the several States." And if it be a just principle that every government *ought to possess the means of executing its own provisions by its own authority* it will follow that in order to the inviolable maintenance of that equality of privileges and immunities to which the citizens of the Union will be entitled, the national judiciary ought to preside in all cases in which one State or its citizens are opposed to another State or its citizens. To secure the full effect of so fundamental a provision against all evasion and subterfuge, it is necessary that its construction should be committed to that tribunal which, having no local attachments, will be likely to be impartial between the different States and their citizens and which, owing its official existence to the Union, will never be likely to feel any bias inauspicious to the principles on which it is founded.

The fifth point will demand little animadversion. The most bigoted idolizers of State authority have not thus far shown a disposition to deny the national judiciary the cognizance of maritime causes. These so generally depend on the laws of nations and so commonly affect the rights of foreigners that they fall within the considerations which are relative to the public peace. The most important part of them are, by the present Confederation, submitted to federal jurisdiction.

The reasonableness of the agency of the national courts in cases in which the State tribunals cannot be supposed to be impartial speaks for itself. No man ought certainly to be a judge in his own cause, or in any cause in respect to which he has the least interest or bias. This principle has no inconsiderable weight in designating the federal courts as the proper tribunals for the determination of controversies between different States and their citizens. And it ought to have the same operation in regard to some cases between the citizens of the same State. Claims to land under grants of different States, founded upon adverse pretensions of boundary, are of this description. The courts of neither of the granting States could be expected to be unbiased. The laws may have even prejudged the question and tied the courts down to decisions in favor of the grants of the State to which they belonged. And even where this had not been done, it would be natural that the judges, as men, should feel a strong predilection to the claims of their own government.

Having thus laid down and discussed the principles which ought to regulate the constitution of the federal judiciary we will proceed to test, by these principles, the particular powers of which, according to the plan of the convention, it is to be composed. It is to comprehend "all cases in law and equity arising under the Constitution, the laws of the United States, and treaties made or which shall be made, under their authority; to all cases affecting ambassadors, other public ministers, and consuls; to all cases of admiralty and maritime jurisdiction; to controversies to which the United States shall be a party; to controversies between two or more States; between a State and citizens of another State; between citizens of different States; between citizens of the same State claiming lands under grants of different States; and between a State or the citizens thereof and foreign states, citizens, and subjects." This constitutes the entire mass of the judicial authority of the Union. Let us now review it in detail. It is, then, to extend:

First. To all cases in law and equity, *arising under the Constitution* and *the laws of the United States*. This corresponds to the two first classes of causes which have been enumerated, as proper for the jurisdiction of the United States. It has been asked what is meant by "cases arising under the Constitution," in contradistinction from those "arising under the laws of the United States"? The difference has been already explained. All the restrictions upon the authority of the State legislatures furnish examples of it. They are not, for instance, to emit paper money; but the interdiction results from the Constitution and will have no connection with any law of the United States. Should paper money, notwithstanding, be emitted, the controversies concerning it would be cases arising under the Constitution and not the laws of the United States, in the ordinary signification of the terms. This may serve as a sample of the whole.

It has also been asked, what need of the word "equity"? What equitable causes can grow out of the Constitution and laws of the United States? There is hardly a subject of litigation between individuals which may not involve those ingredients of *fraud, accident, trust,* or *hardship,* which would render the matter an object of equitable rather than of legal jurisdiction, as the distinction is known and established in several of the States. It is the peculiar province, for instance, of a court of equity to relieve against what are called hard bargains: these are contracts in which, though there may have been no direct fraud or deceit sufficient to invalidate them in a court of law, yet there may have been some undue and unconscionable advantage taken of the necessities or misfortunes of one of the parties which a court of equity would not tolerate. In such cases, where foreigners were concerned on either side, it would be impossible for the federal judicatories to do justice without an equitable as well as a legal jurisdiction. Agreements to convey lands claimed under the grants of different States may afford another example of the necessity of an equitable jurisdiction in the federal courts. This reasoning may not be so palpable in those States where the formal and technical distinction between LAW and EQUITY is not maintained as in this State, where it is exemplified by every day's practice.

The judiciary authority of the Union is to extend:

Second. To treaties made, or which shall be made, under the authority of the United States and to all cases affecting ambassadors, other public ministers, and consuls. These belong to the fourth class of the enumerated cases, as they have an evident connection with the preservation of the national peace.

Third. To cases of admiralty and maritime jurisdiction. These form, altogether, the fifth of the enumerated classes of causes proper for the cognizance of the national courts.

Fourth. To controversies to which the United States shall be a party. These constitute the third of those classes.

Fifth. To controversies between two or more States; between a State and citizens of another State; between citizens of different States. These belong to the fourth of those classes, and partake, in some measure, of the nature of the last.

Sixth. To cases between the citizens of the same State, *claiming lands under grants of different States.* These fall within the last class, and *are the only instances in which the proposed Constitution directly contemplates the cognizance of disputes between the citizens of the same State.*

Seventh. To cases between a State and the citizens thereof, and foreign States, citizens, or subjects. These have been already explained to belong to the fourth of the enumerated classes and have been shown to be, in a peculiar manner, the proper subjects of the national judicature.

From this review of the particular powers of the federal judiciary, as marked out in the Constitution, it appears that they are all conformable to the principles which ought to have governed the structure of that department and which were necessary to the perfection of the system. If some partial inconveniences should appear to be connected with the incorporation of any of them into the plan it ought to be recollected that the national legislature will have ample authority to make such *exceptions* and to prescribe such regulations as will be calculated to obviate or remove these inconveniences. The possibility of particular mischiefs can never be viewed, by a well-informed mind, as a solid objection to a general principle which is calculated to avoid general mischiefs and to obtain general advantages. PUBLIUS

No. 81: Hamilton

LET us now return to the partition of the judiciary authority between different courts and their relations to each other.

"The judicial power of the United States is" (by the plan of the convention) "to be vested in one Supreme Court, and in such inferior courts as the Congress may, from time to time, ordain and establish." *

That there ought to be one court of supreme and final jurisdiction is a proposition which has not been, and is not likely to be contested. The reasons for it have been assigned in another place and are too obvious to need repetition. The

* Article 3, Section 1.

only question that seems to have been raised concerning it is whether it ought to be a distinct body or a branch of the legislature. The same contradiction is observable in regard to this matter which has been remarked in several other cases. The very men who object to the Senate as a court of impeachments, on the ground of an improper intermixture of powers, advocate, by implication at least, the propriety of vesting the ultimate decision of all causes in the whole or in a part of the legislative body.

The arguments or rather suggestions, upon which this charge is founded are to this effect: "The authority of the proposed Supreme Court of the United States, which is to be a separate and independent body, will be superior to that of the legislature. The power of construing the laws according to the *spirit* of the Constitution will enable that court to mould them into whatever shape it may think proper; especially as its decisions will not be in any manner subject to the revision or correction of the legislative body. This is as unprecedented as it is dangerous. In Britain the judicial power, in the last resort, resides in the House of Lords, which is a branch of the legislature; and this part of the British government has been imitated in the State constitutions in general. The Parliament of Great Britain, and the legislatures of the several States, can at any time rectify, by law, the exceptionable decisions of their respective courts. But the errors and usurpations of the Supreme Court of the United States will be uncontrollable and remediless." This, upon examination, will be found to be made up altogether of false reasoning upon misconceived fact.

In the first place, there is not a syllable in the plan under consideration which *directly* empowers the national courts to construe the laws according to the spirit of the Constitution, or which gives them any greater latitude in this respect than may be claimed by the courts of every State. I admit, however, that the Constitution ought to be the standard of construction for the laws, and that wherever there is an evident opposition, the laws ought to give place to the Constitution. But this doctrine is not deducible from any circumstance peculiar to the plan of convention, but from the general theory of a limited Constitution; and as far as it is true is equally applicable to most if not to all the State governments. There can be no objection, therefore, on this account to the federal judicature which will not lie against the local judicatures in general, and which will not serve to condemn every constitution that attempts to set bounds to the legislative discretion.

But perhaps the force of the objection may be thought to consist in the particular organization of the proposed Supreme Court; in its being composed of a distinct body of magistrates, instead of being one of the branches of the legislature, as in the government of Great Britain and in that of this State. To insist upon this point, the authors of the objection must renounce the meaning they have labored to annex to the celebrated maxim requiring a separation of the departments of power. It shall, nevertheless, be conceded to them, agreeably to the interpretation given to that maxim in the course of these papers, that it is not violated by vesting the ultimate power of judging in a *part* of the legislative body. But though this be not an absolute violation of that excellent rule, yet it verges so nearly upon it as on this account alone to be less eligible than the mode preferred by the convention. From a body which had had even a partial agency in passing bad laws we could rarely expect a disposition to temper and moderate them in the application. The same spirit which had operated in making them would be too apt to operate in interpreting them; still less could it be expected that men who had infringed the Constitution in the character of legislators would be disposed to repair the breach in the character of judges. Nor is this all. Every reason which recommends the tenure of good behavior for judicial offices militates against placing the judiciary power, in the last resort, in a body composed of men chosen for a limited period. There is an absurdity in referring the determination of causes, in the first instance, to judges of permanent standing; and in the last, to those of a temporary and mutable constitution. And there is a still greater absurdity in subjecting the decisions of men, selected for their knowledge of the laws, acquired by long and laborious study, to the revision and control of men who, for want of the same advantage, cannot but be deficient in that knowledge. The members of the legislature will rarely be chosen with a view to those qualifications which fit men for the stations of judges; and as, on this account, there will be great reason to apprehend all the ill consequences of defective information, so, on account of the natural propensity of such bodies to party divisions, there will be no less reason to fear that the pestilential breath of faction may poison the fountains of justice. The habit of being continually marshaled on opposite sides will be too apt to stifle the voice both of law and of equity.

These considerations teach us to applaud the wisdom of those States who have committed the judicial power, in the last resort, not to a part of the legislature, but to distinct and independent bodies of men. Contrary to the supposition of those who have represented the plan of the convention, in this respect, as novel and unprecedented, it is but a copy of the constitutions of New Hampshire, Massachusetts, Pennsylvania, Delaware, Maryland, Virginia, North Carolina, South Carolina, and Georgia; and the preference which has been given to these models is highly to be commended.

It is not true, in the second place, that the parliament of Great Britain, or the legislatures of the particular States, can rectify the exceptionable decisions of their respective courts, in any other sense than might be done by a future legislature of the United States. The theory, neither of the British, nor the State constitutions, authorizes the revisal of a judicial sentence by a legislative act. Nor is there anything in the proposed Constitution, more than in either of them, by which it is forbidden. In the former, as well as in the latter, the impropriety of the thing, on the general principles of law and reason, is the sole obstacle. A legislature, without exceeding its province, cannot reverse a determination once made in a particular case; though it may prescribe a new rule for future cases. This is the principle and it applies in all its consequences, exactly in the same manner and extent, to the State governments, as to the national government now under consideration. Not the least difference can be pointed out in any view of the subject.

It may in the last place be observed that the supposed danger of judiciary encroachments on the legislative authority which has been upon many occasions reiterated is in reality a phantom. Particular misconstructions and contraventions of the will of the legislature may now and then happen; but they can never be so extensive as to amount to an inconvenience, or in any sensible degree to affect the order of the political system. This may be inferred with certainty from the general nature of the judicial power, from the objects to which it relates, from the manner in which it is exercised, from its comparative weakness, and from its total incapacity to support its usurpations by force. And the inference is greatly fortified by the consideration of the important constitutional check which the power of instituting impeachments in one part of the legislative body, and of determining upon them in the other, would give to that body upon the members of the judicial department. This is alone a complete security. There never can be danger that the judges, by a series of deliberate usurpations on the authority of the legislature, would hazard the united resentment of the body intrusted with it, while this body was possessed of the means of punishing their presumption by degrading them from their stations. While this ought to remove all apprehensions on the subject it affords, at the same time, a cogent argument for constituting the Senate a court for the trial of impeachments.

Having now examined, and, I trust, removed the objections to the distinct and independent organization of the Supreme Court, I proceed to consider the propriety of the power of constituting inferior courts,* and the relations which will subsist between these and the former.

The power of constituting inferior courts is evidently calculated to obviate the necessity of having recourse to the Supreme Court in every case of federal cognizance. It is intended to enable the national government to institute or *authorize,* in each State or district of the United States, a tribunal competent to the determination of matters of national jurisdiction within its limits.

But why, it is asked, might not the same purpose have

* This power has been absurdly represented as intended to abolish all the county courts in the several States which are commonly called inferior courts. But the expressions of the Constitution are to constitute "tribunals INFERIOR TO THE SUPREME COURT"; and the evident design of the provision is to enable the institution of local courts, subordinate to the Supreme, either in States or larger districts. It is ridiculous to imagine that county courts were in contemplation.

been accomplished by the instrumentality of the State courts? This admits of different answers. Though the fitness and competency of those courts should be allowed in the utmost latitude, yet the substance of the power in question may still be regarded as a necessary part of the plan, if it were only to empower the national legislature to commit to them the cognizance of causes arising out of the national Constitution. To confer the power of determining such causes upon the existing courts of the several States would perhaps be as much "to constitute tribunals," as to create new courts with the like power. But ought not a more direct and explicit provision to have been made in favor of the State courts? There are, in my opinion, substantial reasons against such a provision: the most discerning cannot foresee how far the prevalency of a local spirit may be found to disqualify the local tribunals for the jurisdiction of national causes; whilst every man may discover that courts constituted like those of some of the States would be improper channels of the judicial authority of the Union. State judges, holding their offices during pleasure, or from year to year, will be too little independent to be relied upon for an inflexible execution of the national laws. And if there was a necessity for confiding the original cognizance of causes arising under those laws to them, there would be a correspondent necessity for leaving the door of appeal as wide as possible. In proportion to the grounds of confidence in or distrust of the subordinate tribunals ought to be the facility or difficulty of appeals. And well satisfied as I am of the propriety of the appellate jurisdiction in the several classes of causes to which it is extended, by the plan of the convention I should consider everything calculated to give, in practice, and *unrestrained course* to appeals, as a source of public and private inconvenience.

I am not sure but that it will be found highly expedient and useful to divide the United States into four or five or half a dozen districts, and to institute a federal court in each district in lieu of one in every State. The judges of these courts, with the aid of the State judges, may hold circuits for the trial of causes in the several parts of the respective districts. Justice through them may be administered with ease and dispatch and appeals may be safely circumscribed within a narrow compass. This plan appears to me at present the most eligible of any that could be adopted; and in order to it, it is necessary that the power of constituting inferior courts should exist in the full extent in which it is to be found in the proposed Constitution.

These reasons seem sufficient to satisfy a candid mind, that the want of such a power would have been a great defect in the plan. Let us now examine in what manner the judicial authority is to be distributed between the supreme and the inferior courts of the Union.

The Supreme Court is to be invested with original jurisdiction only "in cases affecting ambassadors, other public ministers, and consuls, and those in which A STATE shall be a party." Public ministers of every class are the immediate representatives of their sovereigns. All questions in which they are concerned are so directly connected with the public peace, that, as well for the preservation of this as out of respect to the sovereignties they represent, it is both expedient and proper that such questions should be submitted in the first instance to the highest judicatory of the nation. Though consuls have not in strictness a diplomatic character, yet, as they are the public agents of the nations to which they belong, the same observation is in a great measure applicable to them. In cases in which a State might happen to be a party, it would ill suit its dignity to be turned over to an inferior tribunal.

Though it may rather be a digression from the immediate subject of this paper, I shall take occasion to mention here a supposition which has excited some alarm upon very mistaken grounds. It has been suggested that an assignment of the public securities of one State to the citizens of another would enable them to prosecute that State in the federal courts for the amount of those securities; a suggestion which the following considerations prove to be without foundation.

It is inherent in the nature of sovereignty not to be amenable to the suit of an individual *without its consent*. This is the general sense and the general practice of mankind; and the exemption, as one of the attributes of sovereignty, is now enjoyed by the government of every State in the Union. Unless, therefore, there is a surrender of this immunity in the plan of the convention, it will remain with the States and the danger intimated must be merely ideal. The circumstances which are necessary to produce an alienation of State sovereignty were discussed in considering the article of taxation and need not be repeated here. A recurrence to the principles there established will satisfy us that there is no color to pretend that the State governments would, by the adoption of that plan, be divested of the privilege of paying their own debts in their own way, free from every constraint but that which flows from the obligations of good faith. The contracts between a nation and individuals are only binding on the conscience of the sovereign, and have no pretensions to a compulsive force. They confer no right of action independent of the sovereign will. To what purpose would it be to authorize suits against States for the debts they owe? How could recoveries be enforced? It is evident that it could not be done without waging war against the contracting State; and to ascribe to the federal courts, by mere implication, and in destruction of a pre-existing right of the State governments, a power which would involve such a consequence, would be altogether forced and unwarrantable.

Let us resume the train of our observations. We have seen that the original jurisdiction of the Supreme Court would be confined to two classes of cases, and those of a nature rarely to occur. In all other cases of federal cognizance the original jurisdiction would appertain to the inferior tribunals; and the Supreme Court would have nothing more than an appellate jurisdiction "with such *exceptions* and under such *regulations* as the Congress shall make."

The propriety of this appellate jurisdiction has been scarcely called in question in regard to matters of law; but the clamors have been loud against it as applied to matters of fact. Some well-intentioned men in this State, deriving their notions from the language and forms which obtain in our courts, have been induced to consider it as an implied supersedure of the trial by jury, in favor of the civil-law mode of trial, which prevails in our courts of admiralty, probate, and chancery. A technical sense has been affixed to the term "appellate" which, in our law parlance, is commonly used in reference to appeals in the course of the civil law. But if I am not misinformed, the same meaning would not be given to it in any part of New England. There, an appeal from one jury to another is familiar both in language and practice, and is even a matter of course until there have been two verdicts on one side. The word "appellate" therefore will not be understood in the same sense in New England as in New York, which shows the impropriety of a technical interpretation derived from the jurisprudence of any particular State. The expression, taken in the abstract, denotes nothing more than the power of one tribunal to review the proceedings of another, either as to the law or fact, or both. The mode of doing it may depend on ancient custom or legislative provision (in a new government it must depend on the latter), and may be with or without the aid of a jury, as may be judged advisable. If, therefore, the re-examination of a fact once determined by a jury should in any case be admitted under the proposed Constitution, it may be so regulated as to be done by a second jury, either by remanding the cause to the court below for a second trial of the fact, or by directing an issue immediately out of the Supreme Court.

But it does not follow that the re-examination of a fact once ascertained by a jury will be permitted in the Supreme Court. Why may not it be said, with the strictest propriety, when a writ of error is brought from an inferior to a superior court of law in this State, that the latter has jurisdiction of the fact as well as the law? It is true it cannot institute a new inquiry concerning the fact but it takes cognizance of it as it appears upon the record and pronounces the law arising upon it.* This is jurisdiction of both fact and law; nor is it even possible to separate them. Though the common-law courts of this State ascertain disputed facts by a jury, yet they unquestionably have jurisdiction of both fact and law; and accordingly when the former is agreed in the pleadings they have no recourse to a jury but proceed at once to judgment. I contend therefore, on this ground, that the expressions, "appellate jurisdiction, both as to law

* This word is composed of JUS and DICTO, *juris, dictio,* or a speaking or pronouncing of the law.

and fact," do not necessarily imply a re-examination in the Supreme Court of facts decided by juries in the inferior courts.

The following train of ideas may well be imagined to have influenced the convention in relation to this particular provision. The appellate jurisdiction of the Supreme Court (it may have been argued) will extend to causes determinable in different modes, some in the course of the COMMON LAW, others in the course of the CIVIL LAW. In the former, the revision of the law only will be, generally speaking, the proper province of the Supreme Court; in the latter, the re-examination of the fact is agreeable to usage, and in some cases, of which prize causes are an example, might be essential to the preservation of the public peace. It is therefore necessary that the appellate jurisdiction should, in certain cases, extend in the broadest sense to matters of fact. It will not answer to make an express exception of cases which shall have been originally tried by a jury because in the courts of some of the States *all causes* are tried in this mode; * and such an exception would preclude the revision of matters of fact, as well where it might be proper as where it might be improper. To avoid all inconveniences, it will be safest to declare generally that the Supreme Court shall possess appellate jurisdiction both as to law and *fact*, and that this jurisdiction shall be subject to such *exceptions* and regulations as the national legislature may prescribe. This will enable the government to modify it in such a manner as will best answer the ends of public justice and security.

This view of the matter, at any rate, puts it out of all doubt that the supposed *abolition* of the trial by jury, by the operation of this provision, is fallacious and untrue. The legislature of the United States would certainly have full power to provide that in appeals to the Supreme Court there should be no re-examination of facts where they had been tried in the original causes by juries. This would certainly be an authorized exception; but if, for the reason already intimated, it should be thought too

* I hold that the States will have concurrent jurisdiction with the subordinate federal judicatories in many cases of federal cognizance as will be explained in my next paper.

extensive, it might be qualified with a limitation to such causes only as are determinable at common law in that mode of trial.

The amount of the observations hitherto made on the authority of the judicial department is this: that it has been carefully restricted to those causes which are manifestly proper for the cognizance of the national judicature; that in the partition of this authority a very small portion of original jurisdiction has been reserved to the Supreme Court and the rest consigned to the subordinate tribunals; that the Supreme Court will possess an appellate jurisdiction, both as to law and fact, in all the cases referred to them, but subject to any *exceptions* and *regulations* which may be thought advisable; that this appellate jurisdiction does, in no case, *abolish* the trial by jury; and that an ordinary degree of prudence and integrity in the national councils will insure us solid advantages from the establishment of the proposed judiciary without exposing us to any of the inconveniences which have been predicted from that source.

PUBLIUS

No. 82: Hamilton

THE erection of a new government, whatever care or wisdom may distinguish the work, cannot fail to originate questions of intricacy and nicety; and these may, in a particular manner, be expected to flow from the establishment of a constitution founded upon the total or partial incorporation of a number of distinct sovereignties. 'Tis time only that can mature and perfect so compound a system, can liquidate the meaning of all the parts, and can adjust them to each other in a harmonious and consistent WHOLE.

Such questions, accordingly, have arisen upon the plan proposed by the convention, and particularly concerning the judiciary department. The principal of these respect the situation of the State courts in regard to those causes which are to be submitted to federal jurisdiction. Is this to be exclusive, or are those courts to possess a concurrent jurisdiction? If the latter, in what relation will they stand to the national tribunals? These are inquiries which we meet with in the mouths of men of sense, and which are certainly entitled to attention.

The principles established in a former paper * teach us that the States will retain all *pre-existing* authorities which may not be exclusively delegated to the federal head; and that this exclusive delegation can only exist in one of three cases: where an exclusive authority is, in express terms, granted to the Union; or where a particular authority is granted to the Union and the exercise of a like authority is prohibited to the States; or where an authority is granted to the Union with which a similar authority in the States would be utterly incompatible. Though these principles may not apply with the same force to the judiciary as to the legislative power, yet I am inclined to think that they are, in the main, just with respect to the former, as well as the latter. And under this impression, I shall lay it down as a rule that the State courts will *retain* the jurisdiction they now have, unless it appears to be taken away in one of the enumerated modes.

The only thing in the proposed Constitution, which wears the appearance of confining the causes of federal cognizance to the federal courts, is contained in this passage:—"THE JUDICIAL POWER of the United States *shall be vested* in one Supreme Court, and in *such* inferior courts as the Congress shall from time to time ordain and establish." This might either be construed to signify that the supreme and subordinate courts of the Union should alone have the power of deciding those causes to which their authority is to extend; or simply to denote that the organs of the national judiciary should be one Supreme Court, and as many subordinate courts as Congress should think proper to appoint; or in other words, that the United States should exercise the judicial power with which they are to be invested, through one supreme tribunal, and a certain number of inferior ones to be instituted by them. The first excludes, the last admits, the concurrent jurisdiction of the State tribunals; and as the first would amount to an alienation of State power by implication, the last appears to me the most natural and the most defensible construction.

* No. 32.

But this doctrine of concurrent jurisdiction is only clearly applicable to those descriptions of causes of which the State courts have previous cognizance. It is not equally evident in relation to cases which may grow out of, and be *peculiar* to, the Constitution to be established; for not to allow the State courts a right of jurisdiction in such cases can hardly be considered as the abridgement of a pre-existing authority. I mean not therefore to contend that the United States, in the course of legislation upon the objects intrusted to their direction, may not commit the decision of causes arising upon a particular regulation to the federal courts solely, if such a measure should be deemed expedient; but I hold that the State courts will be divested of no part of their primitive jurisdiction further than may relate to an appeal; and I am even of opinion that in every case in which they were not expressly excluded by the future acts of the national legislature, they will of course take cognizance of the causes to which those acts may give birth. This I infer from the nature of judiciary power, and from the general genius of the system. The judiciary power of every government looks beyond its own local or municipal laws, and in civil cases lays hold of all subjects of litigation between parties within its jurisdiction, though the causes of dispute are relative to the laws of the most distant part of the globe. Those of Japan, not less than of New York, may furnish the objects of legal discussion to our courts. When in addition to this we consider the State governments and the national governments, as they truly are, in the light of kindred systems, and as parts of ONE WHOLE, the inference seems to be conclusive that the State courts would have a concurrent jurisdiction in all cases arising under the laws of the Union where it was not expressly prohibited.

Here another questions occurs: What relation would subsist between the national and State courts in these instances of concurrent jurisdiction? I answer that an appeal would certainly lie from the latter to the Supreme Court of the United States. The Constitution in direct terms gives an appellate jurisdiction to the Supreme Court in all the enumerated cases of federal cognizance in which it is not to have an original one, without a single expression to confine its operation to the inferior federal courts. The objects of appeal, not the tribunals from which it is to be made, are alone contemplated. From this circumstance, and from the reason of the thing, it ought to be construed to extend to the State tribunals. Either this must be the case or the local courts must be excluded from a concurrent jurisdiction in matters of national concern, else the judiciary authority of the Union may be eluded at the pleasure of every plaintiff or prosecutor. Neither of these consequences ought, without evident necessity, to be involved; the latter would be entirely inadmissible, as it would defeat some of the most important and avowed purposes of the proposed government and would essentially embarrass its measures. Nor do I perceive any foundation for such a supposition. Agreeably to the remark already made, the national and State systems are to be regarded as ONE WHOLE. The courts of the latter will of course be natural auxiliaries to the execution of the laws of the Union, and an appeal from them will as naturally lie to that tribunal which is destined to unite and assimilate the principles of national justice and the rules of national decisions. The evident aim of the plan of the convention is that all the causes of the specified classes shall, for weighty public reasons, receive their original or final determination in the courts of the Union. To confine, therefore, the general expressions giving appellate jurisdiction to the Supreme Court to appeals from the subordinate federal courts, instead of allowing their extension to the State courts would be to abridge the latitude of the terms, in subversion of the intent, contrary to every sound rule of interpretation.

But could an appeal be made to lie from the State courts to the subordinate federal judicatories? This is another of the questions which have been raised, and of greater difficulty than the former. The following considerations countenance the affirmative. The plan of the convention, in the first place, authorizes the national legislature "to constitute tribunals inferior to the Supreme Court." * It declares, in the next place, that "the JUDICIAL POWER of the United States *shall be vested* in one

* Section 8, Article 1.

Supreme Court, and in such inferior courts as Congress shall ordain and establish"; and it then proceeds to enumerate the cases to which this judicial power shall extend. It afterwards divides the jurisdiction of the Supreme Court into original and appellate, but gives no definition of that of the subordinate courts. The only outlines described for them are that they shall be "inferior to the Supreme Court," and that they shall not exceed the specified limits of the federal judiciary. Whether their authority shall be original or appellate, or both, is not declared. All this seems to be left to the discretion of the legislature. And this being the case, I perceive at present no impediment to the establishment of an appeal from the State courts to the subordinate national tribunals; and many advantages attending the power of doing it may be imagined. It would diminish the motives to the multiplication of federal courts and would admit of arrangements calculated to contract the appellate jurisdiction of the Supreme Court. The State tribunals may then be left with a more entire charge of federal causes; and appeals, in most cases in which they may be deemed proper, instead of being carried to the Supreme Court may be made to lie from the State courts to district courts of the Union. PUBLIUS

No. 83: Hamilton

THE objection to the plan of the convention, which has met with most success in this State, and perhaps in several of the other States, is *that relative to the want of a constitutional provison* for the trial by jury in civil cases. The disingenuous form in which this objection is usually stated has been repeatedly adverted to and exposed but continues to be pursued in all the conversations and writings of the opponents of the plan. The mere silence of the Constitution in regard to *civil causes* is represented as an abolition of the trial by jury, and the declamations to which it has afforded a pretext are artfully calculated to induce a persuasion that this pretended abolition is complete and universal, extending not only to every species of civil but even to *criminal causes*. To argue with respect to the latter would, however, be as vain and fruitless as to attempt the serious proof of the *existence* of *matter,* or to demonstrate any of those propositions which, by their own internal evidence, force conviction when expressed in language adapted to convey their meaning.

With regard to civil causes, subtleties almost too contemptible for refutation have been adopted to countenance the surmise that a thing which is only *not provided for* is entirely *abolished.* Every man of discernment must at once perceive the wide difference between *silence* and *abolition.* But as the inventors of this fallacy have attempted to support it by certain *legal maxims* of interpretation which they have perverted from their true meaning, it may not be wholly useless to explore the ground they have taken.

The maxims on which they rely are of this nature: "A specification of particulars is an exclusion of generals"; or, "The expression of one thing is the exclusion of another." Hence, say they, as the Constitution has established the trial by jury in criminal cases and is silent in respect to civil, this silence is an implied prohibition of trial by jury in regard to the latter.

The rules of legal interpretation are rules of *common sense,* adopted by the courts in the construction of the laws. The true test, therefore, of a just application of them is its conformity to the source from which they are derived. This being the case, let me ask if it is consistent with reason or common sense to suppose that a provision obliging the legislative power to commit the trial of criminal causes to juries is a privation of its right to authorize or permit that mode of trial in other cases? Is it natural to suppose that a command to do one thing is a prohibition to the doing of another, which there was a previous power to do, and which is not incompatible with the thing commanded to be done? If such a supposition would be unnatural and unreasonable, it cannot be rational to maintain that an injunction of the trial by jury in certain cases is an interdiction of it in others.

A power to constitute courts is a power to prescribe the mode of trial; and consequently, if nothing was said in the Constitution on the subject of juries, the legislature would be at liberty either to adopt that institution or to let it alone. This discretion, in regard to criminal causes, is abridged by the express injunction of trial by jury in all such cases; but it is, of course, left at large in relation to civil causes, there being a total silence on this head. The specification of an obligation to try all criminal causes in a particular mode excludes indeed the obligation or necessity of employing the same mode in civil causes, but does not abridge *the power* of the legislature to exercise that mode if it should be thought proper. The pretense, therefore, that the national legislature would not be at full liberty to submit all the civil causes of federal cognizance to the determination of juries is a pretense destitute of all just foundation.

From these observations this conclusion results: that the trial by jury in civil cases would not be abolished; and that the use attempted to be made of the maxims which have been quoted is contrary to reason and common sense, and therefore not admissible. Even if these maxims had a precise technical sense, corresponding with the ideas of those who employ them upon the present occasion, which, however, is not the case, they would still be inapplicable to a constitution of government. In relation to such a subject, the natural and obvious sense of its provisions, apart from any technical rules, is the true criterion of construction.

Having now seen that the maxims relied upon will not bear the use made of them, let us endeavor to ascertain their proper use and true meaning. This will be best done by examples. The plan of the convention declares that the power of Congress, or, in other words, of the *national legislature,* shall extend to certain enumerated cases. This specification of particulars evidently excludes all pretension to a general legislative authority, because an affirmative grant of special powers would be absurd as well as useless if a general authority was intended.

In like manner the judicial authority of the federal judicatures is declared by the Constitution to comprehend certain cases particularly specified. The expression of those cases marks the precise limits beyond which the federal courts cannot extend their jurisdiction, because the objects of their cognizance being enumerated, the specification would be nugatory if it did not exclude all ideas of more extensive authority.

These examples might be sufficient to elucidate the maxims which have been mentioned, and to designate the manner in which they should be used. But that there may be no possibility of misapprehension upon this subject, I shall add one case more, to demonstrate the proper use of these maxims, and the abuse which has been made of them.

Let us suppose that by the laws of this State a married woman was incapable of conveying her estate, and that the legislature, considering this as an evil, should enact that she might dispose of her property by deed executed in the presence of a magistrate. In such a case there can be no doubt but the specification would amount to an exclusion of any other mode of conveyance, because the woman having no previous power to alienate her property, the specification determines the particular mode which she is, for that purpose, to avail herself of. But let us further suppose that in a subsequent part of the same act it should be declared that no woman should dispose of any estate of a determinate value without the consent of three of her nearest relations, signified by their signing the deed; could it be inferred from this regulation that a married woman might not procure the approbation of her relations to a deed for conveying property of inferior value? The position is too absurd to merit a refutation, and yet this is precisely the position which those must establish who contend that the trial by juries in civil cases is abolished, because it is expressly provided for in cases of a criminal nature.

From these observations it must appear unquestionably true that trial by jury is in no case abolished by the proposed Constitution, and it is equally true that in those controversies between individuals in which the great body of the people are likely to be interested, that institution will remain precisely in the same situation in which it is placed by the State constitutions, and will be in no degree altered or influenced by the adoption of the plan under consideration. The foundation of this assertion is that the national judiciary will have no cognizance of them, and of course they will remain determinable as heretofore by the State courts only, and in the manner which the State constitutions and laws prescribe. All land causes, except where claims under the grants of different States come into question, and all other controversies between the citizens of the same State, unless where they depend upon positive violations of the articles of union by acts of the State legislatures, will belong exclusively to the jurisdiction of the State tribunals. Add to this that admiralty causes, and almost all those which are of equity jurisdiction, are determinable under our own government without the intervention of a jury, and the inference from the whole will be that this institution, as it exists with us at present, cannot possibly be affected to any great extent by the proposed alteration in our system of government.

The friends and adversaries of the plan of the convention, if they agree in nothing else, concur at least in the value they set upon the trial by jury; or if there is any difference between them it consists in this: the former regard it as a valuable safeguard to liberty; the latter represent it as the very palladium of free government. For my own part, the more the operation of the institution has fallen under my observation, the more reason I have discovered for holding it in high estimation; and it would be altogether superfluous to examine to what extent it deserves to be esteemed useful or essential in a representative republic, or how much more merit it may be entitled to as a defense against the oppressions of an hereditary monarch, than as a barrier to the tyranny of popular magistrates in a popular government. Discussions of this kind would be more curious than beneficial, as all are satisfied of the utility of the institution, and of its friendly aspect to liberty. But I must acknowledge that I cannot readily discern the inseparable connection between the existence of liberty and the trial by jury in civil cases. Arbitrary impeachments, arbitrary methods of prosecuting pretended offenses, and arbitrary punishments upon arbitrary convictions have ever appeared to me to be the great engines of judicial despotism; and these have all relation to criminal proceedings. The trial by jury in criminal cases, aided by the *habeas corpus* act, seems therefore to be alone concerned in the question. And both of these are provided for in the most ample manner in the plan of the convention.

It has been observed that trial by jury is a safeguard against an oppressive exercise of the power of taxation. This observation deserves to be canvassed.

It is evident that it can have no influence upon the legislature in regard to the *amount* of taxes to be laid, to the *objects* upon which they are to be imposed, or to the *rule* by which they are to be apportioned. If it can have any influence, therefore, it must be upon the mode of collection and the conduct of the officers intrusted with the execution of the revenue laws.

As to the mode of collection in this State, under our own Constitution the trial by jury is in most cases out of use. The taxes are usually levied by the more summary proceeding of distress and sale, as in cases of rent. And it is acknowledged on all hands that this is essential to the efficacy of the revenue laws. The dilatory course of a trial at law to recover the taxes imposed on individuals would neither suit the exigencies of the public nor promote the convenience of the citizens. It would often occasion an accumulation of costs, more burdensome than the original sum of the tax to be levied.

And as to the conduct of the officers of the revenue, the provision in favor of trial by jury in criminal cases will afford the security aimed at. Wilful abuses of a public authority, to the oppression of the subject, and every species of official extortion, are offenses against the government, for which the persons who commit them may be indicted and punished according to the circumstances of the case.

The excellence of the trial by jury in civil cases appears to depend on circumstances foreign to the preservation of liberty. The strongest argument in its favor is that it is a security against corruption. As there is always more time and better opportunity to tamper with a standing body of magistrates than with a jury summoned for the occasion, there is room to suppose that a corrupt influence would more easily find its way to the former than to the latter. The force of this consideration is, however, diminished by others. The sheriff, who is the summoner of ordinary juries, and the clerks of courts, who have the nomination of special juries, are themselves standing officers, and, acting individually, may be supposed more accessible to the touch of corruption than the judges, who are a collective body. It is not difficult to see that it would be in the power of those officers to select jurors who would serve the purpose of the party as well as a corrupted bench. In the next place, it may fairly be supposed that there would be less difficulty in gaining some of the jurors promiscuously taken from the public mass, than in gaining men who had been chosen by the government for their probity and good character. But making every deduction for these considerations, the trial by jury must still be a valuable check upon corruption. It greatly multiplies the impediments to its success. As matters now stand, it would be necessary to corrupt both court and jury; for where the jury have gone evidently wrong, the court will generally grant a new trial, and it would be in most cases of little use to practice upon the jury unless the court could be likewise gained. Here then is a double security; and it will readily be perceived that this complicated agency tends to preserve the purity of both institutions. By increasing the obstacles to success, it discourages attempts to seduce the integrity of either. The temptations to prostitution which the judges might have to surmount must certainly be much fewer, while the co-operation of a jury is necessary, than they might be if they had themselves the exclusive determination of all causes.

Notwithstanding, therefore, the doubts I have expressed as to the essentiality of trial by jury in civil cases to liberty, I admit that it is in most cases, under proper regulations, an excellent method of determining questions of property; and that on this account alone it would be entitled to a constitutional provision in its favor if it were possible to fix the limits within which it ought to be comprehended. There is, however, in all cases, great difficulty in this; and men not blinded by enthusiasm must be sensible that in a federal government, which is a composition of societies whose ideas and institutions in relation to the matter materially vary from each other, that difficulty must be not a little augmented. For my own part, at every new view I take of the subject I become more convinced of the reality of the obstacles which, we are authoritatively informed, prevented the insertion of a provision on this head in the plan of the convention.

The great difference between the limits of the jury trial in different States is not generally understood; and as it must have considerable influence on the sentence we ought to pass upon the omission complained of in regard to this point, an explanation of it is necessary. In this State, our judicial establishments resemble, more nearly than in any other, those of Great Britain. We have courts of common law, courts of probates (analogous in certain matters to the spiritual courts in England), a court of admiralty, and a court of chancery. In the courts of common law only, the trial by jury prevails, and this with some exceptions. In all the others a single judge presides, and proceeds in general either according to the course of the canon or civil law, without the aid of a jury.* In New Jersey, there is a court of chancery which proceeds like ours, but neither courts of admiralty nor of probates, in the sense in which these last are established with us. In that State the courts of common law have the cognizance of those causes which with us are determinable in the courts of admiralty and of probates, and of course the jury trial is more extensive in New Jersey than in New York. In Pennsylvania, this is perhaps still more the case, for there is no court of chancery in that State, and its common-law courts have equity jurisdiction. It has a court of admiralty, but none of probates, at least on the plan of ours. Delaware has in these respects imitated Pennsylvania. Maryland approaches more nearly to New York, as does also Virginia, except that the latter has a plurality of chancellors. North Carolina bears most affinity to Pennsylvania; South Carolina to Virginia. I believe, however, that in some of those States which have distinct courts of admiralty, the causes depending in them are triable by juries. In Georgia there are none but common-law courts, and an appeal of course lies from the verdict of one jury to another, which is called a special jury, and for which a particular mode of appointment is marked out. In Connecticut, they have no distinct courts either of chancery or of admiralty, and their courts of probates have no jurisdiction of causes. Their common-law courts have admiralty and, to a certain extent, equity jurisdic-

* It has been erroneously insinuated, with regard to the court of chancery, that this court generally tries disputed facts by a jury. The truth is that references to a jury in that court rarely happen, and are in no case necessary but where the validity of a devise of land comes into question.

tion. In cases of importance, their General Assembly is the only court of chancery. In Connecticut, therefore, the trial by jury extends in *practice* further than in any other State yet mentioned. Rhode Island is, I believe, in this particular, pretty much in the situation of Connecticut. Massachusetts and New Hampshire, in regard to the blending of law, equity, and admiralty jurisdictions, are in a similar predicament. In the four Eastern States, the trial by jury not only stands upon a broader foundation than in the other States, but it is attended with a peculiarity unknown, in its full extent, to any of them. There is an appeal *of course* from one jury to another, till there have been two verdicts out of three on one side.

From this sketch it appears that there is a material diversity, as well in the modification as in the extent of the institution of trial by jury in civil cases, in the several States; and from this fact these obvious reflections flow: first, that no general rule could have been fixed upon by the convention which would have corresponded with the circumstances of all the States; and secondly, that more or at least as much might have been hazarded by taking the system of any one State for a standard, as by omitting a provision altogether and leaving the matter, as it has been left, to legislative regulation.

The propositions which have been made for supplying the omission have rather served to illustrate than to obviate the difficulty of the thing. The minority of Pennsylvania have proposed this mode of expression for the purpose—"Trial by jury shall be as heretofore"—and this I maintain would be absolutely senseless and nugatory. The United States, in their united or collective capacity, are the OBJECT to which all general provisions in the Constitution must necessarily be construed to refer. Now it is evident that though trial by jury, with various limitations, is known in each State individually, yet in the United States, *as such,* it is at this time altogether unknown because the present federal government has no judiciary power whatever; and consequently there is no proper antecedent or previous establishment to which the term *heretofore* could relate. It would therefore be destitute of a precise meaning, and inoperative from its uncertainty.

As, on the one hand, the form of the provision would

not fulfil the intent of its proposers, so, on the other, if I apprehend that intent rightly, it would be in itself inexpedient. I presume it to be that causes in the federal courts should be tried by jury, if, in the State where the courts sat, that mode of trial would obtain in a similar case in the State courts; that is to say, admiralty causes should be tried in Connecticut by a jury, in New York without one. The capricious operation of so dissimilar a method of trial in the same cases, under the same government, is of itself sufficient to indispose every well-regulated judgment towards it. Whether the cause should be tried with or without a jury would depend, in a great number of cases, on the accidental situation of the court and parties.

But this is not, in my estimation, the greatest objection. I feel a deep and deliberate conviction that there are many cases in which the trial by jury is an ineligible one. I think it so particularly in cases which concern the public peace with foreign nations—that is, in most cases where the question turns wholly on the laws of nations. Of this nature, among others, are all prize causes. Juries cannot be supposed competent to investigations that require a thorough knowledge of the laws and usages of nations; and they will sometimes be under the influence of impressions which will not suffer them to pay sufficient regard to those considerations of public policy which ought to guide their inquiries. There would of course be always danger that the rights of other nations might be infringed by their decisions so as to afford occasions of reprisal and war. Though the proper province of juries be to determine matters of fact, yet in most cases legal consequences are complicated with fact in such a manner as to render a separation impracticable.

It will add great weight to this remark, in relation to prize causes, to mention that the method of determining them has been thought worthy of particular regulation in various treaties between different powers of Europe, and that, pursuant to such treaties, they are determinable in Great Britain, in the last resort, before the king himself, in his privy council, where the fact, as well as the law, undergoes a re-examination. This alone demonstrates the impolicy of inserting a fundamental provision in the Constitution which would make the State systems a standard for the national government in the article under consideration, and the danger of encumbering the government with any constitutional provisions the propriety of which is not indisputable.

My convictions are equally strong that great advantages result from the separation of the equity from the law jurisdiction, and that the causes which belong to the former would be improperly committed to juries. The great and primary use of a court of equity is to give relief *in extraordinary cases,* which are *exceptions* * to general rules. To unite the jurisdiction of such cases with the ordinary jurisdiction must have a tendency to unsettle the general rules, and to subject every case that arises to a *special* determination; while a separation of the one from the other has the contrary effect of rendering one a sentinel over the other, and of keeping each within the expedient limits. Besides this, the circumstances that constitute cases proper for courts of equity are in many instances so nice and intricate that they are incompatible with the genius of trials by jury. They require often such long, deliberate, and critical investigation as would be impracticable to men called from their occupations, and obliged to decide before they were permitted to return to them. The simplicity and expedition which form the distinguishing characters of this mode of trial require that the matter to be decided should be reduced to some single and obvious point; while the litigations usual in chancery frequently comprehend a long train of minute and independent particulars.

It is true that the separation of the equity from the legal jurisdiction is peculiar to the English system of jurisprudence, which is the model that has been followed in several of the States. But it is equally true that the trial by jury has been unknown in every case in which they have been united. And the separation is essential to the preservation of that institution in its pristine purity. The nature of a court of equity will readily permit the extension of its jurisdiction to matters of law; but it is

* It is true that the principles by which that relief is governed are now reduced to a regular system; but it is not the less true that they are in the main applicable to SPECIAL circumstances, which form exceptions to general rules.

not a little to be suspected that the attempt to extend the jurisdiction of the courts of law to matters of equity will not only be unproductive of the advantages which may be derived from courts of chancery, on the plan upon which they are established in this State, but will tend gradually to change the nature of the courts of law, and to undermine the trial by jury, by introducing questions too complicated for a decision in that mode.

These appeared to be conclusive reasons against incorporating the systems of all the States in the formation of the national judiciary, according to what may be conjectured to have been the attempt of the Pennsylvania minority. Let us now examine how far the proposition of Massachusetts is calculated to remedy the supposed defect.

It is in this form: "In civil actions between citizens of different States, every issue of fact arising in *actions at common law* may be tried by a jury if the parties, or either of them, request it."

This, at best, is a proposition confined to one description of causes; and the inference is fair, either that the Massachusetts convention considered that as the only class of federal causes in which the trial by jury would be proper; or that if desirous of a more extensive provision, they found it impracticable to devise one which would properly answer the end. If the first, the omission of a regulation respecting so partial an object can never be considered as a material imperfection in the system. If the last, it affords a strong corroboration of the extreme difficulty of the thing.

But this is not all: if we advert to the observations already made respecting the courts that subsist in the several States of the Union, and the different powers exercised by them, it will appear that there are no expressions more vague and indeterminate than those which have been employed to characterize *that* species of causes which it is intended shall be entitled to a trial by jury. In this State, the boundaries between actions at common law and actions of equitable jurisdiction are ascertained in conformity to the rules which prevail in England upon that subject. In many of the other States the boundaries are less precise. In some of them, every cause is to be tried in a court of common law, and upon that foundation every action may be considered as an action at common law, to be determined by a jury, if the parties, or either of them, choose it. Hence the same irregularity and confusion would be introduced by a compliance with this proposition that I have already noticed as resulting from the regulation proposed by the Pennsylvania minority. In one State a cause would receive its determination from a jury, if the parties, or either of them, requested it; but in another State a cause exactly similar to the other must be decided without the intervention of a jury, because the State judicatories varied as to common-law jurisdiction.

It is obvious, therefore, that the Massachusetts proposition upon this subject cannot operate as a general regulation until some uniform plan, with respect to the limits of common-law and equitable jurisdictions, shall be adopted by the different States. To devise a plan of that kind is a task arduous in itself, and which it would require much time and reflection to mature. It would be extremely difficult, if not impossible, to suggest any general regulation that would be acceptable to all the States in the Union, or that would perfectly quadrate with the several State institutions.

It may be asked, Why could not a reference have been made to the constitution of this State, taking that which is allowed by me to be a good one, as a standard for the United States? I answer that it is not very probable the other States would entertain the same opinion of our institutions as we do ourselves. It is natural to suppose that they are hitherto more attached to their own, and that each would struggle for the preference. If the plan of taking one State as a model for the whole had been thought of in the convention, it is to be presumed that the adoption of it in that body would have been rendered difficult by the predilection of each representation in favor of its own government; and it must be uncertain which of the States would have been taken as the model. It has been shown that many of them would be improper ones. And I leave it to conjecture whether under all circumstances it is most likely that New York, or some other State, would have been preferred. But admit that a judicious selection could have been effected in the convention, still there would have been great danger of jealousy and disgust in the other States at the partiality which had been shown to the institutions of one. The enemies of the plan would have been furnished with a fine pretext for raising a host of local prejudices against it which perhaps might have hazarded, in no inconsiderable degree, its final establishment.

To avoid the embarrassment of a definition of the cases which the trial by jury ought to embrace, it is sometimes suggested by men of enthusiastic tempers that a provision might have been inserted for establishing it in all cases whatsoever. For this, I believe, no precedent is to be found in any member of the Union; and the considerations which have been stated in discussing the proposition of the minority of Pennsylvania must satisfy every sober mind that the establishment of the trial by jury in *all* cases would have been an unpardonable error in the plan.

In short, the more it is considered the more arduous will appear the task of fashioning a provision in such a form as not to express too little to answer the purpose, or too much to be advisable; or which might not have opened other sources of opposition to the great and essential object of introducing a firm national government.

I cannot but persuade myself, on the other hand, that the different lights in which the subject has been placed in the course of these observations will go far towards removing in candid minds the apprehensions they may have entertained on the point. They have tended to show that the security of liberty is materially concerned only in the trial by jury in criminal cases which is provided for in the most ample manner in the plan of the convention; that even in far the greatest proportion of civil cases, and those in which the great body of the community is interested, that mode of trial will remain in its full force as established in the State constitutions, untouched and unaffected by the plan of the convention; that it is in no case abolished* by that plan; and that there are great if not insurmountable difficulties in the

* *Vide* No. 81 in which the supposition of its being abolished by the appellate jurisdiction in matters of fact being vested in the Supreme Court is examined and refuted.

way of making any precise and proper provision for it in a Constitution for the United States.

The best judges of the matter will be the least anxious for a constitutional establishment of the trial by jury in civil cases, and will be the most ready to admit that the changes which are continually happening in the affairs of society may render a different mode of determining questions of property preferable in many cases in which that mode of trial now prevails. For my own part, I acknowledge myself to be convinced that even in this State it might be advantageously extended to some cases to which it does not at present apply and might as advantageously be abridged in others. It is conceded by all reasonable men that it ought not to obtain in all cases. The examples of innovations which contract its ancient limits as well in these States as in Great Britain afford a strong presumption that its former extent has been found inconvenient, and give room to suppose that future experience may discover the propriety and utility of other exceptions. I suspect it to be impossible in the nature of the thing to fix the salutary point at which the operation of the institution ought to stop, and this is with me a strong argument for leaving the matter to the discretion of the legislature.

This is now clearly understood to be the case in Great Britain, and it is equally so in the State of Connecticut; and yet it may be safely affirmed that more numerous encroachments have been made upon the trial by jury in this State since the Revolution, though provided for by a positive article of our Constitution, than has happened in the same time either in Connecticut or Great Britain. It may be added that these encroachments have generally originated with the men who endeavor to persuade the people they are the warmest defenders of popular liberty, but who have rarely suffered constitutional obstacles to arrest them in a favorite career. The truth is that the general GENIUS of a government is all that can be substantially relied upon for permanent effects. Particular provisions, though not altogether useless, have far less virtue and efficacy than are commonly ascribed to them; and the want of them will never be, with men of sound discernment, a decisive objection to any plan which exhibits the leading characters of a good government.

It certainly sounds not a little harsh and extraordinary to affirm that there is no security for liberty in a Constitution which expressly establishes the trial by jury in criminal cases, because it does not do it in civil also; while it is a notorious fact that Connecticut, which has been always regarded as the most popular State in the Union, can boast of no constitutional provision for either.

PUBLIUS

No. 84: Hamilton

IN THE course of the foregoing review of the Constitution, I have taken notice of, and endeavored to answer most of the objections which have appeared against it. There however remain a few which either did not fall naturally under any particular head or were forgotten in their proper places. These shall now be discussed; but as the subject has been drawn into great length, I shall so far consult brevity as to comprise all my observations on these miscellaneous points in a single paper.

The most considerable of these remaining objections is that the plan of the convention contains no bill of rights. Among other answers given to this, it has been upon different occasions remarked that the constitutions of several of the States are in a similar predicament. I add that New York is of this number. And yet the opposers of the new system, in this State, who profess an unlimited admiration for its constitution, are among the most intemperate partisans of a bill of rights. To justify their zeal in this matter they allege two things: one is that, though the constitution of New York has no bill of rights prefixed to it, yet it contains, in the body of it, various provisions in favor of particular privileges and rights which, in substance, amount to the same thing; the other is that the Constitution adopts, in their full extent, the common and statute law of Great Britain, by which many other rights not expressed in it are equally secured.

To the first I answer that the Constitution proposed by the convention contains, as well as the constitution of this State, a number of such provisions.

Independent of those which relate to the structure of

the government, we find the following: Article 1, section 3, clause 7—"Judgment in cases of impeachment shall not extend further than to removal from office and disqualification to hold and enjoy any office of honor, trust, or profit under the United States; but the party convicted shall, nevertheless, be liable and subject to indictment, trial, judgment, and punishment according to law." Section 9, of the same article, clause 2—"The privilege of the writ of *habeas corpus* shall not be suspended, unless when in cases of rebellion or invasion the public safety may require it." Clause 3—"No bill of attainder or *ex post facto* law shall be passed." Clause 7—"No title of nobility shall be granted by the United States; and no person holding any office of profit or trust under them shall, without the consent of the Congress, accept of any present, emolument, office, or title of any kind whatever, from any king, prince, or foreign state." Article 3, section 2, clause 3—"The trial of all crimes, except in cases of impeachment, shall be by jury; and such trial shall be held in the State where the said crimes shall have been committed; but when not committed within any State, the trial shall be at such place or places as the Congress may by law have directed." Section 3, of the same article—"Treason against the United States shall consist only in levying war against them, or in adhering to their enemies, giving them aid and comfort. No person shall be convicted of treason, unless on the testimony of two witnesses to the same overt act, or on confession in open court." And clause 3, of the same section—"The Congress shall have power to declare the punishment of treason; but no attainder of treason shall work corruption of blood, or forfeiture, except during the life of the person attainted."

It may well be a question whether these are not, upon the whole, of equal importance with any which are to be found in the constitution of this State. The establishment of the writ of *habeas corpus,* the prohibition of *ex post facto* laws, and of TITLES OF NOBILITY, *to which we have no corresponding provision in our Constitution,* are perhaps greater securities to liberty and republicanism than any it contains. The creation of crimes after the commission of the fact, or, in other words, the subjecting of men to punishment for things which, when they were done, were breaches of no law, and the practice of arbitrary imprisonments, have been, in all ages, the favorite and most formidable instruments of tyranny. The observations of the judicious Blackstone,* in reference to the latter, are well worthy of recital: "To bereave a man of life [says he] or by violence to confiscate his estate, without accusation or trial, would be so gross and notorious an act of despotism as must at once convey the alarm of tyranny throughout the whole nation; but confinement of the person, by secretly hurrying him to jail, where his sufferings are unknown or forgotten, is a less public, a less striking, and therefore a *more dangerous engine* of arbitrary government." And as a remedy for this fatal evil he is everywhere peculiarly emphatical in his encomiums on the *habeas corpus* act, which in one place he calls "the BULWARK of the British Constitution." †

Nothing need be said to illustrate the importance of the prohibition of titles of nobility. This may truly be denominated the cornerstone of republican government; for so long as they are excluded there can never be serious danger that the government will be any other than that of the people.

To the second, that is, to the pretended establishment of the common and statute law by the Constitution, I answer that they are expressly made subject "to such alterations and provisions as the legislature shall from time to time make concerning the same." They are therefore at any moment liable to repeal by the ordinary legislative power, and of course have no constitutional sanction. The only use of the declaration was to recognize the ancient law and to remove doubts which might have been occasioned by the Revolution. This consequently can be considered as no part of a declaration of rights, which under our constitutions must be intended as limitations of the power of the government itself.

It has been several times truly remarked that bills of rights are, in their origin, stipulations between kings and their subjects, abridgments of prerogative in favor of privilege, reservations of rights not surrendered to the

* *Vide* Blackstone's *Commentaries,* Vol. 1, Page 136.
† Idem, Vol. 4, Page 438.

prince. Such was MAGNA CHARTA, obtained by the barons, sword in hand, from King John. Such were the subsequent confirmations of that charter by subsequent princes. Such was the *Petition of Right* assented to by Charles the First in the beginning of his reign. Such, also, was the Declaration of Right presented by the Lords and Commons to the Prince of Orange in 1688, and afterwards thrown into the form of an act of Parliament called the Bill of Rights. It is evident, therefore, that, according to their primitive signification, they have no application to constitutions, professedly founded upon the power of the people and executed by their immediate representatives and servants. Here, in strictness, the people surrender nothing; and as they retain everything they have no need of particular reservations, "WE, THE PEOPLE of the United States, to secure the blessings of liberty to ourselves and our posterity, do *ordain* and *establish* this Constitution for the United States of America." Here is a better recognition of popular rights than volumes of those aphorisms which make the principal figure in several of our State bills of rights and which would sound much better in a treatise of ethics than in a constitution of government.

But a minute detail of particular rights is certainly far less applicable to a Constitution like that under consideration, which is merely intended to regulate the general political interests of the nation, than to a constitution which has the regulation of every species of personal and private concerns. If, therefore, the loud clamors against the plan of the convention, on this score, are well founded, no epithets of reprobation will be too strong for the constitution of this State. But the truth is that both of them contain all which, in relation to their objects, is reasonably to be desired.

I go further and affirm that bills of rights, in the sense and to the extent in which they are contended for, are not only unnecessary in the proposed Constitution but would even be dangerous. They would contain various exceptions to powers which are not granted; and, on this very account, would afford a colorable pretext to claim more than were granted. For why declare that things shall not be done which there is no power to do? Why, for instance, should it be said that the liberty of the press shall not be restrained, when no power is given by which restrictions may be imposed? I will not contend that such a provision would confer a regulating power; but it is evident that it would furnish, to men disposed to usurp, a plausible pretense for claiming that power. They might urge with a semblance of reason that the Constitution ought not to be charged with the absurdity of providing against the abuse of an authority which was not given, and that the provision against restraining the liberty of the press afforded a clear implication that a power to prescribe proper regulations concerning it was intended to be vested in the national government. This may serve as a specimen of the numerous handles which would be given to the doctrine of constructive powers, by the indulgence of an injudicious zeal for bills of rights.

On the subject of the liberty of the press, as much as has been said, I cannot forbear adding a remark or two: in the first place, I observe, that there is not a syllable concerning it in the constitution of this State; in the next, I contend that whatever has been said about it in that of any other State amounts to nothing. What signifies a declaration that "the liberty of the press shall be inviolably preserved"? What is the liberty of the press? Who can give it any definition which would not leave the utmost latitude for evasion? I hold it to be impracticable; and from this I infer that its security, whatever fine declarations may be inserted in any constitution respecting it, must altogether depend on public opinion, and on the general spirit of the people and of the government.*

* To show that there is a power in the Constitution by which the liberty of the press may be affected, recourse has been had to the power of taxation. It is said that duties may be laid upon the publications so high as to amount to a prohibition. I know not by what logic it could be maintained that the declarations in the State constitutions, in favor of the freedom of the press, would be a constitutional impediment to the imposition of duties upon publications by the State legislatures. It cannot certainly be pretended that any degree of duties, however low, would be an abridgment of the liberty of the press. We know that newspapers are taxed in Great Britain, and yet it is notorious that the press nowhere enjoys greater liberty than in that country. And if duties of any kind may be laid without a violation of that liberty, it is evident that the extent must depend on legislative discretion, regulated by public opinion; so that, after all, general declarations respecting the liberty of the press will give it no greater security than it will have without them. The same invasions of it may be

And here, after all, as is intimated upon another occasion, must we seek for the only solid basis of all our rights.

There remains but one other view of this matter to conclude the point. The truth is, after all the declamations we have heard, that the Constitution is itself, in every rational sense, and to every useful purpose, A BILL OF RIGHTS. The several bills of rights in Great Britain form its Constitution, and conversely the constitution of each State is its bill of rights. And the proposed Constitution, if adopted, will be the bill of rights of the Union. Is it one object of a bill of rights to declare and specify the political privileges of the citizens in the structure and administration of the government? This is done in the most ample and precise manner in the plan of the convention; comprehending various precautions for the public security which are not to be found in any of the State constitutions. Is another object of a bill of rights to define certain immunities and modes of proceeding, which are relative to personal and private concerns? This we have seen has also been attended to in a variety of cases in the same plan. Adverting therefore to the substantial meaning of a bill of rights, it is absurd to allege that it is not to be found in the work of the convention. It may be said that it does not go far enough though it will not be easy to make this appear; but it can with no propriety be contended that there is no such thing. It certainly must be immaterial what mode is observed as to the order of declaring the rights of the citizens if they are to be found in any part of the instrument which establishes the government. And hence it must be apparent that much of what has been said on this subject rests merely on verbal and nominal distinctions, entirely foreign from the substance of the thing.

Another objection which has been made, and which, from the frequency of its repetition, it is to be presumed is relied on, is of this nature: "It is improper [say the

---

effected under the State constitutions which contain those declarations through the means of taxation, as under the proposed Constitution, which has nothing of the kind. It would be quite as significant to declare that government ought to be free, that taxes ought not to be excessive, etc., as that the liberty of the press ought not to be restrained.

objectors] to confer such large powers as are proposed upon the national government, because the seat of that government must of necessity be too remote from many of the States to admit of a proper knowledge on the part of the constituent of the conduct of the representative body." This argument, if it proves anything, proves that there ought to be no general government whatever. For the powers which, it seems to be agreed on all hands, ought to be vested in the Union, cannot be safely intrusted to a body which is not under every requisite control. But there are satisfactory reasons to show that the objection is in reality not well founded. There is in most of the arguments which relate to distance a palpable illusion of the imagination. What are the sources of information by which the people in Montgomery County must regulate their judgment of the conduct of their representatives in the State legislature? Of personal observation they can have no benefit. This is confined to the citizens on the spot. They must therefore depend on the information of intelligent men, in whom they confide; and how must these men obtain their information? Evidently from the complexion of public measures, from the public prints, from correspondences with their representatives, and with other persons who reside at the place of their deliberations. This does not apply to Montgomery County only, but to all the counties at any considerable distance from the seat of government.

It is equally evident that the same sources of information would be open to the people in relation to the conduct of their representatives in the general government, and the impediments to a prompt communication which distance may be supposed to create will be overbalanced by the effects of the vigilance of the State governments. The executive and legislative bodies of each State will be so many sentinels over the persons employed in every department of the national administration; and as it will be in their power to adopt and pursue a regular and effectual system of intelligence, they can never be at a loss to know the behavior of those who represent their constituents in the national councils, and can readily communicate the same knowledge to the people. Their disposition to apprise the community of whatever may prejudice its interests from another quarter may be relied upon, if it were only from the rivalship of power. And we may conclude with the fullest assurance that the people, through that channel, will be better informed of the conduct of their national representatives than they can be by any means they now possess, of that of their State representatives.

It ought also to be remembered that the citizens who inhabit the country at and near the seat of government will, in all questions that affect the general liberty and prosperity, have the same interest with those who are at a distance, and that they will stand ready to sound the alarm when necessary, and to point out the actors in any pernicious project. The public papers will be expeditious messengers of intelligence to the most remote inhabitants of the Union.

Among the many extraordinary objections which have appeared against the proposed Constitution, the most extraordinary and the least colorable one is derived from the want of some provision respecting the debts due *to* the United States. This has been represented as a tacit relinquishment of those debts, and as a wicked contrivance to screen public defaulters. The newspapers have teemed with the most inflammatory railings on this head; and yet there is nothing clearer than that the suggestion is entirely void of foundation, and is the offspring of extreme ignorance or extreme dishonesty. In addition to the remarks I have made upon the subject in another place, I shall only observe that as it is a plain dictate of common sense, so it is also an established doctrine of political law, that *"States neither lose any of their rights, nor are discharged from any of their obligations, by a change in the form of their civil government."**

The last objection of any consequence, which I at present recollect, turns upon the article of expense. If it were even true that the adoption of the proposed government would occasion a considerable increase of expense, it would be an objection that ought to have no weight against the plan.

The great bulk of the citizens of America are with reason convinced that Union is the basis of their political

* *Vide* Rutherford's Institutes, Vol. 2, Book II, Chapter X, Sections XIV and XV. *Vide* also Grotius, Book II, Chapter IX, Sections VIII and IX.

happiness. Men of sense of all parties now with few exceptions agree that it cannot be preserved under the present system, nor without radical alterations; that new and extensive powers ought to be granted to the national head, and that these require a different organization of the federal government—a single body being an unsafe depositary of such ample authorities. In conceding all this, the question of expense must be given up; for it is impossible, with any degree of safety, to narrow the foundation upon which the system is to stand. The two branches of the legislature are, in the first instance, to consist of only sixty-five persons, which is the same number of which Congress, under the existing Confederation, may be composed. It is true that this number is intended to be increased; but this is to keep pace with the increase of the population and resources of the country. It is evident that a less number would, even in the first instance, have been unsafe, and that a continuance of the present number would, in a more advanced stage of population, be a very inadequate representation of the people.

Whence is the dreaded augmentation of expense to spring? One source pointed out is the multiplication of offices under the new government. Let us examine this a little.

It is evident that the principal departments of the administration under the present government are the same which will be required under the new. There are now a Secretary at War, a Secretary for Foreign Affairs, a Secretary for Domestic Affairs, a Board of Treasury, consisting of three persons, a treasurer, assistants, clerks, etc. These offices are indispensable under any system and will suffice under the new as well as under the old. As to ambassadors and other ministers and agents in foreign countries, the proposed Constitution can make no other difference than to render their characters, where they reside, more respectable, and their services more useful. As to persons to be employed in the collection of the revenues, it is unquestionably true that these will form a very considerable addition to the number of federal officers; but it will not follow that this will occasion an increase of public expense. It will be in most cases nothing more than an exchange of State officers for national officers. In the collection of all duties, for instance, the persons employed will be wholly of the latter description. The States individually will stand in no need of any for this purpose. What difference can it make in point of expense to pay officers of the customs appointed by the State or those appointed by the United States? There is no good reason to suppose that either the number or the salaries of the latter will be greater than those of the former.

Where then are we to seek for those additional articles of expense which are to swell the account to the enormous size that has been represented to us? The chief item which occurs to me respects the support of the judges of the United States. I do not add the President, because there is now a president of Congress, whose expenses may not be far, if anything, short of those which will be incurred on account of the President of the United States. The support of the judges will clearly be an extra expense, but to what extent will depend on the particular plan which may be adopted in practice in regard to this matter. But it can upon no reasonable plan amount to a sum which will be an object of material consequence.

Let us now see what there is to counterbalance any extra expense that may attend the establishment of the proposed government. The first thing that presents itself is that a great part of the business which now keeps Congress sitting through the year will be transacted by the President. Even the management of foreign negotiations will naturally devolve upon him, according to general principles concerted with the Senate, and subject to their final concurrence. Hence it is evident that a portion of the year will suffice for the session of both the Senate and the House of Representatives; we may suppose about a fourth for the latter and a third, or perhaps a half, for the former. The extra business of treaties and appointments may give this extra occupation to the Senate. From this circumstance we may infer that, until the House of Representatives shall be increased greatly beyond its present number, there will be a considerable saving of expense from the difference between the constant session of the present and the temporary session of the future Congress.

But there is another circumstance of great importance in the view of economy. The business of the United States has hitherto occupied the State legislatures, as well as Congress. The latter has made requisitions which the former have had to provide for. Hence it has happened that the sessions of the State legislatures have been protracted greatly beyond what was necessary for the execution of the mere local business of the States. More than half their time has been frequently employed in matters which related to the United States. Now the members who compose the legislatures of the several States amount to two thousand and upwards, which number has hitherto performed what under the new system will be done in the first instance by sixty-five persons, and probably at no future period by above a fourth or a fifth of that number. The Congress under the proposed government will do all the business of the United States themselves, without the intervention of the State legislatures, who thenceforth will have only to attend to the affairs of their particular States, and will not have to sit in any proportion as long as they have heretofore done. This difference in the time of the sessions of the State legislatures will be all clear gain, and will alone form an article of saving, which may be regarded as an equivalent for any additional objects of expense that may be occasioned by the adoption of the new system.

The result from these observations is that the sources of additional expense from the establishment of the proposed Constitution are much fewer than may have been imagined; that they are counterbalanced by considerable objects of saving; and that while it is questionable on which side the scale will preponderate, it is certain that a government less expensive would be incompetent to the purposes of the Union.

PUBLIUS

No. 85: Hamilton

ACCORDING to the formal division of the subject of these papers announced in my first number, there would appear still to remain for discussion two points: "the analogy of the proposed government to your own State constitution," and "the additional security which its adoption will afford to republican government, to liberty, and to property." But these heads have been so fully anticipated and exhausted in the progress of the work that it would now scarcely be possible to do anything more than repeat, in a more dilated form, what has been heretofore said, which the advanced stage of the question and the time already spent upon it conspire to forbid.

It is remarkable that the resemblance of the plan of the convention to the act which organizes the government of this State holds, not less with regard to many of the supposed defects than to the real excellences of the former. Among the pretended defects are the re-eligibility of the executive, the want of a council, the omission of a formal bill of rights, the omission of a provision respecting the liberty of the press. These and several others which have been noted in the course of our inquiries are as much chargeable on the existing constitution of this State as on the one proposed for the Union; and a man must have slender pretensions to consistency who can rail at the latter for imperfections which he finds no difficulty in excusing in the former. Nor indeed can there be a better proof of the insincerity and affectation of some of the zealous adversaries of the plan of the convention among us who profess to be the devoted admirers of the government under which they live than the fury with which they have attacked that plan, for matters in regard to which our own constitution is equally or perhaps more vulnerable.

The additional securities to republican government, to liberty, and to property, to be derived from the adoption of the plan under consideration, consist chiefly in the restraints which the preservation of the Union will impose on local factions and insurrections, and on the ambition of powerful individuals in single States who might acquire credit and influence enough from leaders and favorites to become the despots of the people; in the diminution of the opportunities to foreign intrigue, which the dissolution of the Confederacy would invite and facilitate; in the prevention of extensive military establishments, which could not fail to grow out of wars between the States in a disunited situation; in the express guaranty of a republican form of government to each; in the absolute and universal exclusion of titles of nobility; and in the precautions against the repetition of those practices on the part of the State governments which have undermined the foundations of property and credit, have planted mutual distrust in the breasts of all classes of citizens, and have occasioned an almost universal prostration of morals.

Thus have I, fellow-citizens, executed the task I had assigned to myself; with what success your conduct must determine. I trust at least you will admit that I have not failed in the assurance I gave you respecting the spirit with which my endeavors should be conducted. I have addressed myself purely to your judgments, and have studiously avoided those asperities which are too apt to disgrace political disputants of all parties and which have been not a little provoked by the language and conduct of the opponents of the Constitution. The charge of a conspiracy against the liberties of the people which has been indiscriminately brought against the advocates of the plan has something in it too wanton and too malignant not to excite the indignation of every man who feels in his own bosom a refutation of the calumny. The perpetual changes which have been rung upon the wealthy, the well-born, and the great have been such as to inspire the disgust of all sensible men. And the unwarrantable concealments and misrepresentations which have been in various ways practiced to keep the truth from the public eye have been of a nature to demand the reprobation of all honest men. It is not impossible that these circumstances may have occasionally betrayed me into intemperances of expression which I did not intend; it is certain that I have frequently felt a struggle between sensibility and moderation; and if the former has in some instances prevailed, it must be my excuse that it has been neither often nor much.

Let us now pause and ask ourselves whether, in the course of these papers, the proposed Constitution has not been satisfactorily vindicated from the aspersions thrown upon it; and whether it has not been shown to be worthy of the public approbation and necessary to the public safety and prosperity. Every man is bound to answer these questions to himself, according to the best of his conscience and understanding, and to act agreeably to the genuine and sober dictates of his judgment. This is a duty from which nothing can give him a dispensation. 'Tis one that he is called upon, nay, constrained by all the obligations that form the bands of society, to discharge sincerely and honestly. No partial motive, no particular interest, no pride of opinion, no temporary passion or prejudice, will justify to himself, to his country, or to his posterity, an improper election of the part he is to act. Let him beware of an obstinate adherence to party; let him reflect that the object upon which he is to decide is not a particular interest of the community, but the very existence of the nation; and let him remember that a majority of America has already given its sanction to the plan which he is to approve or reject.

I shall not dissemble that I feel an entire confidence in the arguments which recommend the proposed system to your adoption, and that I am unable to discern any real force in those by which it has been opposed. I am persuaded that it is the best which our political situation, habits, and opinions will admit, and superior to any the revolution has produced.

Concessions on the part of the friends of the plan that it has not a claim to absolute perfection have afforded matter of no small triumph to its enemies. "Why," say they, "should we adopt an imperfect thing? Why not amend it and make it perfect before it is irrevocably established?" This may be plausible enough, but it is only plausible. In the first place I remark that the extent of these concessions has been greatly exaggerated. They have been stated as amounting to an admission that the plan is radically defective and that without material alterations the rights and the interests of the community cannot be safely confided to it. This, as far as I have understood the meaning of those who make the concessions, is an entire perversion of their sense. No advocate of the measure can be found who will not declare as his sentiment that the system, though it may not be perfect in every part, is, upon the whole, a good one; is the best that the present views and circumstances of the country will permit; and is such a one as promises every species of security which a reasonable people can desire.

I answer in the next place that I should esteem it the extreme of imprudence to prolong the precarious state of our national affairs and to expose the Union to the jeopardy of successive experiments in the chimerical pursuit of a perfect plan. I never expect to see a perfect work from imperfect man. The result of the deliberations of all collective bodies must necessarily be a compound, as well of the errors and prejudices as of the good sense and wisdom of the individuals of whom they are composed. The compacts which are to embrace thirteen distinct States in a common bond of amity and union must as necessarily be a compromise of as many dissimilar interests and inclinations. How can perfection spring from such materials?

The reasons assigned in an excellent little pamphlet lately published in this city * are unanswerable to show the utter improbability of assembling a new convention under circumstances in any degree so favorable to a happy issue as those in which the late convention met, deliberated, and concluded. I will not repeat the arguments there used, as I presume the production itself has had an extensive circulation. It is certainly well worth the perusal of every friend to his country. There is, however, one point of light in which the subject of amendments still remains to be considered, and in which it has not yet been exhibited to public view. I cannot resolve to conclude without first taking a survey of it in this aspect.

It appears to me susceptible of absolute demonstration that it will be far more easy to obtain subsequent than previous amendments to the Constitution. The moment an alteration is made in the present plan it becomes, to the purpose of adoption, a new one, and must undergo a new decision of each State. To its complete establishment throughout the Union it will therefore require the concurrence of thirteen States. If, on the contrary, the Constitution proposed should once be ratified by all the States as it stands, alterations in it may at any time be effected by nine States. Here, then, the chances are as thirteen to nine † in favor of subsequent amendment, rather than of the original adoption of an entire system.

This is not all. Every Constitution for the United States must inevitably consist of a great variety of particulars in which thirteen independent States are to be accommodated in their interests or opinions of interest. We may of

* Entitled "An Address to the People of the State of New York."
† It may rather be said TEN, for though two thirds may set on foot the measure, three fourths must ratify.

course expect to see, in any body of men charged with its original formation, very different combinations of the parts upon different points. Many of those who form a majority on one question may become the minority on a second, and an association dissimilar to either may constitute the majority on a third. Hence the necessity of moulding and arranging all the particulars which are to compose the whole in such a manner as to satisfy all the parties to the compact; and hence, also, an immense multiplication of difficulties and casualties in obtaining the collective assent to a final act. The degree of that multiplication must evidently be in a ratio to the number of particulars and the number of parties.

But every amendment to the Constitution, if once established, would be a single proposition, and might be brought forward singly. There would then be no necessity for management or compromise in relation to any other point—no giving nor taking. The will of the requisite number would at once bring the matter to a decisive issue. And consequently, whenever nine, or rather ten States, were united in the desire of a particular amendment, that amendment must infallibly take place. There can, therefore, be no comparison between the facility of affecting an amendment and that of establishing, in the first instance, a complete Constitution.

In opposition to the probability of subsequent amendments, it has been urged that the persons delegated to the administration of the national government will always be disinclined to yield up any portion of the authority of which they were once possessed. For my own part, I acknowledge a thorough conviction that any amendments which may, upon mature consideration, be thought useful, will be applicable to the organization of the government, not to the mass of its powers; and on this account alone I think there is no weight in the observation just stated. I also think there is little weight in it on another account. The intrinsic difficulty of governing THIRTEEN STATES at any rate, independent of calculations upon an ordinary degree of public spirit and integrity will, in my opinion, constantly *impose* on the national rulers the *necessity* of a spirit of accommodation to the reasonable expectations of their constituents. But there is yet a further consideration, which proves beyond the possibility of doubt that the observation is futile. It is this: that the national rulers, whenever nine States concur, will have no option upon the subject. By the fifth article of the plan, the Congress will be *obliged* "on the application of the legislatures of two thirds of the States [which at present amount to nine], to call a convention for proposing amendments which *shall be valid,* to all intents and purposes, as part of the Constitution, when ratified by the legislatures of three fourths of the states, or by conventions in three fourths thereof." The words of this article are peremptory. The Congress "*shall* call a convention." Nothing in this particular is left to the discretion of that body. And of consequence all the declamation about the disinclination to a change vanishes in air. Nor however difficult it may be supposed to unite two thirds or three fourths of the State legislatures in amendments which may affect local interests can there be any room to apprehend any such difficulty in a union on points which are merely relative to the general liberty or security of the people. We may safely rely on the disposition of the State legislatures to erect barriers against the encroachments of the national authority.

If the foregoing argument is a fallacy, certain it is that I am myself deceived by it for it is, in my conception, one of those rare instances in which a political truth can be brought to the test of mathematical demonstration. Those who see the matter in the same light with me, however zealous they may be for amendments, must agree in the propriety of a previous adoption as the most direct road to their own object.

The zeal for attempts to amend, prior to the establishment of the Constitution, must abate in every man who is ready to accede to the truth of the following observations of a writer equally solid and ingenious: "To balance a large state or society [says he], whether monarchical or republican, on general laws, is a work of so great difficulty that no human genius, however comprehensive, is able, by the mere dint of reason and reflection, to effect it. The judgments of many must unite in the work; EXPERIENCE must guide their labor; TIME must bring it to perfection, and the FEELING of inconveniences must correct the mistakes which they *inevitably* fall into in their first trials and experiments." * These judicious reflections contain a lesson of moderation to all the sincere lovers of the Union, and ought to put them upon their guard against hazarding anarchy, civil war, a perpetual alienation of the States from each other, and perhaps the military despotism of a victorious demagogue, in the pursuit of what they are not likely to obtain, but from TIME and EXPERIENCE. It may be in me a defect of political fortitude but I acknowledge that I cannot entertain an equal tranquillity with those who affect to treat the dangers of a longer continuance in our present situation as imaginary. A NATION, without a NATIONAL GOVERNMENT, is, in my view, an awful spectacle. The establishment of a Constitution, in time of profound peace, by the voluntary consent of a whole people, is a PRODIGY, to the completion of which I look forward with trembling anxiety. I can reconcile it to no rules of prudence to let go the hold we now have, in so arduous an enterprise, upon seven out of the thirteen States, and after having passed over so considerable a part of the ground, to recommence the course. I dread the more the consequences of new attempts because I KNOW that POWERFUL INDIVIDUALS, in this and in other States, are enemies to a general national government in every possible shape.

PUBLIUS

* Hume's *Essays*, Vol. I, Page 128: "The Rise of Arts and Sciences."

The Constitution of The United States of America
(Collated with *The Federalist Papers*)

WE THE PEOPLE of the United States, in Order to form a more perfect Union, establish Justice, insure domestic Tranquility, provide for the common defence, promote the general Welfare, and secure the Blessings of Liberty to ourselves and our Posterity, do ordain and establish this CONSTITUTION for the United States of America. 513

ARTICLE I.

SECTION 1. All legislative Powers herein granted shall be vested in a Congress of the United States which shall consist of a Senate and House of Representatives. 292

SECTION 2. The House of Representatives shall be 242, 244,
composed of Members chosen every second Year by the 291; 326-36
People of the several States, and the Electors in each 325-26, 351
State shall have the Qualifications requisite for Electors of the most numerous Branch of the State Legislature.

No Person shall be a Representative who shall not have attained to the Age of twenty-five Years, and been seven Years a Citizen of the United States, and who shall not, when elected, be an Inhabitant of that State in which he shall be chosen. 326, 371

[Representatives and direct Taxes shall be appor- 336
tioned among the several States which may be included within this Union, according to their respective Numbers, which shall be determined by adding to the whole
Number of free Persons, including those bound to Serv- 336-41
ice for a Term of Years, and excluding Indians not taxed, three fifths of all other Persons.] The actual Enumeration shall be made within three Years after the
first Meeting of the Congress of the United States, and 356
within every subsequent Term of ten Years, in such
Manner as they shall by Law direct. The Number of 341-50
Representatives shall not exceed one for every thirty Thousand, but each State shall have at Least one Repre-

sentative; and until such enumeration shall be made, the State of New Hampshire shall be entitled to chuse three, Massachusetts eight, Rhode-Island and Providence Plantations one, Connecticut five, New-York six, New Jersey four, Pennsylvania eight, Delaware one, Maryland six, Virginia ten, North Carolina five, South Carolina five, and Georgia three.

When vacancies happen in the Representation from any State, the Executive Authority thereof shall issue Writs of Election to fill such Vacancies.

474 The House of Representatives shall chuse their Speaker and other Officers; and shall have the sole Power of Impeachment.

242, 244, SECTION 3. The Senate of United States shall be
291, 368, composed of two Senators from each State, chosen by
377-90 the Legislature thereof, for six Years; and each Senator shall have one Vote.

365 Immediately after they shall be assembled in Consequence of the first Election, they shall be divided as equally as may be into three Classes. The Seats of the Senators of the first Class shall be vacated at the Expiration of the second Year, of the second Class at the Expiration of the fourth Year, and of the third Class at the Expiration of the sixth Year, so that one-third may
410-11 be chosen every second Year; and if Vacancies happen by Resignation, or otherwise, during the Recess of the Legislature of any State, the Executive thereof may make temporary Appointments until the next Meeting of the Legislature, which shall then fill such Vacancies.

376, 391 No Person shall be a Senator who shall not have attained to the Age of thirty Years, and been nine Years a Citizen of the United States, and who shall not, when elected, be an Inhabitant of that State for which he shall be chosen.

The Vice President of the United States shall be President of the Senate, but shall have no Vote, unless they be equally divided.

The Senate shall chuse their other Officers, and also a President pro tempore, in the absence of the Vice President, or when he shall exercise the Office of President of the United States.

242, 396- The Senate shall have the sole Power to try all Im-
407, 474-75 peachments. When sitting for that Purpose, they shall be on Oath or Affirmative. When the President of the
399 United States is tried, the Chief Justice shall preside: And no Person shall be convicted without the Concurrence of two thirds of the Members present.

Judgment in Cases of Impeachment shall not extend further than to removal from Office, and disqualification to hold and enjoy any Office of honor, Trust or Profit under the United States: but the Party convicted shall nevertheless be liable and subject to Indictment, Trial, Judgment and Punishment, according to Law. 511

SECTION 4. The Times, Places and Manner of holding Elections for Senators and Representatives, shall be prescribed in each State by the Legislature thereof; but the Congress may at any time by Law make or alter such Regulations, except as to the Place of Chusing Senators. 361-76

The Congress shall assemble at least once in every Year, and such Meeting shall be on the first Monday in December, unless they shall by Law appoint a different Day.

SECTION 5. Each House shall be the Judge of the Elections, Returns and Qualifications of its own Members, and a Majority of each shall constitute a Quorum to do Business; but a smaller number may adjourn from day to day, and may be authorized to compel the Attendance of absent Members, in such Manner, and under such Penalties as each House may provide.

Each House may determine the Rules of its Proceedings, punish its Members for disorderly Behavior, and, with the Concurrence of two thirds, expel a Member.

Each House shall keep a Journal of its Proceedings, and from time to time publish the same, excepting such Parts as may in their Judgment require Secrecy; and the Yeas and Nays of the Members of either House on any question shall, at the Desire of one fifth of those Present, be entered on the Journal.

Neither House, during the Session of Congress, shall, without the Consent of the other, adjourn for more than three days, nor to any other Place than that in which the two Houses shall be sitting.

SECTION 6. The Senators and Representatives shall receive a Compensation for their Services, to be ascertained by Law, and paid out of the Treasury of the United States. They shall in all Cases, except Treason, Felony and Breach of the Peace, be privileged from Arrest during their Attendance at the Session of their respective Houses, and in going to and returning from the same; and for any Speech or Debate in either House, they shall not be questioned in any other Place.

No Senator or Representative shall, during the Time 345, 459
for which he was elected, be appointed to any civil

Office under the Authority of the United States, which shall have been created, or the Emoluments whereof shall have been encreased during such time; and no Person holding any Office under the United States, shall be a Member of either House during his Continuance in Office.

404 SECTION 7. All Bills for raising Revenue shall originate in the House of Representatives; but the Senate may propose or concur with Amendments as on other Bills.

416-17, Every Bill which shall have passed the House of Rep-
442-47 resentatives and the Senate, shall, before it becomes a Law, be presented to the President of the United States; If he approve he shall sign it, but if not he shall return it, with his Objections to that House in which it shall have originated, who shall enter the Objections at large on their Journal, and proceed to reconsider it. If after such Reconsideration two thirds of that House shall agree to pass the Bill, it shall be sent, together with the Objections, to the other House, by which it shall likewise be reconsidered, and if approved by two thirds of that House, it shall become a Law. But in all such Cases the Votes of both Houses shall be determined by Yeas and Nays, and the Names of the Persons voting for and against the Bill shall be entered on the Journal of each House respectively. If any Bill shall not be returned by the President within ten Days (Sundays excepted) after it shall have been presented to him, the Same shall be a Law, in like Manner as if he had signed it, unless the Congress by their Adjournment prevent its Return, in which Case it shall not be a Law.

416-17, Every Order, Resolution, or Vote to which the Con-
442-47 currence of the Senate and House of Representatives may be necessary (except on a question of Adjournment) shall be presented to the President of the United States; and before the Same shall take Effect, shall be approved by him, or being disapproved by him, shall be repassed by two thirds of the Senate and House of Representatives, according to the Rules and Limitations prescribed in the Case of a Bill.

188-223, SECTION 8. The Congress shall have Power To lay
261-64 and collect Taxes, Duties, Imposts and Excises, to pay
347 the Debts and provide for the common Defence and general Welfare of the United States; but all Duties, Imposts and Excises shall be uniform throughout the United States;

To borrow money on the credit of the United States;

To regulate Commerce with foreign Nations, and 267-69, 292,
among the several States, and with the Indian Tribes; 347

To establish an uniform Rule of Naturalization, and 199 269-71
uniform Laws on the subject of Bankruptcies through- 271
out the United States;

To coin Money, regulate the Value thereof, and of 269
foreign Coin, and fix the Standard of Weights and
Measures;

To provide for the Punishment of counterfeiting the 269
Securities and current Coin of the United States;

To establish Post Offices and post Roads; 271

To promote the Progress of Science and useful Arts, 271-72
by securing for limited Times to Authors and Inventors
the exclusive Right to their respective Writings and
Discoveries;

To constitute Tribunals inferior to the supreme 481, 485
Court;

To define and punish Piracies and Felonies com- 265-66
mitted on the high Seas, and Offenses against the Law
of Nations;

To declare War, grant Letters of Marque and Re- 256
prisal, and make Rules concerning Captures on Land
and Water;

To raise and support Armies, but no Appropriation 153, 158,
of Money to that Use shall be for a longer Term than 171-74, 256-
two Years; 60

To provide and maintain a Navy; 260-61

To make Rules for the Government and Regulation
of the land and naval Forces;

To provide for calling forth the Militia to execute the 182-87
Laws of the Union, suppress Insurrections and repel
Invasions;

To provide for organizing, arming, and disciplining 182-87, 348
the Militia, and for governing such Part of them as may
be employed in the Service of the United States, re-
serving to the States respectively, the Appointment of
the Officers, and the Authority of training the Militia
according to the discipline prescribed by Congress;

To exercise exclusive Legislation in all Cases what- 198, 272-73
soever, over such District (not exceeding ten Miles
square) as may, by Cession of particular States, and the
acceptance of Congress, become the Seat of the Govern-
ment of the United States, and to exercise like Authority
over all Places purchased by the Consent of the Legis- 273
lature of the State in which the Same shall be, for the
Erection of Forts, Magazines, Arsenals, dock-Yards,
and other needful Buildings;—And

183, 201-04 To make all Laws which shall be necessary and
283-86 proper for carrying into Execution the foregoing Powers, and all other Powers vested by this Constitution in the Government of the United States, or in any Department or Officer thereof.

266-67 SECTION 9. The Migration or Importation of such Persons as any of the States now existing shall think proper to admit, shall not be prohibited by the Congress prior to the Year one thousand eight hundred and eight, but a tax or duty may be imposed on such Importation, not exceeding ten dollars for each Person.

499, 511-12 The privilege of the Writ of Habeas Corpus shall not be suspended, unless when in Cases of Rebellion or Invasion the public Safety may require it.

511-12 No Bill of Attainder or ex post facto Law shall be passed.

No capitation, or other direct, Tax shall be laid, unless in Proportion to the Census or Enumeration herein before directed to be taken.

No Tax or Duty shall be laid on Articles exported from any State.

199 No Preference shall be given by any Regulation of Commerce or Revenue to the Ports of one State over those of another: nor shall Vessels bound to, or from, one State, be obliged to enter, clear, or pay Duties in another.

No Money shall be drawn from the Treasury, but in Consequence of Appropriations made by Law; and a regular Statement and Account of the Receipts and Expenditures of all public Money shall be published from time to time.

242, 511-12 No Title of Nobility shall be granted by the United States: And no Person holding any Office of Profit or Trust under them, shall, without the Consent of the Congress, accept of any present, Emolument, Office, or Title, of any kind whatever, from any King, Prince, or foreign State.

201, 280-83 SECTION 10. No State shall enter into any Treaty, Alliance, or Confederation; grant Letters of Marque and Reprisal; coin Money; emit Bills of Credit; make any Thing but gold and silver Coin a Tender in Payment of Debts; pass any Bill of Attainder, ex post facto Law, or Law impairing the Obligation of Contracts, or grant any Title of Nobility.

199, 283 No State shall, without the Consent of the Congress, lay any Imposts or Duties on Imports or Exports, except what may be absolutely necessary for executing it's inspection Laws: and the net Produce of all Duties and Imposts, laid by any State on Imports or Exports, shall be for the Use of the Treasury of the United States; and all such Laws shall be subject to the Revision and Controul of the Congress.

No State shall, without the Consent of Congress, lay any duty of Tonnage, keep Troops, or Ships of War in time of Peace, enter into any Agreement or Compact with another State, or with a foreign Power, or engage in War, unless actually invaded, or in such imminent Danger as will not admit of delay.

ARTICLE II.

SECTION 1. The executive Power shall be vested in **242, 244,**
a President of the United States of America. He shall **424-35, 519**
hold his Office during the Term of four Years, and, to- **416, 434-35**
gether with the Vice-President, chosen for the same **415**
Term, be elected, as follows

Each State shall appoint, in such Manner as the **244, 291,**
Legislature thereof may direct, a Number of Electors, **411-14, 464**
equal to the whole Number of Senators and Representatives to which the State may be entitled in the Congress: but no Senator or Representative, or Person holding an Office of Trust or Profit under the United States, shall be appointed an Elector.

[The Electors shall meet in their respective States, and vote by Ballot for two persons, of whom one at least shall not be an Inhabitant of the same State with themselves. And they shall make a List of all the Persons voted for, and of the Number of Votes for each; which List they shall sign and certify, and transmit sealed to the Seat of the Government of the United States, directed to the President of the Senate. The President of the Senate shall, in the Presence of the Senate and House of Representatives, open all the Certificates, and the Votes shall then be counted. The Person having the greatest Number of Votes shall be the President, if such Number be a Majority of the whole Number of Electors appointed; and if there be more than one who have such Majority, and have an equal Number of Votes, then the House of Representatives shall immediately chuse by Ballot one of them for
President; and if no Person have a Majority, then from **404**
the five highest on the List the said House shall in like Manner chuse the President. But in chusing the President, the Votes shall be taken by States, the Represen-

tation from each State having one Vote; A quorum for this Purpose shall consist of a Member or Members from two-thirds of the States, and a Majority of all the States shall be necessary to a Choice. In every Case, after the Choice of the President, the Person having the greatest Number of Votes of the Electors shall be the Vice President. But if there should remain two or more who have equal Votes, the Senate shall chuse from them by Ballot the Vice-President.]

The Congress may determine the Time of chusing the Electors, and the Day on which they shall give their Votes; which Day shall be the same throughout the United States.

No person except a natural born Citizen, or a Citizen of the United States, at the time of the Adoption of this Constitution, shall be eligible to the Office of President; neither shall any Person be eligible to that Office
391 who shall not have attained to the Age of thirty-five Years, and been fourteen Years a Resident within the United States.

In Case of the Removal of the President from Office, or of his Death, Resignation, or Inability to discharge the Powers and Duties of the said Office, the same shall devolve on the Vice President, and the Congress may by Law provide for the Case of Removal, Death, Resignation or Inability, both of the President and Vice President, declaring what Officer shall then act as President, and such Officer shall act accordingly, until the Disability be removed, or a President shall be elected.

441-42, 473 The President shall, at stated Times, receive for his Services, a Compensation, which shall neither be encreased nor diminished during the Period for which he shall have been elected, and he shall not receive within that Period any other Emolument from the United States, or any of them.

Before he enter on the Execution of his Office, he shall take the following Oath or Affirmation:—"I do solemnly swear (or affirm) that I will faithfully execute the Office of President of the United States, and will to the best of my Ability, preserve, protect and defend the Constitution of the United States."

417-18, 447 SECTION 2. The President shall be Commander in Chief of the Army and Navy of the United States, and of the Militia of the several States, when called into the actual Service of the United States; he may require the
447 Opinion in writing, of the principal Officer in each of the executive Departments, upon any subject relating

to the Duties of their respective Offices, and he shall
have Power to Grant Reprieves and Pardons for Of- 417-19
fenses against the United States, except in Cases of 447-49
Impeachment.

He shall have Power, by and with the Advice and 264-65, 390-
Consent of the Senate, to make Treaties, provided two- 96, 402, 405-
thirds of the Senators present concur; and he shall nom- 407
inate, and by and with the Advice and Consent of the
Senate, shall appoint Ambassadors, other public Min- 264-65, 403-
isters and Consuls, Judges of the supreme Court, and all 405, 420-21,
other Officers of the United States, whose Appointments 454-62, 464
are not herein otherwise provided for, and which shall
be established by Law: but the Congress may by Law
vest the Appointment of such inferior Officers, as they
think proper, in the President alone, in the Courts of
Law, or in the Heads of Departments.

The President shall have Power to fill up all Vacan- 408-11, 454
cies that may happen during the Recess of the Senate,
by granting Commissions which shall expire at the End
of their next Session.

SECTION 3. He shall from time to time give to the 463
Congress Information of the State of the Union, and
recommend to their Consideration such Measures as he 417, 463
shall judge necessary and expedient; he may, on ex-
traordinary Occasions, convene both Houses, or either 463
of them, and in Case of Disagreement between them, 417, 419,
with Respect to the Time of Adjournment, he may ad- 463
journ them to such Time as he shall think proper; he 264-65, 420
shall receive Ambassadors and other public Ministers; 463
he shall take Care that the Laws be faithfully executed, 417, 463
and shall Commission all the Officers of the United 467
States.

SECTION 4. The President, Vice President and all 242, 416
civil Officers of the United States, shall be removed
from Office on Impeachment for, and Conviction of,
Treason, Bribery, or other high Crimes and Misde-
meanors.

ARTICLE III.

SECTION 1. The judicial Power of the United States, 481-95
shall be vested in one supreme Court, and in such in- 398-400
ferior Courts as the Congress may from time to time
ordain and establish. The Judges, both of the supreme
and inferior Courts, shall hold their Offices during good 465-72
Behaviour, and shall, at stated Times, receive for their 472-74

Services a Compensation which shall not be diminished during their Continuance in Office.

475-81 SECTION 2. The judicial Power shall extend to all Cases, in Law and Equity, arising under this Constitution, the Laws of the United States, and Treaties made, or which shall be made, under their Authority;—to all Cases affecting Ambassadors, other public Ministers and Consuls;—to all Cases of admiralty and maritime Jurisdiction;—to Controversies to which the United States shall be a Party;—to Controversies between two or more States;—between a State and Citizens of another State;—between Citizens of different States;—between Citizens of the same State claiming Lands under Grants of different States, and between a State, or the Citizens thereof, and foreign States, Citizens or Subjects.

487-88 In all Cases affecting Ambassadors, other public Ministers and Consuls, and those in which a State shall be Party, the supreme Court shall have original Jurisdiction. In all the other Cases before mentioned, the supreme Court shall have appellate Jurisdiction, both as to Law and Fact, with such Exceptions, and under such Regulations as the Congress shall make.

495-510, The trial of all Crimes, except in Cases of Impeach-
511 ment, shall be by Jury; and such Trial shall be held in the State where the said Crimes shall have been committed; but when not committed within any State, the Trial shall be at such Place or Places as the Congress may by Law have directed.

273, 511 SECTION 3. Treason against the United States, shall consist only in levying War against them, or in adhering to their Enemies, giving them Aid and Comfort. No Person shall be convicted of Treason unless on the Testimony of two Witnesses to the same overt Act, or on Confession in open Court.

273, 511 The Congress shall have power to declare the Punishment of Treason, but no Attainder of Treason shall work Corruption of Blood, or Forfeiture except during the Life of the Person attainted.

ARTICLE IV.

SECTION 1. Full Faith and Credit shall be given in each State to the public Acts, Records, and judicial Proceedings of every other State. And the Congress
271 may by general Laws prescribe the Manner in which

such Acts, Records and Proceedings shall be proved, and the Effect thereof.

SECTION 2. The Citizens of each State shall be en- 478
titled to all Privileges and Immunities of Citizens in the several States.

A Person charged in any State with Treason, Felony, or other Crime, who shall flee from Justice, and be found in another State, shall on demand of the executive Authority of the State from which he fled, be delivered up, to be removed to the State having Jurisdiction of the Crime.

No Person held to Service or Labour in one State, under the Laws thereof, escaping into another, shall, in Consequence of any Law or Regulation therein, be discharged from such Service or Labour, but shall be delivered up on Claim of the Party to whom such Service or Labour may be due.

SECTION 3. New States may be admitted by the 273-74
Congress into this Union; but no new State shall be formed or erected within the Jurisdiction of any other State; nor any State be formed by the Junction of two or more States, or parts of States, without the Consent of the Legislatures of the States concerned as well as of the Congress.

The Congress shall have Power to dispose of and 274
make all needful Rules and Regulations respecting the Territory or other Property belonging to the United States; and nothing in this Constitution shall be so construed as to Prejudice any Claims of the United States, or of any particular State.

SECTION 4. The United States shall guarantee to 242, 274-78
every State in this Union a Republican Form of Government, and shall protect each of them against Invasion; and on Application of the Legislature, or of the Executive (when the Legislature cannot be convened) against domestic Violence.

ARTICLE V.

The Congress, whenever two-thirds of both Houses 246, 278-79
shall deem it necessary, shall propose Amendments to 524-26
this Constitution, or, on the Application of the Legislatures of two-thirds of the several States, shall call a 526
Convention for proposing Amendments, which, in either Case, shall be valid to all Intents and Purposes, as part of this Constitution, when ratified by the Legislatures of three-fourths of the several States, or by Conventions

in three-fourths thereof, as the one or the other Mode of Ratification may be proposed by the Congress; Provided that no Amendment which may be made prior to the Year One thousand eight hundred and eight shall in any Manner affect the first and fourth Clauses in the
279 Ninth Section of the first Article; and that no State, without its Consent, shall be deprived of its equal Suffrage in the Senate.

ARTICLE VI.

278 All Debts contracted and Engagements entered into, before the Adoption of this Constitution, shall be as valid against the United States under this Constitution, as under the Confederation.

177, 201, 204-205, 245, 286-87 This Constitution, and the Laws of the United States which shall be made in Pursuance thereof; and all Treaties made, or which shall be made, under the Authority of the United States, shall be the supreme Law of the Land; and the Judges in every State shall be bound thereby, any Thing in the Constitution or Laws of any State to the Contrary notwithstanding.

177, 287 The Senators and Representatives before mentioned, and the Members of the several State Legislatures, and all executive and judicial Officers, both of the United States and of the several States, shall be bound by Oath or Affirmation, to support this Constitution; but no religious Test shall ever be required as a Qualification to any Office or public Trust under the United States.

ARTICLE VII.

243, 244, 251, 279 The Ratification of the Conventions of nine States shall be sufficient for the Establishment of this Constitution between the States so ratifying the Same.

DONE in Convention by the Unanimous Consent of the States present the Seventeenth Day of September in the Year of our Lord one thousand seven hundred and Eighty seven and of the Independence of the United States of America the Twelfth. In Witness whereof We have hereunto subscribed our Names.

Go WASHINGTON
Presidt and deputy from Virginia

New Hampshire.

JOHN LANGDON
NICHOLAS GILMAN

Massachusetts.

NATHANIEL GORHAM
RUFUS KING

Connecticut.

WM SAML JOHNSON
ROGER SHERMAN

New York.

ALEXANDER HAMILTON

New Jersey.

WIL: LIVINGSTON
DAVID BREARLEY
WM PATTERSON
JONA: DAYTON

Pennsylvania.

B. FRANKLIN
ROBT. MORRIS
THOS FITZSIMONS
JAMES WILSON
THOMAS MIFFLIN
GEO. CLYMER
JARED INGERSOLL
GOUV MORRIS

Delaware.

GEO: READ
JOHN DICKINSON
JACO: BROOM
GUNNING BEDFORD jun
RICHARD BASSETT

Maryland.

JAMES MCHENRY
DANL CARROLL
DAN: of ST THOS JENIFER

Virginia.

JOHN BLAIR—
JAMES MADISON Jr.

North Carolina.

WM BLOUNT
HU WILLIAMSON

RICHD DOBBS SPAIGHT,

South Carolina.

J. RUTLEDGE
CHARLES PINCKNEY
CHARLES COTESWORTH PINCKNEY
PIERCE BUTLER.

Georgia.

WILLIAM FEW
ABR BALDWIN

Attest:

WILLIAM JACKSON, *Secretary.*

ARTICLES IN ADDITION TO, AND AMENDMENT OF, THE CONSTITUTION OF THE UNITED STATES OF AMERICA, PROPOSED BY CONGRESS, AND RATIFIED BY THE LEGISLATURES OF THE SEVERAL STATES, PURSUANT TO THE FIFTH ARTICLE OF THE ORIGINAL CONSTITUTION.

[ARTICLE I.]

Congress shall make no law respecting an establishment of religion, or prohibiting the free exercise thereof; or abridging the freedom of speech, or of the press; or the right of the people peaceably to assemble, and to petition the Government for a redress of grievances.

[ARTICLE II.]

A well regulated Militia, being necessary to the security of a free State, the right of the people to keep and bear Arms, shall not be infringed.

[ARTICLE III.]

No Soldier shall, in time of peace be quartered in any house, without the consent of the Owner, nor in time of war, but in a manner to be prescribed by law.

[ARTICLE IV.]

The right of the people to be secure in their persons, houses, papers, and effects, against unreasonable searches and seizures, shall not be violated, and no

Warrants shall issue, but upon probable cause, supported by Oath or affirmation, and particularly describing the place to be searched, and the persons or things to be seized.

[ARTICLE V.]

No person shall be held to answer for a capital, or otherwise infamous crime, unless on a presentment or indictment of a Grand Jury, except in cases arising in the land or naval forces, or in the Militia, when in actual service in time of War or public danger; nor shall any person be subject for the same offence to be twice put in jeopardy of life or limb; nor shall be compelled in any criminal case to be a witness against himself, nor be deprived of life, liberty, or property, without due process of law; nor shall private property be taken for public use, without just compensation.

[ARTICLE VI.]

In all criminal prosecutions, the accused shall enjoy the right to a speedy and public trial, by an impartial jury of the State and district wherein the crime shall have been committed, which district shall have been previously ascertained by law, and to be informed of the nature and cause of the accusation; to be confronted with the witnesses against him; to have compulsory process for obtaining witnesses in his favor, and to have the Assistance of Counsel for his defence.

[ARTICLE VII.]

In suits at common law, where the value in controversy shall exceed twenty dollars, the right of trial by jury shall be preserved, and no fact tried by a jury, shall be otherwise re-examined in any Court of the United States, than according to the rules of the common law.

[ARTICLE VIII.]

Excessive bail shall not be required, nor excessive fines imposed, nor cruel and unusual punishments inflicted.

[ARTICLE IX.]

The enumeration in the Constitution, of certain rights, shall not be construed to deny or disparage others retained by the people.

[ARTICLE X.]

The powers not delegated to the United States by the Constitution, nor prohibited by it to the States, are reserved to the States respectively, or to the people.

ARTICLE XI.

The Judicial power of the United States shall not be construed to extend to any suit in law or equity, commenced or prosecuted against one of the United States by Citizens of another State, or by Citizens or subjects of any foreign State.

ARTICLE XII.

The Electors shall meet in their respective states and vote by ballot for President and Vice-President, one of whom, at least, shall not be an inhabitant of the same state with themselves; they shall name in their ballots the person voted for as President, and in distinct ballots the person voted for as Vice-President, and they shall make distinct lists of all persons voted for as President, and of all persons voted for as Vice-President, and of the number of votes for each, which lists they shall sign and certify, and transmit sealed to the seat of the government of the United States, directed to the President of the Senate;—The President of the Senate shall, in presence of the Senate and House of Representatives, open all the certificates and the votes shall then be counted;—The person having the greatest number of votes for President, shall be the President, if such number be a majority of the whole number of Electors appointed; and if no person have such majority, then from the persons having the highest numbers not exceeding three on the list of those voted for as President, the House of Representatives shall choose immediately, by ballot, the President. But in choosing the President, the votes shall be taken by states, the representation from each state having one vote; a quorum for this purpose shall consist of a member or members from two-thirds of the states, and a majority of all the states shall be necessary to a choice. And if the House of Representatives shall not choose a President whenever the right of choice shall devolve upon them, before the fourth day of March next following, then the Vice-President shall act as President, as in the case of the death or other constitutional disability of the President.—The person having the greatest number of votes as Vice-President, shall be the Vice-President, if such number be a majority of the whole number of Electors appointed, and if no person have a majority, then from the two highest numbers on the list, the Senate shall choose the Vice-President; a quorum for the purpose shall consist of two-thirds of the whole number of Senators, and a majority of the whole number shall be necessary to a choice. But no person constitutionally ineligible to the office of President shall be eligible to that of Vice-President of the United States.

ARTICLE XIII.

SECTION 1. Neither slavery nor involuntary servitude, except as a punishment for crime whereof the party shall have been duly convicted, shall exist within the United States, or any place subject to their jurisdiction.

SECTION 2. Congress shall have power to enforce this article by appropriate legislation.

ARTICLE XIV.

SECTION 1. All persons born or naturalized in the United States, and subject to the jurisdiction thereof, are citizens of the United States and of the State wherein they reside. No State shall make or enforce any law which shall abridge the privileges or immunities of citizens of the United States; nor shall any State deprive any person of life, liberty, or property, without due process of law; nor deny to any person within its jurisdiction the equal protection of the laws.

SECTION 2. Representatives shall be apportioned among the several States according to their respective numbers, counting the whole number of persons in each State, excluding Indians not taxed. But when the right to vote at any election for the choice of electors for President and Vice-President of the United States, Representatives in Congress, the Executive and Judicial officers of a State, or the members of the Legislature thereof, is denied to any of the male inhabitants of such State, being twenty-one years of age, and citizens of the United States, or in any way abridged, except for participation in rebellion, or other crime, the basis of representation therein shall be reduced in the proportion which the number of such male citizens shall bear to the whole number of male citizens twenty-one years of age in such State.

SECTION 3. No person shall be a Senator or Representative in Congress, or elector of President and Vice-President, or hold any office, civil or military, under the United States, or under any State, who, having previously taken an oath, as a member of Congress, or as an officer of the United States, or as a member of any State legislature, or as an executive or judicial officer of any State, to support the Constitution of the United States, shall have engaged in insurrection or rebellion against the same, or given aid or comfort to the enemies thereof. But Congress may by a vote of two-thirds of each House, remove such disability.

SECTION 4. The validity of the public debt of the United States, authorized by law, including debts incurred for payment of pensions and bounties for services in suppressing insurrection or rebellion, shall not be questioned. But neither the United States nor any State shall assume or pay any debt or obligation incurred in aid of insurrection or rebellion against the United States, or any claim for the loss or emancipation of any slave; but all such debts, obligations and claims shall be held illegal and void.

SECTION 5. The Congress shall have power to enforce, by appropriate legislation, the provisions of this article.

ARTICLE XV.

SECTION 1. The right of citizens of the United States to vote shall not be denied or abridged by the United States or by any State on account of race, color, or previous conditions of servitude—

SECTION 2. The Congress shall have power to enforce this article by appropriate legislation.

ARTICLE XVI.

The Congress shall have power to lay and collect taxes on incomes, from whatever source derived, without apportionment among the several States, and without regard to any census or enumeration.

ARTICLE XVII.

The Senate of the United States shall be composed of two Senators from each State, elected by the people thereof, for six years; and each Senator shall have one vote. The electors in each State shall have the qualifications requisite for electors of the most numerous branch of the State legislatures.

When vacancies happen in the representation of any State in the Senate, the executive authority of such State shall issue writs of election to fill such vacancies: *Provided,* That the legislature of any State may empower the executive thereof to make temporary appointments until the people fill the vacancies by election as the legislature may direct.

This amendment shall not be so construed as to affect the election or term of any Senator chosen before it becomes valid as part of the Constitution.

ARTICLE XVIII.

SECTION 1. After one year from the ratification of this article the manufacture, sale, or transportation of intoxicating liquors therein, the importation thereof into, or the exportation thereof from the United States and all territory subject to the jurisdiction thereof for beverage purposes is hereby prohibited.

SECTION 2. The Congress and the several States shall have concurrent power to enforce this article by appropriate legislation.

SECTION 3. This article shall be inoperative unless it shall have been ratified as an amendment to the Constitution by the legislatures of the several States, as provided in the Constitution, within seven years from the date of the submission hereof to the States by the Congress.

ARTICLE XIX.

The right of citizens of the United States to vote shall not be denied or abridged by the United States or by any State on account of sex.

Congress shall have power to enforce this article by appropriate legislation.

ARTICLE XX.

SECTION 1. The terms of the President and Vice President shall end at noon on the 20th day of January, and the terms of Senators and Representatives at noon on the 3d day of January, of the years in which such terms would have ended if this article had not been ratified; and the terms of their successors shall then begin.

SECTION 2. The Congress shall assemble at least once in every year, and such meeting shall begin at noon on the 3d day of January, unless they shall by law appoint a different day.

SECTION 3. If, at the time fixed for the beginning of the term of the President, the President elect shall have died, the Vice President elect shall become President. If a President shall not have been chosen before the time fixed for the beginning of his term, or if the President elect shall have failed to qualify, then the Vice President elect shall act as President until a President shall have qualified; and the Congress may by law provide for the case wherein neither a President elect nor a Vice President elect shall have qualified, declaring who shall then act as President, or the manner in which one who is to act shall be selected, and such person shall act accordingly until a President or Vice President shall have qualified.

SECTION 4. The Congress may by law provide for the case of the death of any of the persons from whom the House of Representatives may choose a President whenever the right of choice shall have devolved upon them, and for the case of the death of any of the persons from whom the Senate may choose a Vice President whenever the right of choice shall have devolved upon them.

SECTION 5. Sections 1 and 2 shall take effect on the 15th day of October following the ratification of this article.

SECTION 6. This article shall be inoperative unless it shall have been ratified as an amendment to the Constitution by the legislatures of three-fourths of the several States within seven years from the date of its submission.

ARTICLE XXI.

SECTION 1. The eighteenth article of amendment to the Constitution of the United States is hereby repealed.

SECTION 2. The transportation or importation into any State, Territory, or possession of the United States for delivery or use therein of intoxicating liquors, in violation of the laws thereof, is hereby prohibited.

SECTION 3. The article shall be inoperative unless it shall have been ratified as an amendment to the Constitution by conventions in the several States, as provided in the Constitution, within seven years from the date of the submission hereof to the States by the Congress.

ARTICLE XXII.

SECTION 1. No person shall be elected to the office of the President more than twice, and no person who has held the office of President, or acted as President, for more than two years of a term to which some other person was elected President shall be elected to the office of the President more than once. But this Article shall not apply to any person holding the office of President when this Article was proposed by the Congress, and shall not prevent any person who may be holding the office of President, or acting as President, during the term within which this Article becomes operative from holding the office of President or acting as President during the remainder of such term.

SECTION 2. This article shall be inoperative unless it shall have been ratified as an amendment to the Constitution by the legislatures of three-fourths of the several States within seven years from the date of its submission to the States by the Congress.

ARTICLE XXIII.

SECTION 1. The District constituting the seat of Government of the United States shall appoint in such manner as the Congress may direct:

A number of electors of President and Vice President equal to the whole number of Senators and Representatives in Congress to which the District would be entitled if it were a State, but in no event more than the least populous State; they shall be in addition to those appointed by the States, but they shall be considered, for the purposes of the election of President and Vice President, to be electors appointed by a State; and they shall meet in the District and perform such duties as provided by the twelfth article of amendment.

SECTION 2. The Congress shall have power to enforce this article by appropriate legislation.

ARTICLE XXIV

SECTION 1. The right of citizens of the United States to vote in any primary or other election for President or Vice-President, or for Senator or Representative in Congress, shall not be denied or abridged by the United States or any State by reason of failure to pay any poll tax or other tax.

SECTION 2. The Congress shall have the power to enforce this article by appropriate legislation.

Index of Ideas